THE MEDIEVAL
THEATER OF CRUELTY

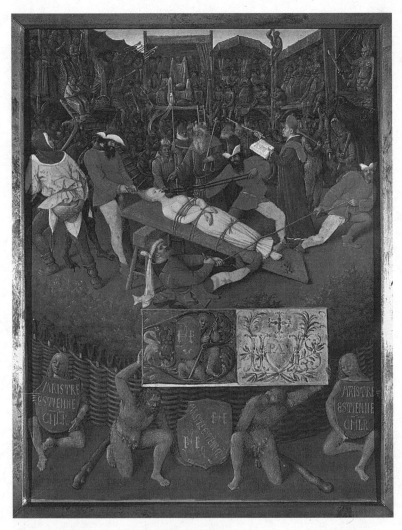

Jean Fouquet, *The Martyrdom of Saint Apollonia.* From the *Livre d'heures d'Etienne Chevalier.* Courtesy of the Musée Condé, Chantilly.

THE MEDIEVAL THEATER OF CRUELTY

RHETORIC, MEMORY, VIOLENCE

Jody Enders

CORNELL UNIVERSITY PRESS

ITHACA AND LONDON

THIS BOOK HAS BEEN PUBLISHED WITH THE AID
OF A GRANT FROM THE UNIVERSITY OF CALIFORNIA,
SANTA BARBARA.

First published 1999 by Cornell University Press.

Printed in the United States of America.

Library of Congress Cataloging-in-Publication Data
Enders, Jody, 1955 –
     The medieval theater of cruelty : rhetoric, memory, violence /
Jody Enders.
        p.   cm.
     Includes bibliographical references and index.
      ISBN 0-8014-3334-7 (cloth : alk. paper)
      1. Drama, Medieval—History and criticism.   2. Violence in
literature.   3. Violence in the theater.   I. Title.
PN1751.E49   1999
809.2'9355—dc21   98-26024

Cornell University Press strives to use environmentally responsible suppliers
and materials to the fullest extent possible in the publishing of its books. Such
materials include vegetable-based, low-VOC inks and acid-free papers that are
recycled, totally chlorine-free, or partly composed of nonwood fibers.

Clothing printing   10 9 8 7 6 5 4 3 2 1

To the memory of Daniel Poirion

Contents

Illustrations

Preface

Strange things happen when the discussion turns to violence. And because this is a book about violence, torture, medieval drama, and the dark side of rhetoric, some prefatory remarks may prove appropriate.

Over the past several years, as I have presented various stages of this project in various public forums, I have never known whether colleagues were going to break into amused guffaws or gasp in horror. Sometimes, in a phenomenon that is endemic to performance, the way an audience responds and the way I choose to present the material become part of the Q and A. If audiences titter, it is because I have smiled during the presentation. If audiences are mortified, it is because I have stressed the horror of the real events to which dramatic scenes of torture allude. If audiences are put off, it is because I have been too preachy. If they are angry, it is because I have trivialized the real suffering that medieval plays represent by proposing a "mere verbal" connection with the rhetorical tradition.

Similarly, if an audience member laughs when I am stressing horror, that person is accused of being morally defective. If another audience member deems problematic the pleasure it is possible to take in one's work—even when that work treats a horrific subject—then it is I who become morally defective. If someone else finds that my judgment has been too pronounced, the presence of evaluative standards becomes an invitation to dismiss the argument on the grounds that twentieth-century morality is no way to approach the Middle Ages. And yet someone else deems that any verdict I may have rendered is not strong enough—indeed, that the moral obligation to distance oneself from the horrors of torture is so urgent that to fail to do so is to be complicit.

I thus acknowledge the problematic place of the personal in literary theory . . . the better, I hope, to move beyond it. All the responses cited above (each of which I have seen) can be reduced to two polarized and polarizing stances. The first is "How can one *fail* to take a position?" It operates under the assumption that the absence of a critical stand against torture is tantamount to silent approval or consent. The second is "How dare one *take* a position?" It operates under the assumption that there is no place in the academy for an individual with a modern contextualized self who stands back and makes aesthetic, logical, or moral judgments. Needless to say, the only critical response that can satisfy both objections is silence. And silence is not the purpose of literary criticism or, I submit, a suitable moral response to torture.

Throughout this book I endeavor to occupy a middle ground, which in fact is impossible to occupy when I seek neither to trivialize nor to pontificate about suffering. In this respect, David Nirenberg elaborates the problematic of speaking of violence so eloquently and so sensibly in *Communities of Violence* that I cannot say it better: "It is never easy to think or write about violence, however meaningful one believes it to be. Throughout the writing of this book I have tried to find sense in horrors, to place acts of violence in cultural and social contexts that would give them meanings beyond the literal ones which emerge with such visceral force" (16). Nirenberg hopes that the quest to understand the ideology of violence will not be misperceived as a denial of its horrific physicality. So do I. Nor does that wish stop him from emphasizing "how rare and strange a similarity the nightmares of a distant past bear to our own" (17).

In the classical, medieval, and modern theories that inform the pages that follow, it is my goal to do justice to the nightmarish violence of the medieval theater of cruelty. In aiming for measured assessments about aesthetics, rhetorical efficacy, and contextualized morality, I also attempt to respect similarities as well as differences between medieval and modern times along the lines articulated by Louise Fradenburg. As critics, she urges, we "need to concede some significant differences between modern theory and medieval texts. If we fail not only to concede these incompatibilities but to inform our interpretations with them, we lose our capacity to conduct cultural analyses of the Middle Ages, analyses that draw partly on differences for their interrogative power."[1] The contemporary world provides a variety of intellectual avenues for exploring a culture, from psychoanalysis to folklore to anthropology. I have opted for a model that the Middle Ages frequently chose as a means of explaining itself to itself: the rhetorical tradition.

If I am fortunate enough to convey humor, despair, hope, or fear when early texts convey them, I hope also to be fortunate enough to point out (and without myself doing violence to the sociocultural contexts of these texts) that sometimes fear is the dark side of hope and suffering the dark side of pleasure. To those who may ask: "Why the dark side? What about all the beauty of medieval aesthetics? What about the positive rather than the negative examples?" I can but respond that I do not see beauty and positivity as the primary side of the artifacts to be analyzed in this book. The dark side is not the only side. And it is not my intention to discount the influence of brightness, beauty, and non-

---

[1] Fradenburg is extrapolating from Elaine Scarry's groundbreaking *Body in Pain* in "Criticism, Anti-Semitism, and the Prioress's Tale," 74.

violent things. But since the dark side of aesthetics is still with us today, it merits inclusion within the larger scholarly dialogue.

Once upon a time Peter Brook cautioned that "there is a deadly element everywhere; in the cultural set-up, in our inherited artistic values, in the economic framework, in the actor's life, in the critic's function."[2] Rhetoric, law, and drama also betray a deadly element; and that is the subject of the medieval theater of cruelty.

I have profited enormously over the past several years from the insights and expertise of numerous colleagues. My intellectual debt to the inspiring work of R. Howard Bloch will be only too apparent, as will that to my various mentors: Stephen Nichols, Douglas Kelly, James J. Murphy, Robert Francis Cook, and David Lee Rubin. I am also grateful to Sarah Beckwith for her challenging reading of the manuscript for Cornell University Press, and to the remarkably generous colleagues who took the time to critique parts of this work in its various stages: Mary Carruthers, Rita Copeland, John Ganim, Richard Helgerson, Bruce Holsinger, Michal Kobialka, Michael Lieb, David Marshall, D. Vance Smith, Eugene Vance, and Kathleen Welch. I also owe three very special debts: to Robert Gaines, my first rhetoric teacher, because he paused to puzzle over Aristotle's treatment of torture; to Alan Knight, who not only discovered seventy-two plays from Lille in the library at Wolfenbüttel but was willing to share their texts pending publication of his own edition; and to Clifford Davidson, who in 1992 invited me to contribute an essay to a special issue of *Comparative Drama* devoted to the theme of classical survivals in the Middle Ages. When we spoke of my suspicions about a connection between torture, violence, and rhetoric on the medieval stage, he urged me to follow that hunch—one that led to *The Medieval Theater of Cruelty*.

It is perhaps with the greatest pleasure of all that I recognize the community of scholars I was fortunate enough to find at the University of California, Santa Barbara. When I needed to brainstorm about memory, Louise Fradenburg regaled me with her insights into psychoanalysis. When Sharon Farmer learned that I was working on torture, a photocopied passage from the *Miracles de Saint Loys* appeared in my mailbox; Jeffrey Burton Russell was there to sort out medieval Heaven from medieval Hell, and Paul Sonnino told me everything I needed to know about Philip II. When I was perplexed by the phenomenology of impersonation, Bert States talked it through with me, and Simon Williams cheerfully spearheaded an institutional effort to bring together colleagues in theater studies. When I needed to track down what Charles Nodier had really said about the theatricality of the French Revolution, Catherine Nesci knew immediately. When I realized that my own dean had pondered the topic of virtual performance, Paul Hernadi's *Cultural Transactions* arrived in intramural mail. When

---

[2] Brook, *Empty Space*, 17.

it came to the continuity of violence as aesthetics, Didier Maleuvre stirred me with contemporary philosophy. When I needed to ask about snuff films and urban legends, Constance Penley shared her resources; and when it was time to broach larger ideological questions of risk and censorship, Lizzie MacArthur shared her own work in progress. Meanwhile, my colleague William Ashby never once lost his astonishing ability to answer any philological question I have ever had. I also thank Bernie Kendler and Barbara Salazar, with whom it is always a pleasure to work; the Aspen Center for Physics for generously sharing their office resources with me each summer; and the Institute for Advanced Study in Princeton, where some of my research was conducted.

My first teacher of the Middle Ages was Daniel Poirion, and it is with pleasure that I acknowledge the life and spirit of a pedagogue who treated a class of undergraduates at the University of Virginia to the performance of a lifetime when he played every single role in the courtroom scene of the *Farce de Pathelin*. It is also with the deepest sadness that I mourn the passing of this remarkable man with whom I feel privileged to have studied.

Finally, I am grateful for the love and support of my husband, Eric D'Hoker, who spent countless hours listening to discussions of torture—proving once again that things of beauty can come from pain.

JODY ENDERS

Santa Barbara, California

Abbreviations

HLC   *A History of Literary Criticism in the Italian Renaissance,*
        by Bernard Weinberg
HMS   *Histoire de la mise en scène dans le théâtre religieux français du
        Moyen-Age,* by Gustave Cohen
HTB   *Histoire du théâtre en Belgique depuis son origine jusqu'à nos
        jours,* by Frédéric Faber
HTDW   *How to Do Things with Words,* by J. L. Austin
IO   *Institutio oratoria,* by Quintilian
LC   *The Lives of the Caesars,* by Suetonius
LFWP   *The Language of Fiction in a World of Pain,* by Barbara J. Eckstein
LM   *Les Mystères,* vols. 1 and 2 of *Histoire du théâtre en France,*
        by L. Petit de Julleville
MCV   *Milton and the Culture of Violence,* by Michael Lieb
MFLL   *Medieval French Literature and Law,* by R. Howard Bloch
MM   *The Master and Minerva,* by Helen Solterer
MS   *Mervelous Signals,* by Eugene Vance
NLH   *New Literary History*
PCC   *The Play Called Corpus Christi,* by V. A. Kolve
PCM   *Poetry and the Cult of the Martyrs,* by Michael Roberts
PDMA   *Pour une dramaturgie du Moyen-Age,* by Henri Rey-Flaud
PEL   *The Practice of Everyday Life,* by Michel de Certeau
PN   *Poetria nova,* by Geoffrey of Vinsauf
POLF   *The Philosophy of Literary Form,* by Kenneth Burke
PP   *Power and Persuasion in Late Antiquity,* by Peter Brown
QJS   *Quarterly Journal of Speech*
RAH   *Rhetorica ad Herennium,* by [Cicero]
RCPP   *Réflexions critiques sur la poésie et sur la peinture,*
        by Jean-Baptiste Du Bos
RIMA   *Rhetoric in the Middle Ages,* by James J. Murphy
RMDD   *Ramus, Method, and the Decay of Dialogue,* by Walter Ong
ROMD   *Rhetoric and the Origins of Medieval Drama,* by Jody Enders
RPI   *Role Playing and Identity,* by Bruce Wilshire
RRT   *Rhetoric, Romance, and Technology,* by Walter Ong
SES   *The Surprising Effects of Sympathy,* by David Marshall
SRT   *Staging Real Things,* by Geoff Pywell
ST   *Stages of Terror,* by Anthony Kubiak
SV   *The Subject of Violence,* by Peter Haidu
SW   *Selected Writings,* by Jean Baudrillard
TD   *The Theater and Its Double,* by Antonin Artaud
TFW   *Trial by Fire and Water,* by Robert Bartlett
TM   *Théâtre de la mort,* by André de Lorde
TMA   *The Theatre in the Middle Ages,* by William Tydeman
TO   *Theater of the Oppressed,* by Augusto Boal

TT	*Torture and Truth*, by Page duBois
VH	*The Vanishing Hitchhiker*, by Jan Harold Brunvand
VS	*Violence and the Sacred*, by René Girard
WD	*Writing and Difference*, by Jacques Derrida
YFS	*Yale French Studies*

The Medieval Theater of Cruelty

If we are what people say we are, let us take our delight in the blood of men.

—Tertullian, *De spectaculis*

A Polemical Introduction

Once a connection is assumed between violence and rhetoric, the two terms begin to slide, and, soon enough, the connection will appear to be reversible.

— Teresa de Lauretis, *Technologies of Gender*

In the *Topica*, one of the classical texts most widely accessible in the European Middle Ages, Cicero makes the following remarkable statement about an experience that was and would remain all too well known. He speaks of torture:

Nam et verberibus, tormentis, igni fatigati quae dicunt ea videtur *veritas ipsa dicere*, et quae *perturbationibus animi, dolore*, cupiditate, iracundia, *metu*, qui necessitatis vim habent, afferunt auctoritatem et fidem.[1]

For what men say when they have been worn down by stripes, the rack, and fire, seems to be spoken by truth itself; and what they say under stress of mind—grief, lust, anger or fear—lends authority and conviction, because these emotions seem to have the force of necessity.

The context of the passage is quite precise: Cicero is proffering future lawyers advice about how to advance convincing arguments based on necessities that "may be either physical or mental" (facit etiam necessitas fidem, quae tum a corporibus tum ab animis nascitur). But for students of the Middle Ages and of

---

[1] The most enduring "polemical introduction" I know of was written by Northrop Frye in 1957 to preface his *Anatomy of Criticism*. Different times call for different polemics, as do different understandings of different anatomies.

The citation from Cicero's *Topica*, 74, is discussed briefly in Mellor, *Torture*, 70–71. Such works as the *Topica*, *De inventione*, and the Pseudo-Ciceronian *Rhetorica ad Herennium* were available in France as early as the eleventh century (see, e.g., Clerval, *Écoles de Chartres*, 115–17). The finest introductions to the general history of rhetoric remain Murphy, *Rhetoric in the Middle Ages* (hereafter *RIMA*); Kennedy, *Classical Rhetoric*; and Fumaroli, *L'Age de l'éloquence*.

theater history, his words are hauntingly familiar. His description of torture as a factual, "extrinsic," or "inartificial" rhetorical proof is a disturbing echo of that quintessential Aristotelian description of tragedy—the art form that, through the manipulation of pity and fear, grants "relief to these and similar emotions." [2] Cicero's invocation of the "disturbances of mind" (*perturbationi animi*) that accompany such emotions as pain and fear takes on a hitherto unsuspected significance when we discover the philological parallels offered by a sixteenth-century Latin translation of Aristotle's *Poetics* 1449b. Tragedy functions by purging pity and fear through catharsis: "non per enarrationem rei, sed per misericordiam, metumque factis expressum, eius modi vehementes *animorum perturbationes* unasquasque purgans expiansque" (not through narrating the thing, but through pity and fear expressed by the deeds, in that way purging and relieving all such violent disturbances of the soul).[3] Even at the level of philology, a connection emerges between torture, law, rhetoric, drama, and what Isidore of Seville (ca. 570–636) once termed "the spectacle of cruelty." [4] That connection was conspicuous centuries before Antonin Artaud pronounced that "without an element of cruelty at the root of every spectacle, the theater is not possible." [5]

That the rhetorician's legalistic view of torture could be so similar to the dramatist's literary view of theater has ramifications for the history of aesthetics that are harrowing, to say the least. Is it not possible, then, that this evidence might provide a partial explanation for why learned medieval authors of mystery plays, moralities, and farces wove so many scenes of torture into their plays? At a time when prescriptive literary treatises such as Aristotle's *Poetics* were largely unavailable, did they turn instead to a system of rhetorical discovery, imagery, and performance that included discussions of torture? [6] Beyond the obvious desire of the religious dramatist to render faithfully the biblical accounts of the tortures of Christ, is it conceivable that, like his rhetorician colleagues, he concluded from his university training in rhetoric as a "general theory of literature" that torture was a dramatic and effective means of conceiving, proving, and enact-

---

[2] Aristotle, *Poetics*, ed. Fyfe, 1449b. For the traditional definitions of extrinsic/inartificial proof (*atechnoi*) as opposed to intrinsic/artificial or invented proofs (*entechnoi*), see Aristotle, *"Art" of Rhetoric* (hereafter *Rhetoric*), 1355b; and Quintilian, *Institutio oratoria* (hereafter *IO*), V, 4.1–2.

[3] Aristotle, *De poetica*, ed. Harles, 1449b; see also D. S. Margouliouth's edition of *The Poetics of Aristotle*. Quintilian also speaks of *animi perturbatio* in *IO*, V, pr. 1; and of pity and fear: e.g., IV, 1.20 and 42; VI, 1.28.

[4] *Isidori Hispalensis Episcopi Etymologiarum* (hereafter Isidore, *Etymologarium*), vol. 2, bk. 18, "De bello et ludis," chap. 59. I discuss the "De bello et ludis" at length in *Rhetoric and the Origins of Medieval Drama* (hereafter *ROMD*), 77–89.

[5] Artaud, *Theater and Its Double* (hereafter *TD*), trans. Mary Caroline Richards, 99. Needless to say, the title of this book is inspired by Artaud's treatise.

[6] There is some evidence to suggest that portions of the *Poetics* may have been available in the early Middle Ages via Averroës and Hermann the German, although details on the circulation of those works often remain elusive. For Hermann's text and a helpful critical commentary, see Minnis, Scott, and Wallace, *Medieval Literary Criticism*, chap. 7, esp. their discussion of catharsis, 285.

ing the didactic messages of ecclesiastical drama?[7] Finally, might not such an approach help to repudiate the opinions advanced by such early historians of the theater as L. Petit de Julleville, who denounced the "fuzzy and dormant sensibilities of the medieval public," and Gustave Cohen, who proclaimed that the medieval stage reflected "a universally cruel tendency. . . . As far as a lofty moral and social conscience is concerned, it is betrayed nowhere."[8]

Those questions may be answered in the affirmative once we reunite two disciplines that have characteristically remained separate but that are in fact conjoined by the influential forensic rhetorical tradition: the histories of medieval stagecraft and of torture. The European Middle Ages inherited a classical rhetorical legacy that characterized torture as a hermeneutic legal quest for truth, a mode of proof, a form of punishment enacted by the stronger on the weaker, and a genre of spectacle or entertainment.[9] Historians of torture have increasingly perceived the great instability of the relationship between torture and truth,[10] but they have devoted far less attention to one of the foundational causes of that instability: the role of dramatic theory and spectacle in the rhetorical discovery, interpretation, enactment, and even theatricalization of torture. As we shall see, the rhetorical tradition poses fundamental problems concerning the aesthetic nature of "truth production." By looking to the myriad connections among rhetoric, drama, and violence in terms of the rhetorical interplay among hermeneutics, imagery, and performance, I argue that the "truth" of medieval torture is cast in terms of dramatic verisimilitude, probability, character, and catharsis and adumbrated with a panoply of theatrical, illusory, subjective, and aesthetic terms while the "truth" of highly rhetoricized medieval plays is frequently enhanced by scenes of torture. In other words, the spectacularity of violence was

[7] Curtius, *European Literature* (hereafter *EL*), 71; see also Trimpi, "Quality of Fiction." I am by no means suggesting that medieval legal practice was identical to that of the Romans. On this subject see, e.g., Langbein, "Origins of Judicial Torture," in *Torture and the Law of Proof*, 5–8. Still, it is clear that during their rhetorical training, medieval students of literature (like their peers who aspired to be lawyers, priests, and politicians) would have been exposed to classical views of torture—especially in such widely circulated texts as the *Rhetorica ad Herennium* and Cicero's *Topica*. For university training in rhetoric, see, e.g., Paetow, *Arts Course at Medieval Universities*, 23–25; and Kelly, *Arts of Poetry and Prose*.

[8] Petit de Julleville, *Les Mystères* (hereafter *LM*), 1:224; and Cohen, *Histoire de la mise en scène* (hereafter *HMS*), 276.

[9] In addition to Mellor and Langbein, see esp. Peters, *Torture, The Magician, the Witch, and the Law* and *Inquisition*. Peters demonstrates that in the theory of torture, the distinction between interrogation, investigation, and punishment was confused very early on (*Torture*, 28). He also provides two helpful bibliographic essays: in *Torture*, 188–91; and in *Magician*, app. 3. Other useful introductions to the history of torture include Lea, *Inquisition of the Middle Ages* and *Superstition and Force*; Bartlett, *Trial by Fire and Water*; Garnsey, *Social Status and Legal Privilege in the Roman Empire*; Asad, *Genealogies of Religion* and "Notes on Body, Pain, and Truth"; duBois, *Torture and Truth* (hereafter *TT*); Fiorelli, *Tortura giudiziaria*; and Ullman, "Reflections on Medieval Torture."

[10] Particularly sensitive approaches to that instability include Peters, *Torture*, 33; duBois, *TT*; Hanson, "Torture and Truth"; and Spierenburg, *Spectacle of Suffering*.

embedded in the very language of the law, and the violence of law was expressed in the theater.

Even though rhetoric was ostensibly concerned with persuasive probabilities, its extrinsic proofs did indeed purport to reveal truths. Violently imagined and extracted through torture, those truths lent authority to a legal rhetoric that often relied on the so-called "factual evidence" of torture, however theatrically and prejudicially that "evidence" was constructed. As a discipline, rhetoric thus constitutes a complex epistemological matrix by which learned medieval writers theatricalized real legal ordeals and concomitantly codified legal practice as theatricality—and all that with a view toward discovering, disseminating, and performing truths that themselves become dramatic fictions.[11] In the end, the most powerful vehicle for perpetuating the illusion of truth inherent in torture may well be the literary genre with the ontology that draws strength from the truth of its own illusions: drama.

Using key rhetorical and theatrical texts from antiquity through the early Renaissance, I propose to return to the violent, ideological foundations of an everelliptical rhetorical Truth to show that the medieval understanding of torture both enabled and encouraged the dramatic representation of violence as a means of coercing theater audiences into accepting the various "truths" enacted didactically in mysteries, miracles, and even farces.[12] Of special importance here are three of the five constitutive parts or canons of the legal or forensic rhetorical genre. In theoretical treatments of invention (*inventio*), memory (*memoria*), and delivery (*actio, pronuntiatio*, or *hypokrisis*), the subject of torture was regularly interspersed with larger themes of hermeneutics, communication, violence, law, creation, creativity, truth, and performance.[13] *Inventio* was the site of hermeneutic discovery and creation, and it foregrounded torture at the level

---

[11] By "learned," I mean medieval men who were trained in rhetoric during a formal university education. I return shortly to the complexities of this term. Here I also extend Michael Riffaterre's concept of "fictional truth" in linguistics, semantics, or diegesis to the cultural praxis of jurisprudence (*Fictional Truth* [hereafter *FT*], 5–6).

[12] This is not to say, of course, that all medieval drama was coercive, although see Jelle Koopmans's contextual introduction to the *Théâtre des exclus au Moyen Age*, 15–36. Moreover, the traditional period divisions of "Middle Ages" and "Renaissance" tend to mask certain continuities, esp. in the religious drama of the fifteenth and sixteenth centuries, which are the literary focus of this book. Hence I use the term "medieval" for an expanded period.

[13] For the five rhetorical canons of invention, disposition, style, memory, and delivery (discussions of which frequently occur in treatments of the forensic or legal genre of rhetoric as opposed to the deliberative or epideictic genres), see, e.g., [Cicero], *Ad C. Herennium* (hereafter *RAH*), I, 3; Quintilian, *IO*, III, 3.1–3; Cicero, *De inventione*, I, 9; Martianus Capella, *De nuptiis*, 141g; Alcuin, *Rhetoric of Alcuin and Charlemagne*, 71–83. Philologically, *actio, pronuntiatio*, and especially *hypokrisis* implied impersonation and counterfeit, *hypokrisis* referring to the theatrical register of "acting" (*hypokritike*). In Chapter 2, I propose a metaphorical reading of *dispositio* as a "body" or corporeal incarnation of rhetoric, leaving aside only *elocutio* in light of Marc Fumaroli's assessment that that canon was primarily responsible for the marginalization of rhetoric in contemporary culture (*Age de l'éloquence*, 10).

of ideological and linguistic conception. There, an elliptical truth was fabricated violently and dramatically in such a way that it came into direct conflict with the probabilities that composed the province of rhetoric. *Memoria* provided the mental space in which the violently discovered "truths" of invention were visualized and deceptively authorized through detailed visualizations which functioned as virtual performances. *Actio* offered a means by which real bodies with real voices translated the violent imagery of an inventional memory into the speech and action of the courtroom, the classroom, and the stage. With the profusion of rhetorical lore available in the Middle Ages, it is thus probable that a learned dramatist staging the violent Passion of Christ or even the scenes of abuse in a farce may readily have turned to the violence of rhetoric. He may have done so conceptually at the level of invention, visually in the memory, and performatively in the praxis of delivery.

Once one has restored the rhetorical connections among the violent discovery of truth during invention, its storage in the memory, and its dramatic staging during delivery, one is better able to explain (if not to explain away) how medieval religious theater might have come to include the portrayal of physical suffering as a pivotal means by which to reveal its own truths. Indeed, I show that much of that theater not only *was* violent but that, at some level, it *had to be* violent because it was unable to escape the conceptual and philological similarities among creative invention, dramatic catharsis, and human suffering that emerged from the rhetorical treatments of torture (which circulated in the classical, medieval, and early Renaissance educational systems). The study of rhetoric then bears out John Gatton's choice of "Il faut du sang" (there must be blood) as an epigraph for medieval drama.[14] It further helps us uncover the conceptual foundations for dramatic and human violence in a variety of cultural arenas, including literature and literary criticism.

While the notion of a tortured and torturing medieval theater might initially sound sensational, there is nothing sensational about the complicity of torture, rhetoric, and law in the construction of a Truth that is as violent as it is theatrical. Kenneth Burke once perceived that the relation between theater and law was a forensic correspondence born of spectacularity and performance.[15] Howard Bloch theorized that one of the primary functions of medieval literary discourse was to verbalize and to poeticize the legal ordeal.[16] I have shown elsewhere that

[14] The line is from the vast fifteenth-century cycle of the *Mistère du Vieil Testament*; see Gatton's essay of the same title, " 'There Must Be Blood,' " 77. It was Gustave Cohen, however, who first proposed this idea when he wrote that "one may extend to all the mystery plays this stage direction [*rubrique*] which appears in the 'Mystère du Vieil Testament': 'il faut du sang' " (*HMS*, 152).

[15] Burke, *Attitudes toward History*, 39. For an important discussion of Burke's views, see Kubiak, *Stages of Terror* (hereafter *ST*), 27–28.

[16] Bloch, *Medieval French Literature and Law* (hereafter *MFLL*), 153–66. See also Bartlett following T. F. T. Plucknett on thirteenth-century judicial torture as a "newer sort of ordeal" (*Trial by Fire and Water* [hereafter *TFW*], 139).

forensic rhetoric was indivisible from the very origins of drama, characterized as it was by a constant shifting among legal statute, performance, and the poetic imitation of justice (*ROMD*, chap. 1). The historian Edward Peters is the first to admit that "our chief sources for the torture of slaves are the legal orators and the comic playwrights" (*Torture*, 14). Much of the historical evidence about torture, then, has been culled from rhetoric and theater history. That practice may actually have served to camouflage the notion that the truths of the law and of its rhetoric are profoundly theatrical as well as violent.

Page duBois finds, for instance, that forensic discourse and practice have always been indivisible from "the deliberate infliction of human suffering" (*TT*, 4). In light of the compatibility of forensic rhetoric with theatrical discourse and practice, a similar contention might be made for the indivisibility of human suffering and drama. As a violent, creative, and dramatic process, rhetoric promises to illuminate substantially such an oft-staged moment as the scourging of Christ in medieval religious drama. On one hand, that scene exemplifies the rich if frightening union of word and action, investigation and punishment, epistemology and violence, torture and truth. On the other hand, in the reciprocal relationship between rhetoric and literature which has long been affirmed by historians of rhetoric, a violent literary (and in this case, dramatic) moment might also have influenced the conception of new rhetorical treatises.

It does bear mentioning at this point, however, that some might argue that in directing attention to the most violent moments of medieval and early Renaissance drama, I have somehow decontextualized those moments, created a freeze frame, divorced them from the religiosity that inspired such a genre as the *mystère*. I would counter that moments of extreme violence are always "decontextualized." It is not the literary critic who selects them out but rather the scourging scenes that select themselves out. To a medieval audience as to a modern one, a beating was never associated exclusively with the theater. Instead, it recalled other spectacles of punishment (legal or illegal) in which bodies in pain were displayed: school bullies, court cases, public punishments and executions. Singled out for special attention (negative or positive) by aficionados, audiences, and critics over the ages, a scourging is meant to stand apart and always has done. In that sense, if the representative texts cited here as evidence are more parts than wholes, more moments than durations, and more snapshots than entire pictures, it is because these powerful scenes symbolize a problem that pervades entire works. While I cannot pretend to propose anything resembling a complete account of the conception and reception of medieval and Renaissance dramatic works, I do believe that the sustained inquiry into the historical and philological interrelations of rhetoric, law, and drama can help us to understand why torture must stand out.

Whether the representations are dramatic, cinematic, literary, or juridico-political, nothing reviles the imagination more than torture. Yet nothing titillates it more. In the histories of rhetoric, law, religion, and theater, it is the tension of that moment of simultaneous attraction and revulsion, of acknowledgement and denial that provides one important key to understanding both the violence and the drama of medieval representation. Scholars of drama in particular are only too familiar with the commonplace aesthetic theory that there is pleasure in watching pain. For Aristotle, pain, mimesis, and catharsis came together in the theory that "we enjoy looking at accurate likenesses of things which are themselves painful to see, obscene beasts, for instance, and corpses" (*Poetics* 1448b). For Lucian of Samosata, the mime presented violence "in a way that is less risky and at the same time more beautiful and pleasurable." [17] Perhaps most telling of all, for Plato mimesis and catharsis were key components of law and legal discourse as lawyers became the "authors of a tragedy [*tragoidias*]" and forensic discourse or policy a "representation [*mimesis*] of the fairest and best life, which is in reality, as we assert, the truest tragedy." [18] Platonic law itself (along with its links to violence) became a cathartic enterprise: "when men are investigating the subject of laws their investigation deals almost entirely with pleasures and pains, whether in States or in individuals" (*Laws*, I, 636d).[19] A new critical orientation toward the troublingly fluid boundaries among drama, torture, truth, the law, and its secular or religious politics suggests that it is often impossible to distinguish a specific ontological status for theater that is separate from violence. Even so, ever since Plato, critics have tried.

Largely influenced by Michel Foucault's *Discipline and Punish* and Elaine Scarry's *Body in Pain*, literary critics have devoted much attention to the spectacular nature of violence, transgression, discipline, and punishment. Wendy Lesser is "drawn to the increasingly blurry borderline between real murder and fictional murder . . . but it is not clear that these categories were ever easily separable." [20] William B. Worthen speculates that "the relations between theater and torture seem complex and multiple"; and Scarry, who motivates his remark, employs a theatrical lexicon in her work on torture: since it is built on "repeated acts of display and [has] as its purpose the production of a fantastic illusion of power, torture is a grotesque piece of compensatory drama." [21] If one were to limit discussion of this subject to modern or even postmodern theory, however, one would overlook the vital insights imparted by classical and medieval rhetoric. As it happens, the rhetorico-dramatic ideology of torture proves extremely

[17] See his second-century "Saltatio," 71. Also, Bert States concludes his *Pleasure of the Play* with a chapter headed "The Pleasure of Pain."

[18] Plato, *Laws*, II, 817B. For an excellent discussion of theories of drama raised in Plato's *Laws*, see Eden, *Poetic and Legal Fiction*, 29–30.

[19] Important medieval, Renaissance, and early modern descendants of that principle are discussed in Chapter 1.

[20] Lesser, *Pictures at an Execution*, 1. On transgression, see also Stallybrass and White, *Politics and Poetics of Transgression*; and on its politics, Steiner, *Scandal of Pleasure*, 71–93.

[21] Worthen, *Modern Drama and the Rhetoric of Theater*, 134n, who also cites Scarry, *Body in Pain* (hereafter *BP*), 28. These citations represent only a glimpse of the overpowering contemporary interest in this topic.

relevant to such modern theories as Artaud's "theater of cruelty," Kubiak's "theatre of punishment" (*ST*, 49), and Foucault's "spectacle of the scaffold" (*DP*, chap. 2). What we shall see, though, is that the rhetorical tradition played a crucial role in the creation of precisely that sort of cultural moment in which the theatricality of violence and the violence of theatricality are coterminous. Kubiak surmises in his brilliant *Stages of Terror* that the affiliation between theater and law can be traced rather to a hidden system of pain production (24–25). I mean to establish that one such system of pain production was rhetoric.[22]

I thus bring together what the current academic matrix has usually separated. Because of the occasionally arbitrary disciplinary divisions endemic to academia, legal historians, theater historians, classicists, medievalists, historians of rhetoric, anthropologists, philosophers, and modern theorists of literature, culture, and performance have mostly worked independently toward understanding torture. Not surprisingly, the results (however perceptive) have been characterized by fragmentation rather than synthesis. Historians from Piero Fiorelli and Alec Mellor to Henry Lea and Edward Peters have long recognized that torture "evidently connoted a kind of necessary critical inquiry."[23] Theater historians have consistently documented the violence (either deftly imitated or real) of medieval dramatic representation.[24] Meanwhile, Page duBois has scrupulously reestablished the connections between torture and theater in ancient Greece (*TT*, chap. 2). Finally, modern theorists have shared a concern with the performative violence of language—whether that concern is represented in theater studies, as in Artaud's "theater of cruelty" and Jean Baudrillard's "simulations"; in theater anthropology through the work of Victor Turner, Erving Goffman, and Richard Schechner; in theater phenomenology (Bruce Wilshire and Herbert Blau); in the sociology of the quotidial theater of violence (Elaine Scarry and Anthony Kubiak); or in the more general literary philosophies of Kenneth Burke, Michel Foucault, René Girard, Gilles Deleuze and Félix Guattari, and Jacques Derrida.[25] It is rhetoric that provides the necessary materials

[22] In this connection, see also Derrida's *Writing and Difference* (hereafter *WD*), chap. 4; and de Lauretis, *Technologies of Gender*, chap. 2. Throughout this book I will be employing such terms as "rhetorico-dramatic" and "rhetorico-literary." This is not the same thing as suggesting that forensic rhetoric is identical to theater or to any other literary genre. Forensic rhetoric would, of course, play out its juridical proceedings ritually with "real" results, while theatrical genres presumably would "just represent" them. But, as we shall see, the similarities between certain legalistic and theatrical representations readily collapse that helpful distinction.

[23] The citation is from Peters, *Torture*, 14, as he considers evidence from Aristotle and Thucydides about the interrogation of slaves.

[24] For example, the work of Rey-Flaud, Faber, Petit de Julleville, Gustave Cohen, and Meredith and Tailby is discussed at length in Chapter 3.

[25] Here I refer in particular to Baudrillard, "Simulacra and Simulations," in his *Selected Writings* (hereafter *SW*); Turner, *From Ritual to Theatre*; Goffman, *Frame Analysis*; Schechner, *Performance Theory*; Wilshire, *Role Playing and Identity*; Blau, *Audience* and *Blooded Thought*; Burke, *Philosophy of Literary Form* (hereafter *POLF*); Girard, *Violence and the Sacred* (hereafter *VS*)—a work to be read in connection with, e.g., Vernant and Vidal-Naquet, *Tragedy and Myth in Ancient*

for reunification; for it is rhetoric that documents the commingling of legal, political, or theological process, literary invention, violence, and dramatic performance. Rhetoric is the theoretical site at which the violence of representation is articulated as theory, rehearsed in the imagination, and concretized dramatically.

In essence, all the scholars mentioned above (and many more besides) address one and the same notion (albeit in manifestly different ways): that there was and is a hermeneutic of torture which exploits the relationship between language and pain; and that that relationship can be elucidated (and perhaps changed) through language itself. By no means, of course, do I wish to imply that the infliction of physical pain can or should be reduced to a series of linguistic or aesthetic constructs. The perniciousness of the critical proclivity toward exalting language above all things has been forcefully indicted by both Elaine Scarry and Barbara J. Eckstein, the former insisting that "pain is pain, and not a metaphor of pain"; and the latter that "the daily assault on human flesh and all physical facts of life are not simply battles of words." [26] Nor do I posit any sort of purity or distance for the critical language used in the service of describing torture—even to condemn it. As Simon Goldhill cautions, "there is no position beyond such norms and institutions [of the law] from which to speak of violence. We are all always already implicated in the system and rhetoric of power." [27] Moreover, suspicions about the discourses condemning cruelty considerably antedate our own era; the Christian apologist Tertullian (ca. 160–225) already voiced his own in the *De spectaculis*: "If these tragedies and comedies, bloody and lustful, impious and prodigal, teach outrage and lust, the study of what is cruel or vile is no better than itself. What in action is rejected, is not in word to be accepted." [28] His contemporary, Saint Cyprian, was even more cynical, hinting that "the same persons are accusers in public and the defendants in secret, both their own critics and the guilty." [29] Nevertheless, the words used to theorize torture can tell us a great deal; and, once understood, may be harnessed to social change.

Greece; Frazer, *Scapegoat*, Deleuze and Guattari, *Anti-Oedipus*; and Derrida, *Of Grammatology* and *WD*.

[26] Here I borrow the résumé of Scarry's thesis (*BP*, 51–56) offered in Blau, *Audience*, 165. The citation from Eckstein appears in her *Language of Fiction in a World of Pain* (hereafter *LFWP*), 181. See also duBois's eloquent refusal to lyricize, sensationalize, exoticize, or celebrate torture (*TT*, 141).

[27] Goldhill, "Violence in Greek Tragedy," 26, in which he argues that "the notion of 'violence' needs to be carefully situated within a cultural, rhetorical and ideological system" (15). For an excellent overview of tragedy in general, see Kelly, *Ideas and Forms of Tragedy*.

[28] Tertullian, *De spectaculis*, chap. 17.

[29] Cyprian, "To Donatus," chap. 9, p. 15. His cynicism was echoed on the sixteenth-century English stage by Philip Massinger (b. 1584), whose actor Latinus paraphrases Tertullian: "Pleasures of worse natures / Are gladly entertayn'd, and they that shun vs, / Practise, in priuate sports the *Stewes* would blush at" ("Roman Actor," Act I, scene 1, p. 21).

According to the late Paul Zumthor, theater is the literary genre that is the "most receptive to changes in the social structure, and the most revelatory of those changes." [30] My point is that no real critique of violence can lead to social change unless the pervasive linguistic and ideological foundations of violence are exposed. [31] Such a critique necessarily goes beyond even the sophisticated inquiries of a Derrida into the inherent violence of language. It must also call into question the enactment of the violence of language on the entire stage of popular culture in what Michel de Certeau terms "the practice of everyday life." [32] It must refute a widespread conservative tendency to focus in the name of the law on the acts criminals committed in order to "deserve" their ordeals. [33] Yet, at the same time, it must also question some of the more optimistic conclusions of a largely liberal New Historicism, which has sometimes privileged the recovery of contestation, subversiveness, rebellion, humor, and dialogism over its oft-violent sources and contexts. [34] Although I do not wish to insinuate that the medieval theater offered no possibility of metadramatic critique in the form of rebellion, I do mean quite deliberately to suggest we have not finished circumnavigating the paradoxes of violence. That is, even when it is possible to reconstruct the contexts of specific medieval performances, it seems unlikely that representations of torture glorified by hegemonies are sinister while those glorified by other classes and communities are not. [35] Caught up in the current vogue for critiquing the politics of the oppressor (in which my own book participates, at least in part), we are not always well served if we focus exclusively on the reconstructed voices of communities that have been marginalized or persecuted and fail to explore the possibility that those very communities were also capable of replicating oppressive structures.

Somewhere in this nexus of mutual influences lies the critical work necessary for deciphering violence. Only then will it be possible to assess Simon Richter's conclusion that "pain is beauty's story": "no matter what classicism says to the contrary, the condition for ideal beauty is material pain." [36] Only then will we

[30] Zumthor, *Essai de poétique médiévale*, 447.

[31] I allude deliberately here to Frank Lentricchia's *Criticism and Social Change*, esp. to his prefatory "Provocations" (even though he abjured them in an essay in *Lingua Franca*).

[32] I refer to de Certeau's book of the same title, *The Practice of Everyday Life* (hereafter *PEL*).

[33] As historians such as Esther Cohen (*Crossroads of Justice*) and Bartlett (*TFW*) have amply shown, few things are more impressionistic than medieval justice.

[34] Of many scholars conducting superb reconstructive work related to the field of early English drama, one thinks, e.g., of Justice, *Writing and Rebellion*; Rubin, *Corpus Christi* (hereafter *CC*); Copeland, *Rhetoric, Hermeneutics, and Translation* and the collection of essays Copeland edited, *Criticism and Dissent*; Scherb, "Violence and the Social Body"; Travis, "Social Body of the Dramatic Christ"; and Sarah Beckwith's forthcoming *Signifying God*.

[35] After all, it is a commonplace of the anthropology of Christianity that the cult imposed itself initially by superimposing its own festivities on days when pagan feasts were already held. Regrettably, the questions why, when, and how popular anxieties about violence exert themselves in response to precise hegemonic structures lie beyond the scope of this book.

[36] Richter, *Laocoon's Body*, 198.

be in a position to understand the genesis of the pleasures of pain, for which audiences have consistently had a taste. Only then will the inadequacy of certain comforting modern distinctions become perceptible, such as William Ian Miller's statement that "violence can bear positive moral significations in certain settings; cruelty seldom can. Cruelty always bears with it a sense of disproportionality." [37] If torture, drama, rhetoric, and violence have habitually been linked, then cruelty is difficult to escape.

In his reevaluation of the historian Marc Bloch's statement that violence was "deep-rooted in the social structure and in the mentality" of the Middle Ages, Peter Haidu protests that "we will not begin to make headway with our own versions of the issue [of violent transgression] until we grasp the continuity between those contemporary versions and the bases laid down in the Middle Ages upon which our struggles with violence are founded." [38] John Gatton finds that the necessity for bloodshed still obtains in such a contemporary drama as *Agnes of God*, which "follows the crimson path blazed and trod by its centuries-old theatrical ancestors, with its familiar and popular horrific landmarks of physical agony, infanticide, mutilation, and death" ("There must be blood," 89). And, when questioning the beauty of classicist aesthetics, Simon Richter alleges that the crucified Christ and the victim of rape or torture are "the radically unclassical counterparts of the Laocoon, riveted together through pain. Each stands for a heterogenous discourse that pierced the tranquillity of classical aesthetics" (*Laocoon's Body*, 190). The rhetorical tradition, characterized by bloodshed, assaults, and piercing, provides a particularly effective way to prove those claims historically as it disproves the intuition that there was ever any such tranquillity in classical aesthetics. Hence my primary emphasis on a "medieval theater of cruelty" as a mental rhetorical theater, a memory theater, and a theater of rhetoric which exists as a *theory* of virtual performance. [39] That virtuality is repeatedly "translated" into actual medieval dramatic practice (which impels my reliance on theatrical examples throughout). But it is not limited to drama or even to the learned theatrical illustrations to be invoked in this book. Concentrated within the principally male, hegemonic world of medieval learning, the rhetorical theater of cruelty accounts for a great deal of medieval theatrical practice, but not all of it.

Still, modern theorists often imply that Artaud's theater of cruelty or its current descendants are something new, with each generation seemingly committed to singling out the novelty of whatever violent art forms predominate in their day. When the director Charles Nonon was interviewed about the closing

---

[37] Miller, *Humiliation*, 70.

[38] Haidu, *Subject of Violence* (hereafter *SV*), 195. The citation to Bloch is to *Feudal Society*, 2:411.

[39] Of special importance here is the role of memory, which Frances Yates described as a theater in her pathbreaking *Art of Memory* (esp. chaps. 6 and 7) and *Theatre of the World*. On the practical problems of the concept of virtual performativity, see Alter, *Sociosemiotic Theory of Theatre*, 178.

of the scandalous Parisian theater of the Grand Guignol, he had this to say about a popular actress who had been bound, gagged, whipped, and had the tips of her breasts "clipped off with hedge shears and her eyes scooped out with a soup spoon and a jackknife": "We are very proud of that sequence. . . . We consider it *original*, at least onstage."[40] André de Lorde, a dramatist for that theater, contended in 1928 that "the theater that seeks fear as its principal mode of action—I am not saying as its goal—is a recent invention; it responds to a need characteristic of the times we live in."[41] Richter notes that before Winckelmann, "theories of beauty abounded, but a theory of classical beauty that relies on pain as a self-representing force is *something altogether new*, so new, in fact, that Winckelmann himself was uncomfortable with it" (*Laocoon's Body*, 47; my emphasis). And with regard to avant-garde theatrical performances of bodily mortification, Herbert Blau posits a "*new* foregrounding of the body" which confounds traditional artistry by grounding the dramatic image in "the visceral immediacy of its pain" (*Audience*, 164; emphasis mine). Such work valuably situates theatrical violence within specific sociohistorical contexts, but there is little novel here. Indeed, throughout literary history, critics have just as steadily (if paradoxically) named violence as something that audiences want and need, despite its apparent newness.

For example, if we survey several periods, we find that in the first century Tacitus was already deploring the "peculiar and characteristic vices of this metropolis of ours, taken on, as it seems to me, almost in the mother's womb [*in utero matris*]—the passion for play actors, and the mania for gladiatorial shows and horse-racing."[42] Gustave Cohen considered torture a constitutive part of any medieval mystery play (*HMS*, 148) and declared that "we cannot insist upon this emphatically enough: if the people hadn't liked torture, they could not have tolerated the sight of it" (*HMS*, 275). Jonas Barish remarks of the ubiquitous violence in Shakespeare that "something about physical injuries inflicted on human bodies seems to exercise a kind of mesmerism, both over Shakespeare's generation and our own."[43] Jean Rousset, the literary historian of the French Baroque, dubbed its drama "a theater of cruelty" that "tends toward the drama of horror."[44] The eighteenth-century aesthetic critic Jean-Baptiste Du Bos looked back in horror to the ancient Roman gladiatorial practice of fattening up future victims "so that the blood would flow more slowly through the wounds they would receive, and so that the spectator could thus enjoy for a longer time the

---

[40] "Outdone by Reality," *Time*, 30 November 1962, 78, 80 (emphasis mine), cited in Callahan, "Ultimate in Theatre Violence," 170.

[41] De Lorde, *Théâtre de la mort* (hereafter *TM*), 13; emphasis mine.

[42] Tacitus, *Dialogus de oratoribus*, 29. He also transfers both blame and agency to women and, more precisely, to the uterus (a point I explore in Chapter 2).

[43] Barish, "Shakespearean Violence," 101.

[44] Rousset, *L'Age baroque*, 6; I thank Rachael Siciliano for bringing this text to my attention.

horrors of their agony."[45] In the nineteenth century, Jules Michelet stated that the public persecution of witches linked pleasure with both outrage and outrageousness, and Charles Nodier cast the French Revolution as "the greatest drama of all time," a "bloody play" whose spectators/participants "needed conspiracies, dark cells, scaffolds, fields of battle, gunpowder, and blood."[46] In twentieth-century Paris, the theater of the Grand Guignol regaled its thrilled crowds with such spectacles as the following: "A butcher reels out a woman's intestines, two novice nuns are raped and one subsequently impaled on a blood-drenched meat hook, and a crone gouges out the eye of a starving old man and feeds it to him. . . . And all the while the audience gasps, and cheers and bursts into nervous laughter."[47] In fact, André de Lorde dreamed of composing a play that was "so terrifying that, a few instants after the curtain rose, the spectators would be constrained to flee the theater screaming, incapable of seeing and hearing such a drama any longer" (*TM*, 11–12).

Violence has underpinned the aesthetics of theater since the earliest times. Nor did that violence subside in the wake of ubiquitous critiques or of the still more vehement counsel of Tertullian that aficionados of the stage replace the *fabula* of pagan wrestling with the truth of the agonistic spectacle of Christianity: "See . . . perfidy slain by faith, cruelty crushed by pity. . . . Have you a mind for blood? You have the blood of Christ" (*De spectaculis*, chap. 29).[48] Tertullian is suggesting that the pagan spectacle of immoral violence be replaced by a Christian spectacle of moral violence—an effort that may be profitably analyzed in light of René Girard's discussion of the "good violence" of religious ritual in service of "bad violence." "Even the wildest aberrations of religious thought," writes Girard, "still manage to bear witness to the fact that evil and the violent measures taken to combat evil are essentially the same. . . . Ritual is nothing more than the regular exercise of 'good' violence" (*VS*, 37). Nevertheless, how audiences were to discern which violent, bloody struggles it was acceptable to enjoy is a question to which writers keep returning. It is a question that continues to preoccupy the United States as the Congress grapples with legislating morality in the entertainment industry. It is a question explored in even the most unsophisticated of media venues, as when a local California television station aired a news story about the reenactment of Christ's Passion in the Philippines. The smiling anchor, Dean Mignola, reported that, in connection with

[45] Du Bos, *Réflexions critiques sur la poésie et sur la peinture* (1770) (hereafter *RCPP*), 1:15; cited and translated by David Marshall in his important discussion of Du Bos in *The Surprising Effects of Sympathy* (hereafter *SES*), 24–25.

[46] Michelet, *Sorcière*, 1:56; and Nodier, quoted in English in Brown, *Theater and Revolution*, 88–89.

[47] "As the Stomach Turns," *Newsweek*, 18 March 1974, 22, cited in Emeljanow, "Grand Guignol and the Orchestration of Violence," 151.

[48] In *De spectaculis*, Tertullian (95–96) attempted to ban drama entirely. Isidore of Seville echoed him in *Etymologiarum*, bk. 18, chap. 59.

the celebration of Easter in 1995, a group of believers carried their "reenact-ment a step farther" by allowing themselves to be nailed to crosses before a crowd of some five thousand spectators. Thin nails previously soaked in alco-hol were used in order to prevent infection. Mignola dubbed the event "pretty shocking by our standards."[49]

What standards? Some two years earlier, in a San Francisco club called The Quake, a young, possibly underage woman had her nipples pierced publicly as she was stretched upon a cross while rock music blared against a backdrop of drugs and alcohol. Several hundred people were riveted to the ongoing spec-tacle; and an observer reports that the protagonist/star/victim later joined the audience to view the next performance: a man having his testicles pierced (he later disappeared without a trace).[50] Several decades earlier, theatergoers had been treated to a variety of Christological—even hagiographical—images of violence at the theater of the Grand Guignol in which "a nude and lissome ac-tress [was] nailed to a cross and carved to pieces by a group of gypsy magicians chanting something that sounded like a Protestant hymn sung backwards" (Callahan, "Ultimate in Theatre Violence," 170). While I do not argue that the violent medieval dramatizations of the Passion of Christ are identical to modern performances or rituals in which actors, artists, and participants stage their own self-mutilation, these theatrical events are not really so far from the violent spec-tacularity of what Erich Auerbach once termed "the great drama of Christian-ity."[51] Nor are they so far from the pleasure, obsession, or fascination eternally aroused in audiences. There was a reason why, as early as the Roman empire, Tiberius failed in his efforts to pacify the brutal tendencies of his monstrously cruel son, Caligula. Even in his youth, writes Suetonius, Caligula "could not control his natural cruelty and viciousness, but he was a most eager witness of the tortures and executions of those who suffered punishment, revelling at night in gluttony and adultery, disguised in a wig and a long robe, passionately de-voted besides to the *theatrical arts of dancing and singing,* in which Tiberius very willingly indulged him, in the hope that *through these his savage nature might be softened.*"[52]

Caligula's father clung to a false hope. He believed that a theatrical interven-tion might tame a ferocious nature through its promise of catharsis. Nor was Tiberius alone in his optimism. Even in as radically different a work as the *De doctrina christiana,* Saint Augustine subscribed to the view that theater might, after all, have the capacity to improve human nature. He imagined a potentially virtuous Christian theater where attendees would ultimately love and defend God as the model actor by analogy to their heartfelt love and defense of their

---

[49] This broadcast was aired on KCOY, Channel 12, serving California's counties of Santa Barbara, Santa Maria, and San Luis Obispo.

[50] I thank Chad Percival for sharing his research on these events of Saturday, 16 January 1993.

[51] Auerbach, *Mimesis,* 158.

[52] Suetonius, "Gaius Caligula," chap. 11 in *Lives of the Caesars* (hereafter *LC*); my emphasis.

own favorite actors. By that logic, a spectator loves an actor, loves those who love him, hates opposition to him, and endeavors to remove indifference toward him by exciting the skeptic "as much as he can with the praises of the actor. . . . Does not this pattern of behavior befit the action of us who are united in the brotherhood of the love of God, to enjoy whom is to live the blessed life. . . ?" [53]

In the end, a taste for theater could not replace a taste for violence because the two were (and perhaps still are) too similar, too intertwined. Since theater had always been of a piece with the theoretical language of torture, it was rather more likely that the stage would cultivate Caligula's viciousness and prompt confusion in Tertullian's or Augustine's audiences. No matter how sincere or how fiercely fought the struggle to overcome violence, it seems that the first casualty is the presumed distinction between "good" and "bad" violence, because the two are equally theatrical. So the issue is not whether torture spawns theater or theater spawns torture—even though that is the essence of the contemporary political intuition that threatens the music and television industries with censorship (the allegation being that forms of entertainment that depict violence cause violent crimes). Rather, the issues are that the boundaries between rhetoric, law, and spectacle are blurred by a common violence of representation and that the critical scapegoating of rhetoric, theater, or even the contemporary media contents itself with condemning variegated parts of a whole that may well be too disquieting to identify. Underlying rhetorical narratives of torture is the insight that "human nature" thirsts after spectacles that help to institutionalize legal systems that are as unreliable as they are dramatic.

Perhaps most germane of all, then, to the present inquiry is the fact that the very debate about the "good" or "bad" violence of the theater locates us at the same theoretical impasse that has long plagued the history of rhetoric. According to James Berlin, that discipline is characterized even today by a dialectic of praise and self-loathing as "the enemies of rhetoric argue that it is inherently corrupt (usually because they want to conceal or naturalize their own rhetoric)" while "the defenders of rhetoric too often take the opposite tack, insisting that it is inherently good." [54] In the cultural territories of law, pedagogy, and drama, rhetoric turns out to be compellingly (and disagreeably) at odds with itself at the deepest epistemological and ontological levels. Quintilian might well have written that "rhetoric is not self-contradictory. The conflict is between case and case, not between rhetoric and itself" (*IO*, II, 17.33). But rhetoric really was self-contradictory—hence the eternal critical battle about defining, redefining, and even marginalizing it. Part of that love-hate relationship may be traced to its interrelations with theater and torture.

---

[53] *De doctrina christiana*, I, 29, as translated by D. W. Robertson, *On Christian Doctrine*, 24. For a discussion of this passage, see also Barish, *Anti-theatrical Prejudice*, 58.

[54] James A. Berlin suggests that that dichotomy is ahistorical in "Revisionary Histories of Rhetoric," 115.

Subtending the compatibility of rhetoric, drama, and torture were profound anxieties about their commingling. As we shall see, theorists betray a need to camouflage the violence on which rhetoric depends and to attribute a positive valence to that violence. Each canon is built upon a violent originary narrative: the bodily tortures involved in *inventio*, the imagistic reenactments of death and dismemberment of *memoria*, and the legendary first *actio* of rhetoric, which subjugated early man to the discursive politics of civilization.[55] Each canon thus rehearses a fundamental paradox by which rhetoric is constructed as a nonviolent way to mediate the violence that it condemns, requires, and even ennobles. In invention, rhetors and dramatists could learn to conceal the instability of the "truths" they discovered; in memory, they could obscure the revelation that rhetorico-literary creation depended on a primordial scene of dismembered bodies; and in delivery, they could create an illusion by which a rhetorical performance devoted to empowerment, domination, and discipline was, in reality, peacekeeping and mediatory. In those ways, each canon hands down a different strategy for convincing audiences of the beauty of violence and even the beauty of literature. Rhetorical production is reconfigured as the positive creation of the very violence that engenders it and that is occasionally denied in favor of the idealized ends of salubriousness, social order, peace, or creation.

Implicit in all these narratives is the identification of rhetoric with various modes of violence, spectacle, torture, and indoctrination, including those historically imbricated in law, religion, and a rhetorical medieval drama that can never quite divorce itself from that originary violence.[56] Sometimes, then, the history of rhetoric becomes a history of dramatic subterfuge and even coercion insofar as the rhetorics of law and religion cannot call into question some of their tortured inventions and continue to generate, enact, and preserve the Truth. To explore such paradoxes, I offer three chapters devoted to the theatrical enactments of invention, memory, and delivery in antiquity and in late medieval and early Renaissance France. I do so with the following caveats and precisions.

All footnotes include author, short title, and any relevant numbers for pages, verses, lines, or sections of classical works. Complete data are found in the list of works cited. When practical, abbreviated titles are used parenthetically in the text; they are identified in the list of abbreviations. In general, when a bilingual edition of a work (such as those in the Loeb Classical Library) is readily accessible, I do not reproduce the original except when philology is utterly cru-

---

[55] I refer here to the fact that rhetorical discussions of torture most frequently occur under the rubric of *invention*; that the violent Simonides legend gives rise to *memoria*, and that the first delivery is associated with tales of colonization told by Cicero, *De inventione* I.3; and Alcuin, *Dialogue*, 33–51.

[56] For example, in Eusebius's *Ecclesiastical History*, the foundational moment of Christianity is connected to the imposition of legal and political structures; while James L. Kinneavy hypothesizes that rhetoric informed the structure of New Testament theology in *Greek Rhetorical Origins of Christian Faith*, 20–21.

cial to the argument. Nor do I include the original of most sources in modern French. Translations of French and Latin materials are my own unless otherwise indicated.

My primary focus on the French-language corpus as opposed to other European vernaculars is inspired by its rich philological complexities. Those are especially evident in the polysemy of the term *la question*, which signified torture, debate, legal question, and investigation, and in the widespread poetic pairing of such words as *battre* (to beat) and *esbatre* (to have fun, take pleasure), *lier* (to bind) and *liesse* (joy). I was somewhat tempted to divide this work along the period lines of antiquity, Middle Ages, and Renaissance. I have opted instead to consider together different historical moments of the dramatic violence of rhetoric, the better to convey the continuity of that tradition. Needless to say, this approach emphasizes similarities over differences, but it does have the advantage of elucidating patterns and paradigms that inform the history of the cultural response to violence. The differences—great and small, chronological and geographical, theoretical and practical—may then be investigated further by others. Moreover, when it comes to the myriad theatrical genres of the fourteenth through sixteenth centuries, a preference for similarities over differences encourages more flexibility in the use of such terms as "medieval," "Renaissance," and "early modern" because it promotes a way of identifying influential medieval models rather than pale forerunners of the French classical theater of Racine and Corneille.

There are other caveats. While I replicate in the structure of my chapters the standard rhetorical sequence from inventional conception to mnemonic rehearsal to delivered performance, it is crucial to bear in mind that that chronology is often arbitrary and artificial. The rhetorical canons are interconnected in ways that are more concentric than sequential. Even the meticulous Cicero observed poetically that "a division into parts is more indefinite, like drawing streams of water from a fountain" (*Topica*, 7.33–34). Both invention and memory engendered rhetorico-literary creation; and delivery concretized mnemonic visions as it simultaneously reconsigned them to what Mary Carruthers prefers to call an inventional memory.[57] Therefore, one of the great advantages of rhetoric as a critical approach to drama is its ability to provide models and sketches of pre-performance, or virtual performance, or intentions of performance.[58] Ideally, the dissemination of particular rhetorical, didactic, and theatrical messages to particular audiences would remain firmly rooted in the geographical, social, and historical specificity of individual performances. But, in the face of so many lost medieval performances in circumstances that are notoriously difficult to reconstruct, carefully articulated rhetorical intentions do constitute a kind of evidence. Notwithstanding the hard times on which any intentional fal-

---

[57] See, e.g., Carruthers, *Book of Memory*, 20 (hereafter *BM*).
[58] I return to intentionality and its fallacies in Chapter 3.

lacy has fallen, rhetoric at least grants a way of getting beyond the question of how, when, where, or even if a given play was actually performed.

Finally, since a "learned" medieval man was someone who was trained in rhetoric during a formal university education, it has been natural here to privilege the manifestations of violence in the context of a hegemonic world of learning. On that basis, I have emphasized the *theory*—articulated by an intelligentsia—of the theater of cruelty rather than the entirety of its variegated practices. However, the omnipresent lexicon of violence that pervades the materials under analysis here is by no means limited to the "learned realm."

Beginning, then, with the precise linguistic connections between torture and invention in Chapter 1, I show that theories of torture were cast in terms of drama and rhetoric; theories of drama in terms of torture and rhetoric; and theories of rhetorico-literary invention in terms of torture and drama. The first rhetorical canon extended to all who were exposed to it an important mechanism for investigating the interrelations among language, truth, torture, agency, literary creation, theatricality, and pain. Classical and medieval legal theorists linked torture hermeneutically to the truth, as in Ulpian's definition from the Justinian *Digest*: "'Quaestionem' intelligere debemus tormenta et corporis dolorem ad eruendam veritatem" (By 'torture' we should understand torment and corporeal suffering and pain employed to extract the truth).[59] At the same time, though, rhetoricians consistently asserted in their treatments of legal *inventio* that the ideal of a truth extracted by means of torture was open to interpretation because of its reliance on such dramatic criteria as probability, verisimilitude, and catharsis. That was the connection and the paradox that medieval dramatists staged time and time again in the scourgings of Christ, to the terror and delight of their public.

Equally important to an understanding of the medieval theater of cruelty is *memoria*, which is the subject of Chapter 2. Memory's intermediary position between the inventional conception and the performative delivery of what torture creates explains its placement as the centerpiece of this book. Inasmuch as the key function of the memory image was, as Longinus reminds us, to "engender speech," *memoria* served as a pictorial script whence rhetors were to deliver their orations by translating its imagery into dramatic performances.[60] Yet the vast mnemonic repertoire of vivid architectural spaces housing veritable casts of dramatic characters (*imagines agentes*) was also rife with imagery of de-

---

[59] Justinian, *Digest*, 47.10.15.41; vol. iv, p. 779. This text is discussed in Peters, *Torture*, 28; and in Garnsey, *Social Status*, 141n. As we shall see, the function of rhetorical *inventio* was traditionally extended to literary invention.

[60] Longinus, *On the Sublime*, chap. 15, pp. 1–2. This is the main argument of my *ROMD*, in which I suggest that, in antiquity and the Middle Ages, delivery was the canon that enacted the veritable protodrama of memory. Those two rhetorical canons codified such crucial components as theatrical space, conflict, audience adaptation, reenactment, and impersonation (see, e.g., *IO*, VI, 1.25–27).

struction, mutilation, dismemberment, and bodies in pain on which the lessons of rhetoric could be inscribed—violently.[61] In that sense, the memory script may have "set the stage" for torture, engendering not only violent speech but the violent actions of legal proceedings, of early pedagogy, and of the rhetorically charged pieces of the medieval stage. In the floggings endured by students, in the graphic details of the scourging of Christ, in the countless wife-beating scenes of medieval farce, learned drama provides compelling support of Friedrich Nietzsche's dictum that pain was "the strongest aid to mnemonics," which then becomes an appropriate orientation to theater studies.[62]

Next, if invention and memory helped the orator to imagine and rehearse images of tortured bodies, it was delivery that helped him to stage them with all the verisimilitude, all the aesthetic power, and all the potential for catharsis that inhered in torture itself. In Chapter 3 I problematize the theory and practice of *actio*, which codified for orators the important principles of how the acting body communicated violence through voice, gesture, rhythm, musicality, reenactment, and even impersonation. Since, as Cicero affirmed, "by action the body talks" (est enim actio quasi sermo corporis),[63] the ways in which the body "talked" emphasized the association among rhetoric, torture, and aesthetics. When he wrote that the orator "played" the body like a harp during delivery (*De oratore*, III, 216), his invocation of the stringed musical instrument (ut nervi in *fidibus*) also recalls the stringed instrument of torture known as the *fidiculae*.[64] Here concepts of music and aesthetic pleasure are implicated in the interplay among rhetoric, torture, performance, and even performativity. Indeed, medieval theatrical performances regularly blurred the lines between real and aesthetic violence in their graphic stage effects, in accidental close calls, and even in an onstage execution ostensibly carried out during the biblical drama of Judith, to thunderous applause.[65] When we read of such phenomena in con-

[61] On the *imagines agentes*, see *RAH*, III, 37; and Yates's discussion of this passage, *AM*, 10. While I do not concentrate on the classic conception of *dispositio* per se as the canon that regulated the structure of an oration, I propose a metaphorical reading of rhetorical disposition as a literal but also literary body of eloquence. See in this connection duBois, *TT*, 113; and the powerful work of Rita Copeland on the literal "body" of rhetoric in "Pardoner's Body." For the traditional concept of *dispositio* as, e.g., exordium, narration, proof, and peroration, see Cicero, *De oratore*, I, 142–43.

[62] Nietzsche, *Genealogy of Morals* (hereafter *GM*), 193.

[63] Cicero, *De oratore*, III, 222–23. Thus Jacques Le Goff's observation that "the body provided medieval society with one of its principal means of expression" had already been confirmed in antiquity (*Medieval Civilization*, 357; trans. by Julia Barrow). I offer a brief history of delivery in chap. 1 of *ROMD*.

[64] The *fidiculae* as both binding cords and musical chords also appear in Isidore's *Etymologiarum*, vol. 1, bk. 5, 27.21–22. I discuss them later in connection with the musicality of the body in pain.

[65] The "execution" is discussed in Rey-Flaud, *Pour une dramaturgie du moyen âge* (hereafter *PDMA*), 17–19; and, before him, in Faber, *Histoire du théâtre en Belgique*, 14–15. I later discuss it from the standpoint of Austinian performativity (see, e.g., *How to Do Things with Words* [hereafter *HDTW*]).

junction with the fact that, in medieval France, a bishop watching a civic spectacle from on high might be empowered to force men to accept Christ through flogging,[66] those moments betray a sense of imminent danger, a level of pity, fear, and terror that one can only begin to imagine. Or rather, one cannot begin to imagine it.

Nevertheless, at some level, it might be argued that one should be able to imagine it, given the abundant contemporary examples of the theater of cruelty in which authors, directors, performers, and spectators continuously experiment with staging violence on the tenuous borderline between fiction and real life. Ironically, it often seems that the reason one cannot imagine it is that it chips away at one of the generic cornerstones of theater—aesthetic distance—and at one of the critical cornerstones for the medievalist—alterity. That irony then provides the rationale for my Conclusion, devoted to "vicious cycles" or the historical continuity of the conflation of torture, rhetoric, and drama.

Medievalists have come to pride themselves of late on respecting what Rainer Warning elegantly dubbed the "alterity" of the Middle Ages.[67] Many devotedly attempt to avoid anachronism, while preaching respect for its "otherness" and emphasizing the fluidity of literary genres that collapse the boundaries between rhetoric, law, history, literature, and religion. For most, this is a good thing. It has substantially raised critical consciousness through a better anthropological understanding of ritual violence, as exemplified in Girard's work on surrogate victims, Kenneth Burke's on violence and the "consubstantiality" of social hierarchies (*POLF*, 107–9), and Victor Turner's on ritual dramas.[68] While respect for the alterity of the Middle Ages is an admirable goal that no one would reasonably dispute, I submit nonetheless that that very perception of difference has become problematic for the medievalist.

The violence of representation has remained caught in an ageless ideological circle, deplored or rationalized even as it is uncovered and analyzed by critics. It is true that the pat denunciations of early historians of the theater are no longer allowed to stand: the Abbé Du Bos's accusation that Roman gladiatorial display was "a spectacle we could not imagine today without horror"; Gaston Paris's and Gaston Raynaud's revulsion in the face of the "tortures, as atrocious as they are disgusting, to which Jesus is subjected for seven thousand verses."[69]

[66] For a discussion of the *Cap. Duo Incerta*, a Frankish capitulary that probably dates from the late ninth century, see Goebel, *Felony and Misdemeanor*, 170–71.

[67] In addition to Warning's "On the Alterity of Medieval Religious Drama," see Jauss, "Alterity and Modernity of Medieval Literature."

[68] The anthropological work of Turner and Goffman has proved particularly inspirational in medieval drama studies, as exemplified in the work of Kathleen M. Ashley. See, e.g., her introduction to the edited volume *Victor Turner and the Construction of Cultural Criticism.*

[69] The citations are from Du Bos, *RCPP*, 1:15, translated and discussed by Marshall in *SES*, 25; and Paris and Raynaud, in their edition of Arnoul Gréban's fifteenth-century *Mystère de la Passion*, xvii.

But the "corrected" view now set forth by such a critic as Henri Rey-Flaud is not without moral ambiguities of its own: that "it is not complicity which medieval men bring to the theater, it is faith." [70] Acknowledging the "unheard-of sadism" of the medieval stage, Rey-Flaud rationalizes its scenes of cruelty, persecution, and dismemberment by attributing to them the exaggeratedly lofty motivations of a Christian "price to pay for collective salvation" (*PDMA*, 153). Elsewhere, Victor Scherb professes skepticism about the critical tendency to view violence as part of the affective piety of the late Middle Ages, only to conclude in regard to the relentless mutilations of the Croxton *Play of the Sacrament* that "violence is de-ritualized and given bloody form once again so that the action of the play can in effect both *mirror and heal* the divisions within the contemporary Suffolk community." [71]

Still, if torture somehow assists in the formation of civilized Christian communities, then it does so on the backs of mutilated bodies, variously deemed deserving or undeserving of their ordeals. As it mirrors, heals, and makes communities it just as readily unmakes other communities—pagan, Jewish, female, lower-class.[72] Over three centuries before Elaine Scarry defined torture as the "making and unmaking" of the world, the English king James I had proposed a making and unmaking of his own in a statement to Parliament concerning the laws, pleasures, pains, and powers in the monarch's charge. And just as Plato believed that all law was a question of "pleasures and pains, whether in States or in individuals" (*Laws*, I, 636d), James compared the king to God in 1609 by virtue of his divine power "to create, or destroy, *make, or vnmake at his pleasure*, to giue life, or send death, to iudge all, and to be iudged nor accomptable to none . . . but God onely." [73] There is nothing so terribly "other" about such making and unmaking. The critical gesture by which the horrific is transformed into the noble, the positive, or the curative replaces one problem with another.

Throughout this book I argue that the prevalent critical tendency to view the Middle Ages as a distant, irrecuperable Other has actually masked certain disturbing affinities. Modern responses to the medieval aesthetics of violence sometimes disclose a pitched sense of alienation from the Middle Ages that is as intriguing for what it reveals as for what it denies. "Aesthetic distance" and "alterity" may even function as flattering terms that conceal what might better be termed a kind of ellipsis of the self. For example, when such a critic as Francis Barker dares to tackle the moral and ethical problems of Shakespeare's "culture

[70] Rey-Flaud, *PDMA*, 19. John Gatton raises a similar objection against treating spectacular bloodshed as "exempla of Christian fortitude and faith" in "'There Must Be Blood,'" 79.

[71] Scherb, "Violence and the Social Body," 77.

[72] These points have been explored in, e.g., Biddick, "Genders, Bodies, Borders"; and duBois, *TT*, chap. 14.

[73] *The Political Works of James I*, 307–8. I thank Patricia Marby for sharing this reference with me.

of violence" in moral and ethical terms, the reviewer William Gruber cynically denounces him for narcissism and "an excessive and sometimes offensive piousness." [74] Barker concludes his chapter on *Titus Andronicus* with the impassioned statement that "I, for one, will not be party to that violence, nor to its occlusion" (*CV*, 206). Gruber responds with deliberate contrariness that "if all I keep hearing is how wicked the theater has been, what I think of is Plato, Tertullian, Stephen Gosson, and Jeremy Collier, and my reaction is 'It can't be *that* bad'" (533; emphasis his). In an eerie latter-day response to the very objections raised by Tertullian and Cyprian, the reviewer's message is that twentieth-century literary critics are basically "good," but that somehow the challenges posed by the likes of Barker occasion their "unnatural" transmutation from a state of goodness to one of perversity.

Helpful in this respect is Peter Haidu's advice that we distinguish the contemporary moralistic pairing of violence and transgression from the medieval pairing of violence and norms: "the rough, injurious, or unjust use of force did not invariably bear coded, moral disapproval, however much individuals may have suffered from it. Our term 'violence' perforce bears a seme of disapproval, of condemnation: our culture assumes peace as the desired and desirable norm, and negativizes its opposite" (*SV*, 3). By reintegrating the violence of rhetorical theory into the critical enterprise, we are better able to look to the origins of that disapproval and to its own theatrical construction. Consequently, we are also better able to come to terms with the philosophical need to condemn violence, to find it "natural" or "unnatural," or to distance ourselves from it even as so many aesthetic or ritual diversions rely on it.

It has become somewhat ordinary these days to read in scholarly analysis of both medieval literature and the modern media that the ubiquity of violence dulls an audience's senses to violence. One common charge is that entertainment genres are violent because violence is (or because violence was) everywhere. Peter Brown reminds us that in Roman households, "violence surrounded men of the elite at every level of their lives. They grew up in households where slavery had remained a domestic school of cruelty." [75] The theater historian Richard Beacham gathers that brutality was fashionable on the Roman stage because "violence was a part of everyday existence for the Roman audience. Slaves were indeed tortured, even executed for trivial offences." [76] Long before them, Petit de Julleville attributed the cruelty of the medieval theater to the popularity of the judicial ordeal, whose "frequency, cruelty, and highly public nature [*grande publicité*] . . . partially explain how the sight of the tortures inflicted at length [*longuement*] upon Christ remained tolerable" (*LM*, 224). John Gatton went on to note that the miracle plays and *mystères* of the Middle Ages were "violent

---

[74] Gruber, review of Francis Barker, *Culture of Violence*, 532.

[75] Brown, *Power and Persuasion in Late Antiquity* (hereafter *PP*), 51.

[76] Beacham, "Violence on the Street," 47.

theatre for a violent era" (" 'There Must Be Blood,' " 80). But cultural topoi are not explainable by their ubiquity; nor does ubiquity guarantee a lack of contestation and conflict. Rather, as Curtius emphasized following the wisdom of Quintilian, topoi are "storehouses of chains of thought" (*IO*, V, 10.20; *EL*, 70). The chains of thought associated with violence and torture must also be reconstructed.

When it comes to a seemingly omnipresent violence that manages nonetheless consistently to generate outrage and shock, the current debate about violence typically focuses on whether or not peaceful civilization is indeed the norm. Yet one cannot argue simultaneously that violence is the norm and that it is not the norm, or that violence is outrageous and shocking at the same time that its spectators are jaded by the sight of it. Hence the insufficiency of even some of the more eloquent arguments about transgression and the relevance of Haidu's warning that "in respect to the practices of violence, *modernity is medieval*: it continues the practices of the Middle Ages, differentiating itself primarily in the amount of violence produced, and in its hypocritical disguisement" (*SV*, 193–94; his emphasis).

In the final analysis, what is at stake here is the demystification of both the aesthetics of violence and the critical response to it. In the case of torture, the critical tendency to condemn, to overexplain, or to excuse might ultimately derive less from a true sensitivity to the Middle Ages than from a false notion of our own moral superiority. Even if one does not go so far as to accept Page duBois's pronouncement that our entire civilization is based on barbarism (*TT*, 142–43), it is difficult not to accept her succinct refutation of Foucault's claim that "we are now far away from the country of tortures, dotted with wheels, gibbets, gallows, pillories" (*DP*, 307). Eloquently debunking the myth of alienation, she offers a simple rejoinder: "Tell it to the El Salvadorans" (154). Perhaps it is easier to affect alienation than to come face to face with the possibility that a Louis-Fernand Céline in the full throes of his most virulent anti-Semitic writings may have been right about the course violence would take: "Take it from me, the right time to have been born is 100 B.C.! . . . the stories we tell are a bore! . . . our plays, more yawns! and the movies and TV . . . disaster! what the people want and the élite too is Circuses! the gory kill! . . . honest-to-God death rattles, tortures, guts all over the arena! . . . the real stuff, blood and entrails . . . no more of your rigged brawls . . . no! the Circus will put the theaters out of business."[77]

Just as classical and medieval writers wrestled with the paradoxes of violence, so too does Maria Tatar in her work on *Lustmord* in the Weimar Republic. Articulating a question that may well dominate future American presidential elections, she asks: To what extent do works of art depicting scenes of murder, rape,

---

[77] Céline, *North*, 3. I thank Philip Watts for bringing this text to my attention.

death, and violation "legitimize murderous violence, providing for it a socially acceptable outlet?"[78] Even now, the American television audience is stimulated by a plethora of reality-based crime shows that promise dramas of life and death which are no less appalling than the great games played with daggers, blindfolds, and blows by torturers on the medieval stage. A commercial for a police drama tempts viewers with the guarantee that "in this dramatic story someone's life is on the line"; a cable television network airs (among other dramas) rape and murder trials; the network brass debates the issue of whether or not capital executions should be televised; a snuff-film video series titled *Faces of Death* is a best-seller in video stores nationwide; a Time-Life book series invites us to enter the tortured minds of serial killers and the suffering souls of their victims; the trial of Jeffrey Dahmer induced several entrepreneurs to market trading cards bearing his image; and, in anticipation of the airing of the O. J. Simpson murder trial, one television producer proudly proclaimed that it had "all the elements of great TV-movies: sex, murder, race, money, the ultimate fall from grace—every driving force in America wrapped up in one."[79] Finally, under the guise of investigative reporting, television journalism no longer stops with the playback of 911 tapes that preserve the sounds of near-death and attempted murder. Now the media air home videos of police beatings, abusive babysitters, hate crimes, and, in February 1993, an actual murder in a Miami cemetery.[80] Notwithstanding the dignity of Rainer Warning's observation that the medieval integration of torture into the mystery play bespeaks a "unity of play and reality [that] is no longer accessible to our experience" (285), that statement is surely false in view of such phenomena. If the modern media continue to cultivate often-unarticulated desires for such taboo forms as the snuff film,[81] so did the early equivalents of the media: rhetoric, law, and theater.

In the case of the medieval theater, a well-intentioned deference to the concept of alterity may well have masked a very real denial of the contemporary spectacle of violence and of contemporary complicity in the history of that violence. As repugnant as the modern reader claims to find the "entertainment potential" of torture, that claim is resolutely denied by our own culture. And as comforting as one might find the notion of aesthetic distance, the purpose of this book is to show that it is quite simply not there in the interrelations of rhetoric and drama, torture and truth.

[78] Tatar, *Lustmord*, 18.

[79] Michael O'Hara, quoted in *TV Guide*, 2 July 1994, 34.

[80] At least three times the ABC news program *20/20* offered video evidence of actual murders: one neighbor killing another (25 September 1992); a murder in a Miami cemetery (February 1993); and video surveillance tapes from convenience stores that recorded three deaths, two by shooting and one by stabbing (9 February 1996).

[81] See Schechner, *Between Theater and Anthropology*, 295–324. I explore this point at greater length in "Medieval Snuff Drama."

CHAPTER 1

The Dramatic Violence of Invention

Ego porro ne invenisse quidem credo eum, qui non iudicavit.

For my own part I do not believe that invention can exist apart from judgment.

— Quintilian, *Institutio oratoria*, III, 3.5–6

The skill of invention, writes Geoffrey of Vinsauf in the thirteenth-century *Poetria nova*, "does not come easily or without labor." In a treatise that fashions literature as a rhetorical enterprise and rhetoric as a literary one, he explains that poetry, rhetoric, and rhetorical poetics are generated brutally through a kind of self-torture in which the poet/rhetor is both agent and victim:

> Non venit ex facili res ista nec absque labore:
> Sed mens quando studet, tanquam pugil, anxia pugnat.
> Pugnat enim secum. Petit ut sibi consulat, et non
> Consulit ipsa sibi. Repetit patiturque repulsam
> Ipsa secunda sibi: ferventius instat et ipsa
> Perstat adhuc contra se, curis anxia torquet
> Se, tandem quod vult extorquet vi violenta
> A se. Sicque simul victrix et victa triumphat
> De se.[1]

The matter does not come easily or effortlessly; but when the mind is eager, like a champion, it struggles over-anxiously. For it fights with itself. It desires to take counsel of itself, and it does not. It tries again, and suffers repulse, being its own worst enemy. More determinedly it presses on, and yet it still stands firm against itself; *it torments itself*, afflicted by cares; *with violent force it finally wrests what it seeks from itself*. Thus at once conqueror and conquered, it triumphs over itself.

[1] Geoffrey of Vinsauf, *Poetria nova* (hereafter *PN*), ed. and trans. Ernesto Gallo, 109.

Most striking is Geoffrey's mention of the violent extraction of literature (*extorquere vi violenta*) in terms that recall the juridical vocabulary of the Justinian *Digest*. There Ulpian had defined torture as a hermeneutic theory of discovery: "'Quaestionem' intellegere debemus tormenta et corporis dolorem ad eruendam veritatem"[2] (By "torture" we should understand torment and corporeal suffering and pain employed to extract the truth). Ulpian configures torture as an epistemological extraction of truth; Geoffrey associates that epistemological extraction with literary works of beauty and stature. Moreover, although the victim of Geoffrey's creative search is not Ulpian's slave but another side of himself, there were other victims of a pain that was not always self-inflicted.

The very idea that a violent, tortured, inventional scene could engender the useful or beautiful discourses of law, drama, or poetry suggests that—troubling though the linkage of torture, truth, inventional discovery, and creativity may be—the innumerable medieval scenes of torture that have so revolted the modern reader actually enact that scenario. In the rhetorical invention of both torture and drama, learned medieval authors rehearsed and re-rehearsed an inexorably violent and even protodramatic creational conflict (with all its attendant ellipsis of agency). In a long history of instability played out in rhetorico-legal theory and dramatic practice, torture is cast as a dramatic process of invention, rhetorical invention constitutes a dramatic process analogized to torture, and drama (as demonstrated by many a medieval and early Renaissance scourging scene) frequently stages the inventions of torture. Specifically, one of the things learned French dramatists appear to have discovered in invention was a model that taught them not only to harm themselves metaphorically but to harm their audiences more than metaphorically by perpetuating the ultimate legal illusion: that torture could indeed lead to truth.

The cultural stakes here are enormous, if only in the intuition that Geoffrey's vision of torture anticipates Friedrich Nietzsche's statement that "the creative instinct excites both a desire to harm *ourselves*, self-violation, and a desire to harm others."[3] At the same time, his literary vision of torture is radically different from Elaine Scarry's realistic one, which warrants that "physical pain does not simply resist language but actively destroys it, bringing about an immediate reversion to a state anterior to language, to the sounds and cries a human being makes before language is learned."[4] In the medieval rhetorical tradition, torture does not destroy language but creates it, and, most germane of all to the present inquiry, creates it dramatically.

---

[2] Justinian, *Digest*, 47.10.15.41. Here the term *eruo/eruendam*—meaning tearing, plucking out, digging up—underscores the idea that "bringing something to light" was a violent process of extraction.

[3] Nietzsche elaborates on the "art of terrifying" in his *Will to Power*, 802, discussed in a most interesting way by Amy Newman in "Aestheticism, Feminism, and the Dynamics of Reversal," 24.

[4] Scarry, *BP*, 4.

Torture has always been intertwined with rhetoric, law, and theater at the levels of etymology, ideology, and performance.[5] First, I analyze the theatrical view of torture that emerges from discussions of rhetorical invention. Since the paradoxical presence of theatrical components both falsifies and aestheticizes the information extracted through torture, this poses problems of rhetorical "truth," the subject of the second section. Despite the traditional belief that rhetoric was the science of probabilities, forensic invention relies on torture to prove the "truth" in criminal cases, that truth being an elusive entity characterized by creativity, verisimilitude, probability, pity, fear, and catharsis. Next, I consider historical narratives of the origins of drama that are inextricably linked to torture and invention. I then turn to selected scourging scenes from the late medieval stage to show that, if torture undermines its own pretensions to truth, so too do various medieval didactic works that enact torture, including certain dramatic, dialogic, and hagiographic forms.

Ultimately, all those aspects of *inventio* inform the rhetorical canons of memory and delivery—hence my emphasis on a medieval theater of cruelty, a theater devised by learned dramatists schooled in rhetoric for whom the violent, inventional hermeneutics of rhetoric might have served as both a "general theory of literature," as Curtius maintained, and a theory of drama.[6] At this juncture, however, my concern is with the semantic and epistemological (rather than the iconographic and performative) manifestations of torture. The widespread philological association of torture, theater, and rhetorical invention may then uncover early presumptions not only about the violent origins of language and law but about the construction and—always theatrical—performance of violence.

Such authors as Geoffrey of Vinsauf might well have refigured inventional violence as positive, creational, and generative of aesthetic beauty. But in the end, to study the rhetorical invention of torture is to reevaluate in the context of rhetoric (including its mnemonic and performance systems) Simon Richter's claim that once pain is removed, "beauty becomes invisible or dead."[7] Pain was always an integral part of medieval aesthetics. And it is to resituate Jacques Derrida's remark that "eschato*logy* is not possible, except *through violence*" within the historical framework of one medieval art form that dramatized a part of eschatology: the mystery play.[8]

---

[5] General introductions to the importance of grammar and etymology in the Middle Ages include Gehl, *Moral Art*, and Irvine, *Making of Textual Culture*. On the ideology of philology, see Bloch, *Etymologies and Genealogies*, 53–62; Asad on the genealogical vision of torture, "Notes on Body, Pain, and Truth," 294; and Page duBois's discussion of Emile Benveniste's theory that Greek philosophy was coterminous with Greek linguistic categories in *TT*, 6.

[6] Curtius, *EL*, 70–71. For the status of rhetorical theory as a hermeneutic enterprise, see the masterful introduction to Copeland, *Rhetoric, Hermeneutics, and Translation*.

[7] Richter, *Laocoon's Body*, 48.

[8] Derrida, *WD*, 130; emphasis his.

The Inventional Drama of Torture

From the standpoint of the history of rhetoric, the presence of dramatic elements in discussions of torture presents a tremendous predicament for scholars, who have long been troubled by Aristotle's casual inclusion of torture as one of any number of factual, "inartificial," or "extrinsic" proofs to be discovered by orators during the inventional process. On the face of it, his statement seems straightforward enough. Inartificial proofs (*atechnoi*) are those "which have not been furnished by ourselves but were already in existence, such as witnesses, tortures [*basanoi*], contracts, and the like." They are opposed to the "artificial" or "intrinsic" proofs (*entechnoi*) that were to be "invented" by the rhetorician.[9] Aristotle has designed a helpful distinction that depends on further distinctions of fact from fiction, truth from lies, objective from subjective, provable from unprovable, empirical from emotional. What is so striking, however, about the evidence supplied by rhetorico-legal descriptions of torture is that during *inventio*, the ostensibly *extrinsic* proof of *basanos* often functions as an avowedly unreliable *intrinsic* proof. In an activity analogous to dramatic creation, the rhetorician theorizes the inventional proof of torture as a verisimilar process that causes torture to *appear* to be an unshakable extrinsic proof when in reality it is just as "intrinsic," just as "creative," just as fictional, just as "dramatic" as other modes of rhetorical invention.[10]

In antiquity and the Middle Ages, the rhetorical theory of torture offered lawyers, orators, and writers a means to discover, to *invent*, and to enact a verisimilar scenario for the construction of "truth." Even though intuited in advance, that truth was thought nonetheless to be hiding somewhere inside another person, upon whose body a torturer, judge, or questioner might intervene violently to squeeze it out, all the while casting himself as the victim.[11] But, as we shall see, the secret bodily contents drawn out through torture are subject to the same criteria of creation, interpretation, and reception as rhetoric and drama. The "inartificial" proof of torture is constructed "artificially," subjectively, and aesthetically through verisimilitude, probability, pity, and fear. Its "facts" are evaluated on the basis of their potential persuasiveness as fashioned

---

[9] Aristotle, *Rhetoric*, 1355b. For a useful discussion of the complex transmission of Aristotle in the Middle Ages, see Murphy, "Aristotle's *Rhetoric* in the Middle Ages."

[10] Here I question duBois, whose focus on the body as a kind of extrinsic space leads her to accept the classical notion that torture was indeed a mode of extrinsic proof (*TT*, 65–68).

[11] Although rhetoric is ostensibly concerned with probabilities and not truth, the existence of inartificial proofs in general and of torture in particular actually suggests the contrary. For introductions to the tenuous relationship between torture and truth, see Asad, "Notes" and *Genealogies of Religion* (hereafter *GOR*); Peters, *Torture* and *The Magician, the Witch, and the Law*; Garnsey, *Social Status*; duBois, *TT*; Hanson, "Torture and Truth"; Bartlett, *TFW*; Lea, *Inquisition of the Middle Ages*; Fiorelli, *Tortura giudiziaria*; Foucault, *Discipline and Punish* (hereafter *DP*); and Scarry's discussion of the reversal of agent and victim in the ideology of torture (*BP*, 50–59).

probabilities, and then, in a process of reaffirmation, judged as factual on the basis of their verisimilitude. At issue, then, is less the truth of the law than the spectacular probabilities of its rhetorical presentation, which is born of materials extracted less through questioning than through punishment. The two primary questions, then, are: How do theorists and practitioners of torture manage to ignore or disguise the well-documented imperfections of their own violent methods? And by what *spectacular* means do they represent and re-present those flaws as truth and beauty? Plato once identified lawyers as the rivals of poets in that both are masters of illusion: "we are composers of the same things as yourselves, rivals of yours as artists and actors of the fairest drama." [12] Quintilian summarized the problem more succinctly still when he identified the goal of oratorical instruction as "the imitation of truth." [13] The place where young boys learned to construct truth dramatically was *inventio*.

As rhetoricians, torturers, and dramatists struggled to construct illusions that were more or less plausible, the violence of invention and the invention of violence fused in a dramatic process of creation that bears striking similarities to the theory of torture. For example, in the *Rhetorica ad Herennium*, one of the most widely circulated rhetorical texts of the European Middle Ages, the Pseudo-Cicero is explicit on the subject, using the word *invenire* in his discussion of torture. "We shall speak in favour of the testimony given under torture," he writes, "when we show that it was in order to *discover* the truth that our ancestors wished investigations to make use of torture and the rack, and that men are compelled by violent pain to tell all they know" (a *quaestionibus* dicemus cum demonstrabimus maiores veri *inveniendi* causa tormentis et cruciatu voluisse quaeri, et summo dolore homines cogi ut quicquid sciant dicant).[14] But if torture was a violent process of discovery, then rhetoric had a disciplinary name for "discovery": *heuresis* or *inventio*. According to Marcus Tullius Cicero, *inventio* was the first and the most important of all the divisions of rhetoric, by means of which the orator was "to discover [*invenire*] how to convince the persons whom he wishes to persuade and how to arouse their emotions." [15] It can scarcely be coincidental, then, that when the fifth-century Greek orator Isaeus stated that the truth could be established "by putting the slaves to torture," he

[12] Plato, *Laws*, 817b; see also Eden, *Poetic and Legal Fiction*, 29–30.

[13] Quintilian, *IO*, V, 12.22. Even though the *Institutio oratoria* was only partially accessible to the early Middle Ages in the mutilist tradition, Quintilian's influence at that time was much greater than once thought, as Murphy argued in "The Influence of Quintilian in the Middle Ages and Renaissance." On the availability of Quintilian, see also Murphy, *RIMA*, 123–26; Woods, "Among Men," 19; Reynolds, ed., *Texts and Transmissions*, 332–36; and most recently, two special numbers of *Rhetorica* 13 devoted exclusively to Quintilian (1995; nos. 2 and 3)—especially Ward, "Quintilian and the Rhetorical Revolution of the Middle Ages."

[14] *RAH*, II, 10.

[15] Cicero, *De partitione* I, 5. Martianus Capella agreed about the power of invention in his *De nuptiis*, 141g. See also in this connection Monika Otter's recent work on the blurring of "factual truth," "invention," and "fiction" in twelfth-century English historical writing in *Inventiones*, 6.

referred to *heuresis* (*heurein tên alêtheian*).[16] In fact, the term *invenire* appears elsewhere as late as the fourteenth-century sorcery trial of Alice Kyteler. The report of that inquest begins with the results of an inquisitorial invention by Richard, bishop of Ossory, who "held the customary inquest [*invenit per inquisitionem solennem*] in which five knights and a large number of other nobles took part. The bishop discovered that in the town of Kilkenny there had been for long time, and still were, very many heretical sorceresses who practised all kinds of sorceries and were well-versed in all kinds of heresies."[17]

Nor can it be coincidental that the violent invention of rhetorical materials liable to persuade a judge was also based on such cornerstones of theater as probability and verisimilitude, the latter of which had once been defined by Aristotle as follows: in tragedy, "a convincing impossibility is preferable to that which is unconvincing though possible."[18] For his part, the *Ad Herennium* author maintained that *inventio* was "the devising of matter, true or plausible, that would make the case convincing" (inventio est excogitatio rerum verarum aut *veri similium* quae causam *probabilem* reddant) (*RAH*, I, 3).[19] Yet that description is virtually identical to the "appearance of plausibility" he invokes later in the context of torture. Explaining how orators might introduce the evidence drawn out from torture into a given courtroom performance, the Pseudo-Cicero notes that it "will have the greater force if we give the confessions elicited under torture an appearance of plausibility [*ad veri similem suspicionem*] by the same argumentative procedure as is used in treating any question of fact" (*RAH*, II, 10).

At such moments, the interplay among torture, rhetorico-poetic invention, and drama is crystal clear, yet the clarity of that interplay stands to undermine the integrity of the entire rhetorical tradition. That is, the similarity between finding the truth in a tortured victim's body and finding a rhetorical proof in one's own mind through the dramatic procedures of invention was (and is) too disquieting to acknowledge overtly. It would lead to an inescapable yet unacceptable logical conclusion: either torture was a discursive, cerebrally constructed

---

[16] Isaeus 8.12, quoted by duBois, *TT*, 64–65; and also by Peters, *Torture*, 16. While Elizabeth Hanson observes that torture in England was "conceptually allied to the epistemology of discovery" ("Torture and Truth," 54), she does not explicitly invoke the rhetorico-juridical register of invention itself.

[17] L. S. Davidson and J. O. Ward, eds. and trans., *The Sorcery Trial of Alice Kyteler: A Contemporary Account (1324)*, 26. In this connection, see also Bloch's section "Text as Inquest" in *MFLL*, chap. 4.

[18] Aristotle, *Poetics*, ed. Fyfe, 1461b. Although I limit my discussion here to probability and verisimilitude, the dramatic criterion of character is also invoked in rhetorical treatments of torture. See, e.g., *RAH*, II, 10; Aristotle, *Rhetoric*, 1377a; Quintilian, *IO*, V, 4.1–2. As I state in my Introduction, the medieval dissemination of Aristotle's *Poetics* is difficult to trace, but medieval allusions to pity and fear might suggest a mediated influence.

[19] For similar discussions of rhetorical verisimilitude, see Quintilian, *IO*, IV, 2.34; 2.89. On the concept of credibility, see also Trimpi, "Quality of Fiction," 60–61.

phenomenon (which it is clearly not); or the law that relied on torture for its inventional systems was both dramatic and violent (which it may well be). Furthermore, if torture was (at least conceptually) an inventional drama, *inventio* was also a tortured drama. Its so-called truths were dramatic inventions, verisimilar dramas masquerading as truth.

So it is that we read in a particularly vivid discussion from the *Ad Herennium* that torture was especially useful in deciphering what would come to be known today as circumstantial evidence. The Pseudo-Cicero claims merely to be explaining the efficacy of the rhetorical figure of *exornatio* in pleas to a jury. But his "facts" add up with all the episodic coherence of a dramatic plot as he sets the scene:

> If, before the victim was murdered, the defendant was seen, alone, in the place [*in eo loco*] in which the murder was committed; if soon afterward, during the very commission of the crime, the voice of the victim was heard [*vox illius qui occidebatur audita*]; if it is established that then, after the murder, the defendant returned home, at dead of night; that on the next day he spoke of the man's murder haltingly and inconsistently . . ." (*RAH*, IV, 53)[20]

Torture enters the scenario with its own important role to play in the transformation of hypothesis into fact. Information, belief, and judgment—at least, so the lawyer hoped—would be confirmed partly by the dramatic evocation of the scene of the crime, and partly by the use of torture which was itself dependent on preexisting public opinion. Just as Talal Asad affirms that torture was "intended to confirm and to elaborate what was independently known to the court—or rather, to transform its suspicion into knowledge" ("Notes," 297), the Pseudo-Cicero's speechmaker asserts that

> if all these indications are proved, partly by witnesses, and partly by the confessions upon torture [*quaestionibus*] which have been adduced in confirmation, and by public opinion, which, born of evidence, must necessarily be true [*ex argumentis natum necesse est esse verum*]; then, gentlemen, it is your duty to gather all these indications into one, and arrive at *definite knowledge*, not suspicion, of the crime [*scientiam, non suspicionem maleficii*]. (*RAH*, IV, 53; emphasis mine)

Here the theories of torture and invention alike are concerned with the discovery and *invention* of a probable or verisimilar scenario for the construction of a "truth" already intuited in advance by the orator/creator and already confirmed by public opinion. When the Pseudo-Cicero concludes that a confession

---

[20] In this passage, which may be fruitfully compared to the excerpt from Cicero's *Topica* that opened this book, the Pseudo-Cicero is analyzing one of the key inventional questions of forensic rhetoric known as the conjectural stasis, to which I return shortly. This passage is also rich in imagery that assumes greater importance in connection with memory, where loci, vocality, and the formation of public opinion or doxa also functioned as an "inventional drama."

made under torture "must necessarily be true" because it confirms evidence and public opinion, he also confirms that torture discovers not judgment but *pre-*judgment. Moreover, in the theories of rhetoric that informed the forensic and learned literary speech of the Middle Ages, both the orator and the Christian dramatist (who reanimated the tortures of Christ) were thought to be the makers and interpreters of signs. They were well versed in the common consent necessary to read and enforce the meaning of signs, as when Saint Augustine himself recognized that even in the context of mimicry, "it is true that everyone seeks a certain verisimilitude in making signs so that these signs, in so far as is possible, may resemble the things that they signify. But since one thing may resemble another in a great variety of ways, signs are not valid among men except *by common consent*."[21] The "common consent" necessary for interpretation is preemptive in the decipherment of forensic signs, signs which signify thanks to the *rumor populi*. After all, early rhetorico-literary invention was about finding what was already there; and that conundrum was shared by the history of torture.

Defined with such terms as *heurein* and *invenire*, torture can never be a legitimate "invention" in that its truths are not "discovered" at all, but posited in advance by common consent. In Quintilian's oratory, there can *never* be a question of truth but only of individually invented judgments about what the truth might be: "some have added a sixth department [of rhetoric], subjoining *judgment* to *invention*, on the ground that it is necessary first to *invent* and then to *exercise our judgment*. For my own part I do not believe that invention can exist apart from judgment" (*IO*, III, 3.5; editor's emphasis). In the inventional drama of torture, facts and proofs depend on interpretation, judgment, and even prejudgment—so crucially that Quintilian claimed that the understanding of torture relied on the ability to determine "whether the confession was credible or consistent, whether the witness stuck to his first statement or changed it under the influence of pain, and whether he made it at the beginning of the torture or only after it had continued some time [*an procedente cruciatu*]" (*IO*, V, 4.2). As he concludes his own discussion of the role of rumors in the courtroom, he also articulates a fundamental problem in the nature of truth production, one that has dogged rhetoric ever since the earliest denunciations of the Sophists. Even in contemporary jokes about lawyers who sometimes confirm and sometimes doubt the veracity of DNA evidence, Quintilian's theory is very much alive: namely, that a good orator can argue just as readily for something as against it. "It will be easy," he avers of gossip and rumor, "for both parties to produce precedents to support their arguments," which leads him to the topic of torture: "A like situation arises in the case of evidence extracted by torture:

[21] Augustine, *De doctrina Christiana*, chap. 25, 61; emphasis mine. Augustine is speaking here of the occasional need for an expositor to interpret the performance of a mime. Nowadays, American society is rather more concerned about a different kind of "common consent," like that to the rape of Kitty Genovese or to the "wilding" attack on a Central Park jogger.

one party will style torture an infallible method of discovering the truth, while the other will allege that it also often results in false confessions, since with some their capacity of endurance makes lying an easy thing, while with others weakness makes it a necessity" (*IO*, V, 4.1).

How to find one's way around two such compelling arguments, one for and one against? The situations cited above broach fascinating questions of motive, victimization, and agency as Quintilian gives voice to what might be called the subjectivity of subjection: "for if the point at issue is whether torture should be applied, it will make all the difference who it is who demands or offers it, who it is that is to be subjected to torture, against whom the evidence thus sought will tell, and what is the motive for the demand" (*IO*, V, 4.2). Indeed, as Eckstein infers from Scarry's work, "because pain does not relate to other people and cannot depend upon their testimony, its factual nature can be perceived as illusion or opinion by those who witness it and those who hear tell of it. In other words, they can doubt it."[22] The truth of legal rhetoric was a matter of prejudice; and reading the bodily signs which marked its way was a matter of violence: "just as blood is the result of a wound . . . anything that springs from the matter under investigation and comes to our notice, may properly be called an indication" (cum signum id proprie sit, quod ex eo, de quo quaeritur, natum sub oculos venit ut sanguis et caede) (*IO*, V, 9.14).[23] If torture was an inventional prejudgment, invention was also a prejudgment of torture, both of which were dramatically conceived.

The great French historian Jules Michelet once conceived torture as a kind of decorative supplement to the juridical process without which victims would have confessed anyway: "torture will come, but afterward, as a complement and ornament to the proceeding."[24] What the "invention" of torture implies, however, is that the converse was also true. Torture could come first. Such a vision of torture is consistent with the views of contemporary scholars, who disagree about the chronological placement of torture in the interrogative process. Scarry contends, for example, that interrogation was an integral part of torture, while Peters considers that originally torture was a part of interrogation and not the other way around (*Torture*, 27–29). But, as Eckstein points out, "in either case, an answer to this chicken and egg question proves less interesting than another question this controversy implicitly raises: Does torture elicit truth?" (*LFWP*, 75). The history of rhetoric strongly suggests that the answer to Eckstein's question is no, inasmuch as both torture and the truths it seeks are

---

[22] Eckstein, *LFWP*, 72. Eckstein is concerned here with showing that "the experience of pain is factual truth [only] for the person in pain."

[23] Here, Quintilian is referring specifically to reading such signs of effeminacy as depilation, voluptuous gait, and womanish attire. I discuss the gendered ramifications of his assessment in "Delivering Delivery."

[24] Michelet, *Sorcière*, II, 18. His allusion to ornamentation also recalls a much older debate about the placement of style in rhetorical chronologies.

dependent on the fictions of rhetoric and drama. Bound by the need to interpret the very proof that was designed to permit interpretation, torture was extremely persuasive in its tautological manipulations of artifice, power, agency, and spectacle—the precise qualities that underpinned the invention of good rhetoric and good theater (or, depending on one's perspective, bad rhetoric and bad theater).

In the case of the dramatically constructed evidence of torture, legal interpretation relied on a common consent to the truth of the law's illusions. Premier among those illusions was this: that something that was *not* an invention could be represented as one while something that was *not* a fact could also be represented as one. To put it another way, torture and invention are both concerned with discovery. But if torture cannot produce truth and if its inventional processes yield no real discovery, then the only functions that remain viable enough to justify the very ontologies of torture and forensic rhetoric are their drama and their violence. What is truly "artificial" and definitely dramatic is the process by which artifice is refigured as fact when there is nothing necessarily factual in statements emitted under torture—nothing, that is, except the necessity of interpreting the relationship between pain and speech. In that sense, while even the most enlightened historians of torture have tended to focus on how it came to pass that a practice so long acknowledged as so dubious could come to be associated with the truth, the problem is still more complex. Edward Peters rightly reminds us that there was "no absolute conviction of the reliability of evidence elicited [under torture]" (*Torture*, 33), but what remains insufficiently understood is the notion that the violent yet ineffective modes of "truth production" that characterize the history of torture are shared—in both their inadequacies and their violence—by rhetoric and drama. The very disciplines that have traditionally been demonized—rhetoric and drama—actually aid immeasurably in both the construction and the deconstruction of Truth. Appalling as it may seem in the context of a rhetorical tradition presumably devoted to justice, torture itself becomes part of a larger theatrical vision of proof and even of knowledge, an idea that coincides with Kubiak's belief that theater is the essential condition of all knowledge (*ST*, 64).

Therefore, despite numerous theoretical protestations to the contrary, the extrinsic proofs of *inventio* make no real discovery. That line of reasoning, however, leads to an impossible conclusion: that no manner of forensic rhetorical inquiry is ever viable or necessary because everything is known in advance. The most factual part of torture and forensic invention, then, is the existence in both of a persuasive and dramatic pretense of discovery which is strengthened by probability and verisimilitude. Even at the end of the passage from the *Rhetorica ad Herennium* analyzed above, the Pseudo-Cicero expresses some doubts amidst his claims of certainty when all the "signs" of guilt come together: "To be sure, some one or two of these things can by chance have happened in such a way as to throw suspicion upon this defendant; but for everything to coincide from first to last, he must have been a participant in the crime. This cannot be the result of chance" (*RAH*, IV, 53). Such theoretical anomalies persisted; Tertullian found a new way to condemn the spectacle of punishment by questioning its legitimacy. "But who will pledge himself to me," he asks, "that it is always the guilty who are condemned to the beasts, or whatever the punishment, and that it is never inflicted on innocence too, through the vindictiveness of the judge it may be, the weakness of the advocate, the severity of *torture?*"[25] Later, in 724, the theft laws of the Frankish king Liutprand addressed the possibility of a reversal of legal fortune, should new evidence arise to contradict the dubious evidence extracted under torture. One edict even prescribed financial restitution in the event that someone "accuses another of theft and defeats him in combat, or if perhaps the theft was revealed through torture (*districtione*) by a public official and composition has been paid, and if afterwards it is found that the theft was committed by another man."[26] If legally imposed tortures really could lead reliably to the truth, then such problematic legal remedies to problematic legal practices could not exist.

When the law renders itself accountable for the unreliability of its own methods, it compromises its own existence, because a presumably just legal system could not be based on prejudgment. Modern perceptions of democracy or Christian justice notwithstanding, within the classical and scholastic legal systems that staged extensive verbal discoveries of legal and religious truths, discovery could not be based on pretense. Even so, it was imperative that the legal structures associated with hegemonies perpetuate the illusion that the truth (however illusory) was on their side. In fact, according to some contemporary revisionist theories, the very project of rhetoric is involved in perpetuating precisely such illusions. Numerous caveats have been issued of late by critics who have called into question the very nature of early democracies. James Berlin is emphatic in his reminder that, for all their lofty philosophical ideals, Aristotle "favored an educated and wealthy elite, and his rhetoric teaches this elite to dominate and control their inferiors," while Cicero was "a dirty politician among dirty politicians, supporting in his intellectual and political work one of the cruelest, most violently repressive governments ever to exist."[27] Even if it is anachronistic for Augusto Boal to chastise Aristotle for failing to transform preexisting inequalities,[28] and even if it is impossible within the scope of this book to undertake a social history of torture, it is certainly possible to probe the theoretical foundations of some of those inequalities.

One dominant theme of the theory of torture over the ages is its association with the strong, the empowered, the hegemonic who typically intervene upon

---

[25] Tertullian, *De spectaculis*, chap. 19.

[26] The text of Edict 56.III appears in Drew, trans., *Lombard Laws*, 167.

[27] Berlin, "Revisionary Histories of Rhetoric," 115. In his comment on Cicero, he quotes from Dorey, "Honesty in Roman Politics."

[28] See Boal, *Theater of the Oppressed* (hereafter *TO*), 23.

the bodies of the weaker, the disempowered, the disenfranchised. "The right to 'question,'" asserts Hans-Robert Jauss in reference to the Middle Ages, "is a prerogative that remains on the side of the lords; to be obliged to respond and to be unable to speak until one is interrogated is the lot of the subjected."[29] According to Peter Brown, beatings and torture in the Roman world might even become weapons in a larger fight for social status among the empowered: "even when less severe, beating inflicted crushing dishonor on a notable. He would be 'stripped and thrown down' to be beaten, as if he were a member of the lower classes; his 'free body' would be sullied, from henceforth, by the marks of punishment."[30] So, even as they conducted inquiries into pain, learned authors (writing largely from a position of economic privilege) belonged to social classes that had the power to inflict it—a phenomenon that continues to polarize political differences about rhetoric even in today's discussions about composition classes and curricular development. For example, the desire to expose the non-democratic tendencies of democratic language seems omnipresent as such a scholar as C. Jan Swearingen advocates the "badly needed" search for a "phenomenology of self and voice that can reconcile contemporary cultural, critical, and disciplinary divergences . . . [and] bridge the curricular gaps that continue to disenfranchise traditionally marginal groups."[31] By dint of its own tortured relationship with the truth, rhetoric constitutes such a phenomenology.

Since torture was an integral part of early jurisprudence, it could not be acknowledged that the legal judgments that were designed to reflect, reveal, and respect Truth were inventions. The overwhelming evidence that torture invented truth dramatically had to be suppressed. During a violent and falsified search for Truth, early theorists actually used their eloquence to camouflage the fact that the legal "truths" dug out by torture might well have been illusions or lies. In other words, where Hanson argues that, by the Renaissance, such ambiguities are connected to a profound epistemological crisis within the law ("Torture and Truth," 53–56), I suggest that the site of that crisis was rhetorical *inventio*. Long before Lucien Goldmann characterized the novel as "the story of a degraded search . . . for authentic values, by a problematic hero, in a degraded world,"[32] long before novels in the modern sense were ever written, rhetorical theorists and early dramatists had rehearsed a falsified search of their

---

[29] "Adam Interrogateur," 160–61. The term *questionner* (question, interrogate, torture) is especially difficult to translate for reasons that will be addressed below. See also Helen Solterer's discussion of this passage in the context of the Hegelian master–slave dialectic in *Master and Minerva* (hereafter *MM*), 98, 238n.

[30] Brown, *PP*, 54, in which he discusses commentaries by Augustine and Libanius.

[31] Swearingen, *Rhetoric and Irony*, 234. See also Page duBois's discussion of "Women, the Body, and Torture" (chap. 14 of *TT*). On class tensions within the medieval university among bourgeois lawyers, upwardly mobile theology students, and villagers, see Murray, *Reason and Society in the Middle Ages*, chap. 10.

[32] Goldmann, *Pour une sociologie du roman*, 26.

own during the inventional process, which gave rise to the spectacular performances of law, politics, pedagogy, theology, and theater.

Similarly Kubiak has argued from the work of Kenneth Burke, Derrida, and Nietzsche that "theatre's perverse claim to truth is that it is not 'real' but is a *true perjury* that is determined and upheld by the conventions of the stage" (*ST*, 28; emphasis his).[33] My point is rather that, for learned medieval authors, the truth of that perjury resides in the shared inventional systems of rhetoric and drama. Invention itself becomes the "truest perjury" of all in that it casts the dramatic illusions of torture as truth and, later, as real-life dramas that render judgments upon bodies. In accordance with techniques advocated in theories of invention, the various dramatic texts to be analyzed here stage judgments (or rather, prejudgments) about the "truth" of the statements drawn out from tortured bodies, as when Pilate of the *Passion* from the Sainte Geneviève Library orders that his henchman make judgment about and upon the body of Christ ("De son corps faictes jugement").[34]

Enlightening in this context is Michael Riffaterre's pronouncement that "the only reason that the phrase 'fictional truth' is not an oxymoron, as 'fictitious truth' would be, is that fiction is a genre whereas lies are not." [35] In antiquity and the Middle Ages, forensic rhetoric was also a genre, a genre concerned with the truth of crimes and punishment, a genre that exploited truths that were indeed "fictitious" because they had come from torture. Those "fictitious truths" could then go on to inform some of the "fictional truths" of medieval didactic literature, especially works that explicitly situate themselves—in both theme and performance—in the hazy area between illusion and reality. Riffaterre goes on to ponder "how the same text can be at once fictional and true, how verisimilitude can substitute an idea of truth for an actual experience of actuality, thus freeing fiction from the shackles of reference and making truth a concept that depends on grammar and is therefore impervious to change, rather than on our subjective, idiosyncratic, and changeable experience of reality" (*FT*, 5–6). In rhetoric, in torture, in theater, far more than grammar is implicated, even though grammar helps light the way today. Nor is their frequently violent content freed of reference. If anything, rhetorical invention provided a mental rehearsal (ultimately assisted by the mnemonic imagination) that might trans-

---

[33] Not all medievalists will agree with Kubiak's contention that such a process is innately terroristic (*ST*, 63–66), but his denunciation of the law's "agonizing trap of a falsely assumed empiricism" (*ST*, 66) resonates compellingly with inventional theories of torture. I submit that rhetoric is an important birthplace for both the falsity and the theatricality of that "empiricism."

[34] *Mystère de la Passion Nostre Seigneur du manuscrit 1131 de la Bibliothèque Sainte-Geneviève*, 1756–59. For the sake of simplicity, I refer to this text as the Sainte Geneviève *Passion*. See in this connection Asad's statement that "torture was not only a demonstration of justice, it was also itself productive of truth" (*GOR*, 88).

[35] Riffaterre, *FT*, 1.

form the shackles of grammar into real implements of pain and punishment during delivery.

Rhetoric and Drama, Torture and Truth

Presumably, the whole point of torture was to extract the truth. Be that as it may, the same persons who wrote its history linked it consistently to dramatic, creative, inventional methods which demonstrate that it was totally unreliable. Despite Demosthenes's assertion that "no statements made as a result of torture [*basanos*] have ever been proved to be untrue," Aristotle had no trouble at all crafting a rhetorical position according to which the "evidence from torture may be considered utterly untrustworthy" (*Rhetoric*, 1377a).[36] Nor did Quintilian, who notes that torture "often results in false confessions" (*IO*, V, 4.1). Following Aristotle's distinction between the extrinsic, inartificial, or factual proofs (*atechnoi*) which lie outside the art of speaking and the intrinsic, artificial, or invented proofs (*entechnoi*) which the orator deduces himself, Quintilian affirms that

> to the first class [*atechnoi*] belong decisions of previous courts, rumours, evidence extracted by torture [*tormenta*], documents [*tabulae*], oaths, and witnesses, for it is with these that the majority of forensic arguments are concerned. But though in themselves they involve no art [*se carent arte*], all the powers of eloquence are as a rule required to disparage or refute them. Consequently in my opinion those who would eliminate the whole of this class of proof from their rules of oratory, deserve the strongest condemnation. (*IO*, V, 1.1–2)[37]

However, a closer look at the words of Quintilian and of other rhetoricians reveals that the *atechnoi* do indeed involve considerable art—and not just the artistry necessary to refute them. They also involve a crucial shift that seems ubiquitous in the rhetorical tradition from intellectual to bodily hermeneutics. The inquiry into a legal subject and its parts becomes an inquiry into the body and its parts, a bodily invention.

Plato's Socrates once advised that the way to reflect on the nature of any complex subject was "to enumerate its parts and observe in respect of each what we observe in the case of a simple object, to wit what its natural capacity, active or passive, consists in."[38] Thus, to hear Quintilian discuss torture is to witness a veritable Platonic heuresis, complete with the requisite investigation into such questions as passivity vs. agency or acting vs. acted upon. "It will make all the

---

[36] See duBois on Demosthenes 30.37 (*TT*, 49–50).

[37] Those *tabulae* assume new importance in connection with the wax tablets of memory, discussed in Chapter 2.

[38] Plato, *Phaedrus*, 270d.

difference," he writes, "who was in charge of the proceedings, who was the victim and what the nature of the torture" (*IO*, V, 4.2). Later, in a work that was to serve as the quintessential encyclopedic reference for the Middle Ages, Isidore of Seville introduced into the *Etymologiarum* his own heuristic investigation into the activity or passivity of the pain of legally inflicted punishment (*poena*). In "De poenis in legibus constitutis," he ruminates on whether *poena* is inflicted or endured: "Dupliciter malum appellatur: unum, quod homo facit, alterum, quod patitur. Quod facit, peccatum est; quod patitur, poena" (Evil is called by two names: one, which man commits, the other which he endures. The one he commits is a sin; the one he endures, a punishment).[39]

Still, the constant alternation between a tortured conception of hermeneutics and a hermeneutic conception of torture foregrounds complex questions of passivity and agency and of masters and subjects. As with Geoffrey of Vinsauf (and numerous medieval representations), torture blurs the categories of "acting" and "acted upon." Its own history bears witness to the transformation of a cerebral, dialectical inquiry into a dramatic, punitive rhetorical intervention involving mutilated bodies in pain. As punishment is equated with the acquisition of knowledge, it seems that the legendary "open hand" of rhetoric could become the "closed fist" of dialectical inquiry—a fist that inflicts pain dramatically.[40]

On these points, the very philology of torture is instructive. The ancient Greek term for torture, *basanos*, denoted the literal "touchstone" that had been used as early as the seventh century B.C. for testing currency for the content of precious metals (*TT*, 9–14).[41] That physical test, conducted by rubbing coins against a special stone, acquired metaphorical connotations as the hermeneutic manipulations of the touchstone for seeking the truth about metallic content became a different kind of test. Metal, it seems, proved equally suited to investigations into the hidden epistemic contents of the human body—normally that of a social inferior or slave—as those bodies were mined in the course of prosecution.[42] That shift in meaning from financial to political inquiry is already clear in Saint Augustine's *City of God*, where he invokes the teachings of Paulinus, bishop of Nola. In Augustine's description of torture as a means by which to coerce victims into revealing their gold and silver, the touchstone of *basanos* is associated with precious metals. Ennobled by Augustine, the victims of torture stand in metonymically for the silver and gold the intellect might conceal from pagan persecutors:

[39] Isidore of Seville, *Etymologiarum*, I, bk. 5, chap. 27.1.

[40] I refer here to the dictum cited by Isidore of Seville—who borrows it from Cassiodorus (*Institutiones*, II.3.2), who attributes it to Varro (*Etymologiarum*, bk. 2, chap. 23). See Murphy's discussion of the open hand/closed fist in *RIMA*, 73.

[41] For an excellent philological introduction to *basanos*, see duBois, *TT*, chap. 2; and Peters, *Torture*, 14–15.

[42] Particularly helpful introductions to the social history of torture as it relates to questions of class and gender include Peters, *Torture*; Garnsey, *Social Status*; duBois, *TT*; and Brown, *PP*.

Some good men, to be sure, even Christian men, have been *put to torture [tor-mentis excruciati sunt]* to make them reveal their property to the enemy. . . . These who endured as much suffering for gold, as they ought to have borne for Christ, should have been warned to learn rather to love him who enriches with eternal happiness all who suffer on his behalf—not to love gold and silver for which in either case it was the height of wretchedness to suffer, whether they lied and kept them concealed or told the truth and surrendered them.[43]

Hence it is difficult to embrace Marie-Christine Pouchelle's statement that in the Middle Ages "the cutting open of bodies in search of knowledge was subject to taboos deeply rooted in the mentality of the time. It could not be accepted . . . that, for the sake of knowledge, one had the right to invade a body."[44] Torture staged precisely that sort of invasion, mutilating bodies in a dramatic, epistemological quest for the illusory truths which informed the legal process. Even in so apparently benign a medieval narrative as that of the eight-year-old deaf-and-dumb boy who is miraculously cured by Saint Louis, torture is linked to the violent quest for the secrets of a human body (in this case, a defective body). One of the *Miracles de Saint Louis* relates the tale of a "vallet de huit anz qui n'avoit oncques oÿ ne parlé, qui recouvra s'oïe au tombel Saint Loys" (an eight-year-old youth who had never heard nor spoken who recovered his hearing at the tomb of Saint Louis). Just as torture consisted of a violent intervention upon a body that was thought to contain a hidden truth, here the "truth" of an illness or defect is subject to the same sort of hermeneutic inquiry. The quest for knowledge about pathology becomes an ordeal played out on the young boy's body—an ordeal that is designed to test his ability to do the very thing that rhetorical invention was supposed to do: make speech possible:

Il estoit sort et muet. Et li cornoit on et buisinoit et crioit d'un cor en l'oreille, mes riens n'en apercevoit ne n'ooit. Et en ce meemes tens l'*en le poignoit et batoit griement pour ce que l'en esprouvast se il parleroit*, et neporquant il ne disoit mot, ançois faisoit tant seulement signes d'omme muet. Et les enfanz du dit Gauchier li getoient les charbons ardanz sus son ventre nu pour esprouver se il parleroit et se il estoit vraiement muet, et riens ne fesoit pour tout ce fors signes de muet et fors que jeter les charbons *loing* de lui.[45]

---

[43] Augustine, *City of God*, bk. I, chap. 10. Later in this passage, even gold and silver are recontextualized in favor of Christian poverty, as Augustine goes on to distinguish true believers from those who worship gold and silver for their own sake. See also Roberts's discussion of torture in Prudentius where "truth is counted a crime" in *Poetry and the Cult of the Martyrs* (hereafter PCM), 47–48.

[44] Pouchelle, *The Body and Surgery in the Middle Ages* (hereafter BSMA), 1. Insofar as her study is devoted to Henri de Mondeville (d. ca. 1320), surgeon to Philip le Bel, Pouchelle is referring specifically to the cutting up of cadavers in the quest for medical knowledge. See also Wilson, "William Harvey's *Prelectiones*."

[45] Guillaume de Saint-Pathus, *Miracles de Saint Louis*, chap. 15, pp. 50–51; emphasis his. I thank Sharon Farmer for bringing this text to my attention. See also Peter Brown's discussion of the "pathology of power" in the context of medicine, class, and the beating of slaves (PP, 51).

He was deaf and dumb. And they poked him and prodded him and screamed in his ear with a horn, but he noticed and heard nothing. And at the same time they punched and beat him harshly in order to test whether he could speak; but for all that, he spoke not a word as he made only the signs of a mute man. And the children of the aforementioned Gauchier threw burning coals on his bare chest in order to determine if he would speak and if he were truly mute and he [still] did nothing for all that except to make the signs of the mute and to throw off the coals far from him.

In the happy ending to this story, the boy is able to speak and commences work in a kitchen, a valuable member of the Christian society for whom Louis's miracles have been compiled.

The transition from intellectual to bodily hermeneutics is also borne out by the latinate terms for torture. As Edward Peters duly notes of the history of torture, the concepts of interrogation, testing, and punishment (*quaestio* and *tormentum/tortura*) became synonymous, a synonymy that was preserved in the French term *la question*: "when *tormentum* was applied in an interrogatory way, the technical term was *quaestio per tormenta* or *quaestio tormentorum*, that is an investigation by means that had originally been strictly a form of punishment, and that of slaves only" (*Torture*, 28).[46] The blurring of those terms would also become painfully clear in a different kind of drama staged throughout medieval and early modern Europe in which countless women were tormented during what H. Trevor Roper calls the "great European witch-craze."[47] In the notorious fifteenth-century inquisitorial manual *Malleus maleficarum*, Heinrich Kramer consistently advocates the torture of witches, even though he acknowledges that the method is unreliable.[48]

Kramer is in the process of explaining to his fellow inquisitors what is to be done to the accused witch. When "neither threats nor such promises [to spare her life] will induce her to confess the truth," he advises that "the officers must proceed with the *sentence*, and she must be *examined* [tunc ministri *sententiam* latam exequantur, & *quaestionetur*]." Here the problem of interpretation lies in determining just what is happening under the "questioning" and just when it is happening. In the Latin original, the "questioning" apparently begins with frightful inducements to speak: "And while she is being questioned about each

---

[46] See duBois, *TT* 21–25; Asad, "Notes," 296–97; Brown on corporal punishment leading to death (*PP*, 54); and Foucault's claim that "it is as if investigation and punishment had become mixed" (*DP*, 41). See also Bartlett on thirteenth-century judicial torture as "an alternative to trial by ordeal" (*TFW*, 139).

[47] Here I invoke the title of chap. 3 of Trevor-Roper, *Crisis of the Seventeenth Century*, "The Great Witch-craze of the Sixteenth and Seventeenth Centuries."

[48] Authorship of the *Malleus* has often been attributed jointly to Kramer and Jakob Sprenger, but historians have largely determined that Sprenger's contribution was minimal. Latin citations are from the 1487 edition of the *Malleus Maleficarum*; and English citations are from Kors and Peters, *Witchcraft in Europe* (who follow Montague Summers).

several point, *let her be often and frequently exposed to torture* [questioning?], beginning with the more gentle of them; for the Judge should not be too hasty to proceed to the graver kind" (Et dum *quaestionatur* de certis articulis super quibus *quaestionatur*, & hoc saepe & frequenter à levioribus incipiendo: quia citius concedet levia quàm graviora). Kors and Peters have translated this questioning as physical "torture" (although it seems equally logical at this stage that it is a verbal torture). Immediately thereafter, Kramer makes the following statement:

> And note that, if she confesses under torture [*per tormenta*], she should then be taken to another place and questioned anew, so that she does not confess only under the stress of torture [*vi tormentorum cognouerit*]. The next step of the Judge should be that, if after being fittingly tortured [*quaestionatus decentur*] she refuses to confess the truth, he should have other engines of torture [*alia tormentorum genera*] brought before her, and tell her that she will have to endure these if she does not confess. If then she is not induced by terror [*ad terrorem*] to confess, the torture must be continued [*questionanda ad continuandum tormenta*] on the second or third day, but not repeated at that present time unless there should be some indication of its probable success. (Kors and Peters, 166–68; *Malleus*, I, 245)

In other words, if torture does not work, torture begins, which seems counterintuitive. It is not logical that additional physical tortures would minimize the chance of lying under the stress of physical torture. Nor does it appear that the instruments of torture are first brought out and displayed to strike terror in the female victim *after* she has already been subjected to them. Then and now, though, the confusion is understandable because of the multiplicity of meanings associated with *quaestio*.

During the Middle Ages, even as it connoted torture, *quaestio* continued to denote such intellectual activities as scholastic debate, legal question, and legal investigation, all of which retained their potentially punitive connotations while they were dramatized in medieval courtrooms, classrooms, and theaters. The *quaestio* was, of course, the bread and butter of forensic inventional theories of *stasis* (the term that designated a thorny problem of legal interpretation). Legal *quaestiones* or *staseis* comprised an extensive system of hermeneutic inquiry that was designed to generate legal arguments. For Cicero, a conflict of pleas entailed considering the nature of the case and then, "when you have found out whether it is simple or complex, and you have seen whether it discusses a written document or involves general reasoning, then you must see what the question in the case is [*quaestio*]" (*De inventione*, I.18).[49] When Isidore of Seville classified various types of *quaestio* in his *Etymologiarum*, the term still evoked various acts of seeking. Isidore specifies in his treatment of various

---

[49] The theory of *stasis* or *status* is attributed to Hermagoras and Hermogenes and was transmitted to the Middle Ages through such treatises as the *Rhetorica ad Herennium*, e.g., I, 18–27; and Cicero's *De inventione*. For a discussion of this tradition, see Murphy, *RIMA*, 3–29.

modes of interpretation that "problemata autem, quae Latine appellantur pro-
positiones, *quaestiones* sunt habentes aliquid quod disputatione solvendum sit.
Quaestio autem est quaesitio, cum quaeritur an sit, quid sit, quale sit" (problems are what are called propositions in Latin, questions are things that have
something to be solved by means of disputation. The question, then, is the thing
sought, when it is asked if a thing is, what it is, how it is) (I, bk. 6, 8.13–16).[50]

Additionally, in the realm of classical and medieval pedagogy, *quaestio* signified the individual intellectual propositions contested during the spectacular
scholastic exercises known in Rome as the *progymnasmata* and in medieval theology faculties as quodlibetal disputations.[51] *Quaestiones* were a time-honored
means of teaching young boys how to take up verbal arms in what Seneca termed
a "school for gladiators" and what John of Salisbury, Abelard, and Henri d'An-
deli later called a battlefield.[52] These philological antecedents have governed the
questioning of questioning over the ages and occasionally emerge in our own
century. Paolo Valesio theorizes in his *Novantiqua*, for instance, that every question "selects a field of battle," while Elaine Scarry contends in *The Body in Pain*
that during torture, "the question, whatever its content, is an act of wounding;
the answer, whatever its content, is a scream" (*BP*, 46).[53] In the case of the
punitive violence of the *quaestio*, torture's dramatic battlefield was the body.

Perhaps nowhere is the commingling of rhetorical invention, torture, spectacle, and punishment more apparent than in Isidore of Seville's treatment of
"De poenis in legibus constitutis." There, Isidore offers a hermeneutic definition of torture by focusing on how it was "invented" as well as on what it invents.
After enumerating various implements of torture, he goes on to explain that torture owes its own *invention* to a need to *find* the truth as it *punishes* the wicked.
Moreover, he situates his entire treatment of crime and punishment in the context of pain and fear (ut sit et *dolor et metus*), the traditional components of
Aristotelian catharsis:

> Ungulae dictae quod effodiant. Haec et *fidiculae*, quia his rei in *eculeo* torquentur,
> ut fides *inveniatur*. Eculeus autem dictus quod extendat. Tormenta vero, quod tor-
> quendo mentem *inveniant*. Est et latomia supplicii genus ad verberandum aptum,
> *inventum* a Tarquinio Superbo ad poenam *sceleratorum*. (*Etymologiarum*, I, bk. 5,
> 27.20–24)

---

[50] As editors Oroz Reta and Casquero point out in their edition, Isidore invokes the distinctions
proposed by Saint Jerome for three types of interpretation from which hidden meanings can be extracted from difficult passages (p. 583, n. 20).

[51] On the *progymnasmata*, see, e.g., Murphy, *RIMA*, 41–42; Kennedy, *Classical Rhetoric*, 163–
64; and Trimpi, "Quality of Fiction," 75–81. The most helpful introduction to the quodlibet remains Glorieux's *Littérature quodlibétique*; see also my "Theatre of Scholastic Erudition."

[52] For a discussion of the intellectual and physical violence of rhetoric by these and other authors, see my *ROMD*, 89–110.

[53] Valesio, *Novantiqua*, 32, as discussed by Covino, "Alchemizing the History of Rhetoric," 49.

The claws are so called because they gouge out. And they are also called the strings or the reins, because, in order that the truth may be found, these kings are tormented on the rack. And the rack or "little horse" is so called because it stretches things out. And torments are so called because they find things in the mind by twisting it. And the latomia [quarry] is a type of ordeal suitable for scourging that was invented by Tarquin the Great as a punishment for the wicked.

In the rich philological intertext of the *Etymologiarum,* the *scelerati* reappear later in Book 18 as the tragedian's objects of imitation in his own songs of pain before spectators: "tragoedi sunt qui antiqua gesta atque facinora sceleratorum regum luctuosa carmine spectante populo concinebant" (tragic poets are those who sang in mournful verses of the ancient deeds and crimes of wicked kings while the people watched) (II, bk. 18, chap. 45).[54] Isidore's subtle shifting among torture, invention, catharsis, performance, and the *similitudes* of punishment (*similitudo* vindictae) (I, bk. 5, 27.24–25) is ideologically consonant with an elaborate rhetorical tradition which emphasized the invention, the performance, and the aesthetics of pain. Indeed, its very fluidity proves highly compatible with the violent scourgings of medieval drama and hagiography.

For example, the medieval producers and spectators of the Towneley Crucifixion certainly seem to have appreciated that interplay as the tortures of Christ were staged in an equestrian setting or *in eculeo*: "Stand thou yonder on yond syde, / And we shall se how he can ryde, / And how to weld a shaft."[55] More gruesome still are the vivid details proposed by the torturers in the *Geu Saint Denis* as they describe how the Saint will get "back in the saddle again." Inviting him to "ride the horsey" (Vien chevauchier ceste buchete), the torturer Masquebignet indicates the method of tortured gaming (*En moustrant le cheaau* [*sic*] *fust*) as his pal Hapelopin announces, "Nous les metrons a la selete" (We'll put them in the saddle). Having promised to suffer whatever comes their way, Denis and his followers hear that they will die (*vous mourrez*) while stage directions call for beatings with sticks (*en batant d'un baston*) and securing the victims upon the *eculeus*: "Cy les defferent et lez metent suz .iii. chevaus de fust ou suz .iii. fourmes qui aient lez piez devant lez plus haus et soient leurs mains liees aus piez dez fourmes, lez piez tirez aval couchiez et estenduz dessus et adens" (Here they strike them and place them on three "horseys" [*cheval de fust* = instrument of torture]; that is, on three forms so that they will have their feet forward and higher and their hands tied to the feet of the devices, with their

---

[54] Isidore's definition of spectacle is based on the gaze of the spectator: "spectacles are so called because something is presented there for the public to look at" (*Etymologiarum*, bk. 18, chap. 16.1). Torturers and tragedians are further united in a veritable song of pain inasmuch as the word for the implements of torture called *fidiculae* also denoted the lyre. I thank Professors Gualtiero Calboli and Laurent Pernot for their assistance with some of the more arcane aspects of Isidore's vocabulary.

[55] *Towneley Plays,* ll. 110–12, p. 261; see also Kolve's discussion of this text in *The Play Called Corpus Christi* (hereafter *PCC*), 192.

feet pulled, laid out, and stretched above and below).[56] Elsewhere, in the omni-present blurring of investigation, punishment, and spectacle that characterizes the *Ecclesiastical History*, Eusebius narrates practices that are more punitive than interrogatory. Even a dead body—that is, a body with supposedly no more information to give—becomes a site of retaliation by torturers: "those who had been strangled in the jail they threw to the dogs, and watched carefully night and day that none should be cared for by us. . . . And some raged and gnashed their teeth at the remains, seeking some further vengeance from them."[57] Alive, dead, or dying martyrs were made a "spectacle to the world" as one such as Blandina "was hung on a stake and offered as a prey to the wild beasts that were let in. She seemed to be hanging in the shape of a cross, and by her con-tinuous prayer gave great zeal to the combatants, while they looked on during the contest" (*EH*, V, 1.40–41).

While my emphasis is not on hagiography but on drama, these accounts speak to a larger cultural problem of dramatic invention that demands closer scrutiny. As we saw earlier, a rhetorical *inventio* that relies on torture yields no real epistemological discovery. And yet, at least for Eusebius, the spectacle of torture as punishment does indeed yield a kind of truth. On one hand, the pa-gan torturers know their own truth in advance—but not the Christian truth that is expounded symbolically through the death of their victims. On the other hand, even if it is not the discovery that the torturers anticipated, the mutilation of Christian bodies yields a *real* discovery of an ostensibly real Christian Truth. Within the larger theological recontextualization of pagan into Christian law—which is, after all, Eusebius's primary subject—the Truth "discovered" in the *Ecclesiastical History* is known in advance not by the torturer but by faithful readers or listeners who strive to build the foundations of a new world order upon martyred bodies. The foundational moment of Christianity is a moment of torture, a moment that transforms an empty pagan method of mangling bod-ies into an ennobled model of exemplary behavior to be imitated by the faith-ful.[58] When pagan tyrants torture the bodies of Christian martyrs, they do so not to discover truth but to punish, not to invent but to destroy, or—to borrow

[56] *Le Geu Saint Denis* (hereafter *GSD*), ed. Bernard James Seubert, 621–27. While I cite Seu-bert's accessible edition throughout, the text reveals a number of anomalies, esp. in punctuation—many of which have been noted by Graham Runnalls in the introduction to his edition of the *Cycle de Mystères des premiers martyrs* (hereafter *CPM*), 16–18.

[57] Eusebius, *Ecclesiastical History* (hereafter *EH*), ed. and trans. Kirsopp Lake, V, 1.59. Even if some truth could have been "discovered" within the live bodies of martyrs through the violent meth-ods of torture, it is now consumed by wild beasts even as another truth is expounded by the Chris-tian apologist. For a superb discussion of torture in hagiographical narrative, see Roberts, *PCM*, "Verbal Examination," 51–55; and his "Punishment and Torture," 55–68.

[58] Another informative treatment of the spectacle of martyrdom in a slightly later period is Knott, *Discourses of Martyrdom in English Literature, 1563–1694*, esp. chap. 1, "John Rogers and the Drama of Martyrdom."

Scarry's terminology—not to make but to "unmake." [59] But if, as Sarah Beckwith has suggested, the companion Christian message relies on Christ's body as a symbol that itself *"makes meaning* for its practitioners and interlocutors," [60] then that tortured body also unmakes its pre-Christian antecedents.

So it is that for Augustine, even the bodily invasions of torture may be figured as positive, desirable, and productive of Christian truth. Martyrs who learn from the experience of physical pain that the true good is Christ and not one's earthly possessions could then be thankful for the lessons of violence: "it may be that the tortures [*tormenta*] which taught them that the good to be held dear is a good that cannot decay were more profitable than those goods of theirs, which without any profitable service at all, brought torture [*torquebant*] upon their owners through love of them" (*City of God*, bk. I, chap. 10).

For Eusebius, martyrdom is an edifying spectacle that discloses to its beholders the virtues of patience, constancy, and a willingness to die. The touchstone of torture actually does extract truth—but a truth that clearly depends on the eye of the beholder: "They say that *those who were standing around* were amazed when they saw that at one time they were torn by scourges down to deep-seated veins and arteries, so that the hidden contents of the recesses of their bodies, their entrails and organs, were exposed to sight" (*EH*, IV, 15.4; emphasis mine). Of special interest here is the presence of "those who were standing around," who indicate that some kind of spectacle is taking place. They even point to a kind of protodrama, anticipating the *circumstantes* described in some of the earliest dramatic texts such as the Fleury Playbook *Herod* in which the *populus circumstantem* is "invited to adore the child." [61] In the passages above, the truth of torture depends quite literally on the *circumstantes*.

As we shall see, at stake in the very language that serves torture, rhetoric, and drama is this troubling perception: if there was no touchstone by which to test the touchstone of *basanos*, then in some cases the genre of drama could become the touchstone, while the *mystère* could offer itself up as a kind of dramatic answer to *la question*. Even so, rhetorically sophisticated Christian dramatists seem to have discovered the undiscoverable or, at least, the unacknowledgeable: that the truth constructed by their plays—however persuasive because of its violence—was also a dramatic fiction. Just as judicial torture was unreliable, so too was the mystery play that staged torture to convey its own presumably truthful messages. Moments of torture, themselves dependent on the interpretation of spectacle, were made more complex by the imitative spectacle of drama. The patently spectacular vocabulary of rhetoric, torture, and drama "invites" audiences to interpret what is already subject to interpretation and to

[59] I refer to the subtitle of Scarry's *Body in Pain: The Making and Unmaking of the World*. Scarry's book is divided into two parts, "Unmaking" and "Making"; see esp. chap. 3.

[60] Beckwith, *Christ's Body* (hereafter *CB*), 3 (emphasis hers), which may usefully be compared with Louis Marin's invocation of "history-making" (*Utopics*, 12).

[61] For a discussion of this text, see Tydeman, *Theatre in the Middle Ages* (hereafter *TMA*), 223.

look at a dramatic illusion that they must not examine too closely even as they are invited to look.

Consequently, the questions that recur throughout this book are these: If neither torture nor invention has the capacity to discover the truth, then what is the interpretive situation of literary works that dramatize the unreliable method of torture within the notoriously unreliable vehicle of drama? What precisely were authors and audiences discovering and inventing in the scourging scenes of religious drama? If the violence of rhetoric, drama, torture, and truth is characterized by a viciously circular logic of verisimilitude proving a truth that then appears verisimilar and therefore truthful, then why even the pretense of truth? To respond to these questions, I turn to the ways in which late medieval French drama compounds the paradoxes of violence. With its extensive rhetorical lexicon of torture and invention, the French corpus comprises a striking case study of how the unstable "truth" of torture is constructed dramatically.

Hannah Arendt once intuited that "persuasion and violence can destroy truth, but they cannot replace it." [62] I propose to show that medieval rhetoricians and dramatists really did replace it. Paradoxically, they "replaced" it with something that had always been a part of persuasion and violence: drama. In the specific context of the histories of torture and rhetoric, it is the presence of a theatrical lexicon and of a genre concerned with masks that in the end unmasks the "lies" to which theatricality gives rise in the interpretation of torture. As it happens, one of the premier ways of turning the dramatic register of torture to advantage was to focus on the spectacle of punishments whose dramatic appeal seemed to detract from the potential falsehood of the discoveries involved. Still, once torture becomes spectacle and takes its place in another birthplace of illusion (the stage), torture also destroys the illusions of the theater. In much the same way that Peter Brook suggests that "theatre is always a self-destructive art, and it is always written on the wind," drama makes and unmakes torture even as torture makes and unmakes drama. [63]

Once the rhetorical aesthetics of violence has been brought to bear upon our readings of medieval drama, we may better understand (even if we can never completely fathom) the anomalous dramatic representations of judicial interrogation and punishment through torture. *Inventio* serves to unite the violent materials extracted from torture with learned medieval conceptions of violence on the stage. Theorists of rhetoric identified the violence of torture as a hermeneutic process with performative ramifications, and medieval learned culture rehearsed and enacted that hermeneutic as dramatists and hagiographers readily trod the same conceptual path from tortured invention to dramatic performance. Some even associated torture with the invention of drama. The representative dramatic examples analyzed below help to establish not only

[62] Arendt, "Truth and Politics, in *Between Past and Future*," 259; see also Eckstein, *LFWP*, 92.
[63] Brook, *Empty Space*, 15.

that drama informed the violence of inventional torture but that tortured invention informed the violence of drama.

The Violent Invention of Drama

Murder, torture, and violence, it seems, have perpetually functioned as theater. In any event, such was the case in three exemplary tales reproduced here because they configure torture as a veritable origin of drama. As early as the second century, Lucian of Samosata elaborated on the drama of torture in his "Tyrannicide." In a tale of brutality, crime, and punishment, he stages before the gaze of a tyrant the invention of a mimetic, juridico-political spectacle of pain:

> Now then, *imagine*, I beg you, what the tyrant no doubt did and what he said before his end. When I sought to slay the son and wounded him again and again in those parts of his body which could be seen, that so I might grieve the parent most, that so I might rend his heart through the first sight, he raised a doleful cry. . . . Before I slipped away, *I had myself composed the whole plot of the tragedy*, but had left to the actor the body, the stage-setting, the sword, and the remainder of the play. When the other made his appearance and saw his only son with but little breath in him, bloodied, covered with gore, his wounds close together, numerous, and vital, he raised this cry.[64]

In Lucian's pathos of law, a bloodied body is an actor, his murder is the drama, and his speeches are wordless cries of pain that prefigure punishment and death. Lucian's description of the very genealogy of tragedy almost anticipates such critical developments as Wendy Lesser's declaration that "murder in real life is, for those directly involved in it, a tragedy, or at the very least a depressingly squalid event, murder in fiction is often a game, and always a drama."[65] More particularly, the whole story of the interplay among rhetoric, drama, and torture was exemplified for the learned Middle Ages by one of the most startling genealogical narratives ever written. As part of his extended discussion of war and play in chapter 18 of the *Etymologiarum* ("De Bello et ludis"), Isidore of Seville mentions the role of the Lydians or the Etruscans in the spread of drama to the West. But his narrative takes an unexpectedly sinister turn when we recall that drama was not the only thing the Lydians were thought to have brought with them during their migration. Their other apocryphal contribution to Western culture was torture.

[64] Lucian of Samosata (ca. 120–180), "The Tyrannicide," in *Works*, V, 20. The emperor Caligula also "forced parents to attend the executions of their sons": Suetonius, *LC*, "Caligula," chap. 27. See also the Pseudo-Quintilianic Declamation 7 on "Tormenta Pauperis," in *Declamationes XIX maiores*, 136–51.

[65] Lesser, *Pictures at an Execution*, 15. My invocation of Nietzschean vocabulary is deliberate.

At first blush, Isidore seems to be presenting a simple narrative of etymological origins. The philological proximity of the terms *ludicra*, *ludi*, *lusi*, and *luctae* set up a semiotic space in which spectacle, political violence, and law are united in their common biological ancestor, the Lydians.[66] In an originary tale of emigration and even colonization, Isidore (like Tertullian before him) equates the theater of a foreign people with idolatry and evil.[67] Even though the derivation of *ludi* from *Lydii* is false, later scholastic authors, philosophers, and theologians had it on Isidore's perceived authority that drama and torture were linked philologically and, therefore, ideologically:

Ludorum origo sic traditur: Lydios ex Asia transvenas in Etruria consedisse duce Tyrreno, qui fratri suo cesserat regni contentione. Igitur in Etruria inter ceteros ritus superstitionum suarum spectacula quoque religionis nomine instituerunt. Inde Romani arcessitos artifices mutuati sunt; *et inde ludi a Lydis vocati sunt.* Varro autem dicit *ludos a luso vocatos*, quod iuvenes per dies festos solebant ludi exultatione *populum delectare.* Unde et eum lusum iuvenum et diebus festis et templis et religionibus reputant. Nihil iam de causa vocabuli, dum rei causa idolatria sit. (II, bk. 18, 16.1–2; emphasis mine)

The traditional origin of these "plays" is that the Lydians [*ludi* < *Lydii* (sic)], refugees from Asia Minor, settled in Etruria under their leader, Tirennus, who had lost to his brother in a struggle over the throne. And so, among other rites in Etruria connected with their superstitions, they also instituted spectacles under the pretext of religion. The Romans had actors brought in from Etruria on loan; consequently, "plays" [*ludi*] are so called from the Lydians [i.e., the Etruscans]. Furthermore, Varro says that "plays" [*ludi*] are so called from "entertainments" [*lusi*], because on holidays, young men habitually amused the people with the verve of their play. Consequently, they considered this "play" by the youth appropriate for holidays, temples, and religious rites. We will say no more about the etymology [*causa*] of this word, since the origin [*causa*] of the practice itself is idolatry.

Of special relevance to the medieval theater of cruelty is Isidore's belief that the same Lydians for whom the first agonistic spectacles of wrestling and gladiatorial display had been named also gave their name to the Latin term for torture. As Page duBois reminds us, the Greek *basanos* was rendered in Latin as *lapis Lydius* (the stone of the Lydians)—apparently in honor of the very people who had invented a touchstone for their metal currency in the seventh century B.C.:

[66] "De spectaculis," *Etymologiarum*, bk. 18, chap. 16. In bk. 18, Isidore groups sixty-nine cultural fields (including warfare, law, sports, the circus, drama, and gladiatorial display) by virtue of their ludic status. Also, on the medieval interplay between *ludus* and *luctae*, see Axton, *European Drama*, 33.

[67] I discuss the colonialist overtones of this passage in Chapter 3 in the context of the foundational moment of rhetorical delivery.

the Lydians.[68] Moreover, the linguistically documented common ancestry of torture and drama is all the richer when we notice the likely origin of Isidore's own narrative of origins. Some five centuries before him, Tertullian (ca. 160–225) had related the identical tale in chapter 5 of his infamous antitheatrical *De spectaculis*. While Latinists have tended to neglect the connection, Isidore's account of the spectacular tale of power, displacement, and appropriation resembles Tertullian's virtually word for word. In the *De spectaculis*, Tirennus's defeat by his brother in their struggle for political supremacy is the event that occasions the exodus of the Lydians from Asia to Etruria along with the their games, the object of Tertullian's condemnation:

> They give this account of the origin of the games. . . . In Etruria, then, among other rites involved by their superstitions, they institute public shows in the name of religion. From Etruria the Romans fetch the performers, and with them they borrow also the time and the name—the *ludii* are so called from the Lydians. Even if Varro derives the *ludii* from *ludus* (that is, from playing)—just as they used to call the Luperci *ludii* because in play they run hither and thither,—he nevertheless reckons this playing of the youths as belonging to festal days, temples and matters of religion. But the verbal issue does not matter, when the real issue is idolatry. (*De spectaculis*, chap. 5; emphasis his)[69]

In addition, then, to their shared lexicon of pity, fear, probability, and verisimilitude, torture and drama share the same originary moment in a legal and political context of violence. If the Lydians brought *basanos* to the West, they also brought theater.

In the same tradition as the Lydian, the innumerable medieval spectacles of the scourging of Christ, the torture of saints, and the beatings of everyday citizens frequently reenact the violent inventional origins of rhetoric, torture, and spectacle (along with all their inherent paradoxes). If *inventio* was the rhetorical canon in which the orator/*actor* traditionally employed the evidence of torture in a spectacular and punitive hermeneutic investigation, learned medieval dramatists regularly exploited such methods. But when they staged the unreliable method of torture by means of drama (its ancestral companion, which had also been deemed unreliable), when they equated literary invention with the tortured invention of classical rhetoric, the results seriously compromised the

---

[68] *TT*, 13. For duBois's complete discussion of the Lydians, see *TT*, 9–13, in which she stresses the importance of the concept of counterfeit to demonstrate the connection of *basanos* to the lexicon of bankers and currency. It cannot help but strike the theater historian that "counterfeit" was also the province of the actor or impersonator (as indicated by the term *hypokrisis*). Within the scope of this book, I cannot treat adequately this suggestive vocabulary of monetary exchange.

[69] Except for rendering certain passive constructions in active form and substituting plurals for singulars, Isidore has changed precious little of Tertullian's narrative (or, hypothetically, of their common source). See also their treatments of the Circus, again, virtually identical in *De spectaculis*, chap. 8, and *Etymologiarum*, bk. 18, chaps. 27–28.

pretensions to Christian truth of a genre like the *mystère*. Just as *la question* was conceived violently, dramatically, and punitively, so too was the rhetorico-literary speech and action it engendered along with all the compromises to legal systems that an ellipsis of truth implies. The discoveries of falsity and artifice then apply to both the violent legal discoveries resulting from torture and the violent literary discoveries extracted through staged torture. At a minimum, if the rhetorical machinations of torture ultimately lead to a kind of truth, it is not necessarily for the reasons one might think.

Emblematic of the phenomenon under discussion here is one of the most concrete references of all to the violence of invention to occur in a *mystère de la Passion*. As Arnoul Gréban links torture to the invention of the *jeu*, he invites the audience of his fifteenth-century play to view the spectacularly violent origins of drama itself. Just before Jesus on the cross commends his spirit, the Devil appears in person to suggest to the torturers the founding of a great new game ("beau jeu nouveau fondé").[70] Christ's robe becomes the prize in this game of chance, skill, and blasphemy as the competitors take the name of a different Person of the Trinity in vain with each blow inflicted (25595–646). Their great game is a game of torture—not unlike that played across the Channel in the English *Ludus Coventriae*, in which one of Christ's torturers declares that: "A and now wole I *a newe game begynne* / þat we mon pley at all þat arn hereinne. / whele and pylle · whele and pylle / comyth to halle ho so wylle / ho was þat."[71] When Gréban's player Griffon asks the equally great onomastic question of what to call the game, Satan himself provides the answer: "Tu le dois appeller ung dé / qui est ung nom de grant haulteur" (Call it a dice-game/God-game, which is a most hallowed name) (25647–48). Nor is knowing the name of the game sufficient. In eminently medieval fashion, the torturers also inquire about its origins and its creator: "Et s'on enquiert de l'*invanteur,* / que diray je?" (And if one inquires about the inventor, what shall I say?) (25649–50; emphasis mine). Satan then identifies himself as the author of the punitive pastime, underscoring the interplay among pleasure, pain, invention, and performance—the very combination that Tertullian and Isidore had once associated with the Lydians.

Even so, when Satan designates himself as the *invanteur* of violent play in the context of a didactic representation of the life of Christ, he points to a crucial aspect of medieval aesthetics. If torture is the Devil's game, it is also the game of the author of the mystery play. In a triumph of counterintuition, the learned medieval dramatist representing the invention and performance of torture has chosen an unreliable vehicle for the staging of Christian truth. At issue here is whether the violent fun and games of Satan's ludic invention of torture offer any

---

[70] Gréban, *Mystère de la Passion*, 25646; Jesus commends his spirit after verse 25862.

[71] *Ludus Coventriae*, 277, 168–72; see Kolve's discussion of this text in *PCC*, 186, and chap. 8. See also Huizinga on gaming in *Homo Ludens* (hereafter *HL*), 82–84; and Woolf, *English Mystery Plays*, 254–55.

substantive epistemological difference from the corresponding activity of the *invanteur* of the mystery play. If torture is an a priori method concerned with the play of punishment rather than with the quest for truth (however falsified that quest), then there is no reason to assume that the staging of a buffeting in a well-intentioned mystery play would be any more reliable and any less "satanic" than the diabolical methods ostensibly rejected. This is not to imply that the mystery play is entirely "diabolical." It is nonetheless to insist that its use of torture is problematic enough to undermine any denunciation within the play of diabolical behavior.

Somewhere, moreover, within the logical circle lies the comic relief imparted by Herod's henchmen in the Mons Passion play who costume Christ for the violent little drama they are about to stage. When Herod himself commands that the costuming be perfect, Christ's tormentors pause to watch the engenderment of comedy as the wisest of fools is forced to don the Fool's outfit: "prens l'[h]abillement / D'un de mes folz qui est bien simple" (take the outfit of one of my fools who's very simple).[72] Grongnart and his cronies are happy to obey: "Lors ilz lui vestent ung habit blan de fol sus sa robe, qui va jusques enmy gambe" (Then they dress him in the garb of a fool under his robe, which goes to knee-length). Christ's costume has the desired effect immediately, even as it would ideally prompt the opposite effect in the audience. "Il a lourde teste et lours dois / assez pour faire une risée," confirms Grongnart (He's heavy headed and heavy-backed—enough to get a laugh); and Gazon agrees as they prepare to remove the "povre fol" from Herod's sight that "Il a maniere desguisé / Droitement pour rire son sol" (He's all dressed up so folks can laugh to their heart's content) (314).

To understand the full implications of the dramatic and metadramatic violence of the medieval religious theater, it is thus necessary to pay special attention to certain philological features which may once have seemed innocuous enough. For example, the polysemous term *la question* often appears in the scourgings of Christians and, for Gréban, supplies the conceptual preface to his entire *Passion*. The lengthy work of some 25,000 verses is introduced from the outset as part of a great *sic et non* debate of question and answer: "S'argurons que sy et que non / comme saint Thomas l'a traictié / soubtillement en son traictié / sur le tiers livre des Sentences" (We will argue *sic et non* as Saint Thomas treated the question in the third book of Sententiae) (1692–95). The notion that the retelling of Christ's Passion can somehow be distilled into the answer to a theological *quaestio* is all the more crucial in that Christ is typically subjected to both forms of *question* during his Passion—torture and disputation.[73] He physically endures the *question* of scourging (with a gory realism that

---

[72] Gustave Cohen, ed., *Le Livre de conduite du Régisseur et Le Compte des dépenses pour le "Mystère de la Passion" joué à Mons en 1501*, p. 314. For the sake of convenience, I refer to this play as the Mons *Passion*.

[73] Here I respectfully disagree with Graham Runnalls, who has criticized my interpretation of these lines.

heightens verisimilitude) and verbally acquits himself with skill in responding to the doctors' oft-dramatized *quaestiones*.[74] So, when the servants of Bishop Annas affirm later in the play that they have beaten Christ and the Bishop announces: "Je le vouldray maintenant veoir / pour luy faire des *questions*" (Now I would like to see him in order to "question" him) (Gréban, 19401–2), the subsequent brutality inflicted on Christ demonstrates that such *questions* indicate considerably more than a desire to "ask a few questions."[75] Rather, Annas will conduct a punitive investigation that includes torture—supposedly to discover a hidden truth inside Christ's body.

A similar interrogation occurs in the *Martire Saint Estienne*. While not a *mystère* per se, the play hands down a parallel spectacle of interrogatory torture at Annas's hands. During the staging of both verbal and physical challenges to Estienne's teachings, the saint offers to respond "de plain sans fictïon / A vostre *triple questïon*" (fully and without fiction to your triple question).[76] That term refers not only to the three questions purportedly being asked but to the tripartite nature of *la question* as pedagogical disputation, punitive interrogation, and torture. "Questioning" in dramatic scenes of interrogation is not just "questioning" as we understand it today: it incorporated all the meanings of *quaestio*, including torture, whose truths are known in advance as they were by the persecutors of Joseph. Torturers Goulu and Bruyant of the anonymous fifteenth-century *Mystère de la Passion de Troyes* could hardly be more explicit on the subject when they, the players of games, accuse Joseph of playing games in a trial that is to be a fait accompli: "Vous estes ung mauvais paillart, / et scet on bien, sans plus parler, / de quel jeu vous sçavez jouer: / *vostre procés est ja tout fait*. / Chascun congnoist ja vostre fait" (you are a bad rogue, and everyone knows, nothing left to say, what game you know how to play. Everybody already knows your story) (Troyes *Passion*, II, t. 3, 768–72).

Also featured in the scourging scenes is one of the primary modes of ideological subterfuge that Elaine Scarry deems inherent in torture. In discussing the commonplace reversal of victim and agent, Scarry maintains that only the most unstable political regimes turn to torture "precisely because the reality of [their] power is so highly contestable" (*BP*, 27). But long before political prisoners were brutalized in contemporary Latin America, mystery plays dramatized the instability of the old pagan laws of torture—even as the new law of a powerful medieval Christian judicial community came to rely on comparable reversals in

[74] The debates between Jesus and the doctors is a standard scene in the Passion play: see, e.g., Kline, "Structure, Characterization, and the New Community in Four Plays of Jesus and the Doctors."

[75] A similar remark is uttered by his counterpart in the anonymous *Passion* from Troyes, vol. II, pt. 2, ll. 7423–24. Citations from the *Mystère de la Passion de Troyes*, hereafter Troyes *Passion*, a reworking of Gréban, are from Jean-Claude Bibolet's edition, 2 vols. References to this edition are somewhat complicated: vol. II contains pts. 2 and 3.

[76] *Martire St. Estienne*, 237–38, in *CPM*, pp. 71–85. This play appears in the same manuscript as the *Geu Saint Denis*, which Runnalls does not include in his edition.

its own uses of torture. In the *Convercïon Saint Pol*, the Jews indict Christ as a danger to the law when, according to the anti-Semitic vision of the play, *their* law is a danger to *him*: "Il pert, il confont nostre loy" (he endangers [loses] and confounds our law).[77] In the scourging of the English Chester "Trial and Flagellation," Annas makes that point with great clarity. "Despyse hym, spurne and spitt. / Lett see, or ye sitt, / who hase happ to hitt / that us this harmed hase."[78] The first Jew responds that it is the victim whom they are in the process of harming who actually represents the real threat: "For his harminge here / nighe will I neere / this famelande fere / that makes our law false" (74–77). In the Sainte Geneviève *Passion*, Annas describes Christ as the *tormentor* of Roman law: "Vecy la personne / Qui sy fort nostre loy *tourmente*" (Here is the person who torments our law so forcefully) (1740–41); and in the same play Herod even goes so far as to refigure the victimized Christ as the megalomaniacal agent who torments *him*—Herod—the upholder of Roman law. He condemns Jesus for attempting to destroy the hegemony when it is Herod who seeks to destroy Him: "Dont te vient or ceste licence, / Que tu fais novelle creance / Et veulz la loy de Dieu *abatre*? / Tu as fain de te faire *batre*, / Se ne respons appertement" (Where do you get the nerve to make a new belief and to want to slaughter God's law? You're asking for a beating if you don't answer fully) (Sainte Geneviève *Passion*, 1887–91).[79]

Such reversals occur often on the late medieval stage as religious dramatists attribute to the persecutors of martyrs a desire to destroy a martyr before they are destroyed. In the *Mystère de Saint Christofle*, where torture is not investigation but punishment, we read the following promise of pain: "*Punition* de ce chrestïen, / *Je vous prometz*, sanz faillir rien, / Que ce n'est qu'un droit enchanteur; / *Tous nous destruira* a douleur, / Se asprement il n'est tenu" (I promise you unflinchingly the punishment of this Christian, that he's nothing but a pure sorcerer; he will destroy us all in pain if he is not held severely).[80] In the relentlessly horrific *Mystère du Roy Advenir*, the Maistre d'Istel Avennir articulates a concept of empowerment that is similarly overdetermined: "Qu'il ont *pouoir* dessus vous? / Vers nostre loy mesprenons / D'acouter voz argumens. / Que *vous ne nous tourmentez* / D'aspres et divers tourmens!" (That they [the Christians] should have power over you? We are not faithful to our law [we misconstrue it] by listening to your arguments. May you not torment us with bitter and various torments).[81]

[77] *Convercïon Saint Pol*, 669, in CPM, 86–102.

[78] *Chester Plays*, ed. Lumiansky and Mills, vol. I, app. IIc, 70–73.

[79] A similar phrase, "Car il veut *vostre loy abatre*," appears in the *Passion de Palatinus*, ed. Frank, 585; ed. Pauphilet, p. 232.

[80] *Mystère de Saint Christofle*, 2107–11. The larger subject of promises, threats, and performativity is treated in Chapter 3.

[81] Jehan du Prier, dit le Prieur, *Mystère du Roy Advenir*, 5319–23. Robert L. A. Clark delivered a splendid paper on this play entitled "Courtly versus Bourgeois Dramaturgy," and I thank him for sharing his ideas with me.

Nor is it uncommon in the mystery play for even the most menial laborer to acknowledge that torture is the only way to reverse Christ's power. Torturer Haquin of the Sainte Geneviève *Passion* parrots the letter of the law to his master: "Rien ne prise vostre menace. / Se ne le faictes tourmenter, / Il vous pourra bien enchanter" (Your threat is worth nothing. If you don't have him tortured, he may well bewitch you) (1894–96). Yet here, the very representation of the torturers is problematic insofar as characters of low social standing (normally the most likely victims of torture) are seemingly empowered enough to inflict torture—only to be condemned later for having carried out that responsibility. In the *Passion d'Auvergne*, Alexandre exhorts his companions to break legs because "De ce faire licence avons / de Pilate" (we have Pilate's permission to do it) while his companion Malque confirms that they are "just doing their job" (farons bon devoir).[82] Thus they cannot lose power that they do not really have: "Si ne perdons nostre *pouvoir*" (Thus we do not lose our power) (Auvergne *Passion*, 31).

Whatever their social standing, all the torturers cited above participate in a larger political effort to translate the "incontestable reality" of the physical pain of torture into a fictional but "wholly convincing spectacle of power" (*BP*, 27). In the Middle Ages, such spectacles were indeed convincing—all the more so because the "truth" of the mystery play's fictional display of fictive discoveries (like the "truth" of torture) was known in advance. In fact, the medieval Christian dramatist seems destined to replay eternally the ambiguous relationship between torture and truth. So it is that, in Gréban, both Christ and the false witnesses are subjected to the same type of punitive legal investigation through *la question*. When Caiaphas, Nathan, and Bannanïas ponder the difficulty of bringing witnesses to speak against Christ, the council rules that the desired testimony will be coerced from them through torture: "que s'il est qui saiche parler / des faiz Jhesus, pour luy ou contre, / viengne devant vous et s'admonstre / pour faire sa relacion, / *sur peine* de privacion / de biens et *grant peine de corps*" (if anyone is willing to speak for or against the acts of Jesus, may he come and show himself before you and give his report under penalty/pain of privation of goods and great bodily pain) (20399–404; emphasis mine). In other words, *la question* obtains truth from Christ and falsehood from the witnesses. It must thus exist apart from any abstract notion of truth. Likewise, when Saint Matthew of the *Convercïon Saint Pol* states that "Vraye amour ne ce puet celer; / Sy ardans est en charité / Que le dos se fait marteler / Souvent pour soustenir verité" (True love cannot conceal this. It is so ardent in charity that the back is often pummeled in order to sustain the truth) (759–62), he too affirms that truth exists independently of torture. Or rather, he affirms that the torture of Christian transgressors is but an affirmation of the truth of their faith.

In light of such scenes, it is possible to theorize in a general way that the Truth transmitted to the spectators of torture (imitated or real) was just as elusive as

---

[82] *Passion d'Auvergne* (hereafter Auvergne *Passion*), 3325–26.

that obtained from torture itself. From the standpoint of the law, if torture obtains truth from Christ and lies from false witnesses, then, like the intrinsically oriented extrinsic proofs of *inventio*, the forensic "questioning" of medieval religious drama ultimately serves to question the law along with the laws of the theatrical works that stage it. In the Sainte Geneviève *Passion*, for example, Christ challenges the legal foundations of his treatment just before Peter denies him: "Tu m'as sanz deserte feru / Vilainement en mon visage. / S'il te samble que die oultrage, / Hardiement sy le tesmoigne" (you struck me without cause, feloniously in my face. If it seems to you that I defame, then bring testimony to prove it) (1392–95). Equally forceful is the question posed by Gréban's Christ after he endures a long *sermon* by Annas which is punctuated by blows from his henchmen. He invokes the very defense against torture that was traditionally associated with Roman freeborn citizens who presumably were exempt from it: "Se j'ay mesprins ou parlé mal, / baille du mal tesmoing et preuve; / et se mon parler vray se treuve, / a quel cause m'as tu feru?" (If I have erred or spoken badly, then give some testimony and proof of the evil; and if it turns out that my words are true, then for what cause did you strike me?) (19565–68).[83] Christ's question, reminiscent of another posed by Saint Paul, serves to call into question the laws of a society that is about to change. When threatened with examination by torture before the Roman courts of Jerusalem and Caesarea, Paul asked the centurion, "Can you legally flog a man who is a Roman citizen and moreover has not been found guilty?"[84] Similarly, toward the end of the *Conversïon Saint Denis*, the narrator proclaims the absence from earth of the very equity pagan torture wrongly intended to restore. At the same time, he alludes to the pain and suffering endured by the virtuous, the torture of whom demonstrates true equity and true Christian faith:

> Or voit on souvent que les bons
> Sont dez mauvaiz et dez felons
> Grevez, troublez et tourmentez.
> Lez mauvaiz font leur volentez
> Et en ce monde cy florissent,
> Et les bonnes gens y languissent.
> Lez maulz n'y sont pas tous punis;
> Lez biens n'y sont pas tous meris.
> (CPM, 975–82)

And thus we often see that the good are aggrieved, harmed, and tormented by the evil and the felonious. The evil do their will and flower here in this world, while

---

[83] Here the term *feru/ferir* also recalls *les fers*—iron implements of torture. This extra dimension is not evident in the similar line from Troyes (II, t. 2, 7586–89).

[84] In his helpful discussion of this incident from Acts 22–26, Edward Peters observes that "Paul merely had to voice the claim to citizenship for the torture to be suspended" (*Torture*, 27).

the good people languish here. All the evil folk are not punished here; all the good folk are not rewarded.

Since the Christian truth expounded by these moments of religious drama is at least partially constructed through torture, it follows that, in the same way that *la question* failed to establish the truth in law, it also failed to establish it on a theatrical stage that mirrored the stages of the divine and terrestrial realms. That was the case not only for the pagan laws enforced by real, historical characters but also for the Christian dramatist who staged their failures in his own quest for a different truth.

Nowadays, of course, a modern audience does not normally think of a play as establishing truth or of its author as necessarily desirous of doing so. Even so, the explicit intention of many early religious dramatists was precisely such a demonstration of truth.[85] In that sense, the tortures staged by the religious dramatist in his presumably edifying message may be as unreliable as those inflicted theatrically by the pagan predecessors he condemns. In an ideology that is consistent with the anthropological commonplace that Christianity depends on "good violence," it is not acceptable that pagans torture Christ and the early martyrs: but it *is* acceptable that a Christian God erase sin and that He identify and exterminate heresy by killing off the bodies that house those vices.[86] In the *Mystère de S. Bernard de Menthon*, for example, an archbishop reverses tormented with tormentor as he identifies the threat posed by "strangers" who practice a different faith: "Encore y a preu de pay[e]ns, / Monseignieur, par ceste montaignie, / Qui ont de créances estrange; / Biem bessoing avons de secors" (There are still plenty of pagans, my Lord, over by that mountain who hold strange beliefs. We are in great need of help).[87] Their bodies exemplify a corrupt legal system:

> Archidiaque, sans arez
> Mectre nous fault en oroysons
> Et en humble devocion,
> Pour empetrer dever Dieu grace
> [Et] *celle erreur ung efface*
> De cest païs, car tam de maulx,
> Tant de *crueux herege faux*
> [Et] ydolatre hors de foy
> Tout *corrumpue il ont la loy*
> Et mis en peril maint cristiens. (1191–1200)

---

[85] This is particularly clear, e.g., in Gréban's insistence on the compatibility between dramatic representation (*monstrer*) and proof (*demonstrer*), which I discuss at length in *ROMD*, 169–82.

[86] See Girard, *VS*, esp. chaps. 2 and 6.

[87] This passage occurs immediately after the martyrs traverse a perilous passage in the *Mystère de S. Bernard de Menthon*, 1201–4.

> Archbishop, we must take to constant prayer and humble devotion in order to obtain grace before God and to efface the error of this land; for so many evils, so many cruel and false heretics and idolators outside the faith have completely corrupted our law and placed many Christians in peril.

For Barbara Eckstein, the paradox of torture is that "the 'power' derived from torturing is violence predicated, paradoxically, on the excuse of eradicating pain and death by creating them" (*LFWP*, 91). That paradox is also evident in medieval religious dramas which stage pre-Christian cultures attempting to eradicate pain by creating it—even as the mystery play participates in the creation and recreation of pain. Like torture itself, the scourging scenes undermine the stability of the so-called truths extracted from suffering bodies—including the truth so near and dear to the mystery play of how to lead a good Christian life.

All the scenes above reaffirm both the potency and the unreliability of interrogatory and punitive torture. Yet it is precisely that potent unreliability that the religious medieval dramatist marshals in support of Christian doctrine. He does so by means of two other disciplines long denounced for both potency and unreliability: forensic rhetoric and drama.[88] Hence, the representation of torture in medieval religious drama constitutes an interpretative *mise en abîme*. However, that does not rule out the possibility that the *mise en abîme* was deliberate. In a very real way, the *mystère* provides a rhetorical strategy for proving Truth that is actually *more* logical than the strategy normally invoked in the rhetorical discussions of torture it imitates. In the specific context of its own brand of dramatic verisimilitude, the *mystère* creates an "illusion of truth." But where forensic rhetorical invention exploited the verisimilitude of torture to validate truth, the mystery play employs torture's verisimilitude in order to validate its verisimilar representation of Christian truth. Validating illusion with illusion (rather than truth with illusion) might thus have enabled learned religious dramatists to buttress their representation of Christian doctrine in a way that was more plausible, more logically consistent, more "true." Theirs is a strange yet persuasive logic according to which the most powerful vehicle for perpetuating torture's illusions of truth becomes a dramatic genre based on the verisimilitude of its illusions.

Therefore, with regard to the conflation in the Passion play of legal inquisition, torture, and spectacle, the medieval religious dramatist shares certain similarities with the forensic rhetorician. Like the lawyer in need of convincing a judge of the reliability of torture, he stages the appearance of the truth of Christ's Passion. And like the truth of confessions extracted from torture, the truth of Christ's story is known in advance. That principle held true not only for the re-

---

[88] Here I invoke not only what Jonas Barish calls the antitheatrical prejudice (see esp. his chaps. 2 and 3), but also the similar debate about whether forensic eloquence was more bent on pleasing than on proving (*ROMD*, chap. 2).

ligious dramatists who recreated the Passion but also for the numerous audiences before whom his tortures were regularly represented in the great agon of the Mass, the *ars praedicandi*, and the Passion play.[89] Contrary, however, to the questionable truths of torture, the truth of the Passion (or of what Erich Auerbach called its "great drama") was not really open to question by medieval Christians.[90] It was not thought to be an illusion. So, unlike his rhetorician colleagues who invoked torture in order to construct dramatically the appearance of a truth already known in advance, the author of a *mystère* employed verisimilitude in order to validate a verisimilar representation of a narrative already known to be strictly true: the Passion of Christ. In forensic rhetoric, the truth of torture is a dramatic illusion; in the Passion play, it is a "true illusion" or, at a minimum, the appearance of a true illusion. And one of the best places to display a fiction of power was within the power of fiction associated with drama. A genre that was traditionally associated with lies uncovered a more viable strategy for the discovery of truth than that of the forensic inventional structures that underpinned the law.[91]

Seen from that perspective, the learned author's assimilation of the problematic legal and dramatic structures of torture might constitute a kind of subversive behavior in that theatrical works which recreate the ideology of torture seem to have enabled dramatists, actors, and producers to take the law into their own hands. In a kind of manifest artistic destiny that occurred during performance, a community of artists who had historically endured attempts to silence their voices apparently annexed the very authority that hegemonies appeared to possess because of their power to torture. That power included numerous efforts to exclude theatrical communities from the exercise of political power of their own. For example, as far as actors were concerned, one Roman edict of the praetor barred the following groups from bringing lawsuits: "homosexuals, procurers, gladiators, those who fought wild beasts in the arena, comic and satirical actors." [92] In the Middle Ages, the dubious ninth-century *Benedictus levita* preserves a statute forbidding *histriones* and *scurrae* from pleading in court.[93] As far as dramatists were concerned, the emperors Tiberius and Caligula not only censored and punished them but occasionally put them

[89] I refer here to the famous description by Honorius Augustodunensis of the Mass as the dramatic struggle of Christ. See, e.g., Hardison, *Christian Rite and Christian Drama* (hereafter CRCD), 39–40.

[90] Auerbach, *Mimesis*, 158. Compare his statement to, e.g., Kubiak, *ST*, 28.

[91] Medieval dramatic representations of torture may, however, lose that edge when the performance becomes "real" rather than "realistic"; i.e., when real violence is introduced onto the stage.

[92] On this text, see Peters, *Torture*, 30–31. Although Isidore does not take up the subject of homosexuality, this is the very cast of characters (procurers, gladiators, and those fighting wild beasts) that appears in Book 18, "De bello et ludis" of the *Etymologiarum*. I am not implying here that all theatrical communities are the same.

[93] For a discussion of the *Benedictus levita*, a "somewhat dubious collection" that may date from the reign of Louis the Pious, see Chambers, *Mediaeval Stage*, I, 37–38.

to death. Caligula "burned a writer of Atellan farces alive in the middle of the arena of the amphitheatre, because of a humorous line of double meaning" (*LC*, "Caligula," chap. 27.4); while his father ensured that a tragedian who had slandered Agamemnon was "at once put to death and [his] works destroyed, although they had been read with approval in public some years before in the presence of Augustus himself" (*LC*, "Tiberius," chap. 61.3). Medieval dramatists were also explicit in articulating the real dangers which faced them as they pursued their talents. In France, a long ecclesiastical campaign against the *mystère* culminated in the banning of the plays in 1548; and in England, the banns before the Chester plays addressed conflicts about censorship and punishment directly: "yet therof in these pagentes to make open shewe, / This moonke and moonke was nothing Afreayde / with feare of hanginge, brenninge or Cuttinge off heade, / to sett out that all maye disserne and see, / and parte good be lefte[?], beleeve you mee" (*Chester Plays*, ed. Deimling, v. 24–28).[94]

On one hand, then, it appears that when a dramatist owned for himself the spectacle of torture, he discovered a means by which to legitimize himself and his enterprise and to acquire greater social agency. When he integrated interrogative or punitive torture into a play, he was imitating real power—even though, as we have seen, the reality of that power was itself a fiction. On the other hand, he was also assimilating the repressive structures of torture against which he might ostensibly have been rebelling. In the verisimilar performance of a true event, the mystery play condemns pagan tortures that oppress Christian martyrs even as it must, at least at some level, subtly praise torture as a means by which to denounce torture and oppression. Unfortunately for those of us who seek to evade the labyrinthine rationalizations of torture, even the intuitions above can but force entry into other paradoxes.

While I explore those paradoxes further in the specific context of performance, they are already visible in the language of torture, the theory of drama, and the rhetoric of invention. For example, with regard to the reversal of agent and victim that characterizes the ideology of torture, even James Kastely's excellent analysis of "Violence and Rhetoric in Euripides's *Hecuba*" leads him to read the statement "let a slave set you free/ from what you fear" (868–69) as follows: "this is one of the most important, though paradoxical, insights of the play—those in power are not free but are, in fact, the most deeply enslaved."[95] While Kastely richly serves his stated goal of exploring the paradoxes of rhetoric when he concludes that "power enslaves those who hold it as well as those who are held by it . . . and this paradox besets rhetoric" (1037), he also subtly perpetuates the fallacy that the oppressor is the victim. One thinks here of Louise Fradenburg's plea that "we have a particular responsibility not to

---

[94] On French censorship of the mystery play, see Lebègue, *Tragédie religieuse en France*, 57.

[95] Kastely, "Violence and Rhetoric in Euripides's *Hecuba*," 1043. Kastely finds that rhetoric is a veritable protagonist in the play (1037).

identify with the kind of 'redescription' of pain characteristic of the language of the torturer and the warrior. . . . We are not thereby sacrificing the pursuit of truth to our values or political commitments. We are, instead, refusing an untruth—that untruth which derealizes, which unmakes the voice, which both brings about and conceals the breaking down of language by pain." [96]

Whether the subject be the glorification of Christianity in miracles, *moralités*, and *mystères* or the punitive investigations conducted by husbands upon wives, masters upon servants, or priests upon parishioners in farces, sotties, and fabliaux, when learned authors staged torture as a means of getting at truth, any truth "discovered" and conveyed by the unreliable method of torture remained elusive. [97] The scourging scenes display the enforcers of pagan law attempting to beat one "truth" *out of* the body of Christ as they beat another into it, while still another Christian truth emerges. That flexible morality must then prompt questions as to how one and the same method can lead to such different conclusions. Which tortures lead to truth and which ones to lies? If torture obtained truth from Christ and lies from false witnesses, how was a viewer to distinguish between the negative examples of Caiaphas, Herod, Pilate, and their henchmen and the presumably positive examples of the mystery play which staged them? Which truth or truths were being beaten metaphorically into the audiences of the mystery play? In light of Tertullian's beautiful Christian blood lust in which "perfidy [is] slain by faith, cruelty crushed by pity" (*De spectaculis*, chap. 29), how were spectators to determine which type of bloodshed it was acceptable to enjoy?

Even though this is not a book about reception, its subject is nonetheless the ways in which rhetoric attempts to fashion models for reception. The contours of those models emerge with greater clarity in discussions of the fourth rhetorical canon of memory. For that reason, any critical attempt to explore the ideological movement from the ad hoc placement of torture in *inventio* to its post hoc representations in delivered language must first take into account the crucial intermediary stage that was theorized in great detail in treatments of *memoria*.

In antiquity and the Middle Ages, *memoria* was the epistemological place where the inventional materials of torture were assembled (*dispositio*) and rehearsed for performance (*actio*). Its richly detailed imagery and iconographies conserved the evidence that had been violently extracted through torture and anticipated the representation and re-presentation of that evidence during delivery. Conceived as a theatrical procession of symbolic, personified, dramatic, and often violent visions, the *ars memorandi* offered orators a pictorial script whence to deliver the performances for which forensic *inventio* had supplied the "facts" (*RAH*, III, 30). As memory looked backward to the tortures of in-

---

[96] Fradenburg, "Criticism, Anti-Semitism, and the Prioress's Tale," 82, as she extrapolates from Scarry's *BP*.

[97] Here and later, I focus primarily on religious drama insofar as it presents a violent truth to be imitated rather than one to be laughed at (even though violence is not necessarily funny).

vention and forward to the creative reenactment of their violence during delivery, it also played a major role in the success or failure of one of the primary goals of rhetoric (and of torture): the creation of the illusion of truth. "The main thing," writes Quintilian of the fourth canon, is "to excite the appropriate feeling in oneself, to form a mental picture of the facts (*imagines rerum*), and to exhibit *an emotion that cannot be distinguished from the truth*" (*IO*, XI, 3.62; emphasis mine).[98]

While theories of invention addressed the discovery (*invenire*) of "how to convince the persons whom he [the orator] wishes to persuade and how to arouse their emotions" (Cicero, *De partitione*, I, 5), theories of memory provided the mental models by means of which that orator might generate strong emotions in the audiences before whom he pled his cases. *Memoria* thus rehearsed the exhibition of violence along with the emotions that were realistically (or verisimilarly) associated with violence. Indeed, if torture was inextricably linked to invention and theatricality, then the fact that *memoria* imagined, stored, and scripted the tortured truths of the inventional process heightens the connections between violent thought and violent action—and all in the context of the transformation of knowledge into theater. Eventually, its imaginary acts of display were translated during delivery into acts of performance in ways that might even have informed the learned medieval dramatic imagination.

In *inventio*, torture was theorized in dramatic terms; and in *memoria*, the inventional theory of torture became an imaginary performance that presaged actual performance practice. Ultimately, then, a revised view of rhetoric enables us to historicize Michel Foucault's suggestion that, rather than treat the "history of penal law and the history of the human sciences as two separate series," we inquire instead as to "whether there is not some common matrix or whether they do not both derive from a single process of 'epistemologico-juridical' formation" (*DP*, 23). Early theorists had already conducted that inquiry and found that the "common matrix" was memory, which staged the inchoate or virtual drama of the emergence of law and language.

[98] Compare this to his remarks on the *imitatio veritatis* in *IO*, V, 12.22, cited above.

CHAPTER 2

The Memory of Pain

There is perhaps nothing more terrible in man's earliest history than his mnemotechnics.

—Friedrich Nietzsche, *Genealogy of Morals*

It is a legend of the origins of mnemotechnics, a legend of how Simonides is
called away from a lovely evening of banquet revelry. No sooner does he cross
the threshold on his way out when the entire building collapses on top of the
guests, crushing and mutilating them to such an extent that the relatives who
come to identify their loved ones are unable to do so from the isolated body
parts protruding here and there from the rubble. According to such dissemina-
tors of the legend as Cicero and Quintilian, the art of memory was born when
Simonides purportedly saved the day through his astonishing gift for revisual-
izing exactly where each guest had been seated at table. In Quintilian's narrative, worth reproducing in its entirety, Simonides is able to *re*member what had
been *dis*membered:

> The first person to discover an art of memory (*ars memoriae*) is said to have been
> Simonides, of whom the following well-known story is told (*cuius vulgata fabula
> est*). He had written an ode of the kind usually composed in honour of victorious
> athletes, to celebrate the achievement of one who had gained the crown for box-
> ing. Part of the sum for which he had contracted was refused him on the ground
> that, following the common practice of poets, he had introduced a digression in
> praise of Castor and Pollux, and he was told that, in view of what he had done, he
> had best ask for the rest of the sum due from those whose deeds he had extolled.
> And according to the story they paid their debt. For when a great banquet was
> given in honour of the boxer's success, Simonides was summoned forth from the
> feast, to which he had been invited, by a message to the effect that two youths who
> had ridden to the door urgently desired his presence. He found no trace of them,
> but what followed proved to him that the gods had shown their gratitude. For he

had scarcely crossed the threshold on his way out, when the banqueting hall fell in upon the heads of the guests and wrought such havoc among them that the relatives of the dead who came to seek the bodies for burial were unable to distinguish not merely the faces but even the limbs of the dead (*sed membra etiam omnia requirentes ad sepulturam propinqui nulla nota possent discernere*). Then it is said, Simonides, who remembered the order in which the guests had been sitting, succeeded in restoring to each man his own dead (*corpora suis reddidisse*).[1]

If ever there were an early articulation of Jacques Derrida's belief that "life is already threatened by the origin of the memory which constitutes it," it is the Simonides legend, which stages the violence of epistemology as *memoria*.[2] Yet at several levels, this story of how an isolated violent incident spawns a *techno* has a happy ending as the act of naming permits a return to order and the beginning of mourning. For the legal and political rhetorics that mnemotechnics later produced and safeguarded, Simonides's gift heralded the advent of the *techne* that codified the principles for remembering places, spaces, and their populations at the same time as a specific community managed to identify, name, bury, and commemorate its dead loved ones. Mnemotechnics was a science born of accidental violence to the body, and it owed its genesis to a cultural need to answer acts of violence with acts of commemoration, iteration, and regeneration.[3] Its codification was to offer the Christian Middle Ages a vast epistemological system of places, spaces, containers, and icons by which means any rhetor could generate and store words, stylistic devices, topoi, proofs, and performances before speaking and enacting them.

In this chapter, I take the Simonides legend as a point of departure for broader speculation about the seemingly ubiquitous violence of late medieval rhetoric, pedagogy, and theater. Given the violent origins of the *ars memorandi* upon which any learned author could have drawn, certain basic questions necessarily arise. If, as Aristotle observed of memory in the *De anima*, the soul "cannot

---

[1] Quintilian, *IO*, XI, 2.11–13. The story of Simonides also appears, e.g., in Cicero's *De oratore*, II, 351–55; and Martianus Capella, *De nuptiis*, 177g. For superb critical introductions to the art of memory, see Yates, *AM*; Carruthers, *BM*; Coleman, *Ancient and Medieval Memories* (hereafter *AMM*); Clanchy, *From Memory to Written Record*; Zumthor and Roy, eds., *Jeux de mémoire*; and Ong, *Rhetoric, Romance, and Technology* (hereafter *RRT*), chap. 4. On the Simonides legend specifically, see Yates, *AM*, 1–2; and Carruthers, *BM*, 147. Still, it bears mentioning that this legend really shows a *short-term* memory in action more than the long-term practices of mnemotechnics. I return later to the "economics" of mnemonic metaphor, the financial ramifications of which recall Page duBois's philological argument about torture (*TT*, 9–13).

[2] Derrida, *WD*, 202.

[3] In the grand scheme of the Simonides legend, however, in which the gods avenge a deserving poet, the disaster is not really an accident. For illuminating general perspectives on commemorative culture, see, e.g., Carruthers, *BM*, chap. 1; Illich, *In the Vineyard of the Text*, chap. 2, "Order, Memory, and History"; and Vance on "violence as semiosis" in commemorative cultures in *Mervelous Signals* (hereafter *MS*), 54.

think without a mental picture," what happens when that picture is violent?[4]
If the fourth rhetorical canon of *memoria* was, for the *Ad Herennium* author,
the "guardian of all the parts of rhetoric," then what are the literary and sociocultural ramifications of its custodianship of violence?[5] If, as Longinus insisted,
the primary function of the image was to concretize any "idea which enters the
mind from any source" and to "engender speech," then just what kind of speech
would a violent image engender?[6] If a quintessentially violent mnemonic scene
could literally "set the stage" for dramatic delivery (as it did for Lucian of
Samosata, who cited Mnemosyne as the premier quality of pantomime), is it
not possible that, in some cases, the memory image would generate not only violent speech but violent action? the violent speech, gestures, enactments, and
reenactments of the pedagogical "rule of the rod" and of medieval drama?[7]

Focusing on the insights of the authors cited above, along with those of Augustine, John of Garland, Hugh of Saint Victor, Thomas Bradwardine, Thomas
Murner, and others, I respond to those questions with the suggestion that both
the theatricality and the violence of memory tendered compelling models of creation and performance for early dramatists schooled in rhetoric. As a primor-
dially violent semiotic scene, the *ars memorandi* might thus have encouraged
learned medieval writers and teachers to translate its images of torture and dismemberment into the theory and praxis of Christian didacticism.

A close reading of some of the notoriously violent scourging scenes of late
medieval religious drama together with the classical and contemporaneous
rhetorics available to the Middle Ages discloses a distinct mnemonic lexicon at
dramatic moments of the juridical process and at juridical moments of the dramatic process. At such moments, when violent imagery anticipates violent performance, brutality is also accompanied by creativity, death by birth, or—as is
so common in a Christological context—death by rebirth. After all, one of the
premier sequences of disfigurement and death to capture the medieval imagination was the Passion of Christ itself, a gruesome scene, habitually staged in
all its gory detail. As in the *quem quaeritis* trope—the staple of the Mass that
today remains for many the origins of liturgical drama—memory's own origins
may be traced to a moment when Simonides's contemporaries who seek the
mutilated dead (*requirentes*) are, at least temporarily, unable to find them.[8] But,
unlike the deaths of Simonides's fellow revelers, the "death" of Christ, like

---

[4] Aristotle, *De anima*, ed. and trans. W. S. Hett, 432a; see also Kathy Eden's discussion of the
De anima in *Poetic and Legal Fiction*, 80; and Yates, *AM*, 32–33.

[5] [Cicero], *RAH*, III, 28.

[6] Longinus, "On the Sublime," 15, 1; see also *RAH*, III, 30.

[7] See Lucian, "Saltatio," 36. In chap. 2 of *ROMD* I argue that mnemotechnics constituted both
a psychodrama and a protodrama characterized by reenactment (51–54). See also Davis, "Art of
Memory and Medieval Dramatic Theory."

[8] For the classic discussion of the trope, "quem quaeritis in sepulchro, o Christicole?" as a likely
origin of medieval drama, see, e.g., Hardison, *CRCD*, esp. essay V.

those of the countless martyred saints who followed his example, was not a
death per se in that, for believers, he did not "die." Nor did he inspire a *techne*
but rather a cult in which resurrection and eternal life were remembered and
commemorated (in love and in violence) by religious institutions and by Christian authors.[9]

In *Rhetoric and the Origins of Drama*, I argued that the talented rhetorician
understood that a mnemonically engendered oration was persuasive because it
was dramatic. Here I suggest a corollary: that the memory image was persuasive and dramatic because it was violent. Whether it be the Simonides legend or
John Lydgate's fifteenth-century calling for mnemonic meditation on the blood,
wounds, and love of Christ—"Ye shall also most louyngly *remembre* / Uppon
hys most peynfull passyoun"—violence often lay (literally and metaphorically)
at the architectural and epistemological foundations of classical and Christian
mnemotechnics.[10] Violence also lay at the foundation of many medieval dramas
that revivified, reenacted, and relived its memory, creating new memories, new
actions, and new memories of action.

To corroborate these claims, I begin with a brief overview of the *ars memorandi* as a virtual spectacle with brutal imaginary scenes that sometimes conserved the inventional evidence from torture as they anticipated its spectacular
enactments during delivery. Next, I return to the Simonides legend as the quintessential backdrop against which mnemotechnics creates an architectural and
figurative space for literary and, more precisely, dramatic representation. I then
explore the violent underpinnings of the numerous forensic theories of memory
that configure that art as an imaginary reenactment of a crime, a protodramatic
rehearsal for its performance, and a paradigm for literary creation and re-creation. As we shall see, that emphasis on creation is evidenced by a panoply of
mnemonic associations among violence, birth, and rhetorico-literary invention
which, in turn, create fascinating gendered models of theatricality, birth, appropriation, and assimilation.

Subsequently, the ubiquitous blows sustained by real and imaginary bodies
in real and imaginary memory spaces set the stage for a number of real enactments of mnemonic techniques within the framework of medieval rhetoric,
drama, and pedagogy. Hence my argument that, since memory is situated between the tortured process of rhetorico-dramatic invention and the performance of violence, its mental rehearsals helped to reenact violence in medieval
courtrooms, classrooms, and theaters. With their frequent manipulation of mnemonic imagery and terminology in genres from the mystery play to the farce,
many learned medieval dramatists suggest in their work that the *ars memorandi*
functioned as a common denominator of rhetoric, violence, and drama. In the

---

[9] Sarah Beckwith, e.g., sees an "extreme cultural ambivalence" in Christ's body, which was "loved
and adored, but . . . also violated repeatedly" (*CB*, 5).

[10] John Lydgate, "*Exortacion to prestys when they shall sey theyr masse*" (composed c. 1430–
40), in *The Minor Poems of John Lydgate*, 86, ll. 33–34; cited and discussed by Rubin, *CC*, 94.

graphic dramatic representations of the scourging of Christ as well as in the notorious beating scenes of fifteenth- and sixteenth-century farce studied here, specific invocations of mnemonic techniques restage, commemorate, and perpetuate various violent lessons, whether these be the great *agon* of Christianity or the
apparent comedy of the submission of servant to master and woman to man.

Finally, I consider medieval and postmedieval conceptions of the status of
memory as the birthplace of both violence and empathy—an apparently paradoxical association that turns out to make a great deal of sense in the context
of the enactment of memories during delivery. As memory theory comes full
circle to its own happy ending, the art of conservation and regeneration that was
born of sudden, violent death sets up an important cultural paradigm which
will be codified and avidly pursued in rhetorical theories of delivery: the correspondence between "good acting" and "acting good." In the contexts of forensic oratory, pedagogy, and medieval drama, *memoria* thus constitutes an important ideological site at which early theorists attempted to resolve the paradoxes
of violence. They did so by reconfiguring violent, theatrical images of destruction and dismemberment as creational, persuasive, salubrious, curative, civilizing, edifying, instructive, and ultimately, all the more beautiful, desirable, and
even entertaining because of those effects. It then enables the additional realization that, if rhetoric is a blueprint for morality, it is also a blueprint for the
social performance of moral behavior, medieval and modern.

As might be expected, however, such a blueprint is so complex that it virtually defies the sort of chronological presentation necessary to any critical line of
reasoning. Even so, everything that follows in this chapter depends on an understanding of how the cyclical structure of memory conflates concepts of spa-
tiality, theatricality, violence, and the law. It will therefore prove useful to fore-
ground those concepts with some specific examples, beginning with what may
well be the most oft-cited description of the artificial memory.

In his advice to future lawyers in the *Rhetorica ad Herennium*, the Pseudo-
Cicero explains that "we ought, then, to set up images of a kind that can ad-
here longest in the memory. And we shall do so if we establish likenesses [*simili-
tudines*] as striking as possible; if we set up images that are not many or vague,
but *doing something* [*agentes*]" (*RAH*, III, 37). Those images have already
taken their places within a vividly demarcated memory space because, as Cicero too recalled, any act of thought required a setting or "an abode, inasmuch
as a material object without a locality is inconceivable" (*De oratore* II, 358). So
rich in detail about measurements, color, and lighting that it inspired Frances
Yates to posit a connection between *memoria* and the actual physical architecture of the sixteenth-century wooden theater, the "abode" of memory set the
scene for forensic oratory and for all manners of learned speaking and writing:
"and these backgrounds ought to be of moderate size and medium extent, for
when excessively large they render the images vague. . . . The backgrounds ought
to be neither too bright nor too dim, so that the shadows may not obscure the
images nor the lustre make them glitter" (*RAH*, III, 31–32).

Nonetheless, an exclusive focus on the exterior concretizations of the architectural metaphor has tended to reify the memory scene. No matter how graphic its spatial design, it is crucial to bear in mind that the memory place existed so that it could highlight the various objects and personifications that would inhabit it. When any orator (or any learned dramatist with rhetorical training) visualized detailed memory backgrounds against which vividly costumed characters moved holding their special props, he discovered in the *ars memorandi* a cognitive process that operated as an early form of dramatic invention.[11] Enter the *imagines agentes*, which, asserts the Pseudo-Cicero, will be remembered more easily "if we assign to them exceptional beauty or singular ugliness; if we dress some of them with crowns or purple cloaks, for example, so that the likeness [*similitudo*] may be more distinct to us" (*RAH*, III, 37).[12] Here, the image-in-action evokes a long historical interplay between memory and theatricality, which may by traced from Aristotle, Longinus, Cicero, and Quintilian to Augustine, Martianus Capella, Geoffrey of Vinsauf, and Hugh of Saint Victor. For example, Quintilian advised that personifications of thoughts be "linked one to the other like dancers hand in hand" (*IO*, XI, 2.20); while Hugh of Saint Victor stressed the importance of a dignified slate of mnemonic *dramatis personae* so as not to "provide on-lookers with a spectacle silly and absurd enough."[13] Insofar as the function of the memory image was to "engender speech" (Longinus, 15, 1), its space comprised a nascent stage that housed not only a psychodrama but a protodrama, a virtual theatrical production which but awaited actualization on the various stages of early culture.

Since, however, the mnemonic psychodrama continuously deployed scenes of torture, death, dismemberment, and murder, one might look anew at Anthony Kubiak's contention that "the interval between theatre and its violence is always a virtual space, unlocatable before the fact and only realized in performance."[14] The rhetorician had already articulated that virtuality each time he described the passage from invention to memory to delivery. Even in the celebrated Pseudo-Ciceronian invocation of the *imagines agentes*, there inheres an unmistakably violent subtext as the author oscillates between beauty and ugliness, formation and deformation, betraying a preoccupation with *disfigurement* that is as intense as that with figures. Images are more memorable, he claims, "if we somehow *disfigure them* [aut si qua re *deformabimus*], as by introduc-

---

[11] For an example of mnemonic visualization exercises in early rhetorical training, see *RAH*, III, 31–32. Douglas Kelly argues for the continuity of that training in "Contextual Environment"; see also Yates, *AM*, 50–76. For what French students read in general, see Lucas, "Medieval French Translations."

[12] Since, in Latin, the phrase begins with *id accidet*, the verb *accidere*, based on falling (*ad + cadere*), is relevant to the foundational accident of the falling building of the Simonides legend.

[13] Hugh of Saint Victor (d. 1141), "De tribus maximis," in Carruthers, *BM*, app. A, p. 261.

[14] Kubiak, *ST*, 50. Other illuminating perspectives on virtual performativity include Austin, *HDTW*; Alter, *Sociosemiotic Theory of Theatre*; and Hernadi, *Cultural Transactions*.

ing one stained with blood or soiled with mud or smeared with red paint, so that its *form* [*forma*] is more striking, or by assigning certain comic effects to our images, for that, too, will ensure our remembering them more readily" (*RAH*, III, 37; emphasis mine). The potential assignment of "certain comic effects" to disfigured, bloodied bodies might eventually have fallen under the rubric of the "silly spectacles" Hugh of Saint Victor would go on to condemn. But there is nothing silly about staining the mind's dramatis personae with blood to enhance their evocative value.

Nor was there anything silly about the notorious Gaius Caligula's discovery that the punitive disfigurement of his victims might proffer a memorable spectacle. Among the "special instances of his innate brutality," Suetonius cites the following practice: "Many men of honourable rank were first *disfigured* with the *marks* of branding-irons (*deformatos* prius *stigmatum* notis ad metalla et munitiones viarum) and then condemned to the mines." [15] And yet the spectacular disfigurement of both imaginary, personified figures and actual living bodies is an essential component not only of pagan brutality but of Christian meditative and dramatic practice (including such grotesque scenes of comic relief as the dart game for Christ's robe in Gréban). [16] The deformed bodies that prompted Simonides to form the art of memory are not so far from the Christian rhetorical memory of the faithful who sought to commemorate a different kind of victim in a different kind of sepulcher.

These days, there no longer seems to be any doubt about the primacy of memory theory in learned medieval literary representation. [17] But those same mnemonic systems placed before the eye of the learned author a primordial scene of death, dismemberment, and violence as a precursor to creativity, aesthetics, and beauty. In a meditation of his own on the emergence of beauty from pain, Saint Bonaventure invokes the disfigurement of the perfect figure of Christ: "Behold how your strong one is broken, your desirable one disfigured [*deformatus est*]; behold your peaceful one dying in battle. Where are now the cheeks flushed with life, the skin fair as snow? Where in this ravaged body will you find [*invenies*] any beauty?" [18]

Beginning with the need to *re*member what had been *dis*membered, enshrined by the Simonides legend, memory became a powerful and ubiquitous art form that influenced numerous literary genres. It played a role in the epic *Song of Roland*, in which Charlemagne's knights commit memorable acts of dismemberment: "Anyone having seen him *dismembering* Saracens, / Piling one

---

[15] Suetonius, *LC*, I, 27.

[16] See Chapter 1, notes 70 and 71.

[17] For image and literary imagination in a mnemonic context, see Trimpi, "Quality of Fiction"; Kelly, *Medieval Imagination*, 45–56; Weber, "Poetics of Memory"; Braccesi, *Poesia e memoria*; and Mullini, *Scena della memoria*.

[18] *Bonaventura Opera omnia*, VIII, 171; translated by José de Vinck in *Works of Bonaventure*, I, 167–68. This text is cited and discussed by Bestul, *Texts of the Passion*, 152.

corpse on top of another, / Would *remember* a true knight. / He does not want to forget Charles's battle cry." (Ki lui veïst Sarrazins *desmembrer*, / Un mort sur altre geter, / De bon vassal li poüst *remembrer*. / *L'enseigne* Carle n'i volt mie *ublïer*).[19] And, with regard to the rhetorical theater of cruelty, it played an especially significant role in constructing a mental forum in which orators, lawyers, authors, pedagogues, and dramatists might learn to create their own art forms in violence.

Even so, the twentieth-century critical imagination has tended to preserve rhetorical *imagines agentes* as if on our own memory stage—and with all the appropriate aesthetic distance a classical theatrical metaphor would imply— erecting a safe barrier between the dramatic illusions of a mnemonic *théâtre vitrine* and our own position as thinking spectators.[20] In spite of the exceptional efforts of Mary Carruthers, Eugene Vance, and D. Vance Smith, virtually nowhere within the space of that critical stage have scholars made room for the memory image that is violent and frightening.[21] Therefore, it becomes particularly urgent that we resituate the memory image within the violent and performative rhetorical contexts for which it was intended, all the while recalling how its virtual violence might be translated into speech. Making room for the frightful image necessarily entails a reevaluation of a certain critical fascination with the beauty of allegory and the beaux-arts, which has largely conjured visions of memory as a stately allegorical dance, a delicate iconography of dramatic images enclosed like a tableau within a painter's frame or a dramatist's theatrical space.[22] While I am by no means insinuating that mnemonic *imagines agentes* could *not* be lovely or stately, I wish nonetheless to stress the importance of the violent context in which many narratives of the origins of mnemotechnics occur. What holds true for beautiful regal figures in crowns and purple cloaks must also hold true for disfigured bodies.

Ultimately, a revitalized focus on virtual performance reanimates the memory scene and underscores its status as an inchoate psychodrama with links to enactment and to the violent Simonides legend that would always remain intact. As one principal means by which learned authors organized, categorized, and hierarchized their world and their thoughts, the memory space was no mere

[19] *Chanson de Roland*, 1970–73; emphasis mine. See also Vance, "Roland, Charlemagne, and the Poetics of Memory."

[20] More recently, modern performance theory has called into question the safety of this barrier, as in Pywell, *Staging Real Things* (hereafter *SRT*); Blau, *Blooded Thought*; and Graver, *Aesthetics of Disturbance*. However, the presence of that barrier is evident in Brian Vickers's surprise about certain treatments of memory and delivery in the *ars dictaminis* (*In Defense of Rhetoric*, 236–38).

[21] Here I refer to Smith, "In Place of Memory"; Carruthers, *BM*, 130–38; Vance, *MS*, 24–26, 53–55; and Roberts, *PCM*, 55–77.

[22] I do not focus here on allegory or the beaux-arts per se but rather on the dramatic and psychodramatic ramifications of the allegorical *imagines agentes* when they are translated into speech. This focus on the performative properties of icons is meant, however, to suggest the close proximity of drama to visual modes and traditionally "nondramatic" representations of torture.

"frame." If anything, it was more akin to the "theatrical frame" described by Erving Goffman as "something less than a benign construction and something more than a simple keying."[23] It was an epistemological system that roused those exposed to it to aestheticize both figuration and disfiguration. As the epistemological framework that allowed a mental image—and often a bloody, forensic image—to be translated into a dramatic one, the *ars memorandi* is fundamental to our understanding of the historical commingling among rhetoric, law, literary invention, theatricality, and brutality. The guardian of the materials discovered during the tortured process of invention that memory was also a place whence new images of torture might be generated and enacted in ways that would inform learned theatrical productions.

Even today, *memoria* offers a model by which to investigate the translation of violent, psychodramatic imagery into the dramatic violence and the violent dramas of the Middle Ages. In the case of torture, violence is foregrounded by invention, later to be rehearsed by memory as a virtual performance, and ultimately to be played out as pleasurable in entertaining trials and dramas. It is thus fruitful to recollect that Antonin Artaud once advocated the abolition of the "rupture between things and words" and urged that it was "essential to put an end to the subjugation of the theater to the text, and to recover the notion of a kind of unique language half-way between gesture and thought."[24] That unique language endured for centuries, as did its cruelty. That language was *memoria*.

Foundational Violence

In his own version of the Simonides legend, Cicero explicitly frames memory as the living architectural space of a crypt. When Simonides experiences the common grave of initially unidentifiable bodies, he discovers (*invenire*) a truth about how people remember and determines that loci and their inhabitants constitute a kind of alphabet:

> The story runs that a little later a message was brought to Simonides to go outside, as two young men were standing at the door who earnestly requested him to come out; so he rose from his seat and went out, and could not see anybody; but in the interval of his absence the roof of the hall where Scopas was giving the banquet fell in, *crushing Scopas himself and his relations underneath the ruins and killing them*; and when their friends wanted to bury them but were altogether unable to know them apart as they had been completely crushed, the story goes that Simonides was enabled by his recollection of the place in which each of them had been reclining at table to identify them for separate interment; and that this circumstance sug-

---

[23] Goffman, *Frame Analysis*, 138.
[24] Artaud, *TD*, 7; 89.

gested to him the *discovery* [*invenisse*] of the truth that the best aid to clearness of memory consists in orderly arrangement. (*De oratore*, II, 353)

Paramount to Simonides's discovery is the status of memory as a sepulcher and its concomitant links with death.[25] In this originary narrative, which would inspire so many early lawyers to perfect their rhetorical skills, the first memory building is a crypt from which dead bodies can speak and can themselves be reborn as their deaths give birth to the imagistic "writing" of a new *techne*. For rhetors, lawyers, politicians, and learned authors, an alphabet of theatrical images would record, inscribe, conserve, and generate representations of ideas upon the "wax tablets of the mind." As Cicero tells the tale, even something as apparently voiceless as a cryptic monument becomes part of the "alphabet" of oral tradition:

> [Simonides] inferred that persons desiring to train this faculty must select localities and form mental images of the facts they wish to remember and store those images in the localities, with the result that the arrangement of the localities will preserve the order of the facts, and the images of the facts will designate the facts themselves, and we shall employ the localities and images respectively as a wax writing tablet and the letters written on it [res autem ipsas rerum *effigies* notaret, atque ut locis pro cera, *simulacris* pro litteris uteremur] (*De oratore*, II, 354).[26]

Still, when Cicero configures the originary violent space of Simonides as a place whence death, new life, and art begin, he does something else. In concluding his version of the legend, he actually problematizes the key dramatic features of mnemotechnics to be analyzed throughout this chapter: that the object of remembrance must first die in order to be brought back to life; that the metaphorically encrypted and subsequently resurrected dead are moving, talking, images or simulacra; that mnemotechnics renders present those who are absent or dead; and that it does so by repainting their picture and by giving them voice. Simonides inaugurates a commemorative model that establishes fascinating parallels between theater and birth, death, and resurrection—a model inchoate in form that was even echoed by Gustave Cohen in his efforts to reconstruct the dramatic patrimony of medieval France. Of the mission of his "Théophiliens," a college theater troupe that has been compellingly analyzed by Helen Solterer, Cohen wrote that "their efforts were not dedicated to the 'dissection of cadavers, but to the resurrection of the dead.'"[27] That was also the mission of memory.

---

[25] For example, D. Vance Smith points out that "from its mythologized inception, memory has formed a link between death and places" ("In Place of Memory").

[26] See, e.g., Eusebius on the "everlasting monuments" and remembrance of martyred Christian bodies (*EH*, V, pr.).

[27] See Solterer, "Waking of Medieval Theatricality," 374.

To the extent to which all memory images are simulacra, I argue in this section that the story of Simonides literally sets the stage for a dramatic, simulated vision of the law as a rhetorical episteme which "call[s] the dead to life [*defunctos excitare*]" (*IO*, IV, 1.28). Mnemonics is the art form that emerged from the rubble, and its apocryphal origins are played out in a tale of dismemberment, corporeal order, reconstruction, reconstitution, and re-creation. It is founded upon a crypt or *conditorium*—a term that, as D. Vance Smith reminds us in an exciting re-reading of Hugh of St. Victor, originally denoted the "container in which a corpse or its ashes were placed. It is neither insignificant nor accidental that this word is derived from *condo*, 'to build' or 'to found.'"[28] What is crucial however, in an art that gives voice to the absent or dead is that, at its own inception, *memoria* can only reanimate what has first been crushed and mutilated. It can only *re*-member what has first been *dis*-membered.

For anyone familiar with how the *artes memorandi* engender speech, it is no surprise to read that they give voice to the dead as well. Theorists of rhetoric long stressed the performative potential of the memory image, within which there inhered the capacity for verbalization and actualization during delivery. For example, the Pseudo-Cicero indicates that "the arrangement and disposition of the images [are] like the script, and the delivery is like the reading" (*RAH*, III, 30). In the Middle Ages, that principle gained currency when Augustine described the personal memory palaces in which, "even though my tongue be quiet, and my throat silent, yet can I sing as much as I will."[29] Martianus Capella went on to train his memory by "muttering" softly to himself in a dimly lit room, while Geoffrey of Vinsauf affirmed that the entire purpose of that art was to translate "wandering images" into languages heard in reciting (*in recitante*).[30] Perhaps most explicit of all on the topic was Quintilian, who had criticized the lawyers of his day for habitually bringing into court "a picture of the crime painted on wood or canvas (*in tabula*)" instead of enriching that picture with language. The Roman rhetorician found that mere pictorial exploitation of violence betrayed a lack of skill and a poor understanding of the power of memory in that he "who prefers a voiceless picture [*mutam illam effigiem*] to speak for him . . . must be singularly incompetent" (*IO*, VI, 1.32). Instead, when a legal advocate sought to "stir all the emotions" less by telling and more by showing characters "as in a picture" (IV, 2.113–14), the picture in question during the scourging of a Roman citizen was not the voiceless pictorial effigy. Rather it implied a vivid staging during a delivery that was engendered, animated, and rehearsed on the orator's memory stage, in the courtroom, and even on the different stages

---

[28] Smith, "In Place of Memory," along with his "Irregular Histories."

[29] Augustine, *Confessions*, vol. 1, bk. 10, chap. 8.

[30] On Martianus, see Yates, *AM*, 52. The passage from Geoffrey is from *PN*, 2022; 2036; "New Poetics," 105. See also John of Garland on memory as the site of the reconstitution of sound in *Parisiana poetria*, II, 94–110.

of early drama. When simulacra reanimated the dead, even a "voiceless" wax effigy could speak volumes, as did the *tableau vivant* described by Appian, which was transformed into a spectacle of cruelty: "Somebody raised above the bier an image of Caesar himself made of wax—for the body, prone on the bier, could not be seen. The image was turned about by a mechanical device, and on the whole body and on the face could be seen the 23 wounds that had been dealt him so brutally. The people could not bear this pitiful sight longer, as it was shown to them, but groaned." [31]

Therefore, despite the cultural preeminence of a theory like *ut pictura poesis*, and despite the wisdom of John Mirk that "ymages and payntours ben lewde menys bokys . . . and I say boldyly þer ben mony þousand of pepul þat *couþ not ymagen* in her hert how Christ was don on þe rood, *but þai lerne hit be syȝt of ymages and payntours*," the memory image assumed its full powers—including the power of its violence—only when it "spoke" during delivery and other spectacles. [32] Memory painted its pictures with voices, as it did in the Pseudo-Cicero's well-known recapitulation of a dictum ascribed to Simonides himself: "a poem ought to be a painting that speaks; a painting ought to be a silent poem" (*RAH*, IV, 39). The same held true for such a medieval author as Richard de Fournival, who repaired to his own house of memory "by painting and by speech" (comment on puist repairier a le maison de memoire et par painture et par parole, si est apparant). [33] Later still, it held true for Denis Coppée, who began his seventeenth-century *poésie dramatique*, *La sanglante et pitoyable tragédie de nostre Sauveur et Rédempteur Jésus-Christ* (1624), by describing himself as an author/painter desirous of representing and memorializing in a speaking picture the "sad and useful" memory of the Passion (Désireux, comme aussi nos amis les acteurs, / De vous *représenter en peinture parlante* . . . *Sa vie nous devons avoir en la mémoire. . . .* / Le souvenir en est utile autant que triste). [34] If memory was the art of speaking pictures, those pictures were rather closer to simulacra, described as follows by the *Ad Herennium* author in his own lengthy treatment of the artificial memory: "an image is, as it were, a figure, mark, or a *simulacrum* of the object we wish to remember" (*RAH*, III, 29). [35]

Those are the simulacra of the classical and medieval memory that became the ghostly similitudes of Christian drama. [36] Indeed, in a phenomenon that proves particularly resonant with medieval Christianity, we learn that the most

---

[31] Appian, *Bell. Civ.*, 2.147, quoted in translation in Slater, "Theatricality of Justice," 150. I thank Alexander MacGregor for bringing this essay to my attention.

[32] *Mirk's Festival*, 186, cited in Rowland, "Art of Memory," 14.

[33] Richard de Fournival, cited in Rowland, "Art of Memory," 24, n. 19). For an important discussion of Fournival, see Solterer, *MM*, chap. 3.

[34] Coppée, as cited and discussed in Faber, *Histoire du théâtre en Belgique* (hereafter *HTB*), 25.

[35] Here I refine Caplan's translation of *simulacrum* as "portrait" insofar as the term has performative dimensions.

[36] See also Neel on Nietzsche's ghostly similitudes (*Plato, Derrida, and Writing*, 166).

important feature of the simulacrum is its capacity to represent and re-present (as it did for Simonides) what is absent and what is dead. In their numerous treatments of the role of memory in forensic orations about criminal acts of violence, such theorists as Quintilian recommend that mnemonic "deposit" or "consignment" be achieved through the mental generation of *visiones* or *phantasmatae* "whereby *things absent* are presented to our imagination [per quas imagines *rerum absentium* ita repraesentantur animo] with such extreme vividness that they seem actually to be before our very eyes" (*IO*, VI, 2.29). Similarly the Pseudo-Cicero clarifies elsewhere in his discussion of personification that simulacra are created dramatically through voicing and imaginary behaviors. *Conformatio*, he writes, "consists in *representing an absent person as present*, or in making a *mute thing* or one lacking form articulate, and attributing to it a definite form and a language or a certain behaviour appropriate to its character" (*conformatio* est cum aliqua quae *non adest persona confingitur quasi adsit*, aut cum res muta aut informis fit eloquens, et forma ei et oratio adtribuitur ad dignitatem adcommodata aut *actio* quaedam) (*RAH*, IV, 66; emphasis mine).[37] The presence of memory thus depends on the absence of things past and on the resurrected presence of the dead who may be brought back to life so that they might speak again. This is especially clear in Fournival's statement that the mnemonic imagination "makes what is past seem as if it were present" (fair chu ki est *trespasse* ausi comme present).[38] His use of the term *trespasse* connotes not only what is past but what is dead.

In that sense, the Simonides legend founds an exemplary epistemological space according to which mnemotechnics makes things present by requiring that they first be absent and revives things by requiring that they first be dead. Considerably more is happening here than what D. Vance Smith terms the direction of the memory "by the knowledge that what once occupied a space is gone, and by the knowledge that it is precisely because the space is unoccupied that it can be registered" ("In Place of Memory").[39] Just because a space is unoccupied does not mean that it participates in what Louis Marin terms "the empty and white space-time [of the] neutral."[40] Neither neutral nor impassable, the memory frame preserves the memory of violence as it facilitates the invention of more violence. In the *techne* that originated with Simonides, even an empty mnemonic space retains its originary violence and registers an absence

[37] The translator Caplan captures the connotations of "form" and "behavior," but equally important are the connotations of *conformatio* as "conforming" and of *actio* as delivery. For a superb discussion of this passage, see Paxson, *Poetics of Personification*, 13–15.

[38] Rowland, "Art of Memory," 24; her translation. In light of the specific focus of forensic oratory on the past (as opposed, e.g., to that of deliberative oratory on the future), this mission is particularly appropriate.

[39] On absent presence in liturgical drama, see Kubiak, *ST*, 51–56; and Solterer, "Revivals: Paris 1935," 74. More generally, see Richter, *Laocoon's Body*, 47.

[40] Marin, *Utopics*, 12, as discussed in Smith, "In Place of Memory."

that exists only because the bodies that once populated it have been extermi-
nated. Since the death of a memory object is a prerequisite for its endurance,
the process by which a memory space resurrects the dead in their crypts is often painful, violent, and strikingly compatible with what is probably the greatest tale of absent presence of all time: the story of Christ.

First of all, the rhetorical figure of *conformatio* or giving body is consistent
with what Sarah Beckwith deems "the most important, indeed the defining aspect of [Christ's] personhood": his embodiment, in which "Christ was imagined as having a life, and this involved having a body" (*CB*, 5). But even more
important than that epistemological connection between mnemotechnics and
embodiment is the widespread medieval fascination with how a body like
Christ's might speak from its crypt. The rhetorical attribution of voices to the
mute and presence to the absent compels us to recall that, like the tale of Simonides in which members of an ancient community sought their dead, the story
of Christ's Resurrection begins with the visitation to an empty sepulcher (*visitatio sepulchri*) and, for countless critics, so too begins liturgical drama. Nor
was the story of Christ the only such tale of absent presence to capture the medieval imagination.

For example, the fourteenth-century English *Life of Saint Erkenwald* presents another story of life rebuilt and resurrected upon the mnemonic foundations of an exemplary crypt. In Erkenwald's legend, the saint discovers a tomb at
the foundation of his abbey which contains a perfectly preserved body of a pagan man of laws, a dead body from another time governed by other principles.
He has long been absent yet always present at the foundations of the new church,
and, once discovered (in this case, uncovered) his absent presence inspires a hagiographic tale. When Erkenwald opens the crypt, his pagan forebear "melts
out of memory" and his reanimated body begins to speak:

> "Lords and ladies, now look! Here is lying a corpse.
> It has lain here, locked up—how long is unknown.
> Yet his color and clothes haven't come, through the years,
> To decay; and his coffin is comely and new!
> But no man here among us *remembers* his reign;
> None has lived here a long enough life to *recall*! . . .
> *It's a marvel he'd melt out memory thus. . . .*"
> Then he turns to the tomb and talks to the corpse,
> While he leans down to lift up the lids of its eyes:
> "In this sepulcher stay in your silence no more! . . ."
> Then the man through a miracle moved in his tomb!
> And with sounds that were solemn, he spoke before all,
> For some great, holy ghost then granted him help.
> The body said . . .[41]

[41] Citations from the *Erkenwald* are from *The Complete Works of the Peal Poet*, 146–93—
although whether it is the work of the same anonymous author has been increasingly questioned.
I thank Kathryn Lavezzo for bringing this text to my attention.

Like the Simonides legend, the story of Erkenwald stages a crypt; but it further points to some highly nuanced differences among the rhetorical origins of memory, the mnemonic origins of hagiography, and the commemorative foundations of liturgical drama. In the Simonides legend, the birth of memory is enacted within a crypt that is fashioned by nature at the command of vengeful gods who see to it that its numerous occupants are dismembered and buried alive. In Erkenwald's story, the crypt—like the highly exploited rhetorical tradition itself—was fashioned by pagan ancestors to house a single, perfect, exemplary body already dead. In the *quem quaeritis* trope, the perfect body of Christ is mutilated, only to regain its perfection when resurrected before the eyes of those who seek to remember it:

> At the end of the Sabbath, when it began to dawn towards the first day of the week, came Mary Magdalene and the other Mary to the sepulcher, alleluia [*venit videre sepulchrum*]. . . . And the angel . . . said to the women: Fear you not; for I know that you seek Jesus who was crucified; he is risen, alleluia.
>
> Jesus whom you seek is not here, but he is risen; *remember* how he spoke to you, when he was in Galilee, alleluia [*recordare qualiter locutus sit vobis*]. (*CRCD*, 295; 165)

All three are tales of pasts made present. In the originary narrative of Simonides, a famous orator created a new *techne* that lent a voice to the mutilated bodies of his dead contemporaries. In the narrative of Erkenwald, an anonymous medieval author engendered the beautiful language of hagiography by reanimating the nonmutilated corpse of a practitioner of the old forensic rhetoric. In the *visitatio sepulchri*, Christ's terrestrial body was subjected to torture. But the traces of his ordeal disappeared along with the body itself, the search for which was expanded and dramatized in centuries of liturgical performance:

> When the third response is finished, the sepulcher is visited with the chants. Two brothers in the role of the women say:
>
> Who will remove the stone from the door that we see covering the holy tomb? [Quis reuoluet nobis ab hostio lapidem quem tegere sacrum cernimus sepulchrum?]
>
> The angels should say:
>
> Whom seek you, O fearful women, weeping at this tomb?
>
> The brothers should reply:
>
> We seek Jesus of Nazareth who was crucified.
>
> Angels:

He whom you seek is not here; but go swiftly, tell the disciples and Peter that Jesus has arisen. . . .

[The two brothers] should hold forth the graveclothes, saying:

Behold, O companions, behold the graveclothes and sudary, and the body is not in the tomb [corpus non est in sepulchro *inuentum*].

Then

He has arisen. (*CRCD*, 299; 231)

When Jules Michelet looked back upon the Middle Ages, he determined that God himself was pulling the strings in the vast symbolic puppet show of medieval theology in which hell was characterized by the absence of God: "the shocking idea of a hell where God utilizes treacherous souls, the most guilty of all, to torture the least guilty whom he delivers to them as a plaything: this beautiful dogma of the Middle Ages was enacted literally. Man felt the absence of God." [42] It might well be that one of the places in which God's absence was most keenly felt was in the theater designed to glorify him. It may also be that, contrary to Peter Haidu's recent assertion that medieval violence was "normalized" because of the "absence of a generalized jurisprudential system of daily life," a highly systematized *presence* of legal rhetoric had, rather, normalized, institutionalized, and dramatized violence. [43]

In each of the stories above, the narrators are concerned with discovering and uncovering, re-covering and re-creating the voices of the dead—a powerful metaphor for spectacle itself. In all three stories of absent presence given voice, the foundations that house dead bodies are *un*covered—metaphorically by Simonides, ritually and mysteriously by the three Marys, and literally by Erkenwald who opens a crypt. Erkenwald builds his church on the foundations of a temple which is to be "torn down and turned to new ends" (36), and the discovery of the stranger's corpse is an architectural extraction performed by masons armed with picks who "dig it out":

All to dig a foundation [*fundement*] of depth for the church.
As they made their way, mining, a marvel they found [*founden*],
As the chronicles clearly record [*memorie*] to this day.
When they'd dug to the depths of the dark, hardened earth,
The men found [*founden*] on a floor at their feet a great tomb. (42–46)

Even the lid of the tomb is surrounded by a mnemonic border or frame of the sort that recently graced the dust jacket of Carruthers's *Book of Memory*: "mas-

[42] Michelet, *Sorcière*, I, 55–56.
[43] Haidu, *SV*, 199.

terfully made out of marble of gray, / With a border embellished with bright, golden words." But those decorative words function within a larger mnemonic space that always frames interpretation and performance. In the case of the *Er-kenwald*, that performance is initially unreadable and untranslatable. The words are "runelike, unreadable, rare, and obscure. / What they meant—although masterfully made and intact— / No one knew; *they could never pronounce them aloud*" (50–54). Melting, digging, or later, for Rabelais, "defrosting" words out of memory is what raises the dead from their final resting places— which turn out to be not so final.[44] And disturbing the dead within their crypts— which lie at the literal foundations of art, architecture, law, rhetoric, and liter-ature—turns out to be the source of devotional speech.

Metaphorically speaking, then, when such a character as Saint John in the Auvergne *Passion* asks the actors and the audience to locate a final resting place for his tortured body not yet dead—"Vous me verrés a mort donner / advant que la journee passe; / pour ce *advisés une place* / pour mectre mon corps, mes amis" (You will see me put to death before the day is over; for that reason, find a place to put my body, my friends)—he is also creating a space for the produc-tion of medieval drama.[45] Indeed, such moments bolster Kubiak's suggestion that "in each new phase or mode of recollection, the theatre so often seems to re-member a *dis-figured* body, a *real* body, in other words, that feels its pain, that is *watched* feeling its pain within the forensic spaces of history, culture, and law" (*ST*, 156; his emphasis). Nor was the phenomenon lost on Jean Rousset, who noted much earlier that on the medieval stage, "death is always reborn, from the first to the final act, mingled with life, present in the bloody, twisted, con-vulsing bodies; it is theatrical death, it is living death."[46] When Vance Smith in-vokes in a general way the concept of "mortuary circulation" as articulated by Deleuze and Guattari, it is in order to assert that memory has always alternated "between the overcoming of death and the subjection to it."[47] Thanks to the *artes memorandi*, the medieval theater seems eternally to defy death as it helps to perpetuate it in an epistemological cycle of violence.

More specifically, with its crypts, spaces, and its giving of voice to mutilated, martyred bodies, memory mediates between life and death in ways that inform the conception and execution of late medieval drama. That an object of re-membrance must first die, the better to be brought anew to life, indicates that scholastic cultivation of mnemotechnics might have contributed significantly to the regulation and normalization of violence as a desirable means of produc-

---

[44] See Rabelais, "Quart Livre," chaps. 55 and 56.

[45] *Passion d'Auvergne*, 11–14.

[46] Rousset, *L'Age baroque*, 84. See also Michael Lieb's argument about generative destruction in *Milton and the Culture of Violence* (hereafter *MCV*), 33.

[47] Smith makes this remark in "In Place of Memory." For the concept of mortuary circulation, see Deleuze and Guattari, *Anti-Oedipus*, 144–45; Krell, on the subject of mourning, *Of Memory*, 283–91; and Geary, *Living with the Dead*.

tion and, specifically, of dramatic production. Medieval dramatists customarily locate memory against a backdrop of birth and destruction in their own invocations of an extensive forensic lexicon of memory images. In the context of their association of mnemotechnics with the preservation, commemoration, and even the engenderment of violence, perhaps the most extraordinary aspect of all is the ability of *memoria* to transmute a theory of absent presence into one of "absent absence." Sometimes mnemotechnics (like torture) recreates something that was never really there. In an intriguing twist to the Simonides legend, Quintilian offers a paradigm not only for the recreation of what is absent or dead but for the invention and, literally, giving birth of things that never existed such as unuttered or inchoate thoughts and feelings:

> This achievement of Simonides appears to have given rise to the observation that it is an assistance to the memory if localities are sharply impressed upon the mind, a view the truth of which everyone may realise by practical experiment. For when we return to a place after considerable absence, we not merely recognise the place itself, but remember things that we did there, and recall the persons whom we met and *even the unuttered thoughts* which passed through our minds when we were there before. Thus, as in most cases, art originates in experiment [Nata est igitur . . . ars ab experimento]. (*IO*, XI, 2.17)

Absent absence is the mirror image of what rhetorical invention is supposed to provide: namely, the discovery of something that is *already* there. The violence of memory discovers something that is *not* there even as it is already always there. Consequently, its violence is epistemologically consonant with the supposedly extrinsic but actually intrinsic proofs of torture because it invents some of the realities upon which it bases the presentation of "facts." Seen from the perspective of the tortures of an equally dramatic scene of *inventio*, it is therefore logical that early theorists so consistently memorialized the creative cycle of death, birth, and rebirth by means of the simulacra of a violent originary scene. By that rebirth, the eternal life of the remembered object could then cloak in forgetfulness the violent originary death whence mnemotechnics had originated, even as it commemorated and glorified that violence in the production of its own unforgettable drama.

Ultimately, what is unforgettable about the foundational memory space that originates with Simonides is that it was and remains a crypt. It is thus reasonable to speculate that the later "foundations" of the later "houses" and "abodes" that pepper the landscapes of mnemotechnics may retain some of the violence of the first cryptic foundations of Simonides's legend of death, dismembering, and remembering. Of course, I am by no means suggesting that *all* inventional memory spaces were violent; nor am I denying the existence of beauty in architecture and drama. But there does endure something more than beauty in such a space as Geoffrey of Vinsauf's house of rhetorico-literary composition, which he subjects to the laws of composition. Like Cicero before him, he adheres so fervently to the forensic principle that any act of thought requires an abode (*De oratore* II, 358) that, from the outset of the *Poetria nova*, literary creation takes place upon an architectural foundation of codified *leges* to be transmitted to poets:

> If anyone is to lay the foundation of a house [*fundare domum*], his impetuous hand does not leap into action: the inner design of the heart measures out the work beforehand, the inner man determines the stages ahead of time in a certain order; and the hand of the heart, rather than the bodily hand, forms the whole in advance, so that the work exists first as a mental model rather than as a tangible thing. In this mirror let poetry itself see what law must be given to poets [*quae lex sit danda poetis*]. (*PN*, 43–49; emphasis mine)[48]

Even the most apparently placid of memory foundations is concerned with the imposition of laws. And this is, after all, the same Geoffrey of Vinsauf who elsewhere likens the act of invention to the violent extractions of torture. If he now holds up a mirror to his literary house, then one reflection he might see in that mirror is an archetypal memory of violence apocryphally founded on a crypt. Since mnemotechnical narratives were founded on violence, they laid violent foundations of their own as the Middle Ages constructed and deconstructed classical theory for its own use in the courtroom, in the classroom, and on the stage.

In his inquiry into death and remembrance, Jacques Derrida asks: "What is a crypt? No crypt presents itself. The grounds are so disposed as to disguise and to hide: something, always a body in some way. But also to disguise the act of hiding and to hide the disguise: the crypt hides as it holds."[49] Throughout this chapter, we shall see that one of the things mnemotechnics hides and holds is a deep cultural need to commemorate life by glorifying or advocating death. It effects the opposite of the words once intoned by Euripides's Medea, who claimed that "pain has little bite if it retains the power to conceal itself. Great sufferings do not lurk in disguise."[50] Great sufferings are frequently disguised—so much so that the history of memory bears out Simon Richter's insight that "the pain of the body is at the center of the aesthetics of beauty, and . . . the desires of this aesthetics are responsible for the infliction of the pain it seeks to hide" (*Laocoon's Body*, 190). In a series of discourses that have particularly striking ramifications for the study of educational institutions, the invention of drama,

[48] I return later to the blurry distinction between the mental action of spiritual hands (*manus cordis*) and the physical action of bodily hands (*manus corporis*).

[49] Peggy Kamuf chooses this epigraph from Derrida's *Fors* to preface her entire study of *Fictions of Feminine Desire*, xi. The Derridean concept of the unnatural space of the crypt also speaks to the long-standing debate in rhetorical theory about the natural vs. the artificial. On literary crypts, see also Vance, *MS*, chap. 3; and Kubiak, *ST*, 69.

[50] See Kubiak's discussion of *Medea*, 155–56 (*ST*, 41–42). See also Mazzaro, "*Mnema* and Forgetting in Euripides' *The Bacchae*."

the cultural construction of gender, and the very nature of transgression, theorists of rhetoric conceal the violence of their own mnemotechnical systems even as they articulate them. Those paradoxes at the prediscursive level then help to lay the foundation for rhetorical modes of didacticism that are violent, coercive, spectacular, and rife with self-contradictions. In that way, the *ars memorandi* becomes paramount to our understanding of how the medieval rhetorical tradition enacts and dramatizes the violence of its own discursive systems, including that of an inventional system now recast in memory as a violent birth. Any analysis of those contradictions at the level of real or imagined performance, however, must delve more deeply into the powerful metaphor of birth itself along with the spaces in which it takes place.

"There are some proofs," writes Quintilian of invention, that are "adopted by the orator which lie outside the art of speaking, and others which he himself deduces or, if I may use the term, begets out of his case [*ex causa traheret ipse et quodam modo gigneret*]. The former therefore have been styled *atechnoi* or *inartificial* proofs, the latter *entechnoi* or *artificial*" (*IO*, V, 1.1; editor's emphasis). The verb *trahere* situates us in the realm of torture and the verb *gignere* in the realm of birth. So, when the living dead of the Simonides legend are reborn, die again, and are "reborn again," their cyclical lives and deaths validate Michael Riffaterre's claim that a consciousness of the "circularity of memory" enables us to "witness the birth of literariness."[51] A key property of the mortuary circulation of memory was to place witnesses at violent originary scenes by alluding to that most enduring metaphor of all for literary creation: childbirth. When theorists of rhetoric moved the mortuary circulation of memory from the crypt to the womb, they also helped to spawn some of the most violent originary narratives imaginable.

Violent Births, Miscarriages of Justice, Tortured Spaces

Perhaps nowhere do we find a more haunting prototype for the mortuary circulation of memory than when Thomas Bradwardine teaches techniques for memorizing the signs of the Zodiac by conflating violence and creation in a series of bloody images of beating and childbirth. In his "De memoria artificiali," Bradwardine stages a bloody Taurus who is being kicked from one side in his engorged testicles by Aries the Ram. On the other side, the bull's blood spills over a woman in painful labor with Gemini's Twins, whose ruptured birth produces Cancer the Crab. Bloody violence gives rise to bloody and violent childbirth, highlighted by the infliction of blows upon male and female reproductive organs. Like the Simonides legend which re-membered what had been dismembered, Bradwardine's text locates mnemotechnics at a moment of simultaneous wounding and creation, disfigurement and figuration:

[51] Riffaterre, "Mind's Eye," 40–41, 44.

Constituat ergo sibi iuxta principium primi loci arietem candidissimum stantem et erectum super posteriores eius pedes cum cornibus si voluerit deauratis. Taurum quoque rubissimum ponat ad dextram arietis cum pedibus posterioribus per-cutientem arietem; *aries vero stans erectus* dextro pede percutiat taurum super *tes-ticulos eius magnos* et ultra modum *inflatos ad effusionem sanguinis copiosam.* Et per *testiculos* memorabitur quod sit taurus, non bos *castratus* nec vacca. Similiter taurum anteponatur mulier quasi *laborans* in partu, et in *utero* eius quasi *rupto* a pectore fingantur duo gemelli *pulcherimi* exeuntes, et cum cancro horribili et in-tense rubro *ludentes*, qui unius parvulorum captam manum detineat, et sic ipsum ad fletum et ad signa talia compellat, reliquo parvulo admirante et nihilominus cancrum pueriliter contrectante.[52]

One places a very red bull to the right of the ram, kicking the ram with his rear feet; standing erect, the ram then with his right foot kicks the bull above his large and super-swollen testicles, causing a copious infusion of blood. And by means of the testicles one will recall that it is a bull, not a castrated ox or a cow. In a similar manner, a woman is placed before the bull as though laboring in birth, and from her uterus as though ripped open from the breast are figured coming forth two most beautiful twins, playing with a horrible, intensely red crab, which holds cap-tive the hand of one of the little ones and thus compels him to weeping and to such signs, the remaining child wondering yet nonetheless caressing the crab in a child-ish way.

In Bradwardine's riveting imagery of astrological violence, the blows inflicted by Aries the Ram upon a fertile (not infertile) Taurus the Bull create a situation in which an unnamed mother in painful labor is stained with blood as the Gem-ini Twins are brutally ripped out from another kind of originary memory space: the uterus.

Eerily, Bradwardine's fabulously violent birth of memory anticipates Antonin Artaud's dark metaphysics of theater. "All the great Myths are dark," writes Ar-taud, "so that one cannot imagine, save in an atmosphere of carnage, torture, and bloodshed, all the magnificent Fables which recount to the multitudes the first sexual division and the first carnage of essences that appeared in creation" (*TD*, 31). Additionally, Bradwardine's fable illustrates Elaine Scarry's "making and unmaking" in that, like Simonides's *conditorium*, it destroys as it creates and vividly depicts the association between death-by-violence and birth-by-art.

In this section, I focus on two important features of mnemotechnics which converge in Bradwardine's surprisingly modern mnemonic cycle and fore-ground my subsequent discussion of bodies, spaces, and performance: the vio-

---

[52] Bradwardine, "De memoria artificiali," Fitzwilliam Museum, Cambridge, MS. McClean 169, quoted in translation by Carruthers in *BM*, app. C, 283–84. For the Latin edition, see Carruthers, "Thomas Bradwardine, 'De memoria artificiale adquirenda,' " p. 37, ll. 93–104. According to some medical lore, the entire zodiac would eventually be localized within a male body, as in, e.g., the Zodiac Man whose figure is reproduced in *La Médecine au Moyen Age*, 61, 63. On Bradwardine, see also Rowland, "Bishop Bradwardine."

lent conflation in mnemonic epistemology of wounding and birth; and the placement of those violent activities within imaginary and often gendered spaces like the womb. The first feature, wounding as birth, is consistent with Scarry's insight that the symbiosis between creation and wounding is one of the "essences" of Judeo-Christian culture. When early theorists equate violence and creation, their own intuition is "obscured and deconstructed, as the activity of creating becomes conflated with the activity of wounding; in turn . . . the deconstruction is itself re-constructed, the original intuition is itself rescued, and creating and wounding are once more held securely in place as separable categories of action" (*BP*, 184). Indeed, that phenomenon recalls Geoffrey of Vinsauf's association of aesthetic pleasure with the pain of creation as he too reimagines the disfiguring impulses of violence as birth, conflating wounding and creation only to separate them in order to engender beautiful poetry (*PN*, 1754–65). The second feature, the womb, suggests an inextricable link between memory and the creational violence of rhetorical invention. When male rhetoricians transfer the birth of memory (itself the birthplace of speech) from the crypt to the womb, their gesture constitutes a crucial means by which to attribute a positive valence to violence. It is a violent, punitive, and appropriative gesture rife with the same self-contradictions that have eternally plagued the history of rhetoric. Even though such a writer as Geoffrey claims that his inventional imagination turns *inward* in an act of self-mutilation that spawned poetry and its pleasures, many theories of memory also turned outward, imagining the infliction of torture upon the real and fantasized bodies of women. Therefore, one cannot fully understand the "birth" of learned literature until the violent nature of its own rhetorico-epistemological moorings for creation have been explored and ultimately realigned with the delivered performances that memory anticipates: violently.

It is, of course, a cultural topos that biological birth is beautiful yet horrifying, creational yet destructive, desired yet feared. The dark, unnatural underside of the cycle of birth and death is as well known as its beauty, a view captured by such enduring myths as the Frankenstein story or the harrowing theatrical visions of a Grand-Guignol presentation such as *L'Horrible Expérience* (1909). As John M. Callahan reports, the play "shows a doctor using electric shock to restore his dead daughter to life, however, the doctor only succeeds in causing his daughter's arms to grab him at the neck and choke him to death."[53] Similarly, in the always spooky imagery of de Lorde, the literary imagination is a haunted, sickly space which destroys even as it engenders: "the deadly fluids of the imagination will eat away little by little at one's mind in the same way that the poisonous rays of radium disintegrate the fingers of scientists."[54] Even so, that topos has been little examined in the realm of rhetorical

[53] Callahan, "Ultimate in Theatre Violence," 168.
[54] De Lorde, *Théâtre de la mort* (hereafter *TM*), 11.

mnemotechnics. One of the first benefits of its reintegration into medieval literary studies is a clarification of the logic behind a whole series of images such as the one that opened this section: the ram kicking the bull in his "large and super-swollen testicles."

The kicking ram has long perplexed modern readers (save all, perhaps, but scholars of François Villon). Even Carruthers does not seem to know what to do with it.[55] "What is most surprising, to a puritan-formed sensibility," she avows, "is the emphasis on violence and sexuality which runs through all the interaction of the figures in each scene" (*BM*, 134). But the violent conjunction of bloodshed and birth is not so surprising when we recall the violent genesis of mnemotechnics itself. When the psychic *mises en scène* of memory bring together testicles, testimony, and embodiment in their bloody and generative seminal spaces, the ram's presence begins to make sense in light of another famous image from the *Rhetorica ad Herennium*.

Despite the critical currency of the Pseudo-Ciceronian *imagines agentes* in current scholarly literature, those are not the first memory images to be invoked in the *Rhetorica ad Herennium*. Rather, in the passage that directly precedes his famous analysis of the artificial memory, the ram appears in the Pseudo-Cicero's presentation of a vision of murder for money which highlights both the motive and the means of death. As the orator commits to his memory a murderous drama that has already happened, he makes it all happen again by staging a scene of impending death in what has proved a somewhat confusing allusion to testicles and testimony:

> For example, the prosecutor has said that the defendant killed a man by poison, has charged that the motive for the crime was an inheritance, and declared that there are many witnesses [*testes*] and accessories to this act. If in order to facilitate our defence we wish to remember this first point, we shall in our first background form an image of the whole matter [*totius imaginem conformabimus*]. We shall picture the man in question as lying ill in bed, if we know his person. . . . And we shall place the defendant at the bedside, holding in his right hand a cup, and in his left tablets, and on the fourth finger a ram's testicles [*medico testiculos arietinos tenentem*]. In this way we can record the man who was poisoned, the inheritance, and the witnesses [*testium*]. (*RAH*, III, 33; emphasis mine)[56]

The ram's testicles signify the presence of witnesses (*testes*) and their testimony, as they do when that ram "runs amok in the middle of Albertus's commentary on Aristotle's *De memoria*" (*BM*, 143): "if we wish to record what is brought against us in a law-suit, we should imagine some ram, with huge horns

---

[55] At the end of the final ballade of the *Testament*, Villon swears by his one remaining testicle (see, e.g., André Mary's edition, p. 137, v. 7–8). I am indebted to Walter Blue for discussing Villon with me.

[56] Murder for money is still another twist in the Simonides legend, which, according to Quintilian, shows the orator avenged after failing to collect proper payment for his poetic composition (*IO*, XI, 2.11–13). Again, the verb *conformabimus* appears, connoting the giving of form, body, and voice.

and testicles, coming towards us in the darkness. The horns will bring to memory our adversaries, and the testicles [*testiculos arietinos*], the dispositions of the witnesses." [57] And what the ram is doing in Albertus, in the Pseudo-Cicero, and in Bradwardine (where he kicks Taurus in the testicles and causes a "copious infusion of blood") is helping to configure a legalistic vision of memory as—quite literally—a *seminal* process. He incarnates the forensic rhetorical principle that, no matter how violent the intervention upon it, a male receptacle or container (*testis*)—is the only true witness (*testes*) (*RAH*, III, 33). By that logic, the woman giving birth becomes a false witness, the very crime which, under the later circumstances of the mystery play, could incite the virulent persecutions of Jews. In fact, woman is so false a witness to the generative activities of her own body that the entire birthing process is wrested from her. In a vision of "economy" that would leave the heads of most postmodern critics spinning, Bradwardine even goes on to sketch a strategy by which men might assimilate the entire birthing process. Birth (mnemonic or otherwise) is more efficient, more profitable, more *economical*, he contends, when women are not involved: "the two twins are placed there born not of a woman but from the bull in a marvellous manner, so that *the principle of economy of material* may be observed [*ut rerum paucitas observetur*]" (l. 106; *BM*, 284; emphasis mine).

At one level, that image evokes the underlying ideology of Caesarean birth, which has been characterized by Renate Blumenfeld-Kosinski as a twofold vision of mutilation and salvation.[58] It also participates in a lengthy tradition of the womb as mnemonic receptacle, as when Honorius Augustodunensis describes the uterus as a mere depository for male impressions: "the womb, indeed, is certainly the receptacle of the semen; it is lined within with villi so as to retain it better, and is composed of seven cells with the shape of a man *stamped* on them as if on a coin." [59] Although Honorius's space for mnemonic imprintation is female, the imprints stamped upon it are those of male agents. Even the quintessentially generative locus of the uterus is construed as a passive female vessel upon which an active male seed may be stamped or branded. That tradition might well have fed the later fears of Nicolas Culpeper, who wrote, as late as 1671, that it was not fitting that woman's spirit inform what was growing within her womb: "The imagination of the Mother operates most forcibly in the Conception of the child. How much the better then were it for women to lead *contented* lives, that so their imaginations may be pure and clear." [60]

---

[57] Albertus Magnus, "Commentary on Aristotle's De memoria et reminiscentia," 90:97–118; cited in translation in Yates, *AM*, 68; and also discussed in Carruthers, *BM*, 143.

[58] See Blumenfeld-Kosinski, *Not of Woman Born*, 1.

[59] Honorius, *De philosophia mundi*, cited in Pouchelle, *BSMA*, 137. For another perspective, see Juan Luis Vives's use of the metaphor of the coin as the incarnation of *doxa* or public opinion in *Vives on Education (De tradendis disciplinis)*, 14.

[60] Culpeper, *Directory for Midwives*, cited in Paster, *Body Embarrassed*, 180; Culpeper's emphasis. I take up the gendered register of rhetoric in "Violence, Silence, and the Memory of Witches"; and "Delivering Delivery." See also Davis, "Questions for a Feminist Methodology in Theatre History"; and Ede, Glenn, and Lunsford, "Border Crossings."

At another level, Bradwardine has recontextualized within a mnemonic context of sexuality and spectatorship the classical rhetorical equation of *testimony* and *testicles* (as in a man swearing by his two testicles or Villon swearing by his one). Just as Quintilian's orator extracts (*traheret*) and begets (*gigneret*) artificial proofs from his case (*IO*, V, 1.1), just as Geoffrey of Vinsauf assumes for himself the tortured birth of poetry, Bradwardine now attributes the pain of creation to men at the same time that he manages to strip women in labor of their own agency. Such mnemotechnical principles might then nurture the pedagogical theories of Juan Luis Vives, who later went so far as to reinvent the male teacher as the intellectual birth mother:

> The affection of the master for his pupil will be that of a father; he will love him truly and from his heart, as if he were his own offspring. Does *he indeed who gives birth to the body do more for the child than he who stirs the mind to action?* In truth, in so far as the mind is more truly the essential part of the man than the body the teacher may be said to be more truly the parent. For we are not men because of our bodies which we have in common with the brutes, but in consequence of the likeness of our mind to God and the angels. (*De tradendis*, 86–87)[61]

In the case of the rhetorical expropriation of memory, birth, and the birthing capacities of memory, male authors like Vives reinvent their own physiology and convert themselves into the birth mothers of literature—no matter what the violent implications for the female body. For René Girard, this type of event constitutes a cyclical replacement of destructive violence with a violence that is "creative and protective in nature" (*VS*, 144). Nonetheless, neither that creativity nor that protection are necessarily extended to women.

Notwithstanding the beauty of the classic metaphor of the poet-creator, when early theorists appropriate for themselves the biologically exclusive power of woman to give birth in pain, they translate labor and birth into the work of literature and recast the entire experience as male. That activity is closer to the appropriative literary births analyzed by Walter Benjamin, who acknowledges that the feminine genius "exhausts itself in accomplishment. It gives life to the work of art, and then it dies." The male artist assimilates that process and emerges reanimated as "the masculine first-born of the work of art, which he once conceived."[62] Troubled by the process, Elisabeth Bronfen postulates that "not only is a text created over a dead, feminine body, but this sacrifice also gives a second birth to the artist."[63]

---

[61] In this vision of pedagogy, Vives also replaces wetnurses with such writers as Cicero and Demosthenes, who had "sucked in their language with their mother's milk" (*De tradendis*, 295). C. Jan Swearingen has also explored the antique topos of motherless children in "Plato's Women." On the birthing metaphor, see also Fantham, "The Concept of Nature and Human Nature," 135–36.

[62] Benjamin, *Denkbilder*, 138; cited in translation in Tatar, *Lustmord*, 35–36.

[63] *Over Her Dead Body*, 124; see also Tatar's discussion of her work in *Lustmord*, 36; and Clover, *Men, Women, and Chain Saws*.

While the problematic relationship between power and motherhood has been the topic of many recent feminist critiques, the role of memory within larger cultural strategies of concomitant abnegation and assimilation has been largely neglected. For example, with regard to the birthing process, Page duBois asserts that, ever since Plato's Socrates, it has been a commonplace of Western philosophy that birth is a male prerogative: Plato "reinscribes the act of generation, of reproduction, and transfers it to the philosopher, whose experience in labor and birth is idealized and made to transcend that of women. . . . The female is both excluded and assimilated to a theory of monistic homoerotics."[64] That is the very nature of maieutics. But since one cannot annex or reannex a power that has not been usurped, the rhetorical motivations that underlie the practice of maieutics can never be disclosed. Instead, the compatible mnemonic convergence of birth, death, and reenactment brings the ram's testicles onto the psychodramatic stage and shrouds its motivations in the "secrecy" of the seminal space of birth.

Instructive in this regard are the linguistic markers for biological mystery and secrecy that Marie-Christine Pouchelle has documented in Brunetto Latini. In his *Livre du Trésor*, Brunetto identifies the egg as an "enclosed space of reproduction," while Geoffrey of Vinsauf designates it a "secret place" or *arcanum*.[65] Elsewhere, Drouart la Vache tries in his *Livres d'amours* to unlock those secrets in a vision of dismembered individual body parts which are then re-membered: "En son cuer recorde et *ramenbre* / La faiture de chascun *menbre*, / Les venues et les alees / Et cerche les *choses secrees*" (In his heart he recalls and remembers the form of each member, its comings and goings, and he searches for their secrets).[66] Later still, the fifteenth-century surgeon Henri de Mondeville takes up identical terminology for the female reproductive organs and actually suggests that "the interior space, be it of the house or of the body, is a feminine place; for the first dwelling-place of man is buried deep in the 'secret places of women'" (*BSMA*, 130; 134). Woman's power to give birth is secret enough, mysterious enough, desirable enough to assimilate; but once it has been assimilated, her role in the creative process is often denied.

So it is that Bernard of Clairvaux (when scrutinized by Caroline Walker Bynum) betrays one such assimilation, albeit one that is kindly phrased: "Learn that you must be mothers to those in your care, not masters [*domini*]; make an effort to arouse the response of love, not that of fear. . . . Show affection as a mother would. . . . Be gentle, avoid harshness, do not resort to blows, expose

---

[64] duBois, *Sowing the Body*, 181; see also Swearingen, "Plato's Feminine," 109; Halperin, "Why Is Diotima a Woman?"

[65] Brunetto Latini, cited in Pouchelle, *BSMA*, 138. The term *arcanum* does indeed denote "secret," as when Geoffrey of Vinsauf writes that "mentis in *arcano* cum rem digesserit ordo" (*PN*, 60). Jane B. Kopp translates this passage as "the secret places of your mind" ("New Poetics," 35). Moreover, as we shall see, *secret* is also the term used to designate certain special effects in the staging of medieval drama.

[66] *Li Livres d'amours*, 237–40; cited and discussed in Solterer, *MM*, 32–33.

your breasts: let your bosoms expand with milk not swell with passion." [67] This Bernard who grows breasts is the same Bernard who, haunted by specters of pleasure, blames women for impressing sins of the flesh upon the male memory: "Sed amara quaedam impressit signa memoriae, sed vestigia foeda reliquit" (Even though the itching of evil pleasure quickly passes and any charm of sensual satisfaction is short-lived, still it *stamps on the memory certain bitter marks*; it leaves filthy traces).[68] Apparently, here woman is stamping her mark upon men, although another tradition conversely warrants that a male seed is stamped mnemonically upon the uterus as the woman herself (like the mutilated unnamed woman in Bradwardine) is stamped out. Nor is Bradwardine's by any means the only unnamed woman in Western culture to spawn creation from her own mutilation. Phyllis Trible, for instance, finds in her study of the Old Testament Book of Judges that the violated and dismembered body of an anonymous concubine "gives birth" in violence to the Israelite tribes.[69]

More germane still to the present inquiry is the possibility that the long-standing connection of memory, imagination, and uterine conception facilitates the comprehension of one of the most bizarre legends ever to grace theater history. According to an anonymous (and perhaps unreliable) commentator, Aeschylus's *Eumenides* was once performed so compellingly that it killed the unborn. In an unforgettable tale that links the promise of birth with the infliction of sudden death, the tale of the *Eumenides* does the Simonides legend one better. Where Simonides was able to give voice to the dead, form to the formless, and presence to the absent (e.g. *RAH*, IV, 66), this particular account hints that there is something so dangerous about theater that it can kill what is not yet alive. This is more than even the "absent absence" described earlier or the "re-creation" of something that never existed (*IO*, XI, 2.17). Here, a theatrical representation—one likely outcome of the memory scene—renders those absent even more absent by commuting their births into their death-sentences: "when, at the performance of *The Eumenides*, Aeschylus introduced the chorus in wild disorder into the orchestra, he so terrified the crowd that children died and women suffered miscarriage." [70] The anonymous Greek spectator describes a fear so potent that it prompts spontaneous abortion. In so doing, he betrays a number of anxieties about the ways in which violence, disorder, women, and birth are symbolized by a theater that has the capacity to threaten the continuation of the populace. Theatrical performance is linked here to broken bloodlines, endangering children not only after but before their birth.

Seen from that perspective, the subsequent commentaries of Bradwardine and Tacitus appear more intelligible. Quintilian's orator *extracts* and *begets* his

---

[67] Sermon 23 as cited in Bynum, *Jesus as Mother*, 118.

[68] Bernard of Clairvaux, *Ad clericos de conversione*, in *Opera*, III, 4, p. 75, as discussed in Smith, "In Place of Memory."

[69] See Trible, *Texts of Terror*, chap. 3.

[70] The text of this citation appears in Nagler, *Sourcebook*, 5.

proofs; Bradwardine's unnamed woman has her uterus ripped apart to give way to Gemini and Cancer; and Tacitus names the womb as the birthplace of a vicious theater, the first home for the "peculiar and characteristic vices of this metropolis of ours, taken on, as it seems to me, almost in the mother's womb [*in utero matris*]—the passion for play actors." [71] In other words, the vicious passion for theater which is stimulated in the womb can and perhaps *should* be responsible for the death of theater and the death of women. In still another exemplary tale from the Bible, dramatized by the Middle Ages, the violent fate of Thamar who is raped by her brother Hamon mutates into a different story about the nefarious role of women in engendering hatred among men. *Comment Thamar fut violee par forche de Amon son Frere* is a play in which a female body in pain becomes a sign of the memory of men:

> Pour conforter les desoléz,
> vous prions que aiiés *souvenance*
> de l'istoire que ouÿ avez
> et dont avons fait remoustrance;
> par laquelle avons congnoissance
> que par amour desordonnee
> Thamar fu en grant desplaisance
> de son frere Amon violee;
> *dont haïne fu engenree*
> entre deux freres tellement
> que par *traïson* approuvee
> mort s'ensievit consequanment. [72]

To comfort the aggrieved, we pray that you remember the story that you have heard and of which we have given a demonstration [remonstrance]. By this story, we have knowledge that, by a disorderly love, Thamar was violated by her brother Amon in great displeasure. Whence such a hatred was engendered between two brothers that, by sure and certain treachery, death followed as a consequence.

All such visions of memory, theater, and the memory of the theater might thus have fueled further the rationale by which male authors commandeered woman's power to give birth. In the Passion play staged at Mons in 1501, for example, ignoble laborers get their jollies by scourging a Christ in his birthday suit: "Vous le vollés avoir au point / Qu'il yssi du ventre sa mere" (You want to have

[71] Tacitus, *Dialogus de oratoribus*, 29. For the transmission of Tacitus in the Middle Ages, see Reynolds, ed., *Texts and Transmissions*, 406–11.

[72] Alan Knight has generously shared with me his edition-in-progress of this play. It appears in a manuscript containing seventy-two plays from Lille, designated as Codex Guelf. 9 Blankenburgensis in the Herzog August Bibliothek in Wolfenbüttel, 603–14; emphasis mine. Another dramatic version of this tale occurs in *Le Mistére du Viel Testament*, ed. James de Rothschild, IV, 214–30. Citations from the *Viel Testament* are from this edition, which spans just over 50,000 verses. The biblical version of the story has been analyzed by Trible in *Texts of Terror*, chap. 2.

him in the state in which he emerged from his mother's womb).[73] The "comic relief" of the birthing metaphor is even played for laughs in such a farce as the *Galant qui fait le coup*, a fifteenth-century selection that invites its audiences to enjoy recognizing the oxymoronic topos of the pregnant husband (*le mari enceint*). In an elaborate ruse by a lecherous husband, his friend and co-conspirator, a doctor, shares the momentous news of the husband's feigned pregnancy to his wife, Crespinette: "Puys qu'il fault que je le vous dye, / Cestuy qui porte maladye / Est enchainct d'un enfant tout vif" (Since I must tell you, the patient [he who is carrying the illness] is pregnant with a fully live child).[74]

As is eminently clear, however, from the *Eumenides* and from Bradwardine, not everything about the convergence of memory, theater, and violence in the "secret places" of women was so funny—especially when combined with the special staging effects called *secrets*, the term used to designate hidden devices containing real or simulated blood. For Gustave Cohen, the zenith of horror (*comble de l'horreur*) was attained in the use of those effects by the *conducteurs de secrets* of the *Mystère de la vengeance et destruction de Jérusalem*. As the ferocious Nero seeks to learn the secrets of his own birth with the assistance of a *tailleur* who is disguised as a disciple of Hippocrates (a butcher/stone-cutter/ doctor), the play offers a horrific metacommentary on theatrical creation in general. A stage direction reads that Agrippina should be "tied up on a bench with her belly facing up (and a *fainte* is required in order to open her up)" (Nota qu'ilz la lyent ici sur ung banc, le ventre dessus [et fault avoir une fainte pour l'ouvrir]). Nero responds as follows to her pleas for mercy: "Mais il faut maintenant quérir / *Le lieu ou les femmes recoipvent* / *La semence* dont *ilz conçoivent* / Les enfans"[75] (But now we must seek the place where women receive the semen by which they [men] conceive children.) "Sire," responds the cutter, "here it is. . . . It's the womb" (Sire le voilà. . . . C'est la matrice). And a mortified Cohen concludes: "One can scarcely go any farther in the repulsive" (*HMS*, 151)—although, by Cohen's own account, horror was the specialty of the medieval stage, which seems to have taken unusual delight in the blood of women.

Maria Tatar begins her *Lustmord* with a quote from Brian De Palma: "I don't particularly want to chop up women but it seems to work" (*Lustmord*, 3). It also worked in antiquity and the Middle Ages—so well that it necessitates at this juncture a parenthetical remark. Oddly enough, the current critical sensitivity to sexist language may actually serve to camouflage the very inequalities that its practitioners propose to rectify. For example, John Gatton includes women in the rapacious group of watchers of violence when he notes that "the sight of cruelty, suffering, and blood attracted rather than repelled *men and*

---

[73] Mons *Passion*, p. 364.

[74] This farce appears in Tissier, ed., *Receuil de farces (1450–1550)*, VI, 309–66, verses 285–87.

[75] Cited and discussed in Cohen, *HMS*, 151–52. Nero even went "so far as to imitate [*imitatus*] the cries and lamentations of a maiden being deflowered" (*LC*, II, "Nero," chap. 29).

women of the Middle Ages"; while Takis Poulakos aspires to account for marginalized groups by reconstructing "the other side of the antagonism or the
other half of the dialogue."[76] Even though it would not be appropriate to imply that women felt distaste for violence whereas men enjoyed it, the violent
conjunction of bloodshed, torture, and birth within the mnemonic receptacle
of the womb suggests a special kind of victimization which is considerably
more complex than William Ian Miller's intuition that "victimizers, according
to our common notions, will tend to be male, and victims, if not female to the
same extent as victimizers are male, will, in many settings, be gendered female
nonetheless."[77] In the numerous accounts of rhetoric, law, and theater that
constitute the evidence marshaled by this book, the causes and consequences of
violence against women are captured almost exclusively by male narrators, a
practice which continues today, albeit more sympathetically. Therefore, to Poulakos's articulation of an admirable goal, one might respond that women did
not always participate in the larger medieval dialogue. Similarly, when Gatton
determines that the medieval theater was "non-discriminatory in its victims,"
he contradicts himself in the same sentence, writing that it "exploited with especially brutal energy, clinical accuracy, and abundant theatricality the ignoble
treatment of holy women" (84). Medieval rhetoric, drama, and law were *not*
nondiscriminatory in their victims.

In addition, then, to bearing in mind C. Jan Swearingen's helpful caveat that
"the discovery of appropriation [might] itself become appropriative,"[78] it is
equally important to remain vigilant to the dangers of certain usages of non-
sexist language. At best, such language promotes an atmosphere of respect
among twentieth-century literary critics. At worst, it can falsify the earlier victimization of women and prolong the epistemological process that sometimes
begins with rhetoric as it helps rhetoric to begin: the revelations and concealments of an *ars memorandi* that activates distinct desires to harm women. In
Bradwardine's Zodiac, in the tales of Thamar and the anonymous concubine
from the Book of Judges, in the horrible scenes of insemination described above,
mnemonic imagery gives birth in violence and to violence, a phenomenon that
may then be brought to bear upon some of the contemporary wisdom about
the medieval stage.

In the case of the medieval theater of cruelty, John Gatton believes that Tertullian's blood of the martyrs was the "*inseminating fluid* [that] likewise engendered and freely flowed in medieval English miracle plays and French *mystères*";
and Eugene Vance defines the general process of cultural commemoration as
"any gesture, ritualized or not, whose end is to recover, in the name of a collec-

---

[76] Gatton, " 'There Must Be Blood,' " 80; and Poulakos, "Human Agency in the History of Rhetoric," 61–62.

[77] Miller, *Humiliation*, 55. For another perspective, see Maus, *Inwardness and Theater in the
English Renaissance*, chap. 6.

[78] Swearingen, "Plato's Feminine," 109.

tivity, some being or event either anterior in time or outside of time in order to fecundate, animate, or make meaningful a moment in the present."[79] As we have seen, insemination, fecundation, animation, and making meaning are violent, theatrical, and occasionally appropriative processes requiring special spaces in which to take place. Shining with regularity in the background of those spaces were scenes of violence, murder, and coercion.

There is thus one sense in which memory was definitely nondiscriminatory in its victims. As the legend of Simonides so forcefully instructs, the mere idea of putting a body in a space could be frightening. Within the originary crypt and the epistemological womb of memory, various *artes* continued to beget new spaces housing new images, many of which would inform the tortured spaces of the late medieval stage. Those spaces belong to a larger theatrical category recently designated by Stanton Garner as "bodied spaces" and prove relevant to Benjamin Bennett's remark that all performances are "located in hermeneutic space."[80] More significantly, if bodies and spaces constituted what Kenneth Burke once termed a "predisposing structure" for drama, they also served as a predisposing structure for violence.[81]

Any space could be memory space: a courtroom, a classroom, an imaginary theater, or a real theater in which orators, pedagogues, and learned dramatists mentally rehearsed and later reenacted their discoveries by performing them in real spaces and addressing the memories of their various audiences through language, vivid demonstrations, and gestures. That was true long before Elaine Scarry noticed that any room could be "converted into a weapon, deconverted, undone" so that "there is no wall, no window, no door," so that "everything is a weapon" (*BP*, 41). The space of torture, she theorizes, is transmuted into a dramatic production when, "in the torturers' idiom the room in which the brutality occurs was called the 'production room' in the Philippines, the 'cinema room' in South Vietnam, and the 'blue lit stage' in Chile" (*BP*, 28). That was just as true of the medieval theater of cruelty—and centuries before Victor Emeljanow reminded readers that, in the infamous Parisian theater of the Grand Guignol, "the stage is the colour of blood."[82] The Sainte Geneviève *Passion* proffered one such model when the blood of a scourged Christ stained the earth along with the collective memory of its audience: "D'escourgees tranchans et dures / Firent sur lui maintes romptures; / Tant le batirent sanz refraindre, / De

[79] Tertullian, *Apologeticus*, 50.13, as discussed by Gatton in "'There Must Be Blood,'" 79; and Vance, "Roland, Charlemagne, and the Poetics of Memory," 374. See also Paster's helpful comments on blood as an "ideologically overdetermined sign" (*Body Embarrassed*, 66).

[80] I refer here to Garner's book of the same title, *Bodied Spaces*; see also Bennett, "Performance and the Exposure of Hermeneutics," 436. Other helpful perspectives include Padel, "Making Space Speak"; and Snyder, "Writing under Pressure," chap. 3 of *Writing the Scene of Speaking*.

[81] According to Burke, even mechanistic considerations were part of the predisposing "*ground* or *scene* upon which the drama is enacted" (*POLF*, 106).

[82] "Speaking of Pictures," *Life*, 28 April 1947, 15; cited in Emeljanow, "Grand Guignol and the Orchestration of Violence," 151. See also Schneider, "Fading Horrors of the Grand Guignol."

son sanc font la terre taindre, / Que contreval son corps coulloit" (With scourges sharp and hard / They made numerous cuts upon him / So much and so relentlessly did they beat him / That they stain the earth with his blood / Which flowed down over his body).[83]

Whatever shape the memory locus might take—"a house, an intercolumnar space, a recess, an arch, or the like" (*RAH*, III, 29), it was frequently stained with blood. Indeed, those were the same words uttered by one early spectator of the *Mistere de la Sainte Hostie* (a little-studied French version of the notorious Croxton *Play of the Sacrament*). He noticed that "le lieu [fut] tout ensanglanté" (the setting was drenched with crimson).[84] As we shall see in the next section, the memory space was to become much more than a series of columns, houses, rooms, and stages. No longer did it simply house bodies by encasing them within its external architectures. Sometimes, the *imagines agentes* that were so habitually envisioned as beaten and disfigured became a kind of meta-architecture. *Memoria* not only housed human bodies within its architecture: the bodies themselves functioned as a sort of architecture and became the ultimate memory space. In a stunning recontextualization of the second rhetorical canon of arrangement or *dispositio* (which was concerned with the structure and order of an oration), theorists corporealized the art of memory as a body upon which intellectual, legal, physical, and literary "inquiries" could be conducted.[85] Often, it was a body in pain.

Of course, it was nothing new for rhetors studying the largely forensic context of mnemotechnics to have bodies before their eyes when they conceived and performed their speeches. By virtue of *dispositio*, rhetoric had traditionally been described in corporeal terms. As early as the *Phaedrus*, Plato had assigned eloquence a body, noting of arrangement that "any discourse ought to be constructed like a living creature, with its own body, as it were; it must not lack either head or feet; it must have a middle and extremities so composed as to suit each other and the whole work."[86] Later, Tacitus reiterated that position in the context of delivery, fancying *actio* the performative bodily incarnation of eloquence: "it is with eloquence as with the human frame [oratio autem, sicut corpus hominis]. There can be no beauty of form where the veins are prominent, or where one can count the bones: sound healthful blood must fill out the limbs, and riot over the muscles, concealing the sinews in turn under a ruddy

---

[83] Sainte Geneviève *Passion*, 85–89.

[84] The testimony of Philippe de Vigneulles appears in the *Gedenkbuch des Metzer Bürgers Philippe von Vigneulles aus den Jahren 1471–1522*, 244. John Gatton discusses the slightly abbreviated passage that appears in Petit de Julleville's *LM*, II, 103–4, in "'There Must Be Blood,'" 83.

[85] This statement follows the thinking of Rita Copeland, who argues in "The Pardoner's Body and the Disciplining of Rhetoric" that there was a need to imagine rhetoric as having a body the better to discipline it.

[86] Plato, *Phaedrus*, 264c.

complexion and a graceful exterior" (*Dialogus*, 21).[87] Elsewhere in the declamatory tradition, any oration was thought to have "bones" (*ossa controversiae*),
which expedited its ready construction as well as its dissection for pedagogical
purposes.[88]

But when the *ars memorandi* drew strength from *dispositio* as the literal
body of eloquence, it also staged the body in ways that happen to be remarkably compatible with dramatic invention in general and with medieval Christian
dramatic invention in particular. As Sarah Beckwith points out in an allusion
to the *imitatio Christi*, "Christ's willingness to be incarnated, his embodiment,
is crucial because it is only this condescension to the flesh which will allow
other images to signify" (*CB*, 49). Once memory metamorphoses into a body
on which rhetorical and physical intrusions may take place, its exploitation by
learned religious dramatists provides a noteworthy meditation on their own
preoccupation with the process of embodiment.

Insofar as mnemonic embodiment is designed to engender speech and action
and to bring the dead back to life by means of their simulacra, the ways in
which the *ars memorandi* stages spaces as bodies and bodies as spaces promises
to tell us a great deal about theater and its own "bodied spaces." In the medieval
theater of cruelty, *dispositio* manifests itself in the bodies in pain of the victims
of torture, the orator, the author, the actor, and even the audience—all of whom
may become the subjects or objects upon whom the lessons of rhetoric are inscribed violently. However blurred the rhetorical distinctions between victims
and victimizers, the medieval theater of cruelty may then be construed as a capable forerunner of Artaud's theater of cruelty, about which he comments that
"if the theater, like dreams, is bloody and inhuman, it is, more than just that,
to manifest and unforgettably root within us the idea of a perpetual conflict, a
spasm in which life is continually lacerated . . . it is in order to perpetuate in a
concrete and immediate way the metaphysical ideas of certain Fables whose very
atrocity and energy suffice to show their origin and continuity in essential principles" (*TD*, 92–93). If blood was the generative stuff of rhetoric and literature,
then, to a certain extent, rhetorical tales of the beauty of rhetorico-literary creation and of the desirability of civilized law have always been disfigured, always
violent.

Ever since its apocryphal origins and lacerations with Simonides, mnemotechnics has linked destruction with birth or generation. For antiquity and the

---

[87] Moreover, *dispositio* was a key term of both rhetoric and medicine, connoting the state of body
and soul. See, e.g., Pouchelle, *BSMA*, 137. Hence additional similarities between bodily *colligantia*
or *compassio* (*BSMA*, 141) and mnemonic "collocations," as described in, e.g., Martianus Capella,
De nuptiis, 177g.

[88] See, e.g., Michael Winterbottom's discussion of the pseudo-Quintilianic *Declamationes mi-
nores,* which were "designed quite consciously to show the *ossa controversiae*" of an oration
("Schoolroom and Courtroom," 66).

Middle Ages, it codified an alphabet of images that enabled the conception of bodied architectural spaces whence speech and action could be engendered in violence. No matter how lovely the pillared memory theater might seem in retrospect, this imaginary and internal art had the potential for a violence that readily turned not only inward but outward so that its images might be felt by rhetor, judge, and audience. Violent imagery engenders the violent speech and actions which are to be imprinted upon the memories (and perhaps even the bodies) of spectators. In the courtroom, in the classroom, and on the medieval stage, *memoria* had the power to imprint (and perhaps to violate) the minds of listeners, audiences, and readers.

The Architecture of the Body in Pain

Memory was the place where orators learned how to invent speeches, to conceive poetry, and to think about law and philosophy by imprinting images through the "skilful arrangement of the several masks [*singulis personis*] that represent them, so that we may grasp ideas by means of images and their order by means of localities" (*De oratore*, II, 359–60). Its "bodied spaces" comprised the alphabet of images proper to an art that branded, as when Cicero insisted that, prior to their actual deliveries in court, orators were to inflict pain and other strong emotions upon themselves as a prerequisite for conveying those emotions to an audience: "it is impossible for the listener to feel indignation, hatred or ill-will, to be terrified of anything, or reduced to tears of compassion, unless all those emotions, which the advocate would inspire in the arbitrator, are visibly *stamped or rather branded* on the advocate himself [*impressi esse atque inusti videbuntur*]" (*De oratore*, II, 189; emphasis mine). With that insight, Cicero demonstrates a penetrating early awareness of the "psychological axiom" that was to be articulated centuries later by Friedrich Nietzsche in his own discussion of the creation of remembrance for a human species that incarnated forgetfulness. How, wonders Nietzsche, does one "create a memory for the human animal" and "impress anything on that partly dull, partly flighty human intelligence—that incarnation of forgetfulness—so as to make it stick?" He determines that "'a thing is branded on the memory to make it stay there; only what goes on hurting will stick'—this is one of the oldest and, unfortunately, one of the most enduring psychological axioms." [89]

In order to inscribe, to imprint, to write, to stamp, or brand, however, memory needed both its imagistic alphabet (born with the memory of Simonides and the deaths of his friends) and a place to write. Before proceeding shortly, then, to the ways in which the medieval theater "burns the mind" and "scorches the memory" of its audiences with its "vicarious infliction of pain both during and

[89] Nietzsche, *GM*, 192.

after performance," I first explore the status of memory as a kind of picto-graphic writing that employed human bodies as its alphabetical "characters" but also wrote on those bodies.[90] Following rhetoric's impressionistic chronol-ogy from idea to image to speech to action, I analyze here the theatrical rami-fications of the transition within mnemotechnics of a theory of bodies *in* spaces to one of bodies *as* spaces. Those spatialized bodies (or embodied spaces) are then subject to the regulatory and disciplinary interventions of rhetoric as the human body itself becomes the ultimate space on which to brand lessons, speeches, feelings, laws, and verisimilar visions of information. As it traced its alphabets upon the soft and malleable wax tablets of schoolboys and upon the figurative "wax tablets of the mind," mnemotechnics eventually traced its let-ters upon the soft and malleable bodies of women and men. For Andreas Capel-lanus, for example, woman herself was "like melting wax [*tanquam cera liques-cens*], always ready to assume fresh shape and to be moulded to the imprint of anyone's seal." [91] Later, in an erotic scene from the fifteenth-century *Farce de Martin de Cambray* which underscores a future memorable birth, a lecherous curé compares the object of his desire to wax as a prelude to sexual intercourse: "Vous estes fait comme de cire, / Quant je vous tien, / je suis si aise, / Acollés-moy" (You're made as if of wax. When I hold you I feel so good. Embrace me).[92] In the gruesome *Mystère du Roy Advenir*, Jehan le Prieur offers a vari-ant of the Platonic "waxen blocks" of the mind as an image of torture: "Dirai ge deux foys une chose? / Faut il tant reschofer *la cire* / Ne faire sur mon parler pose?" (Shall I say the same thing twice? Must I heat up the wax so much or interrupt my speech?) (all emphases mine).[93] Indeed, as Appian's waxen effigy of the murdered Caesar attests, images of wax had long been associated with the memory of pain.[94]

Both writing and written upon, mnemotechnics was an art that traced its al-phabets dramatically on real and imaginary bodies in ways that presaged vari-ous modes of literary and pedagogical enactment, including the scenes analyzed throughout this chapter. Its corporeal register partially sets the stage for the medieval theater of cruelty as an art that marked bodies, much in the way that Pilate endorses when he intones in the Sainte Geneviève *Passion*, "Prenez le et sy l'enmenez. / Selon la loy que vous tenez / *De son corps faictes jugement*" (Take him and bring him here. According to the laws that you uphold, make

[90] These terms, used by Peter Brook in *The Empty Space* (136), struck Stanton B. Garner as em-blematic of drama's "searing effects" on its audiences (*BS*, 161).

[91] Andreas Capellanus, *On Love*, bk. 3, 83–84, p. 313. For memory as wax tablet, see Plato, *Theaetetus*, 190e–195b; Martianus Capella, *De nuptiis*, 177g; and for a brief history of that im-age, see Carruthers, *BM*, 16–32.

[92] The farce of *Martin de Cambray* appears in Cohen, *Receuil de farces françaises*, pp. 317–26, verses 415–17.

[93] *Mystère du Roy Advenir*, 5428–30.

[94] I am not implying that all wax tablet imagery is negative: indeed, I show quite the opposite in "Music, Delivery, and the Rhetoric of Memory."

judgment upon his body) (1757–59). Elsewhere, in the vast fifteenth-century cycle of plays now known as the *Mistére du Viel Testament*, God himself explains that marking the body of Christ constitutes an archetypal activity. In his interpretation of that staple of medieval typology, the tale of Abraham and Isaac, he confirms that the *figuracion* and accomplishment of Old Testament prophesies is a violent, juridical, and aesthetic process to be inscribed upon bodies: "il est *licite* / De *figurer* dessus son corps / Les grandes injures et tors / Que Jesus, mon filz, souffrera" (it is lawful to figure upon his body the great injuries and wrongs which Jesus, my son, will suffer).[95] If memory was an alphabet of spaces and images, it was also an alphabet of bodies in pain which inscribed in blood upon the bodies of its victims. As we shall see, such violent processes of imprintation come to identify the memories (and even the bodies) of future audiences—including theatergoers and students—as victims of that branding in the rhetorical theater of cruelty. But they further suggest that anybody (any body) constitutes its own psychodramatic scene or protodramatic space which is readily adaptable to staging. Long before any kind of avant-garde theater existed, mnemotechnics had promoted the perception that not only was space a body but the body was a space, a potential theatrical site.

Seen from that perspective, the blooded alphabets that pepper Western literary thought assume a new meaning. When such contemporary theorists as Deleuze and Guattari define the ways in which a social organization writes upon bodies in order to create a collective memory, they virtually paraphrase the rhetorical definition of memory as an alphabet of images: it "traces its signs directly on the body, constitutes a system of cruelty, a terrible alphabet" (*Anti-Oedipus*, 144–45). Before them, Jules Michelet looked at medieval accounts of the spectacular torture of witches in his *Sorcière* and imparted to his nineteenth-century readers the secrets of how witches pricked alphabets in blood upon the arm. If one witch wished to communicate with another in secret, all that was needed was to suck the bloody tracings. That sucking reopened the wounds which spelled out "the bloody letters of the desired word. At that very instant, the corresponding letters would start to bleed (so they say) on the arms of the other one" (*Sorcière*, I, 124–25). An eloquent anticipation of DeLeuze and Guattari's notion that the body "becomes the stone and the paper, the tablet and the currency on which the new writing is able to mark its figures, its phoneticism, and its alphabet" (*Anti-Oedipus*, 212), one early blooded alphabet was that of mnemotechnics. It provides concrete testimony in support of their contention that "if one wants to call this inscription in naked flesh 'writing,' then it must be said that speech in fact presupposes writing, and that it is this cruel system of inscribed signs that renders man capable of language, and gives him a memory of the spoken word" (145).

[95] *Mistére du Viel Testament*, II, 17239–42; emphasis mine. See also my analysis of this play in *ROMD*, 193–204. The identical passage appears in the *Moralité du Sacrifice d'Abraham*, verses 101–8, in Craig, *Evolution of a Mystery Play*, 179.

Even so, while critics too numerous to mention have perceptively analyzed the violence committed against actual bodies in the theatrical and judicial arenas, they have tended to neglect early techniques of mnemonic imprintation, which imagined with equal force the violent intervention upon bodies in the name of the Law. For that reason, it proves helpful to reassess the *ars memorandi* along the lines proposed by such a philosopher as Avicenna, for whom there could be no pain without memory. So keen was his intuition to that effect that he localizes suffering within the confines of the mnemonic imagination and decides that there is no body without a memory and no memory without a body:

> One has images of things and by this is meant that one possesses, as images in the soul, the dispositions of things, that is, sadness, pain, memories, which are joined to the body [*sed sunt dispositiones rei coniunctae cum corpore*]. One must have a body to experience such emotions in the soul, the soul possessing these emotions in imitative forms; this is not the same as saying that these emotions come directly from the body.[96]

Nor is there any pain without memory. As the body becomes the primary repository of memories of pain and an "actor" or agent in the spectacle of life, the *techne* that emerged from the rubble and dismembered limbs of Simonides's banquet went on to stage its violence in ways that proved especially compatible to medieval Christianity. Echoed in numerous mystery plays and disseminated in the *ars praedicandi* by such Christian Fathers as Alanus de Insulis, mnemotechnics furnished a virtual spectacle of the memory of Christ's body in pain: "And, just as we must always have the eradication of our sins in mind, so penitence must remember, that repentance may give rise to remembrance, and remembrance cause sorrow" (Et sicut *peccata nostra semper in memoria habenda sunt ad delendum*, ita poenitentia ad *memorandum*; ut poenitentia *memoriam pariat, memoria dolorem eliciat*).[97]

Moreover, the violent theatricality of mnemonic "writing" extended far beyond the learned, discursive realm of rhetoric. It was evident even in such a popular ritual as the English Gangdays or Rogation Days (traditionally the Monday, Tuesday, and Wednesday before the Holy Thursday of Ascension). During the Feast of the Ascension, the Rogation Days marked out and celebrated a civic space for the pleasure and edification of an entire community. They delimited and commemorated the boundaries of a medieval town by inscribing them symbolically and physically upon the bodies of young male citizens—the participants and the victims. As George Homans summarizes, the Gangdays were "led by the priest and carrying the Cross, banners, bells, and lights, the men of a village went in perambulation about the boundaries of the village. They *beat its*

---

[96] *Avicenna Latinus*, IV, 60–61, quoted and discussed in Coleman, *AMM*, 357; emphasis mine.
[97] *Summa de arte praedicatoria*, in *Patrologia Latina*, 210.174; trans. by Gillian R. Evans in *Art of Preaching*, 127; emphasis mine.

bounds. The small boys who went with the procession were thrown into the brooks and ponds or had their buttocks bumped against the trees and rocks which marked the bounds, so that they should *remember* them the better."[98] Here, the legalistic and spatial circumscription of communal living is a violent process of remembrance in which the marked space of young bodies simultaneously marks the larger architectural space of the town. Not only do living bodies solemnly delineate the space to be remembered; they become part of the site, enabling its generation and, indeed, its *germination* with a beating. "At certain customary points in the ganging," recalls Homans, "at every 'Holy Oak or Gospel Tree' the procession stopped, and the priest offered up prayers and blessed the growing crops" (368). In another memory-driven tale of violent origins, an entire town is born.

Just as Nietzsche would later theorize that pain is the "strongest aid to mnemonics" (*GM*, 193), the ritual of the Rogation Days enacted that operation mnemonically. With its explicit bodily equation of remembrance with the spatial demarcation of a community, this ritual supplies compelling early support of the work of such theorists as Deleuze and Guattari, Bert States, and Michel de Certeau. Insofar as it is enacted upon actual bodies, it substantiates the remarks of Deleuze and Guattari to the effect that "the primitive territorial machine codes flows, invests organs, and marks bodies. . . . It makes men or their organs into the parts and wheels of the social machine. The sign is a position of desire; but the first signs are the territorial signs that plant their flags in bodies" (*Anti-Oedipus*, 144–45). From the standpoint of theater phenomenology, it bears out States's insight that "the ritual in theater is based in the community's need for *the thing* that transpires in theater and in the designation, or self-designation, of certain individuals who, for one reason or another, consent to become the embodiment of this thing."[99] With territorial signs flagged upon bodies, the Rogation Days suggest that one of those things is violence. They also establish a mnemonic connection between violence and what de Certeau terms the "marking out of boundaries" for the stories of everyday life.[100] "There is no law," he writes, "that is not inscribed on bodies. Every law has a hold on the body" (*PEL*, 139). Simon Goldhill concurs, surmising in his work on classical tragedy that there is "no notion of violence without a notion of the norms and institutions of power in society, without, indeed, a discourse of the body and its treatment in society."[101]

---

[98] Homans, *English Villagers of the Thirteenth Century*, 368; emphasis mine. See also Nigel M. Kennell on the bloody ritual flagellation at the altar of Artemis Orthia in *The Gymnasium of Virtue*, 124. I thank George Pullman for bringing this reference to my attention.

[99] States, *Great Reckonings in Little Rooms*, 157.

[100] De Certeau, *PEL*, 122; see his complete discussion of the "inscription of the law on the body," 139–41. Additionally, David Nirenberg offers a fascinating analysis of the Rogation Days as a game that "may have served to beat the boundaries between Christian and Jew and to preserve them in memory" (*Communities of Violence*, 226).

[101] Goldhill, "Violence in Greek Tragedy," 26.

Still, the history of rhetoric clearly shows that the interrelations between violence, power, and the body are yet more complex. One of the more troubling undercurrents of mnemotechnical theory is that the converse of Goldhill's proposition appears equally true. Thanks to the foundational legend of Simonides, it seems that there is no notion of the body without a theatricalized discourse of violence—one that is as relentlessly imbricated with remembrance as it is with the theater of cruelty. Whether it be a popular ritual like the Rogation Days, or the learned, medieval dramatic productions that are the focus of this chapter, violent, dramatic acts of commemoration share with the *ars memorandi* an epistemological instability between bodies *in* spaces and bodies *as* spaces.

By virtue of its own traditions, the rhetorical art of memory had perpetually modeled the representation of such bodied spaces. In the *Rhetorica ad Herennium*, memory was the "treasure-house [*thesaurus*] of the ideas supplied by Invention" and the "guardian of all the parts of rhetoric" (*RAH*, III, 28). Such medieval commentators as John of Salisbury and Richard de Fournival later agreed, the former dubbing memory the "mind's treasure chest, a sure and reliable place of safe-deposit for perceptions"; and the latter, the "guardian of the treasures acquired by man's senses through the excellence of his imagination" (memoire . . . est la garde des tresors ke sens d'omme conquiert par bonte d'engien).[102] Otherwise, Hugh of Saint Victor and Brunetto Latini certainly thought it better to associate memory with beauty. Hugh recommended the use of "brief and dependable abstracts to be stored in the little chest of the memory," while Brunetto helped to popularize that notion in his *Trésor*.[103] However, in light of the Simonides legend, even such classic memory loci as treasure-houses, buildings, boxes, pillars, wax blocks, pouches, and theaters oscillated between the beauty of formation and the pain of deformation. Like the *imagines agentes*, even so apparently lovely an image as the treasure chest immediately reveals some of the same ambiguities as inventional theories of torture. When Augustine cites the words of Paulinus, bishop of Nola in his *City of God*, the mnemonic treasure chest becomes a tortured body in pain:

> "Lord, let me not be *tormented* [*excrucier*] for gold and silver, for thou knowest where all my possessions are." He kept all his possessions where he had been taught to *store* and *treasure* [*condere et thesaurizare*] them by him who had foretold that these evils would come to the world. Consequently, those who had obeyed their Lord when he counselled them where and how they should lay up *treasure* [*thesaurizare*], did not lose even their earthly treasures in the invasion of barbarians.[104]

[102] John of Salisbury, *Metalogicon*, trans. McGarry, I.11; and Richard de Fournival, as cited in Rowland, "Art of Memory," 24n. On memory as custodian, see also *RAH*, III, 28; and Martianus Capella, *De nuptiis*, 141g.

[103] Hugh of Saint Victor, *Didascalicon*, bk. 3, chap. 11, p. 94.

[104] Augustine, *City of God*, bk. I, chap. 10. Here it is only the bodily container that is tortured, while its spiritual, mnemonic treasure is assigned to another plane. For a fascinating theatrical example of a violent treasure chest, see "The Roman Actor" by Philip Massinger (b. 1584), act 2, scene 1, 11.286–405.

As it blurs writing and written upon, mnemonic imagery likewise blurs container and contained. It had done so as early as Plato's *Cratylus*, in which the body had gained currency as a rather more frightening container for thought, legal invention, and even punishment (the dénouement of any forensic process):

> Some say that the body is the grave of the soul which may be thought to be buried in our present life; or again the index of the soul, because the soul gives indications to the body; probably the Orphic poets were the inventors of the name, and they were under the impression that the soul is suffering the punishment of sin, and that the body is an enclosure or prison in which the soul is incarcerated, kept safe . . . until the penalty is paid.[105]

A companion vision so haunted André de Lorde, that he gave it new meaning by fantasizing burial alive as the worst conceivable punishment. In his tortured theatrical imagination, the body is the prison of the mind even after death (a fantasy he attributes to Edgar Allan Poe): "after death, the soul remains buried alive in its shroud of flesh . . . which it strikes in vain in order to leave the uncrossable gates of the cadaver" (*TM*, 11).[106] In the Hell of de Lorde's twentieth-century imagination, one may discover a dark but not illogical continuation of certain aspects of medieval thought. All such visions complicate the ideology of torture for medievalist readers of Elaine Scarry, according to whom the production of pain within a body allows torture to bestow "visibility on the structure and enormity of what is usually private and incommunicable, contained within the boundaries of the sufferer's body" (*BP*, 27). In memory, and in the veneration of Christ's body, there was no comparable medieval conception of the body as "private and incommunicable."[107] Contrarily, sometimes the body was a very public space: a building and even a city.

On that topic, Marie-Christine Pouchelle has resolved from her extensive analysis of medieval medical lore that "anatomy and architecture (or the city) had been reciprocal models for a long time." Such pervasive analogies "help[ed] to explain why a professional architect and a surgeon could be models one for another, each with his body-building or building-body" (*BSMA*, 126; 127–28). Indeed, she traces the "deep-rooted analogies" between medicine and architec-

---

[105] Plato, *Cratylus*, 400; see also Krell's discussion of this text, *Of Memory*, 51–52.

[106] See also de Lorde's comments on being buried alive (*TM*, 11).

[107] Even such a religious ritual as transsubstantiation—however contested it would be during the Reformation—was scarcely "private" in the modern sense. Indeed, in light of the work of Caroline Walker Bynum in *Fragmentation and Redemption* and Sarah Beckwith in *Christ's Body*, the boundaries of Christ's body seemed infinite. See Beckwith's discussion of the Council of Constance of 1415, which "helped legitimize the notion that the host on every altar was the *same* body of Christ" (*CB*, 3; her emphasis); and Diehl, *Staging Reform*, chap. 4. At stake here is a historical difference between a relatively public medieval body and a relatively private modern body; the latter is, nonetheless, increasingly "publicized" in certain avant-garde theatrical performances that stage the body in pain.

ture, bodies and buildings back to the first-century writings of Vitruvius, who "used the human body as his favourite model for any building." [108] *Memoria* was similarly concerned with buildings as bodies, bodies as buildings, the building of bodies, and the building upon bodies. In the fourteenth century, for instance, the surgeon Henri Mondeville (d. 1320) reinforced those spatial visions of the body when, as Pouchelle notes, his "architectural images present the body, especially its insides, as a collection of containers one within the other: edifice, cell, cage, coffer, box, pot, etc." (*BSMA*, 129). Columns, strongrooms, treasures, cages, coffers, boxes, cells, and even the bones of crypts had always been the stuff of the *ars memorandi*.[109] So too were individual mnemonic buildings, which stood as both microcosmic sites and part of a larger architectural macrocosm or city. According to the teachings of the eleventh-century Muslim order of Basra, the human body with all its labyrinthine passageways was "a great city, whose *columns* were the 248 bones of the human body. This city had *strongrooms* containing its *treasures* (brain, lungs, heart) and was crisscrossed by 360 streets (arteries) and by 360 fountains and canals (veins)." [110] In 1354, Henry of Lancaster analogized the body of the Christian to a town under siege: "in this town there are six doors through which a man can enter, and six streets by which he can come to the market-place. . . . And these doors which are six, are the passages through which sin enters into me." [111] If human bodies could demarcate towns (as during the Rogation Days), and if rhetorical speeches were human bodies, the *ars memorandi* established that those marked bodies might expand into the larger spaces of entire cities—spaces to be protected and controlled.

So it is that Pouchelle argues from the writings of Mondeville and Hildegard of Bingen that "the Christian ideal is a strict control of all communication between the outside and the inside of the body, or even a complete symbolic closure" to be exercised over a body that "opened onto the outside world via 12 doors, the bodily orifices" (*BSMA*, 150; 127). "Through architectural metaphors," she concludes, "the body becomes a building, ordered and controlled by man" (*BSMA*, 147). Of additional interest here is the fact that, every so often, the entity that regulated one body-as-building was another body-as-building:

[108] *Ten Books of Architecture*, 72–73; cited and discussed in Pouchelle, *BSMA*, 126. It seems, however, that her adherence to the view that the body is but a container for the soul (*BSMA*, 146) actually obfuscates the mnemonic register of her own examples in chap. 8. In reality, a consideration of mnemotechnics tends to collapse Pouchelle's division between container and contained—in much the same way that the old "nut" and "nutshell" or "form" and "content" vision of rhetoric would be discarded. On the last topic, see Woods, "In a Nutshell," 20–22.

[109] See, e.g., Geoffrey of Vinsauf's designation of memory as a *cellula deliciarum* in *PN*, 1977. For a list of mnemonic boxes, coffers, arks, etc., see Carruthers, *BM*, 34–45.

[110] The Order of Basra lived in what is now Iraq; its teachings are cited by Pouchelle (*BSMA*, 126–27).

[111] In Arnould, *Livre des Sainctes Medecines*, 51, 54; cited in Pouchelle, *BSMA*, 127. In this connection, see also the general approach of Vito Fumagalli in *Landscapes of Fear*.

that of the Church. For Honorius Augustodunensis, for example, the Church was a corporeal entity in which "teachers stand for the mouth, while the defenders of the Church are like hands; the peasants are, of course, merely the feet of this fantastical body." [112] This same Honorius articulated what now reigns as the quintessential example of the origins of liturgical drama when he described how a priest/*tragicus* represented *in theatro ecclesiae* the dramatic struggle of Christ. [113] The individual bodies of his priests, teachers, defenders, and peasants are subsumed within a larger category of persons whose collective body further supports a massive Christian architecture which is itself represented as a body. [114] Rhetorically speaking, their destiny is not unlike that of the *imagines agentes* who were correspondingly assimilated into the larger architectural space of mnemotechnics. Nor is it unlike the general vision articulated by John of Garland in his own discussion of the pedagogical ramifications of mnemotechnics in his *Parisiana poetria* (ca. 1220). John imagines a series of columns that denote and embody different socioeconomic groups by a series of columns that form part of a larger speaking, acting body:

> The first section or column is subdivided into three parts, for courtiers, city dwellers, and peasants, with their arms and their respective implements, their concerns and their duties. If any word falls from the mouth of the teacher [*ab ore magistri proferatur*] which means anything which pertains to any one of the three kinds of persons mentioned [*trium personarum predictarum*], there it will be, for later inventing and selecting. (*Parisiana poetria*, chap. 2, 93–98)

It bears more than passing comment here that John's reference to the "mouth" of the master sounds like prayer (*orare*), that his "three persons" reproduce the terminology of the Trinity, and that, like Honorius, he splits the space of the human body into regulators and regulated.

Ultimately, if the body is a building and the building is a body, then animate merges with inanimate, outside with inside, mind with body, and, as in torture, extrinsic with intrinsic activities. The rhetorical and literary spaces of the *ars memorandi* thus tend to efface distinctions between real and imaginary actions, setting the scene for the feigned and literal beatings of the medieval stage and blurring the convenient distinction between spiritual and bodily activities—the very distinction rhetoric was in part commissioned to uphold. Vives deemed that mind and body were so inseparable that he proffered this advice about how to tend to both: "The chief care should be paid to the mind and the memory,

---

[112] Honorius, *Elucidarium*, cited in Pouchelle, *BSMA*, 126. On the body of the Church, see also Schmitt, *Raison des gestes*, 189–93.

[113] Honorius's comment appears in his oft-cited *De tragoediis* from the *Gemma animae* (c. 1100). I discuss this text in *ROMD*, 54–56.

[114] I do not mean "individual" in the modern sense but more along the lines proposed by Sarah Beckwith: Christ's body "provides a language through which the relationship of self to society is articulated on an individualized basis" (*CB*, 41).

which are injured by too much attention to the body. Some wise man has said, 'Great care of the body is great carelessness for the mind.' Nevertheless, the body must not be neglected and brought up in dirt and filth, for nothing is more detrimental both to the health of the body and to that of the mind" (*De tradendis*, 122). As we shall see at greater length in the next section, since the rhetorical memory vision was always a virtual performance, even Geoffrey of Vinsauf's distinction between the mental action of "spiritual hands" (*manus cordis*) and the physical action of "bodily hands" (*manus corporis*) was a fluid one.

As it happens, many medieval literary works betray a confusion between intellectual and physical violence and between pain inflicted by words and pain inflicted by deeds—a confusion that is already apparent in *memoria*.[115] When the narrator of the *Martire Pere et Pol* enjoins the audience that, "en cessant d'euvres corporeles, / Facent les espiritüeles" (ceasing bodily works, they do spiritual works) (2189–90), there is no escape from the memory of pain of the play since its own "spiritual work" is violent.[116] Similarly, the martyred saint-protagonist of the *Conversïon Saint Denis* designates a bodily space for justice when he declares that "Pour ce, raison contraint et muet / A mettre autre vie et espace / Ou Dieu a tous justice face, / Et quant a l'ame et quant au corps" (Therefore, reason constrains and moves us to put forth another life and space where God performs justice for everybody, with regard to both the soul and the body) (*CPM*, 988–91). Whether the "hands" of memory are spiritual or bodily (as in the famous image of the human palm as a mnemonic space), one of the premier functions of those hands was to place bodies in spaces and to brand the minds (and, symbolically, even the bodies) of spectators, students, and readers. The hands of the body of the Church were indeed apt for a discipline that might readily be applied to many sorts of body.

The missions of those hands were all the more pressing in that the bodies they supervised or violated appeared not only in the *ars memorandi* but within a literary genre that had itself been denounced as "out of control": the theater. When it came to the filth condemned by Vives (*De tradendis*, 122), such late fifteenth-century offerings as the *Farce du pect* and the *Tresbonne sottie nouvelle des sots* were not shy. The essence of their comedy derives from the depiction of female and effeminate bodies out of control as they demystify the mne-

---

[115] Scholastic words could wound, and the intellectual competitions of university life were plagued with brawls and fistfights. See, e.g., my discussion of violence in the medieval university in *ROMD*, 91–102; and Helen Solterer's argument that such violence can be profitably viewed in the history of libel (*MM*, ch. 7).

[116] *Martire Pere et Pol*, in *CPM*, 2189–90. Apparently Jean de Meun took greater comfort in the socioeconomic ramifications of that apparent distinction than in anything else. His Faux-Semblant advises poor men: "Mes qu'il ovre de mains itiex, / Non pas de mains espiritiex, / Mes de mains de cors proprement, / Sanz metre double entendement" (*Roman de la Rose*, ed. Daniel Poirion, 11479–82). Harry Robbins renders this passage: "he must / With force corporeal, not spiritual, / Perform his labor. That's no metaphor!" (p. 237). The Dahlberg translation even contains woodcuts of the mnemonic *manus corporalis* on p. 201.

monic *arcanum*.[117] In the former text, litigation ensues when a fart escapes from a wife whose anus is the locus of pleasure for her husband: "Mon cul fut la premiere pièce / Par ou il me print, somme toute" (Briefly, my asshole was the first place he took me [107]). Here the interior spaces of women are played for laughs, revealing a comic take on Pouchelle's very serious observations: "Faeces and the female genitals are intimately associated in the secrecy which covers both: 'secret place of nature' was used to mean latrine, while 'secret places of women' means the female reproductive organs" (*BSMA*, 134).[118] The *Mistere de la Sainte Hostie* contains numerous stage directions calling for the use of *secrets* or hidden places, special effects that cause the lacerated Host to spurt out an abundance of blood "as if it were a child pissing" (comme se ce fut ung enfant qui pissoit).[119] And, even in the most vile scenes of torture of the *Mystère du Roy Advenir*, the portrayal of torture is characterized by gallows humor: "Et le lient par les piez en hault et par les cheveux en bas, et le sang li saura de la teste quant on tournera le vis" (And then they tie him by the feet at the top and by the hair at the bottom, and the blood will rush out from his head when they turn the screw) (after v. 5173). When blood rushes out from the head of the bound victim, the sound effects rival those of farce: "Fy! Je croy qu'il a fait ung pait. / Je croy que son cul se descorde" (Whoa! I think he laid a fart. I think his asshole must be coming undone) (5174–75).

Sometimes, though, the intruder into the body was not a torturer, not a series of infidels, nor a farcical judge litigating bodily sounds and smells but Nature. Her force was potentially as destructive, as terrifying, as divinely motivated, and as generative as it must have been for the ill-fated guests at the Simonides banquet. When the art of memory was born to Simonides and when dismembered limbs became one with pieces of a destroyed building, it canonized the interrelations between corporeality, pain, and the natural (or unnatural) intrusions that might occur within the bodied spaces of all manner of caverns and buildings. As manipulated by variously kindly, variously vengeful deities, nature's intrusions into the body are, for Pouchelle, the "essence of pathology." "Images of sickness," she asserts, "relate to things or places remote from architectural space. . . . The remote 'cavern' is on the other end of the scale from man-made buildings: it opens up unfathomable gulfs within the human body through which Nature and all her *terrors* may enter in" (*BSMA*, 159). Pouchelle invokes Gaston Bachelard's metaphor that, "by following the *labyrinth* of fever that runs through the body, by exploring the *houses* of fever, or the pains that inhabit a hollow tooth, we should learn that imagination local-

---

[117] The *Farce du pect* appears in Viollet-le-Duc, *Ancien théâtre français*, I, 94–110; see my discussion of it in *ROMD*, 216–22.

[118] See also *BSMA*, 147; and Jane Burns on female bodily orifices in *Bodytalk*, chap. 1. As we have already seen, "secret places" (like Geoffrey's *arcanum*) are also memory images.

[119] *Gedenkbuch*, 244; and Petit de Julleville, *LM*, II, 103.

izes suffering and creates and recreates imaginary anatomies."[120] Curiously enough, she concludes that none of the metaphors from the history of surgery "relating to architecture itself have anything to do with pathology" (*BSMA*, 159). As far as the "terror" of natural intrusions is concerned, the bodied spaces of *memoria* really did involve a kind of pathology.

In the *Mystère de Sainte Venice*, for example, the emperor Vaspasien determines from his persecution of Jews that his purge must be remembered, never forgotten:

> Il fault qu'en ayez *souvenance*,
> Puis que Dieu vous a faict aydance.
> Au ciel a sainte intelligence.
> Prïons la que pour nous procure
> Car soubz Dieu a faict telle *cure*
> Qu'il ne fault mettre en *oubliance*,
> Puis que Dieu vous a faict aydance.[121]

You must keep this in your memory, since God has come to your aid. He has holy intelligence in Heaven. Let us now pray that he procure it for us, for under God there has come such a cure that one must never consign it to oblivion, since God has come to your aid.

Just as the mystical body of Honorius's Church incorporated defenders as hands ready to inflict violence, other bodied memory spaces rehearsed curative intrusion as control. If terror is implicated here, it is to be found in part within a mnemonic matrix that responds to violence and its pathologies. It is also to be found in the genesis of memory in the violent intrusion of natural forces upon man-made buildings that housed bodies on the verge of mutilation and death. As an art that featured the interplay between architectural space, politics, and medicine, the essence of *memoria* was to reimagine, replicate, reenact, and re-member such dismembering events.

Just as early theorists of medicine pondered distinctions between the natural and the pathological, theorists of rhetoric struggled with related distinctions between natural vs. inborn abilities, natural vs. unnatural violence, accidental vs. intentional acts, and, as was the case for inventional torture, inartificial vs. artificial proofs. Insofar as the purpose of memory imagery was to reenact the scene of a crime, to bring the dead to life, and to anticipate a theatrical delivery leading to justice, a kind of pathology of memory may inform the various spectacles it engenders, including the bodied spaces of learned medieval dramatic production. In other words, the conflicted mnemonic relationship be-

---

[120] Bachelard, *Poetics of Space*, 225; cited in Pouchelle, *BSMA*, 128. The emphasis is hers in a modification of the translation of M. Jolas.

[121] *Mystère de Sainte Venice*, 837–43; emphasis mine.

tween mind and body, life and death, imagination and reality could mirror that between virtual and actual violence.

These are the bodies, the spaces, the bodied spaces that medieval and early Renaissance writers configured time and time again as threatened, under siege, and all the more in need of regulation. Indeed, that phenomenon is taken literally in a particularly intriguing play from the Reformation period. In the *Moralité a sys personnages*, the character of "Eglise" appears on stage as a building and a personified character who is besieged by Heresie, Simonye, and Force. At the beginning of the play, her bodied space is out of control. By the end, it is brought back under control through violence when an Eglise who is reminiscent of Martianus Capella's ironclad Lady Rhetoric comes forward clad in full armor: "L'Eglise sort armée, et d'aspect terrible." [122] After a puzzled Heresie asks "Comment, l'Eglise, avés vous armes?" (What, Lady Church? you're armed?), the embattled Church responds "Ouy, dea! Aveq le glaive entrant / Du Verbe Divin, penetrant / Jusque au parfons de la lame!" (You bet! With my scepter informed with the Divine Word and piercing to the depths of its blade) (310–13). Scandalle begs for mercy, which Eglise accords, but not without conditions and not without due acknowledgement that people are watching:

> En concluant je vous l'acorde
> Devant ceste noble asistence.
> Contre moy faire resistence,
> Il ne se peult pas faire ainsy.
> Vous en avés bonne avertance:
> Contre moy faire resistence,
> *Entrer dedens par viollence,*
> Il ne se peult pas faire ainsy! (316–23).

And so in conclusion, I submit to you before these noble spectators that nothing can be accomplished by resisting me. You have fair warning: Resisting me or entering into me violently, no way!

With images of penetration, pedagogy, and violence, the armed Church wraps up the play by denouncing the violence of her enemies and threatening violence against them if they fail to comply.[123] Her mystical body has beaten other bodies into submission, trampling some of them in the process and even extending that threat to the *noble assistence*. Nobly or, in this case, ignobly with the menace of anal rape, it is by means of such imagery that classical and medieval

---

[122] See Martianus Capella's famous description of Lady Rhetoric in *De nuptiis*, bk. 5. The *Moralité a sys personnages, c'est ascavoir: Heressye, Frere Symonye, Force, Scandale, Procès, L'Eglise* appears in Beck, *Théâtre et propagande aux débuts de la Réforme*, 185–203; and the citation after verse 304. See also in this connection Roach, "Power's Body."

[123] Here the Reformation inherits its own *imagines agentes*—formed, de-formed, and re-formed to its own cultural projects—as the edifice of the church becomes part of dramatic edification.

thinkers offered tangible proof of a "monumentalization" of language. Mnemo-technics had the capacity to alternate between reification and animation as its bodies in spaces become bodies as spaces. Especially in drama, which offered both processes, one might then surmise that it proved an ideal model for hypo-statizing the body on one hand, and dramatizing it on the other.

In the final analysis, mnemonic paradigms may help to explain the different courses certain types of rhetoric may take in their enactments: dramatic per-formance, visual arts, or written word. They also facilitate responses to a final question: in light of the ubiquity of violence in many medieval arts of com-memoration, why a medieval *theater* of cruelty when cruelty is everywhere; or, for that matter, why theater at all? As Eugene Vance has observed of the oral epic narratives of the *Song of Roland*, violence serves as an "*aide-mémoire* or as a generative force in the production of such narrative" (*MS*, 54). Violence is omnipresent in a genre like hagiography; and, for Beryl Rowland, even the bes-tiary combines word and picture in such a way that "the *assault* was made through both the ear and the eye" ("Art of Memory," 15; emphasis mine). But the way in which drama assaults, dis-members, and re-members, through vo-calization, enactment, imitation, and impersonation harks back to the theatri-cal register of the theory of torture. The rhetorical connection between the dy-namic memory scene and the delivered discourses of forensic oratory is the virtual and verisimilar spectacle of torture.[124] In *memoria*, which *imagined* the infliction of pain upon human bodies, the interplay among wounding, birth, de-struction, and resurrection is seconded only by that between virtual and actual violence. In *actio*, the enacted outcome of inventional and mnemonic systems, there is a real moment in real time when real bodies come alive before other real bodies.

By now, it is clear that medieval dramatists staged bodies and buildings in all manner of combinations of speaking, seeing, and writing. Yet, for many mod-ern critics, the metaphor of choice for the body as the recipient of scorching al-phabets is the book. Michel de Certeau believes that the law

> engraves itself on parchments made from the skin of its subjects. It articulates them
> in a juridical corpus. . . . It makes its book out of them. . . . Books are only
> metaphors of the body. But in times of crisis, paper is no longer enough for the law,
> and it writes itself again on the bodies themselves. The printed text refers to what
> is printed on our body, brands it with a red-hot iron with the mark of the Name
> and of the Law. (*PEL*, 140).

Additionally, in the context of medieval manuscript culture, Stephen Nichols argues that the crucified Christ of the Clermont Ferrand *Passion* is a "textual-ized being" who points to "the signs which allow the disciples to read the story

---

[124] Kubiak even equates theater to terrorism (*ST*, 162); and Michael Lieb is moved to discuss Milton in terms of a "theater of vocal assault" in *MCV*, 179.

of the Crucifixion written in his skin or flesh." [125] To a large extent, these commentaries respond effectively to such phrases as Gréban's conception of his monumental mystery play as a book that is both *dit* and *escript* (34409) or to the lines of the *Roy Advenir*, which characterize the piece as a book ready to be performed at any time: "voiz cy le livre achevé, / Tout prest qu'a jouer ce commence" (*Roy Advenir*, 51–52). However, the book metaphor often risks misunderstanding by a twentieth-century reader who might be more familiar with its current static status.

Before the body was a written book, it was the memory of a book in performance. Such a play as the fifteenth-century *Farce de Digeste Viel et Digeste Neuve* amply supports that statement. It is a tale of how two great legal *Digests* incarnating two great theories battle it out for supremacy and influence, occasionally underscoring their own "bookishness." When Digeste Vielle boasts that "his" text is so authoritative that even its gloss is known everywhere, the upstart Digeste Neufve responds by describing his living book-body: "Noz chappitres tous bien escriptz, / Mon texte bien enluminé. . . . Arrière ce vieulx parchemin" (Our chapters are well written, my text is beautifully illuminated. . . . Back off, you old parchment).[126] In this play, books are actually performers, even as their utterances and their contents are preserved in the manuscripts they represent as well as in the manuscript that preserves their own dramatic story, the *Farce de Digeste Viel et Digeste Neuve*.

One might therefore opt for a kind of middle ground by viewing the relationship between books and performance not as a neat divide but as one that is circular and even viciously circular. Mary Carruthers dedicates her entire *Book of Memory* to the larger topic of how the mnemonic imagination is congruent with both orality and textuality; while Sylvia Huot has painstakingly documented the performative properties of the book.[127] If the body both writes and is written upon, then drama proves a particularly effective site at which to explore its pain as both a system of signs and an agent in performance. No matter how "performative" the medieval book now appears, all the mnemonic branding, all the imprintation of images, all the inculcation of values associated with mnemotechnical interventions appear in theater centuries before their analogues in print culture. Consequently, the reintegration of memory into medieval drama criticism promises to shed considerable light on the long-standing debate

---

[125] Nichols, *Romanesque Signs*, 121–22.

[126] The *Farce de Digeste Viel et Digeste Neuve* appears in Cohen, ed., *Receuil de farces*, pp. 333–40, verses 112–22. Here I allude deliberately to the title Cynthia Brown and I selected for a colloquium at the University of California, Santa Barbara, on 25–26 February 1994: "The Book in Performance: Rethinking Codicology."

[127] Here I refer to Carruthers, *BM*; Huot, *From Song to Book*, 1–7; 83–96; and Gellrich, *Idea of the Book in the Middle Ages*, along with such masterful introductions to the interdependency of orality and literacy as Stock, *Implications of Literacy*, and Ong, *Orality and Literacy*. See also Saenger, "Silent Reading"; and Svenbro, "'Interior' Voice."

about medieval textuality, insofar as it offers detailed evidence as to how early theorists conceived of a kind of symbiosis between image and performance: one that is rehearsed within the memory scene.

And yet, there remains to be reintegrated into this scenario the component of violence. For example, Kubiak sees in the sweep of theater history, a "gradual retranslation of body as text, as 'discourse' or written law" into a "theatricalized metaphor of text *as* body." That metaphor "looks back to and reaffirms the violence applied to a 'real' body in society—the subjective, terrorized theatre-body as 'the site of the inscription of the law'" (*ST*, 59; his emphasis). Such an approach resolves an anomaly that attends Foucault's otherwise astute insistence that, for the early modern world, torture "assured the articulation of the written on the oral . . . [and] made it possible to reproduce the crime on the visible body of the criminal."[128] During the Middle Ages, orality preceded written culture or, at the very least, the two were codependent. Foucault's view of the spectacle of punishment may thus be enriched by a mnemotechnical model that melds the two as it anticipates the delivered enactments of that violence. Its tortured spaces, its architectural bodies in pain derive some of their force from a tortured inventional system. But they also constitute a logical if frightening step in rhetorical epistemology. With its imaginary rehearsals of actual or apocryphal acts of violence, memory actually presages the spectacle of real interventions upon real bodies in pain.

Violent Origins and Virtual Performances

"Let art, then, imitate nature," writes the Pseudo-Cicero of the artificial memory: "find what she desires, and follow as she directs. For in invention nature is never last, education never first; rather the beginnings of things arise from natural talent, and the ends are reached by discipline [*disciplina*]" (*RAH*, III, 36).[129] But how and why a rhetorician would imitate nature in a bloody scene of dismemberment in order to invent, to engender, and to preserve the diverse legal and political discourses of the state was indeed a dilemma—the very dilemma that would undergird numerous Christian rhetorical and dramatic discourses.

Simonides's building was constructed by men and destroyed by nature (or, depending on the version of the story, by vengeful Greek gods). So what rhetori-

---

[128] Foucault, *DP*, 55. Foucault also finds that in modern rituals of execution, "the body now serves as an instrument or intermediary" (*DP*, 11). Compare this statement to, e.g., Merleau-Ponty's that "the body assumes the role of a mediator in memory" ("Monday Course," cited in translation in Krell, *Of Memory*, 101).

[129] *Disciplina* refers not only to the concepts of discipline and disciplinarity, but also to the whip (as we shall see shortly in the context of pedagogy). For a compelling treatment of this topic in the realm of *inventio*, see Fantham, "Concept of Nature and Human Nature," esp. 135.

cians discovered in the rubble was an artificial science that could concern itself with violent acts that were "natural" to nature but "unnatural" to humankind. In other words, while the *mnemotechne* that imitates natural violence is artificial, the initial crypt of Simonides's building—its object of imitation—is not. The *ars memorandi* artificially or "unnaturally" imitates the natural violence of nature so that it may reconstruct and recreate from death. It is because mnemotechnics imitates nature that it is artificial; but it is because it imitates nature so successfully by means of simulacra and reenactments that it too may give rise to violence and may do so dramatically in the polis, in the courtroom, in the classroom, and on the stage.

Given the ways in which both *inventio* and *memoria* extract beautiful creations from their own tortuous imagery through a violence that anticipates that of delivery, Nietzsche's words take on new meaning: "Whenever man has thought it necessary to create a memory for himself, his effort has been attended with torture, blood, sacrifice" (*GM*, 192–93). The Simonides legend exemplifies that principle—as it does that expressed more recently by Gilles Deleuze and Félix Guattari. When Deleuze and Guattari extrapolate from Nietzsche that societies record their essence in the violent operations of "tattooing, excising, incising, carving, scarifying, mutilating, encircling, and initiating" with the design of creating a memory for man, they too stress the importance of a primordial cultural drive to *invent* a collective memory from violence. Reaffirming the belief that memory is a learned rather than an inborn ability (*Anti-Oedipus*, 144), Deleuze and Guattari are surely right to insist that "cruelty has nothing to do with some ill-defined or *natural* violence that might be commissioned to explain the history of mankind; cruelty is the movement of culture that is realized in bodies and inscribed on them, belaboring them. That is what cruelty means" (*Anti-Oedipus*, 145; emphasis mine). In the Simonides legend and its numerous continuations, that is also what memory means. In rhetorical lore, the birthplace of language and literature was memory, whose own birth emerged in naturalized violence.

In this section, I show that, when classical and medieval writers theorize the *ars memorandi*, they do far more than express contentment with the birth of their *techne*. They actually refocus the Simonides legend on the didactic and theatrical ramifications of mnemonic systems, which respond to acts of violence that were not accidental at all but intentional: assaults, rapes, murders. By substituting intention for accident and "unnatural" for "natural," they relegate the paradoxes of violence to intentionality and thereby problematize one of the great debates within the history of rhetoric itself: whether that discipline in general (and memory in particular) is a natural or artificial capacity.[130] They further situate an equally great debate about violence within *memoria* as they investigate the

---

[130] That debate also evokes the inventional distinction between inartificial and artificial proof. See also Roland Barthes on the "naturalness" of medieval artifice in *Image/Music/Text*, 202.

complementary question of whether violence is an inborn or acquired "ability" or taste. Ultimately, a revised reading of memory theory suggests that—despite the best early theoretical efforts to "naturalize" violence as an organic part of life, law, learning, and religion—there was in fact no more artificial construction than that very "naturalness." In the same way that the violent spectacularity of torture obfuscated the so-called distinction between the artificial and inartificial proofs of invention, it made for an equally elusive distinction between natural and artificial memories of violence.

Even when memory was not directly linked to torture, it was directly linked to the violence of a tortured inventional process. It was also a proto-performance that mediated between thought and action, past and future and was thereby endowed with a peculiar epistemological project in forensic rhetoric. Thanks to its emphasis on the dramatic enactments of delivery, on one hand, and the criminal motives and intentionality of invention, on the other, *memoria* dramatized psychically the scenes of various crimes as a way of understanding them, finding their "truth" and staging the discovery of that "truth" before judge and jury. One of the premier cultural contributions of its "mortuary circulation," then, was to enable a violent psychodrama to be cleansed of an originary violence that was seemingly (and deceptively) reserved for delivery.

It is from that perspective that its status as virtual performance may help to explain certain forceful parallels between rhetorical theory and medieval Christian dramatic practice. When medieval and early Renaissance rhetoricians, pedagogues, and dramatists reanimate memory scenes, they return to the violent origins of mnemotechnics as they look forward to the didactic reenactments of forensic oratory and drama. Presumably for a good cause, both disciplines re-present crime, torture, and punishment for the purpose of serving a community. So, for the purposes of the medieval theater of cruelty, a foundational mnemonic system of communication that was violent and theatrical might then inform a medieval theater that was eminently violent in its didacticism, most notably in the explicit pedagogical missions of its religious plays.

Long before fifteenth-century dramatists ever staged the reenacted violence of various Christian martyrs, rhetors had drawn extensively on *memoria* in order to reimagine and re-create visions of crimes during delivery. For his own part, Quintilian had conceived a psychic *mise en scène* of murder in which forensic memory images were fundamentally violent and dramatic. The orator was to re-create a drama of criminal activity on his own memory stage, the better to place the audience of his delivery at the reenacted scene of violence and to make them "feel as if they were actual eyewitnesses of the scene [of the crime]" (*IO*, IV, 2.123). In a vivid redeployment of the Simonides legend, the nascent science of mnemotechnics no longer owes its genesis to an accident but to a deliberate act of criminal violence that the forensic orator "replays" in the courtroom. The art that had originated with Simonides's response to the destructive forces of nature (the collapse of a building) is now independent of a "natural" event moderated by divine beings. Instead, the apparently "unnatural" violence of the narrative below is the result of criminal, human agency:

> I am complaining that a man has been murdered. Shall I not bring before my eyes [*in oculis habebo*] all the circumstances which it is reasonable to imagine must have occurred in such a connexion? Shall I not see the assassin burst suddenly from his hiding-place, the victim tremble, cry for help, beg for mercy, or turn to run? Shall I not see the fatal blow delivered and the stricken body fall? Will not the blood, the deathly pallor, the groan of agony, the death-rattle, be indelibly impressed upon my mind? (*IO*, VI, 2.31)

To introduce the topic of *memoria* in this way is to stage a scene of impending disfigurement: the ultimate and intentional disfigurement of murder. It is also to place that intentionally violent scene at the theoretical foundation of an *ars memorandi* that will translate it into a dramatically delivered rhetorical performance in the courtroom. As in the Simonides legend, dismembered victims are brought back to life so that they can die again . . . only to be reborn again.

For example, Quintilian reserves special admiration for Cicero's talent at enacting the psychodrama of criminal activity. Specifically, he pauses to praise Cicero's exploitation of the actual physical evidence that commemorates and vivifies violent criminal acts through metonymy: "blood-stained swords, fragments of bone taken from the wound, and garments spotted with blood" (*IO*, VI, 1.30). Quintilian is impressed by the way in which Cicero's dramatic display of the blood-stained, purple-bordered toga of the murdered Caesar went well beyond the precept that images in purple cloaks are remembered more readily "if we somehow disfigure them [*deformabimus*], as by introducing one stained with blood or soiled with mud or smeared with red paint, so that its form is more striking" (*RAH*, III, 37). He brought "such a vivid image of the crime before their minds [repraesentavit imaginem sceleris], that Caesar seemed not to have been murdered, but *to be being murdered* before their very eyes" (*IO*, VI, 1.31; emphasis mine). Mnemonic violence is just as overdetermined as that favorite contemporary phrase "déjà vu all over again," and that was so in the Middle Ages when John of Garland seems to have heard the death rattle emanating from Quintilian's man abed.

In the *Parisiana Poetria*, John portrays the typical columnar memory locus in which orators were to inscribe images, voices, languages, etymologies, and the pedagogical circumstances under which they were learned in his "Art of Remembering." [131] But, in another subtle conception of the violent genesis of mnemotechnics, he foregrounds that section with a stylistic discussion of the inten-

---

[131] John's full discussion of "De arte memorandi" appears in bk. 2 of the *Parisiana Poetria*, 92–110. Other discussions of the pillared memory stage include *RAH*, III, 31–34; and Cicero, *De oratore*, II, 358–60.

tional acts of violence to which memory must respond. Immediately preceding his "Art of Remembering" is an illustration of the style of complex embellishment in which memorable figures of disfigurement foretell the performance of the legal process. There "a master complains to his bishop of a violent assault [de violenta manuum iniectione]" (chap. 2, pp. 34–35, 48–50). While the passage in question is ostensibly devoted to the rhetorical canon of style or *elocutio*, it is rife with mnemonic imagery of violation: a groan of agony reminiscent of Quintilian's victimized man, a sword metonymically cast as the "wound-making steel," a series of violent imprints that seem to anticipate eerily the Derridean *trace* and the familiar description of memory as a stomach-like receptacle for the food and drink of the mind—transposed here as a criminal mind feeding on blood.[132] John's example of embellishment becomes a rehearsal for the codification of mnemotechnics as we read the victim's tale of how an Everyman knight attacked him:

> I flee to your Holiness's footsteps, most pious Father, to complain that R., knight of such-and-such a place, brandishing the *wound-making steel*, and his satellites . . . assaulted me with a good deal of sweat. . . . In the end the aforesaid knight, with all his house, *fed his crime-infected mind to satiety on my blood*, and leaving the marks [*uestigia*] of his livid hatred on me, dismissed me for dead. Wherefore, in accordance with your clemency, I beg you to offer "the chalice of salvation" (Ps. 115: 13) to me as I keep my couch by listening to the *gasping groans* of my voice. And I beg you so to purge the bilge water of crime in that knight that through the punishment of one the presumptuous insolence of many may cringe in *terror*. (*Parisiana poetria*, chap. 2, pp. 34–35, 56–68; emphasis mine)

That this passage precedes John's discussion of memory implies a restaging of the Simonides legend in which mnemotechnics no longer deals with violent accidents but with intentional acts of criminal violence. Here, the author assimilates the victim's voice which speaks for an absent body and gaspingly invokes the violence done to it as a way of striking terror in the hearts of future criminals and regulating and correcting their antisocial conduct. Like Cicero and Quintilian, John utilizes visions as a deterrent against criminal behavior and believes in exploiting the metonymic power of the mnemonic object (in this case, the weapon) as a means of generating *visiones*. Like the Pseudo-Cicero, he brings *imagines agentes* to life as disfigured images of the body.

Still, by emphasizing the violently dramatic culmination of memory images in performance, such authors as Quintilian and John of Garland create an ideological cleavage between violent epistemology and violent performance even as they stress the status of memory as the birthplace of performance. After all,

---

[132] For the *trace*, see Derrida, *Memoirs*; and Krell, *Of Memory*, chap. 4. For violence and metonymy, see Girard, *VS*, 144; and for the alimentary register of rhetoric in general, see, e.g., Plato on the subject of cookery in *Gorgias*, 462–66; Quintilian, *IO*, VI, 3.19–20; Geoffrey of Vinsauf, *PN*, 1974–2008; Hugh of Saint Victor, *Didascalicon*, bk. 3, chap. 11; and Vives, *De tradendis*, 122.

forensic rhetors had generated their mnemonic images in order to ensure justice, to punish criminals, and to protect society from the very acts of violence now represented iconically and eventually re-presented before the judges, juries, and audiences in whom they elicit pity and fear. Even so, when Quintilian applauds Cicero's use of actual commemorative objects rather than images (or in addition to images), he names delivery as the moment when real violence is reenacted dramatically. In that sense, when rhetoricians reconceive violence epistemologically as the virtuality of memory, when they designate rhetorical delivery as the locus where violence is enacted, the originary mnemonic images of disfigurement and deformation appear somehow pacified by comparison. Similarly, when they stress the violence of delivery, *memoria* appears somehow cleansed by the purity of its intentions to do what Girard calls "good violence" in the name of the law (*VS*, 37; 144). The virtual violence of the mnemonic image consequently seems almost *nonviolent* as its violence reaches fruition in a delivered dramatization of the crime.

One of the principal anomalies of *memoria*, then, is that it enables rhetorical theorists to camouflage violence by emphasizing the artifice of the performances to which memory gives rise. Paradoxically, it is the culminating moment of performance that seems to reify and neutralize that which must be active and dynamic—the *imagines agentes*. Only after the *imagines agentes* have been translated into speech do they appear in retrospect to be the same "voiceless effigies" against which Quintilian lobbies elsewhere (*IO*, VI, 1.32). To put it another way, rhetoricians do two things. They oppose the virtuality of violent memory epistemology to the performed violence of delivered speeches about violent crime; and they focus (however paradoxically) on the artifice and artistry of the forensic rhetorical performance. In doing those two things, rhetoricians purify the artificial memory by "naturalizing" its violence at the level of epistemology and by stressing the virtual rather than the actual performances of violence. In that way, a violently artificial memory is "naturalized" on account of a delivery which seems more violent, more artificial, and more dramatic. The artifice of the "artificial memory" is consigned to the imitative, theatrical canon of delivery, which additionally housed the eminently "artificial" or mimetic faculty of impersonation.[133]

Theorists therefore manage to obscure their own insight that it is largely *because* of the inventional memory that the violence of delivery is inevitable. At the same time, they achieve another ideological feat: the continued concealment of the realization that the Truth to which the Law aspires is often a dramatically constructed illusion.[134] Violent image and violent performance are linked to the

---

[133] I discuss techniques of impersonation or *prosopopoeia* in detail in *ROMD*, 56–65. For a contemporary discussion of the topic, see Derrida, *Memoirs*, 26–29.

[134] Here I follow Baudrillard's thinking in "Simulacra and Simulations," *SW*, 177. In "The Feminist Mnemonics of Christine de Pizan," I argue that the only possible way to avoid this theoretical cleavage is to insist that performance never occur by assigning violence to eternal virtuality.

violence of an *ars memorandi* that conserved both the "proofs" and the tortured "truths" of forensic rhetoric. Equally inevitable was the realization that rhetoric, an art based on probabilities, was ill-suited to the claims about truth on which forensic discourse depended.

As we have seen, *inventio* creates illusions of Truth according to theatrical criteria; *memoria* rehearses those illusions, giving them shape, character, and even characterization; and *actio* enacts them spectacularly. But *actio* is both the end and the beginning of the process of truth fabrication. If the performance of violence seems artificial or false, then the violence of memory (which preserves the fictive and tortured discoveries of invention) often seems "true" by comparison to the artifice of performance. In eminently self-contradictory fashion, theorists assert that, when memory images born of invention are staged, the illusory qualities of their truth seem more true for having been performed. In a viciously circular process, orators fabricate during invention an illusion of the truth of torture (among other things). Next, they visualize the presentation of that truth in the memory; and finally, they perform their mnemonically rehearsed invention during delivery. When that highly elliptical truth is reconsigned to the memory as stable, instability is cloaked in stability, fiction in fact. Delivered illusions of truth may then be reconsigned to the memory as factual, spawning a vicious logical circle. The protodramatic imagery of the artificial memory *seems* stable, real, and true because the enactments of *actio* seem artificial, but afterward the artifice of delivery itself also seems true because it naturalizes or factualizes the memory image that engenders it. Delivered performances then provide the material for future inventions, which in turn generate future mnemonic images, which in turn generate future verisimilar deliveries in an eternal hermeneutic circle of violence.

Insofar as it is inextricably intertwined with delivery, *memoria* is as profoundly cyclical a process as invention. That fact is evidenced by Quintilian's remark that *actio* gave voice to the very imagery that had previously engendered the voice: "the mind should be kept alert [*excitandus*] by the sound of the voice, so that the memory may derive assistance from the double effort of speaking and listening" (*IO*, XI, 2.33). The function of memory that may thus prove most relevant to drama studies is its fascinating ability to transform an imaginary mental voice into a voice that speaks to an audience. While delivery per se is the subject of chapter 3, any discussion of memory anticipates delivery. Each time learned speakers used their voices to translate a violent mental mnemonic picture into something an audience could see and hear, they created a protodrama that was no longer latent within memory, but actualized in language and action before spectators. *Memoria* is at once the site of an ad hoc rehearsal of violence and its post hoc preservation and reanimation. But after and even *during* delivery, that performance (itself generated within the memory) is reconsigned to the memory for storage so that the violent inventional cycle may be reborn.

In the twentieth century, Antonin Artaud asserted that "a violent and con-centrated action is a kind of lyricism: it summons up supernatural images, a bloodstream of images, a bleeding spurt of images in the poet's head and in the spectator's as well" (*TD*, 82). That process also characterized rhetorical mnemo-technics, which rehearsed what dramatic *actio* would eventually perform. When its virtuality was translated into actual performances and when its bloodied bodies in pain were refigured as aesthetically pleasing dramatic images, one re-sult could have been a medieval theater of cruelty. For Anthony Kubiak, an-other result was a classical theater of cruelty in which the "mise-en-scène that is thought leads, ultimately, to the 'actual' theatrical production. . . . We can see a theatre emerging from the alienated violence of thought" (*ST*, 5–6). That alien-ated violence of thought was housed in the psychodramatic or—for Kubiak (*ST*, 46), de Lorde, and Victor Emeljanow—the psychotic *mise en scène* of the imagination. Emeljanow comments, for instance, that the cruelty of the Grand Guignol "reflects psychotic behaviour and a form of madness" ("Grand Gui-gnol," 155). As far as the scholastic culture of the French Middle Ages is con-cerned, my point is that it did not take Edgar Allan Poe's *imagination déréglée* to spawn violent and frightening literature: "there are haunted minds as there are haunted houses; strange specters inhabit them and one senses there all the groaning of dark larvae engendered by a disorderly imagination" (*TM*, 10). Long before an Artaud, a de Lorde, a Kristeva, or a Kubiak could benefit from the insights of psychoanalysis, medieval drama had solidified that connection.[135]

When violence is personified, when the *imagines agentes* are configured as bodies in pain, and when violence is reimagined, reenacted, and commemo-rated, *memoria* is the place where virtual bodies are mentally staged in virtual pain. Since it both anticipated violence and preserved the pictorial, verbal, and dramatic representations of the body in pain, it could then set the stage for a medieval theater of cruelty in which virtuality became reality. One such mo-ment occurs in the liturgical *Ordo ad peregrinum in secunda feria pasche ad vesperas*, when Thomas's belief in Christ is engendered and reenacted once he touches the wounded body of Christ: "Except I shall see the *print* of the nails, / And shall *touch the wound with my finger*, / And thrust my hand into his side, / Know this: I will never believe."[136] Christ invites him to do just that as the play memorializes both the wounds and the faith it engenders: "Thomas, now *examine closely the wounds of my body*. . . . Put your finger in the place of the wound, / And now be not faithless in me" (67–70).

That is the bloody action of medieval drama, inspired in part by a memory that exemplifies what contemporary theorist Herbert Blau calls "blooded thought." Tertullian described it too, concluding his *De spectaculis* by attempt-

---

[135] Here I refer to Kristeva, *Powers of Horror*.
[136] This text appears in Bevington, ed., *Medieval Drama*, pp. 45–49, verses 62–65; empha-sis mine.

ing to replace the bloodshed of pagan spectacles with the dramatic martyrdom of Christ, "pictured through faith in the imagination of the spirit [*spiritu imaginante repraesentata*]." [137] In her work on Alger, canon of Liège (1050–c. 1132), Miri Rubin reminds us that "the eucharist was not the actual immolation of Christ, which had occurred hundreds of years earlier, but the sacrament which could bring forth an image of it: 'In a figure and imitation [*in figura et imitatione*] of His passion, which Christ did not really suffer twice, but the memory of which [*memoria*] is reiterated to us every day." [138] And John Lydgate calls upon the faithful to meditate upon the mutilated body of Christ: "To thy dyscyplys for a *memoryall*, / For a perpetuall *commemoracyoun*, / Of thy flessh and thy blood." [139] One place where violent theatrical imagery was pictorialized was the mnemonic imagination, where orators and dramatists read the signs of the body in pain. Another place was the *mystère*, in which a vivid memory of violence often furnished the lifeblood of techniques of figuration.

When Pilate of the Auvergne *Passion* invokes a veritable refrain inspired by his dream, he too suggests that blood is the ultimate regenerative substance and image, commemorated only to be spilled anew: "Mes sur vous et sur voz enfans / son sang soit et sa mort, combien / qu'il ne vous en chault, meschans gens!" (May his blood and his death be upon you and your children, no matter how great your indifference, evil folk) (2007–9; also 2015–17). Elsewhere, when Saint Christofle's eyes are blinded with blood in the play that bears his name, that blooded vision constitutes the recovery of true vision: "Sire, par amour, je vous prie, / Si voulez la veue recouvrer, / Il vous convient agenoiller, / Et dorer le corps du geant, / Et *oindre vostre oeil de son sang; / Si recouvrerés la veüe*" (Lord, in the name of love, I pray you, / If you wish to recover your vision / You need to get down on your knees and anoint the body of the giant / And *bathe your eye in his blood*. In that way, you will recover your sight).[140] Such mnemonic imaging lends credence to John Gatton's assertion that a single phrase from the massive cycle of the *Mistére du Viel Testament* encapsulates the aesthetic theory of medieval drama: "il faut du sang" (" 'There Must Be Blood,' " 79). Blooded thought saturated the medieval stage when learned French dramatists (who had typically undergone an extensive university training in rhetoric) staged the violence of that most celebrated tale of all, the Passion of Christ. Hence the logic of Gail Gibson's confession that "what bothers me most about the current scholarly quibbling over which archival documents record biblical 'dramas' and which record visual pageants—'mere' silent tableaux processing in the streets—is that the distinction is not only unmedieval but misses the crucial

---

[137] Tertullian, *De spectaculis*, chap. 30.

[138] "De sacramento altrais," *PL*, 180, cols. 786–87; quoted in Rubin, *CC*, 21. See her entire section "Christ's Body and Wounds," 302–6.

[139] *Minor Poems of John Lydgate*, I, 201–3, c. 26, pp. 66–67; cited and discussed in Rubin, *CC*, 100.

[140] *Mystère de Saint Christofle*, 2412–18; emphasis mine.

point that it is, after all, the *imaging* of scripture in human flesh that is the generating force of the medieval religious drama."[141] Insofar as one key function of memory was to supply an alphabet of precisely such images, that generating force was frequently a mnemonic force—and one that was forceful in its violence.

Dramatic Figuration and Mnemonic Disfigurement in Medieval French Drama

Before its vanquished Satan cries "Las dolent! *Je pers ma memoire!*" (Alas, wretch! I'm losing my memory) (4027)—and before such traditional mnemonic components as pillars, wax, and columns are invoked—the Sainte Geneviève *Passion* catalogs authorial intention to stage before an audience a memory of the pain and martyrdom of Christ's flesh. That pain is unrecountable even as it is recounted:

> Cy ot glorïeuse nessance,
> Quant cil qui a toute puissance
> Vint entre nous par sa franchise,
> Puis souffri que sa char fust mise
> Pour nous au plus crüel martire,
> *Que nulz puisse conter ne dire.*
> Or veul venir a ma *memoire.* (45–51)

Here is the glorious birth, when he who has the almighty strength came among us out of his generosity, and then, on our behalf, he put up with having his flesh subjected to the most cruel of martyrdoms *which no one can relate or recount.* So I want to call [them] up in my *memory.* (Emphases mine)

Likewise, Cleophas and Lucas of the *Mystère de la Résurrection* from Angers can barely contain their grief as their own vivid memories of bloodshed fill their eyes with tears. Cleophas laments, "Je ne pourroye mes yeulx garder / De plourer, quant j'en ay *memoire*" (I cannot keep my eyes from crying when I *remember* it); much as his companion Lucas had cried before him:

> Las! Aussi pleurer m'en convient
> Souventesfoiz piteusement,
> *Quant me souvient du grant tourment*
> Qu'il souffrit tant que on le batoit
> A l'estache ou lÿé estoit,
> Et telement y fut playé

---

[141] Gibson, "Writing Before the Eye," 401–2; her emphasis.

> Que son sang si en a rayé
> Et decouru jusqu'a la terre.[142]

Alas, I must also weep piteously again and again when I am *reminded* of the great torment that he suffered as they were beating him on the stake where he was bound, and he was so wounded there that his blood flowed out greatly from him and flowed all the way down to the earth. (Emphases mine)

Sometimes learned dramatists even go so far as to frame an entire cycle as a kind of memory vision, as is the case for the *Mistére du Viel Testament*. The didactic and dramatic exegesis of its Old Testament tales are to be read as prefiguring those in the New Testament "figurativement / Et correspondant au nouveau" (II, 16958–59). In turn, that process is dependent on the staging of *figures*: "il fault *prefigurer* / Ce qui est dit aux Escriptures; / Quant il est baillé par *figures* / En est beaucop mieulx entendu" (we must prefigure what is said in the Scriptures; When it is given by means of figures, it is much better understood) (II, 16746–49). This is a process that is not only violent and dramatic but mnemonic in its reliance on generative figures.

When I come to analyze learned French theater, I argue that the extensive use of mnemonic terminology to describe disfigured bodies in pain gives rise to a coercive didacticism that substantially illuminates how medieval culture grappled with the paradoxes of violence. All the aspects of memory I have discussed thus far—its foundational spaces, its germination, its bodied scenes, and its status as virtual performance—come together on the late medieval French stage. As learned dramatists associate bleeding (*saigner*) with the homophone *en*seigner (to teach), they too discover in mnemotechnics a powerful model by which to dramatize bodies in pain, the better to teach the collective memory.

Particularly striking in that respect is the fact that so many disfiguring scourgings are played out in a pillared locus—the ultimate memory image as chronicled by Cicero, the Pseudo-Cicero, and Quintilian. In the *Mystère de Saint Christofle*, for example, we read a command that "Or faictes que tost soit liés / A ce fort pillier la devant" (Now see to it that he be bound immediately to that strong pillar just in front of us) (2116–17). In Arnoul Gréban's *Mystère de la Passion*, the torturer Griffon obeys such a command by agreeing and taking the cords (*accorder*): "Je l'accorde. / Or, tire donc ce bout de corde / pour le nouer a ce pillier" (I agree [I tie him up]. So pull on this end of the rope so we can tie him up on this pillar).[143] In 1536, a stage direction from the *Mystère des actes des apôtres* dictates that for the immolation of Cidrat, Titon, and Aristarcus, "[il] fault ung pilier près Paradis . . . et sera assis led. pillier sur une trappe et mis trois corps faincts en leurs lieux attachés aud. pilier qui sera environné

---

[142] *Mystère de la Résurrection Angers (1456)* (hereafter Angers *Résurrection*), I, Day 2, 11640–41, 11608–15.

[143] Gréban, *Mystère de la Passion*, 22712–14.

de fagots" (there must be a pillar near Paradise . . . and the aforementioned pillar will be placed on a trap door and three dummies will be placed there and attached to the aforementioned pillar, which will be surrounded by bundles of wood).[144]

Such moments offer early documentation in support of Kubiak's theory of spatial terrorism, according to which "the constraints of legal statute, the historico-mythic traditions that authorize them, and the limits of theatre are all revealed in a folded, forensic space; the site of the legal hearing and the theatrical performance appear superposed" (*ST*, 26). And they are echoed in the *Passion de Palatinus*. When Pilate gives the order for the bloody correction of Christ, he commands that the victim (figured nonetheless as the agent) be attached to a pillar:

> Gran paine li ferez a faire.
> Et si veil que vous le prenez.
> A ce *piler* le lïerés,
> Et le batés d'unes courgiees
> Si que bien soient ensenglentees.[145]

You will cause great pain to be done to him. And so I want you to take him. You will bind him to this pillar, and you will beat him with some switches so that they become fully drenched in blood.

As the scourging continues—with the brutalizers even asking God's help (*Se Dieu m'ait*), the pillar is literally and conceptually attached to the violence inflicted upon Christ's body. During their conversation, torturer Cayn exhorts: "Or le me tien bien a cest post, / Et je les mains li lïerai / A ces bones cordes que j'ai. / Or fier de ça et de la!;" and his companion Huitacelin exclaims: "Caïn, fors sera Jhesucrist, / Se de ce piler vous eschape!" (So hold him well there at that post, and I'll tie his hands with these good ropes that I have. And then strike here and there! Cain, Jesus Christ will be strong if he manages to get away from you and that pillar) (p. 234; Frank, 648–55).

From the standpoint of the bodied memory space, themes of sexuality run through such scenes when, as in the Sainte Geneviève *Passion*, Christ is undressed and bound to a stake ("Tantost tout nu le despoullierent; / A une estache le lïerent") (81–82). In the *Vengeance de Nostre-Seigneur*, it is the memory of a mutilated oppressor that takes precedence during the gruesome punishment of Pilate himself at a pillar.[146] After being starved during his incarceration so that his progressive suffering over the space of twenty-one days will be enhanced, Pi-

---

[144] *Mystère des actes des apôtres*, bk. 9, p. 23; see also Gatton's discussion of this passage in "'There Must Be Blood,'" 91, n. 26.

[145] *Passion de Palatinus*, ed. Frank, 578–82; ed. Pauphilet, 232.

[146] *Vengeance de Nostre-Seigneur*, 194–211. See also Wright, *The Vengeance of Our Lord*.

late's penis is severed on the third day (1099). On the twentieth day, his tongue is cut out (1114); and on the final day, he is decapitated: "c'om lui face hoster la teste et que hom la face seigner afin qu'il dure plus longuement. Et qu'il soit mis sur le piler en la place afin qu'il en soit *remembrance*, et qu'il soit ars et que les sendres soient gitees au Rousne" (Let him then be decapitated and let him be made to bleed so that it lasts longer. And let him then be placed on a pillar so that he may be remembered, and then let him be burned and his ashes cast into the Rhone) (1115–18; emphasis mine).

Perhaps most importantly, though, memory remains an art that employs bodies to write on bodies as scenes of disfigurement become scenes of ideological coercion. Its traces survive even today when Gréban's Pilate anticipates those that he hopes to leave upon Christ's body: "batez le moy par tel party / que sur tout son corps n'y ait place / ou il n'appere playe ou *trace*" (beat him for me in such a way that there's not a single place on his body where there does not appear a wound or a mark) (22729–31). Indeed, such violent mnemonic traces are everywhere, as in the *Passion de Palatinus*, where Cayn announces: "Sire truant, *sus vostre cors* / Maintenant sera fait li sors, / Li quieus de nous deus l'avera" (Lord Felon, now fate will play out upon your body and show which one of us two will win the day) (p. 233; 609–11). The torturers Marquin and Haquin of the Sainte Geneviève *Passion* allude to the memory of their victims as they witness the physical traces they have just left on Christ's body: "Haquin, je voy de grosses bosses / Sus son dos que faictes luy as. / Non ay, voir! / Par ma foy, sy as! / Je vueil que de moy ly *souveigne*" (I see the big bumps that you made on his back. No really, it's true! Upon my word, so you have! I want him to *remember* me) (1624–27). Bruyant of the Troyes *Passion* threatens that Christ will not be forgotten (although not in the way he supposes): "Chascun congnoist ja vostre fait: / vous ne serés pas *oblÿé*" (Everybody knows what you're up to: *you will not be forgotten*).[147] Their counterparts in the Mons *Passion* invoke *espasse* as they boast that Christ will remember the beating they have been playing at inflicting: "En despit du Dieu de la nue / Soudainement en peu d'*espasse* / Il a jué de passe-passe / Affin que de noz mains eschappe. . . . Se je puis / Qu'il en ara bonne *memore*" (In spite of God in heaven, quickly in little space, he played at hide and seek, trying to slip out of our hands. . . . If it's up to me, he will remember it well) (p. 290). And in the relentlessly violent *Mystère du Roy Advenir*, a provost denigrates the very memory of God when he gives the order "Or le m'esloyez a loisir / Par my les braz de ceste corde. / Temps est que ton dieu se *recorde* / De toy" (So, tie up the chosen one at your leisure by his arms with this rope. It's high time that your God make a record of you) (3713–16; emphases mine).

Framed by the ubiquitous pillars of the Christian memory stage, the scourging scenes are all the more memorable because dramatists stage pagan leaders'

---

[147] Troyes *Passion*, vol. II, bk. 3, 772–73. An identical section appears in Gréban, 19736–41.

efforts to "reform" bodies theatrically by making tracings on the perceived transgressors. They then use that same imagery of reform to transform pagan law into Christian religion. Especially noteworthy here is that the pillar is specifically advanced as the locus where Christ's body will be figured, disfigured, and reconfigured (as were the earliest *imagines agentes*). His body is literally *reformed*: "Vostre paillart corps despiteux / sera maintenant refformé" (Your sleazy and despicable body will now be reformed) (Gréban, 22705–6). In the Mons *Passion*, Pilate gives an analogous order that Christ be bound, to which Griffon responds "Il luy fault mettre le corps nud / Sera maintenant *refourmé*" (He must be stripped and [he] will now be reformed). A chorus of assent ensues from Orillart, Brayart, and Clacquedent, who attach and attack Christ as they state that "Il a beau corps et bien *formé* / C'est domaige qu'il n'est plus saige / Il a le dos à l'avantaige / Pour recepvoir beaux horions. . . . Je l'accorde / Pour l'atacquier à ce *piller*" (He's got a beautiful body, and a well-formed one. Too bad he ain't wiser. His back's made perfect for some nice welts. . . . I'll tie him up [I'll grant you that] and attach him to this pillar) (pp. 326–27; emphases mine). These visions are consistent with Kubiak's finding that "the laws of theatre and the theatre of law determine their limits on the acting body by rehearsing, through the repetition of testimonies, the *appearance* of transgression which is consequently reformed in the staged *appearance* of correction legitimated by convention—the judicial sentence, the tragic 'fall' and resolution" (*ST*, 28; emphasis his). But the Passion of Christ and those of his saintly followers were among the greatest medieval stories ever told of fall and resolution.

In the *Geu Saint Denis*, for example, fall, resolution, and mnemonic reform are chanted almost lyrically. In a legalistic and dramatic act of correction (*reformer*), the body of Christ is *de*formed and *dis*figured just as theorists of mnemotechnics had formed and deformed the *imagines agentes* (*deformabimus/ forma*) (*RAH*, III, 37). Its presumably edifying drama stages a pain that forms, deforms, and reforms bodies (*former/deformer/refourmer*) before the eyes of those in attendance:

> Doulz Jhesucrist qui m'as *fourmé*,
> Qui par grace m'as *refourmé*,
> Qui estoie tout *déformé*,
> Qui en ta loy m'as *enfourmé*,
> Qui m'as tous jours reconforté,
> Qui m'as en tous maulx suporté.[148]

[You,] Sweet Jesus Christ who have *formed* me, who, by your grace have *reformed* me—one who was all *deformed*—you who *informed* me in your law and who always comforted me and supported me in all my troubles.

---

[148] *GSD*, 1011–16; emphasis mine.

Elsewhere, we read in the Sainte Geneviève *Passion* that one faithful servant of Christ remembers being an eyewitness to martyrdom: "Je le *tesmoing*, car *bien m'en membre*, / Qu'il n'y a celui qui ait *membre* / Ne soit lïé de feu ardant" (I can testify to this, because I remember well that there is no one with a single limb who is not bound with [who is not joyful for] the burning fire) (879– 81). In these and many like scenes, the conjugated verb *remembrer* (*bien m'en membre*) is philologically identical to the body part or bodily member (*membre*), and the Christian memory is identified with dismemberment.

To effect the kind of bodily "reform" described above, drama itself emerges as the site at which the memory of dismemberment is figured upon the body. "Doulz Jheuscrist," intones Saint Denis, "je vous rens graces / De cen [*sic*] qui vos plaist que les traces / De vostre sainte passion / Ont en mon corps impression" (Sweet Jesus Christ, I give you thanks for your willingness to have the *traces* of your holy Passion inscribed upon my body) (*GSD*, 518–21). The tortures of Christ form, re-form, and reform ideas and bodies and ideas about bodies. At the end of the play, he is grateful and even joyful to receive the tracings of the Passion upon his body and to offer up that marked body to the good folk (*bonnes gens*) within and without the play who are to follow his example (*GSD*, 522; 527).

Such a vivid corporeal mode of exemplification implies that the audiences of religious plays are being instructed to remember something else, something about the character of medieval imitation. In the bodied spaces of the late medieval French stage, legal and aesthetic judgments are marked on bodies in a special way that enables the mnemonic figure to connect (as it had for Augustine) pagan to Christian representation, image to speech, theology to drama. As a play like the *Geu Saint Denis* retraces the steps from memory image to speech, it further predicts the reformed behavior that Christian memory imagery will presumably inspire an audience to perform. In that connection, perhaps its most extraordinary aspect is that its narrator brings together concepts of memory, body, vision, writing, religion, and enactment in an attempt to distinguish pagans from Christians based on the type of *figures* they worship.

One of the first distinctions proposed by the saintly hero of the *Geu Saint Denis* is that between the types of images or *figures* worshiped by pagans and by Christians, each of which scripts a different type of behavior. Whereas a Christian image (however violent) is designed to establish generative and regenerative devotional acts (even though those good acts may be compromised by violence), the pagan image is conceived as one that engenders false behaviors or *fantasies*, which are counterfeit and *faintes*. So it is that, when Denis is asked by a disciple how it is that so many gods are adored when there is only one God, he explains that when a man fails to submit his entire will to the will of God, he loses God's grace and becomes easy prey for the Devil. The Devil may then trick him into doing evil "in many ways" or "through various disguises" (*deçoit en mainte guise*). One of those "ways" is to sever the very ties that a Christian memory epistemology is designed to foster between image, good acting, and acting good. In a fascinating philological nexus, the *Geu Saint Denis* links the pagan, specifically Muslim cult of *mahomerie* to the hypocritical disguisement of acting (*momerie*). That link serves to transmit the message that only images of Christianity can engender genuine, good behaviors:

> *La question*, frere, est profonde
> Et trop de temps avoir fauroit
> Qui a point *soudre* la vourroit,
> Mez a present je vous dy bien
> Que quant pur home qui n'a rien
> Fors de Dieu sa volenté france
> Ne soubzmet toute a l'ordenance
> Et a la volenté divine
> N'est merveille se mal chemine,
> Car Dieu sa grace ly soutrait
> Et l'anemy a soy le trait
> Qui le deçoit en mainte guise
> Et a mal faire adez l'atise.
> Ainssy fait l'un apostater
> Et ly autres ydolatrer
> Institüer *mahommeries*
> Selonc diversses *fantasies*
> Dont ly uns aourent *figures*
> De pecheresses creatures,
> Lez autres bestes ou serpens.
> Et lez autres, les elemens,
> Les autres, *faintes* vanitez
> Afin que leur iniquitez
> Puissent faire a leur apetis. (GSD, 205–28) [149]

The question, my brother, is mo: ⁺ profound, and he who would wish to resolve it completely would need a great deal of time. But now mark my words that when a pure man who has nothing but God fails to submit his whole free will [*volenté franche*] to God's ordinances and divine will, it is no wonder that he missteps [falls off the straight path], for God withdraws His grace from him. And the Devil, who tricks him in many ways, pulls the man toward him and quickly incites him to do evil. So it is that the Devil gets one man to commit apostasy and another to commit idolatry and institute *mahommeries* [mummeries/"mohammedanisms"] according to diverse illusions [*fantasies*]. Of those fantasies, some people worship figures of sinful creatures, others beasts or snakes, others natural forces [*elemens*], and others false vanities so that they may perform their iniquities to their satisfaction.

---

[149] Of course, the appetite for iniquity as reflected by the worship of false images has always been a key feature of the long-standing debate about the nature of iconoclasm.

Another example is found in the Sainte Geneviève *Passion*, when the Centurion speaks directly to the audience at the end of the play (*prononce l'épilogue aux spectateurs*). He consigns Christ to their memories even as he consigns to Christ himself a revitalized vision of that virtuous audience now in prayer: "Prïons ly tuit que par sa grace / De nos meffais pardon face, / Et nous doint cuer de ly servir / Par quoy nous puissons deservir / Sa tres haulte saintisme gloire, / *Et nous mainteigne en son memoire*" (Let us all pray to him that, by his grace, he grant us pardon for our misdeeds and give us the heart [the courage] to serve him. In that way, we might deserve his highest, most saintly glory, and [deserve] that *he keep us in his memory*) (Sainte Geneviève *Passion*, 4468–73; emphasis mine.) Within the mnemonic cycle, the memory of Christ's pain engenders dramatic actions, which then engender good behaviors that are consigned to His memory.

That also holds true for the *Martire Saint Pere et Saint Pol*, which appears with the *Geu Saint Denis* in the *Cycle des Martyrs*. Peter distinguishes Romans from Christians by taking into account the correct or incorrect worship of *ymagetes*. Pagan visions are mute, and their followers are more akin to the "incompetents" whom Quintilian imagined as preferring that a "voiceless picture" speak for them (*IO*, VI, 1.32). As Saint Peter emphasizes that a healthy and regenerative Christian image is essential to the greater health of the Christian body, he simultaneously dememorializes the pagan image:

> Qui est plus grant forssenerie
> Que d'aourer ces *ymagetes*,
> Que vous faites ou faire faites,
> *Qui ne parlent ne ne cheminent . . . ?*
> C'est l'anemy qui vous deçoit,
> Qui en vos ydoles se boute
> Pour estaindre en vos cuers trestoute
> La lumiere de vraye foy
> Et *sain* entendement, par quoy
> Il vous fait sans cesser pechier
> Et vostre createur leissier,
> Et *ymages* de creatures
> Plaines de pechiez et d'ordure
> Aourer, comme fu Venus.
> (*CPM*, 1382–97; emphasis mine)

What greater outrage is there than to worship these little images that you make or have made, which neither talk nor walk? It is the enemy [the Devil] who tricks you, who rams himself into your idols in order to snuff out in your hearts all traces of the light of true faith and healthy understanding, by which he makes you sin constantly, and abandon your creator and worship images of creatures who are full of sin and corruption, as was Venus.

In terminating his speech by criticizing Venus and her offspring, pagan idolatry, Peter mimics Tertullian, who had written that "the theatre is, properly speaking, the shrine of Venus; and that was how this kind of structure came to exist in the world" (*De spectaculis*, chap. 10).

Ultimately, as the plays above anticipate the performance of speech and morality, they also anticipate the transition within memory from image to speech to action. Just as the audience of the Sainte Geneviève *Passion* was inscribed on Christ's memory, the Amboise *Passion* stages Christ's body as a receptacle for the memory of Dimas's body in pain. When his body is lost, Dimas's soul is commended to the memory of Jesus in a real (not an imitated) act of devotion which is designed to spawn more real (not faked) acts of devotion·

> Et si ay je en ma creance
> Que tu puis bien avoir *vengence*
> De ceulx qui t'ont crufiffié [*sic*]
> Et en la croix si fort lïé.
> Mais tu souffriras passïon
> Pour humaine redemptïon. . . .
> Et pour ce, Jhesu, je te prie
> Que, quant perdray du *corps* la vie,
> Que tu aies de moy *memoire*
> Et mon ame metz en ta gloire.
> En toy je croy sans *faintisce*.[150]

And thus I fully believe that you will have your vengeance on those who crucified you and who bound you so tightly on the cross. But you will suffer the passion for the redemption of humankind. . . . And for that, Jesus, I pray you that, when I lose the life from my body, that you keep a memory of me and that you place my soul in your glory. I believe in you without pretense.

Louise Fradenburg once paused to ponder the definition of history articulated by Thomas Caxton: "For certainly [history] . . . is a great blessedness to a man who can be *reformed* by other and strange men's hurts and injuries, and by the same [injuries] to know what is necessary and beneficial for his life." [151] In an inspired response, she identified the following question as one of unique importance to historians of sexuality: "What does it mean to practice a discipline whose designs on the life and death, the pleasure and suffering of the body, however often effaced or repressed, are nonetheless a central part of its cultural work?" (372). That question must be asked by historians of rhetoric and theorists of drama as well. Indeed, Stanton B. Garner has asked it, admonishing that "if we seek to understand the traumatizing, disruptive presence of the suffering body in the representational modes of contemporary political drama, we must begin

---

[150] Amboise *Passion*, 625–39.
[151] Fradenburg with Freccero, "Pleasures of History," 371; emphasis mine.

with the body as zero-point of the subject's phenomenal world" (*BS*, 162). Crucial in the recovery of that "zero-point" for medieval culture is a mnemonic analysis of one of the oldest political dramas on record: the rhetorical tradition. In particular, its art of memory often had political ramifications as it engineered vivid, spectacular imagery of spiritual or bodily figuration and reform.

Before we move on, however, to the performative and political spectacles of rhetorical drama, it is worthwhile to consider a final dimension of the mnemonic protodrama. If mnemonic invention was linked to law, torture, spectacle, and didactic drama, that was also the case for the didactic techniques of pedagogy as practiced in the medieval university. As we shall see, pedagogy and mnemotechnics were eminently compatible, ensuring that the violence they shared would not be forgotten.

Pedagogy, Spectacle, and the Mnemonic Agon

"And don't you forget it!"

The phrase resonates for almost anyone, conjuring images of the imposition of a moral, pedagogical, parental, or societal lesson. The imperative not to forget is a threat. But it is a threat that implicates the memory and one that has been rehearsed both metaphorically and physically for centuries in the classroom.

In this section, I turn to the mnemonic imagery of the pedagogical "rule of the rod" as yet another example of the virtual performance of violence. In the classroom and on the stage, medieval and Renaissance pedagogues had their own violent ways of ensuring that students would not forget, and their classrooms offered an important site in which to enact their designs on remembrance.[152] Of several elements that contribute to a larger coercive spectacle of early instruction, I begin by considering explicit and implicit analogies of teaching to torture. I then turn to the status of the classroom itself as a kind of Burkean "predisposing structure" for violence (*POLF*, 106). As that space helped to build character, it also fostered the translation of mnemonic visions of virtual discipline into pedagogical performances of actual discipline. Next, I explore some of the larger cultural lessons of violent pedagogical rhetorics, including the notion that victimization is salubrious in different ways for men and women. Finally, I analyze a number of properly "dramatic" representations of the classroom from the late medieval and early Renaissance stage that depict violent pedagogy as an edifying or enjoyable game.

---

[152] For the history of the rule of rod in early education, see, e.g., Ong, *RRT*, chap. 5; Leach, *Schools of Medieval England*; and Miner, *Grammar Schools of Medieval England*. I am not implying that medieval and Renaissance educational practices were identical. Indeed, for some nuanced distinctions between the two, see Durkheim, *Evolution pédagogique* (hereafter *EP*), 198–205; and Riché, "Rôle de la mémoire dans l'enseignement médiéval."

In the numerous beatings of classroom, stage, and classroom-on-stage to be treated below, the veritable counting refrains that accompany the flogging of Christ frequently replicate the violent terminology of both pedagogy and memory. They illustrate more than adequately the theorem articulated by Friedrich Nietzsche in his own enumeration of the brutal tortures, beatings, burnings, and flayings employed by his forebears: "by such methods the individual was finally taught to remember five or six 'I won'ts' which entitled him to participate in the benefits of society; and indeed, with the aid of this sort of memory, people eventually 'came to their senses.'" Nietzsche concludes that "we need only recount some of our ancient forms of punishment . . . [to understand] what an enormous price man had to pay for reason, seriousness, control over his emotions" (*GM*, 192.–94). Furthermore, the violence and spectacularity of the rule of the rod amply bear out Michel de Certeau's intuition that "through all sorts of initiations (in rituals, at school, etc.), it [the law] transforms them [bodies] into tables of the law, into living tableaux of rules and customs, into actors in the drama organized by a social order" (*PEL*, 139). Each time a learned religious dramatist employed mnemonic terminology to memorialize the violent scourging of Christ, he supplied early confirmation of those observations along with Nietzsche's boldest statement of all: that "the cruelest rituals in every religious cult (and all religions are at bottom systems of cruelty)—all these have their origin in that instinct which divined pain to be the strongest aid to mnemonics" (*GM*, 193).

While my intention here is neither to insinuate that all pedagogies were violent nor to perpetuate the recent theories of pedagogy-as-victimization which have been so aptly refined by Marjorie Curry Woods; I wish nonetheless to stress that many of the mnemonic techniques of early pedagogy were indeed violent and oppressive.[153] In a strange—or not so strange—echo of the ideology of torture, early teachers had long reinforced the theoretical equivalency between intervention upon the memory and painful intervention upon the body in order to invent knowledge and, later, to extract that knowledge from their students. Since the body was implicated in forgetting, it could logically be targeted as a place where that weakness might be corrected, as when Plotinus discerned in the *Enneads* that the "memory is impeded by the body and addition of many sensible experiences often brings forgetfulness . . . the shifting and fleeting thing which body is can be cause only of its forgetting, not of its remembering."[154] Subsequently, for Avicenna, memory would prove the faculty by means of which pain—the pain of learning—could be accessed. In the *De anima*, he even chose to explain his theory of mnemotechnics with a beating whose pain was appre-

---

[153] In questioning what she calls the debilitating "fear of teaching topos," in which "having taught" becomes synonymous with "having oppressed," Woods stresses the "ageism and academic self-hatred that we support when we accept the suppression of the pedagogical aspects of the history of our profession," "Among Men," 18.

[154] D. Vance Smith offers an insightful discussion of this text from *Enneads*, 283, in "In Place of Memory."

hended by a mnemonic imagination that was itself linked to any corporeal experience:

> One feels pain from a beating (*verbera*) and the accident of pain is in the body [sed dolorem habet propter verbera et propter permutationem complexionis, et hoc accidens habet esse in corpore], while the pain is had in the (internal) senses according to what it means (intention) to sense something whilst the cause of the pain is in the body. . . . Imagination comes from what is apprehended rather than from what is experienced by the body.[155]

Avicenna's mnemonic definition of the imagination explodes any semblance of a distinction between cause and effect, accident and intention, feeling and understanding, container and contained.[156] In fact, when John of Garland precedes his discussion of memory with a victim's voice recounting that his enemy has wounded him and left "marks [*vestigia*] of his livid hatred" (II, 34; 63), John too recognizes how readily such distinctions are blurred at the level of language. "Cause for effect in the phrase 'livid hatred,'" he writes, is appropriate "because hatred is the efficient cause of the wound. . . . There are plenty of other examples which speak for themselves. The genus is put for the species in the sentence 'I bear good arms,' that is, 'sword' or 'knife'; the species for the genus in the sentence, 'The sword shall avenge this crime,' that is, 'some weapon or other'" (II, 37; 73–86).

Insofar as the blurring of those distinctions was one of the hallmarks of torture, it is productive to emphasize the role of memory in the engenderment of violent and spectacular features of didacticism. Teachers who sought to make their imprints upon the minds of impressionable young men also left traces upon their bodies (as a history of anecdotal evidence about corporal punishment makes clear). In the fourth century, no less an authority than Saint Augustine compared the relationship between master and disciple to that of torturer and victim, invoking the actual *tormenta* "which we school-boys suffered from our masters." "Is there any man," he asked,

> who by devoutly applying himself unto thee, is so resolutely affected, that he can think so lightly of those racks and strappadoes, and such varieties of torments [*ut eculeos et ungulas atque huiuscemodi varia tormenta*], (for the avoiding whereof men pray unto thee with so much fear all the world over), that he can make sport at those who most bitterly fear them; as our parents laughed at these torments, which we school-boys suffered from our masters [*quemadmodum parentes nostri*

---

[155] *Avicenna Latinus*, ed. Simone van Riet, IV, 60–61; quoted and discussed in Coleman, *AMM*, 357; emphasis mine. See also Robert Kilwardby on mnemonic "incorporation" in *On Time and Imagination. De Tempore. De Spiritu Fantastico*, 108, sec. 217.

[156] As Umberto Eco contends in an innovative rereading of the Renaissance memory theories of Raymond Llull and Giulio Camillo Delminio, that was a premier function of mnemotechnics itself ("An *Ars Oblivionalis*? Forget It!" 256).

ridebant tormenta, quibus pueri a magistris affligebamur]? For we were no less afraid of the rod, nor did we less earnestly pray to thee for the scaping of it, than others did of their tortures. (*Confessions*, I, 1.9)

Augustine casts pedagogues as punishers and as the transmitters of both torture and truth. His equation of pedagogy, physical punishment, and the violence of the epistemological process bespeaks the quintessentially coercive status of *la question*.

The history of rhetoric forcefully suggests that mnemotechnics has always linked pedagogy with victimization and violence to bodies. Just as the mnemonic alphabet of images employed bodily imagery to "write" upon bodies, the institutional memories that were the province of pedagogy exploited that principle. Pedagogical materials to be remembered were inculcated in the minds of young boys through the presumed assistance of blows on their bodies—all toward the desired end of building masculine characters fruitful to society. And memory was embroiled in the production of physical traces. According to Peter Brown, for example, late Roman education consisted of "a few great authors (Virgil and Cicero in the West, Homer and Demosthenes in the East) [who] were '*burned into the memory*' at an early age in the schools of the grammarians." [157] As late as 1858, Henry Adams complained of the German *gymnasium* that "the arbitrary training given to the memory was stupefying; the strain that the memory endured was a form of torture." [158] As attractive, then, as one might find some of Derrida's work on the originary violence of discourse, the flogged young men of medieval colleges and universities could scarcely have agreed that discourse "can only *do itself violence*, can only negate itself in order to affirm itself, make war upon the war which institutes it without ever *being able* to reappropriate this negativity, to the extent that it is discourse" (*WD*, 130; emphasis his).

A constitutive part of any student's physical and intellectual training, the tortured aspects of "questioning" were pervasive. Not only could any young man come across torture on a daily basis in the law courts. As Peter Brown reminds us, its history infused his scholarly reading matter: "even a school textbook for Latin boys learning Greek included scenes of torture as part of a day in the life of a well-to-do Roman" (*PP*, 52). One such example was provided by Ausonius: "The governor's seat is set up. The judge ascends the tribunal. . . . A guilty brigand is brought in. He is interrogated according to his deserts. He is put to the torture: the torturer lays into him, his chest is constricted; he is hung up, racked, beaten with clubs. He goes through the full cycle of torture. He denies

---

[157] This phrase from Orosius is cited in Brown, *PP*, 39; emphasis mine. See his complete discussion (37–41) of such writers as Basil of Caesarea, Gregory Nazianzen, Libanius, and Orosius.

[158] Henry Adams's remark of 1858 is quoted by Harry Caplan in "Memoria: Treasure-House of Eloquence," 244.

his crime. He is sure to be punished. . . . He is led out and executed." [159] Punitive and fatal even when the crimes it investigates are denied, torture informed the educational cycle and the fear it induced.

For their own part, medieval masters were expert in glossing the signs of that fear, as Geoffrey of Vinsauf implies in his analysis of the plain style: " 'When the boy saw the switch, ruddiness instantly left him and his face was bloodless [*et facies exsanguis erat*].' This appearance signifies that he himself was afraid" ("New Poetics," trans. Kopp, 87–88; 1554–56). They were just as expert, however, in creating the very signs they wished to gloss. Geoffrey's teacher might well have comprehended the signs of fear *before* the beating, when a raised switch warned that only correct answers would be accepted. Other writers would interpret *afterward* the physical traces of those beatings that scarred the beaten student body. When Guibert of Nogent looks back in his *Memoirs* on the experience of being "pelted almost every day with a hail of blows and harsh words" by his schoolmaster, he cannot help but recall the traces that caused his mother to grieve at "the very savage punishment inflicted on my tender body." Mnemonic preservation of the pedagogical experience of violence is figured in the traces left by switches upon the body of the student/victim: "I went to my mother's knee after a more severe beating than I had deserved. And when, as often happened, she began to ask me repeatedly whether I had been whipped that day, I, not to appear a telltale, entirely denied it. Then against my will she threw off my inner garment (which is called a shirt or *chemise*) and saw my little arms blackened and the skin of my back everywhere puffed up with the cuts from the twigs." [160] In that sense, it is an odd turn of events that Guibert's modern editor, John Benton, prefers to see Guibert's experience of torture as internal, going so far as to doubt the veracity of his testimony. "Without impugning Guibert's good faith," avers Benton, "the reader may still conclude that he was all too ready to accept abusive reports uncritically. . . . Like the later work of Vincent van Gogh, his shapes are distorted, his colors are 'unreal,' and he exhibits some of the tortures of a distressed mind" (Benton, 32–33). The landscape of medieval education was not an impressionist painting, and its violence was both internalized and externalized as mnemotechnics "painted" its various traces on the minds and bodies of young men. As Avicenna had demonstrated as well, traces of violently reinforced lessons are figured upon the bodies of victims, whose memories are targeted as a way to build character within a pedagogical space that could truly be violent.

In the same way that all memory images required "an abode, inasmuch as a material object without a locality is inconceivable" (Cicero, *De oratore*, II, 358), so too did pedagogy require an abode, a space in which to set the scene for the

---

[159] Ausonius, cited in Brown, *PP*, 52 in connection with Dionisotti, "From Ausonius' Schooldays?" See also Marjorie Woods on the prevalence of rape narratives in early education, "Rape and the Pedagogical Rhetoric of Sexual Violence," esp. pp. 66–74.

[160] Guibert of Nogent, *Self and Society in Medieval France*, 47, 49–50.

potentially violent inculcation of intellectual and social norms. While Geoffrey of Vinsauf imagined a mnemonic house of composition founded on a tortured inventional process, such a theorist as John of Salisbury deemed that process compatible with a militaristic space for an educational drill. His master is an architect and brutalizer who coaches his students to become proficient in the verbal weaponry of their craft: "In military matters, a commanding officer must first see that his army is properly supplied with arms and other military equipment. The *architect-builder* with his tools first determines and obtains the materials he will use in his construction" (*Metalogicon*, 189; emphasis mine). According to Edward Erdman, Erasmus would later urge in his *Education of a Christian Prince* that "even the schoolroom walls and the fixtures all around the pupils offered lessons about how one should think and behave." [161] It was not enough to hand out precepts, he urged. Rather, lessons were to be "impressed, crammed in, inculcated, and in one way and another kept before him [the student]. . . . They should be engraved on rings, painted in pictures, appended to the wreaths of honor, and, by using any other means by which that age can be interested, kept always before him" (*ECP*, 144–45; Erdman, 2). As the locus for intellectual edification and the building of character, the classroom thus instilled lessons about how medieval teachers and students might have come to understand that violence was, to paraphrase Marshall McLuhan, both the medium and the message of the medieval classroom.[162]

Additionally, the violent and spectacular features of pedagogy were connoted by the term *gymnasium*, which designated the space of learning. Along with its meaning as the privileged locus where athletes trained, the *gymnasium* signified the forum of the public school, high school, or college. It therefore conjures visions of the athletic space of the entire scholastic arena in which students practiced the disputational and declamatory exercises known as *progymnasmata*. Isidore of Seville explained that "school-exercises in virtually all the arts are called *gymnasia*" by analogy to the athlete's *gymnasium*.[163] And Juan Luis Vives even claimed to prefer a rigorous program of physical exercise to sublimate the violent tendencies inspired by such spaces (*De tradendis*, 176).

Medieval education also built character; and, as a host of militaristic analogies illustrate, character building through memory training was a process as violent as it was spectacular. John of Salisbury's architect-builder created a space for the *campidoctor* to "[stack] in the arena arms for the use of his students . . .

---

[161] Erdman, "Imitation Pedagogy and Ethical Indoctrination," 2, discussing Erasmus, *Education of a Christian Prince* (hereafter *ECP*), 144–45.

[162] I refer here to McLuhan and Fiore, *Medium Is the Message*. They even reproduce an article from a Chicago newspaper headed "Develop a Powerful Memory?" including its assurance that the reader is under "no obligation" to buy the advertised materials (115).

[163] *Etymologiarum*, bk. 18, "De ludo gymnico," 17. From the standpoint of theatricality, the athlete is also an anomalous figure, despised by, e.g., Tertullian in *De spectaculis*, chap. 18; and praised by Eusebius in such a martyr as Blandina (*EH*, V, 1.17–19).

[and] to show his disciples how they may use these instruments, and somehow to teach them the art of engaging in [argumentative] combat" (*Metalogicon*, 189). The prevalence of such imagery has motivated such scholars as Walter J. Ong, Emile Durkheim, Alexander Murray, Istvan Hajnal, and Johan Huizinga to spotlight the violent nature of medieval education (although its spectacular nature is clearly just as important).[164] Ong argues from the works of Augustine, Aelfric, and Aquinas that the entire medieval university functioned as an intellectual battlefield that was as ceremonial as it was contentious: "programmed as a form of ritual male combat centered on disputation" in which boys went to school "to war ceremonially with each other (and with the teacher)" (*RRT*, 17–18). Huizinga contends that medieval law, warfare, literature, and philosophy fused "glorious exhibitionism and agonistic aspiration" (*HL*, 146). Durkheim jogs our memory with the statement that by about 1450, " 'people even reached the point where they kicked, punched and bit one another.' Wounded and dead were left lying on the floor" (trans. Collins, 142). And, at the beginning of our own century, John Burnet protested that a militaristic register of pedagogy had never really lost ground: "to face a boy who has had no sufficient drill, with Homer and Virgil, is . . . as wicked as to send an untrained recruit into the firing-line."[165]

Furthermore, athletics, theatricality, pedagogy, and violence were exemplified by the powerful figure of the master himself, who stood center stage. One of his missions was to ensure that boys would remember their lessons well enough that the speech engendered from their mnemonic repositories would conform to social class. So it is that John of Garland locates the teacher at the second of the three columns he describes in the *Parisiana poetria*. The first column is occupied by "courtiers, city dwellers, and peasants," while the third monumentalizes the reconstitution of sound by housing "all kinds of languages, sounds, and voices of the various living creatures, etymologies, explanations of words, distinctions between words, all in alphabetical order" (II, p. 37, 106–10). Standing impressively between those two columns is the teacher, who operates almost as a human shifter between them. His very person reminds students of what they have read and learned as he comes to represent what he has taught them:

> The second part or column should be imagined as containing, in separate compartments, examples and sayings and facts from the authors, and the teachers from whom we heard them, and the books in which we have read them. If memory should fail us on some point, we must then call to mind the time, be it vivid or hazy, when we learned it, the place [*locus*] in which, the teacher from whom, his dress,

---

[164] I refer here to Ong, *RRT*; Durkheim, *EP*, esp. chaps. 12 and 13; Murray, *Reason and Society*; Hajnal, *L'Enseignement de l'écriture aux universités médiévales*; and Huizinga, *HL*. For classical antecedents, see also Gleason, "Semiotics of Gender," 404.

[165] Burnet's statement of 1929 is cited in Caplan, "Memoria," 245.

his gestures, the books in which we studied it, the page—was it white or dark?—the position on the page and the colors of the letters; because all these will lead to the things that we want to remember and select. (*Parisiana poetria*, II, 37; 98–105).

Such well-demarcated spaces served not only to "engender speech" but to re-engender the entire scenic context in which pedagogical communication takes place. Moreover, within the memory columns of that pedagogical space, the teacher is directly connected to the pages of his book, an association that would be given literal expression in a particularly fascinating image from Thomas Murner's *Logica memorativa* or *Chartiludium logice* (*Mnemonic Logic* or *Logical Card Game*), first published in 1509.

A Franciscan religious satirist and anti-Lutheran writer, Murner (1475–1537) reworked Peter of Spain's thirteenth-century *Summulae logicales* into an emblematized memory game, approximately one-third of which consists of woodcut illustrations.[166] The work begins with a glossary of signs designed to assist the reader in glossing text and pictures: a sleigh bell signifying an enunciation, a lobster a predicable, a fish a predicament, a syllogism an acorn, a coronet a fallacy, and so on. But, as Ong points out, when that key is used to interpret the violent memory image of a schoolmaster holding three bundles of switches, the pedagogical repercussions are "terrifying" (*RRT*, 125)—all the more so in that the virtual violence suggested by the images is not only desirable but playful. In an interplay between orality, literacy, and textuality which is well known to medievalists, Murner's book becomes a visual reminder of the experience of learning. Akin to the common iconographic depiction of the Master of Grammar with whips in hand, Murner's pedagogue holds a whip that is ready to fall and mark the bodies of his students who will be coerced into remembering their lessons.[167]

For Murner's destined readers—the "soft youth" of his generation—the image of the schoolmaster is to be glossed as follows: the weight in his hand is an affirmative proposition, the cord a negative proposition, the birds of different species propositions with no common term, and most relevant here, the three switches signify three questions to be imprinted on and rehearsed within the memory: "What? What kind? and How many?" When Murner affirms that "it is with the aid of the switches that the answers to these questions are extracted from the pupils" (triplici virga: triplex esse quesitium nam virgis iuvenes inquirimus), his terms are reminiscent of the definition of torture from the Justinian *Digest* as "torment and corporeal suffering and pain employed to extract the truth" from the body of the victim.[168] In this pedagogical invocation of

---

[166] Rarely treated by historians of rhetoric, Murner's text is discussed briefly in Ong, *RRT*, 125; and at greater length in his *Ramus, Method, and the Decay of Dialogue* (hereafter *RMDD*), 83–91. Peter of Spain was a contemporary of Aquinas who had also studied with Albert the Great at Paris.

[167] For a discussion of the medieval and Renaissance *magister* of grammar, "always represented armed with switches," see Durkheim, *Evolution pédagogique*, 198–99.

[168] Murner, *Logica memorativa*, fols. Bv^v–Bvi^r, quoted in English in Ong, *RRT*, 125. The *Logica memorativa* is also available in a facsimile edition (Nieuwkoop: Miland, 1967). See Justinian, *Digest*, 47.10.15.41. Relevant to the anti-Semitic register of some early pedagogies and their the-

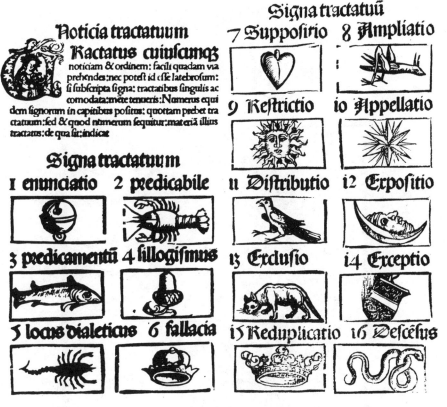

The Logical Card Game. From Thomas Murner, *Logica memorativa.* Courtesy of the Newberry Library, Chicago.

memory, interrogation, beating, and extraction, Murner's woodcut becomes more than a memory image: it is a spectacular memory image of torture or, rather, an image of spectacular torture as the ultimate mnemonic. The "rule of the rod" is itself cast as an *ars memorandi* which is menacing and disciplinary, literally dependent on the whip or *disciplina.* As the schoolmaster incarnates textually the fear felt by Augustine and read in the bloodless young faces evoked by Geoffrey of Vinsauf, he wields his switches as one who is empowered to beat the "truth" not only *out of* but *in to* the bodies of his students— his intended audience, his intended victims.

For Ong, this woodcut constitutes a "curious logical development" in the rise of print culture insofar as Murner's "rules are associated with various designs in ways calculated to *beat* the terms and rules into little boys' heads if not

atricality is a plate in Murner's *Die Entehrung Mariae durch die Juden* depicting a Jew undergoing judicial torture by means of the same weight that is held by Murner's schoolmaster. These images appear in Hsia, *Myth of Ritual Murder* (25, 27, 28), although they are not analyzed.

Primus

Applicatio tertia

The Master of Grammar. From Thomas Murner, *Logica memorativa.*
Courtesy of the Newberry Library, Chicago.

really to teach any genuinely formal logic" (*RMDD*, 85). Even so, it harks back to the rhetorical theory of torture, which was likewise bent on discovering a verisimilar scenario for the construction of a "truth" already known in advance by the torturer. Much as the conception and practice of *la question* had become more punitive than interrogatory, so too did the conception and practice of pedagogy. That view is borne out by scholars of antiquity and the Middle Ages alike. Ong observes of the conflictual tenor of medieval pedagogy, for instance, that "there is evidence that the specifically initiatory cast of the punishment grew more intense and evident" (*RRT*, 124). Distinct antecedents also survive in the "pedagogy" that wealthy Romans had once practiced violently on the bodies of their slaves—presumably as a means of bettering them. According to Saint Basil, "it is involuntary also if a person with a desire of punishing another should beat him with a strap or a pliant rod and he should die from the beating. For . . . he wished to improve the offender, not to kill him." [169] Those "good intentions" were not thwarted by the occasional death of the victims, the alleged recipients of the beneficence.

Still, if Murner's image of the schoolmaster privileges violent process over intellectual content, then one might well wonder what precisely the image teaches, then and now. Among its first lessons is the debunking of a kind of modern myth about nonviolent pedagogies. Even though, at some level, mnemotechnics has consistently addressed the infliction of intentional violence, violence nowadays is nonetheless viewed as "unnatural" to the objective of teaching. Given the ubiquity of salubrious pedagogical violence in early western societies, it is appropriate to ask how the postmedieval world came to substitute for that historical reality the illusion that peaceable dialogue has always been preferable to corporal punishment and violent indoctrination.

Recently, Peter Haidu has exposed the myth of nonviolent pedagogy in the following terms. Whereas the medieval illusion is that violence is salubrious, the contemporary illusion is that the violence of the educational process constitutes an aberration; peace is natural, the "desired and desirable norm"; and violence is its "negativized opposite" (*SV*, 3). Elsewhere, in a reevaluation of the modern tendency to celebrate dialogue over brainwashing, James Berlin identifies a contemporary revisionist fable according to which dialogue has forever been the best and only way to learn: "disruptions in this trajectory [of dialectic] . . . are to be explained away as the products of failed cultures—the most frequently named being that of the Middle Ages and the nineteenth century." [170] Clearly, there was nothing peaceable, dialogic, nor necessarily failed about Murner's schoolmaster with his bundle of switches. Nor could such a scholar as Durkheim refrain from the reluctant acknowledgement that it has

---

[169] Basil, *Epistles*, 188, cited in Brown, *PP*, 52. In fact, Brown reminds us that "deaths of slaves through beating were frequent enough to be cited as usual examples of manslaughter."

[170] James Berlin reevaluates that tendency in the rhetorical scholarship of George Kennedy, Edward Corbett, and Brian Vickers in "Revisionary Histories of Rhetoric," 113.

rather been the efforts to replace early pedagogical violence with something more effective that have failed. One cannot destroy "the whole piece of antique machinery" without finding "other means of stimulating the enthusiasm of the pupils. But why should we fail where the Middle Ages succeeded? Why should the education that we offer be less capable of arousing and sustaining the interest and curiosity of the pupils than the stringent and crude dialectic of medieval Scholasticism?" (trans. Collins, 160).

Since violence was plainly a "natural" part of inventional epistemology and since, by dint of its own foundational narratives, mnemotechnics has always been concerned with the infliction of violence, it is surprising that the violence of the various enactments of classroom rhetoric could have come to be perceived as "unnatural." Be that as it may, from antiquity to the present, powerful discourses against violence steadfastly indict the same violence that societies seem to require. Violence in the classroom is deemed transgressive—notwithstanding the contradictions provided by each daily disclosure in the evening news of beatings, rapes, and abuses in American elementary, secondary, and postsecondary schools. To borrow Girard's general formulation, "if the sacrificial crisis is a universal phenomenon, this hopeful belief [that nonviolent desire is the norm] is clearly without foundation" (*VS*, 144). Civilized societies depend on such hopeful beliefs about the transgressive status of violence. Indeed, it is not so surprising that an intellectual subculture would prefer pathos and empathy to brutality. After all, moral philosophers have traditionally exalted the virtues of compassion and community—however violent their origins. If the explicitly coercive register of pedagogy were acknowledged, those hopes would vanish and Derrida's worst fear would be realized: "the horizon of peace would disappear into the night" (*WD*, 130). Outrage against school violence would become the illusion, since one of its functions is to secure the myth of a nonviolent pedagogy.

In the Middle Ages, a primary epistemological site at which moral and aesthetic responses to learning were constructed and perpetuated violently was the rhetorical memory. As such, it inspires further "lessons" about pedagogical violence in connection with the following phenomena: the distinction between men and women as beneficiaries of violent instruction; and the theatrical representations of on-stage teaching as violent, frightening, and coercive yet pleasurable, playful, and edifying.

Regarding the first phenomenon of gendered learning, the commonplace wisdom of the Middle Ages, of course, was that violence was "good for men." The *magister*'s mnemonic methods of impressing lessons upon his charges, his power to translate the virtual violence of those methods into the actual violence of corporal punishment, his military might and brute physical force were more than beneficial: they were loving. So it is that the same Vives who portrays pedagogues as the birth mothers of their students suckling on Cicero does so without neglecting for a moment the father–son relationship, which he correlated to that of master–disciple: "Thus the son is so devoted to his father by influence and authority that he loves and reverences him, and would not think it right to wish not to reverence him. *The rod of discipline will be constantly raised before the eyes of the boy* and around his back, for it has been wisely declared by Solomon that it is specially good for that age, and extremely salutary" (*De tradendis*, 71; emphasis mine). Although there is no doubt about the highly coercive register of the mnemonic techniques that were harnessed to the schooling of young men, the status of women as possessors of memory and as objects of mnemonic indoctrination was quite different.

As men assimilated the "birthing" dimension of mnemonics, male writers reiterated the important connection between gendered memories and gendered pedagogies. And as the classroom became a locus of spectacular torment, display, and discipline, early pedagogues constructed highly problematic distinctions between men and women as the recipients of education. In addition to such obvious pronouncements by the likes of Vives that woman was to be denied the right to teach young boys "lest when she hath taken a false opinion . . . she spread it into the hearers, by the authority of mastership," all the salubrious aggressivity of pedagogy takes on erotic connotations.[171] That eroticism, existing first among men, ultimately excluded women.

Guibert de Nogent, for example, offers a deliberate contrast between a less desirable male/female love and a more desirable *saevus amor* or male/male love, praised by Virgil and Ovid before him. Guibert professes gratitude for his professorial tormentors. Their cruel and unjust behaviour even engender within him feelings of love for their loving violence—a violence that is ultimately forgotten. His teacher, recollects Guibert,

> had a *harsh love* for me, for he showed excessive severity in his unjust floggings, and yet the *great care* with which he guarded me was evident in his acts. Clearly I did not deserve to be beaten, for if he had had the skill in teaching which he professed, it is certain that I, though a boy, would have been well able to grasp anything that he taught. . . . I conceived much love for him in response, in spite of the many weals with which he furrowed my tender skin, so that not through fear, as is common in those of my age, but through a sort of love deeply implanted in my heart, I obeyed him *in utter forgetfulness* of his severity. (Guibert, 48–49; emphasis mine)[172]

Pedagogical violence is so "good for men" that it facilitates a needed yet counterintuitive outcome of any mnemonic process. Pain stimulates the memory enough to help a student recall his lessons; but, thanks to a sublimated sexual love between student and teacher, that pain is reconfigured as a love which casts into oblivion the very pain that spurs remembrance.

[171] See Joan Gibson's discussion of Vives in "Educating for Silence," 18–19.
[172] A queer reading of *saevus amor* lies beyond the scope of this book.

Even so, Guibert represents his mother as an impediment to his education, while he simultaneously lauds the cruel love of his teacher. When she discovers the traces of her son's classroom beating upon his body, Guibert goes so far as to criticize her maternal pity. Naive about the nature of intellectual indoctrination, Guibert's mother is, moreover, a poor reader of signs since she is unable to interpret the welts upon his body as indicative of salubrious violence: "Troubled, agitated, and weeping with sorrow, she said: 'You shall never become a clerk, nor any more suffer so much to get an education.' At that, looking at her with what reproach I could, I replied, 'If I had to die on the spot, I would not give up studying my lessons and becoming a clerk'" (*Guibert*, 50). The role of Guibert's mother is limited to that of comforter even as the importance of comfort is denied. She incarnates the same feminine or effeminate traits that Murner's whip-bearing schoolmaster would later threaten to expunge.

When Murner reconceives the rule of the rod as a cultural tool by which to purge society of an undesirably "soft male youth," he effects a complex epistemological move that depends on the reconfiguration of unacceptable male traits as feminine or effeminate.[173] Should a young boy display weakness or lack of discipline, his "softness" is called feminine so that an undesirable aspect of his own masculinity may be considered alien when it is not. Re-envisioned as feminine, his softness can then be beaten out at the same time that a more condoned view of masculinity is beaten in. Thus, when Murner reforms the memory by means of the body, he does far more than presage René Girard's theories of "good violence," which depends on surrogate victims who enable societies to fantasize violence as ritualized, "creative and protective in nature" (*VS*, 144). In accordance with an ideal of love for one's "fellow man," he stresses that such necessary cultural illusions as civilization, creativity, goodness, and protection depend on erasing feminine characteristics. Despite other cultural/courtly codes advocating the protection of women, the implication here is that the best and most "natural" way to ensure the continuation of civilization is to beat up on the feminine and, by extension, on the women, who are not even configured as an audience of Murner's book.

Woman's role as comforter survives nonetheless—enough, anyway, to be reconfigured as a male virtue. However defective, denigrated, or discounted the source of comfort may be, young men are indeed comforted by their mothers and surrogate mothers, as when Guibert is virtually suckled on his mother's knee. No such comfort was available to a female charge such as Heloise, whom Abelard identifies in the *Historia calamitatum* as someone "fortunate" enough to be considered a pupil. When the objectified girl is passed from her uncle to her teacher (her future husband), she becomes the victim of pedagogical violence. But instead of receiving comfort, it is she who furnishes sexual comfort

---

[173] This is the subject of my "Delivering Delivery," although it is connected here to the various visions of purgation and pathology invoked earlier.

to her abuser as Abelard transmutes the violence he inflicts upon her memory and body into his personal comforting vision of erotic love:

> For when he handed her over to me not only to teach but to discipline, what else was he doing but giving free rein to my designs, and opportunity, even if I were not seeking it, easily to subdue her by threats and stripes if blandishments did not work . . . ? And the better to prevent suspicion, I sometimes struck her not through anger or vexation but from love and affection which were beyond the sweetness of every ointment. No sign of love was omitted by us. . . .[174]

A violent quest for knowledge need not be as violent as Caligula's blending of love, torture, and the threat of death or cruelty toward women to be real. "Whenever he kissed the neck of his wife or sweetheart," writes Suetonius, "he would say: 'Off comes this beautiful head whenever I give the word' [Tam bona *cervix* simul ac iussero demetur]. He even used to threaten now and then that he would resort to torture [*fidiculis*] if necessary, to find out from his dear Caesonia why he loved her so passionately" (Suetonius, *LS*, "Caligula," chap. 33).

Seen from all these perspectives, a revisionist reading of mnemotechnics actually challenges some of the more optimistic modern readings of the medieval construction of gender. For example, while Carruthers gleans from her interpretation of Heloise that all subjectivity is located in the memory (*BM*, 180–82), the female memory remains elusive insofar as female subjectivity has itself been objectified.[175] Even Martin Irvine's philologically rich reading of Abelard empowers Heloise in a way that is perhaps too hopeful. He finds that she "refuses to be a mere addressee/reader" and becomes "a fully empowered feminine *litteratus*—as grammatically impossible as that phrase may seem—who constructs a voice from the kinds of gendered subjectivity provided by medieval discourse."[176] The oxymoron is more than grammatical: there can be no such thing as objectified subjectivity. And even if there could be, even if medieval theorists could accept that oxymoron, one need not let it pass uncritically today—especially when faced with Andreas Capellanus's analogy of woman to "melting wax, always ready to assume fresh shape and to be moulded to the imprint of anyone's seal" (*On Love*, bk. 3, p. 313, 83–84). His invocation of the traditional mnemonic wax tablet denies to woman the very possession of a memory on which to "write" the lessons of the hegemony. She is not an intellect who endures a mnemonic thrashing but a neutralized mnemonic receptacle on which men inscribe and enact their lessons.

From the classroom beatings endured by Heloise, to the domestic violence of farce, to the prosecution and persecution of witches, to the literal bridling of

---

[174] Abelard, *Historia calamitatum*, 28.

[175] See also Kamuf, *Fictions of Feminine Desire*, Introduction and chap. 1; and the general introduction to the topic by Stephanie Jed in *Chaste Thinking*.

[176] Irvine, "Literate Subjectivity and Conflicting Gender Positions," 107.

the gossip's tongue by means of such a gendered implement of torture as the brank, few things compare to the violence inflicted on woman.[177] Her body is beaten into passivity or oblivion as her memory is eroticized, ridiculed, trivialized, and even demonized. For male students, the purpose of the *disciplina* was to engender speech in the service of the hegemony. The thrashings to which they are subjected enable them to speak, to teach, to act in society. For female students, the same writers who catalog the history of pedagogy conceive beatings as a means to silence, neutralize, and eroticize women, and even to prefigure future violence against them.

Male-on-male violence is healthy, generative, even loving. Male-on-female violence is still generative: but what it generates is the notion that violence is good for women because it is good for men as erotic release. In other words, the male student is both target and targeter, while the female student tends to remain the person targeted. Indeed, even when it is woman who inflicts violence, she does so in the context of the popular or vernacular learning chronicled in such a work as the *Miracles de Saint Louis*. In the story of the deaf-mute cited earlier, the poor lad is subjected to the strict educational discipline of his charwoman/mistress who is "kind enough" to take charge of his upbringing in her kitchen after Louis has miraculously cured him: "Et pour ce qu il apreist a parler ele le mist en sa cuisine, por ce que il fust avec pluseurs, et commanda que il fust enseignié a parler. De quoi cil de la cuisine l'enseignierent en nommant li certaines choses chascun jour, et se il ne les seust nommer l'endemain, *il estoit batu, ausi comme les enfanz sont batus as escoles quant il ne sevent leur leçons.* (And because he learned to talk, she put him in her kitchen, so that he might be with others; and she saw to it that he was taught to speak. Thus, those working in the kitchen taught him by naming several things for him each day, and if he were unable to name them the next day, he was beaten, just as children are beaten in school when they do not know their lessons.)[178]

Therefore, while both men and women endure verbal and physical violence, the male students on whom the lessons of the hegemony are marked are more than victims: they are also future victimizers who inscribe lessons violently and sexually. In the same way that some memory imagery of the body helped early theorists to isolate persons, groups, or races who most deserved to be beaten, it assisted them in rehearsing distinctions about who most deserved to possess the power to inflict violence. The male body and memory are tormented so that young boys may wield the weapons of their trade. They are the militaristic "builders" described by John of Salisbury, the future teachers, future punishers, future inflicters of beatings upon future generations of boys who seek to enter

---

[177] I address the topic of a gendered memory at greater length in "Violence, Silence, and the Memory of Witches." For a full, illustrated treatment of the brank, see Andrews, *Old-Time Punishments*, 38–64.

[178] Guillaume de Saint-Pathus, *Miracles de Saint Louis*, 54. Of course, here the brutalizing teacher is a woman.

the community into which the master had already been initiated. A young man might all the more readily grow up to be the victimizer from his personal knowledge of the traces flogged into his body and memory. He could continue the cycle of violence and sexuality by going on to beat his own students or, as the occasional author of a medieval or Renaissance farce has it, his wife or mistresses.

If gendered theories of pedagogy provided one site at which writers attributed a positive valence to violence, dramatic practice was another. In fact, all the above allusions to memory suggest the ease with which a coercive mnemonic image of pedagogy might readily be transformed into a dramatic one. That returns us to the pedagogical resonances of the virtual performativity of any memory image. Murner's teacher stands ready to mark the minds of his future readers and even to revive the pain of any traces that might endure on their bodies. He promises or threatens a beating—the visible traces of which might later be left by the whip on such a student body as that of Guibert de Nogent. As such, he is no "voiceless effigy" (*IO*, VI, 1.32) but an image that speaks, acts, threatens, and marks. An image like Murner's school-master—even in a printed book—might thus serve as a program for performance as well as a site at which to preserve past performances. The student in whom traces are dormant eventually recalls their effects all the better when he inflicts them as a teacher.

Pedagogically speaking, mnemotechnics aimed specifically to foster the translation from virtual to actual performance, from image to speech, from mental and even printed image to action. So it stands to reason that such translations might occur not only in textbooks and in classrooms but on the stage. In the violent didacticism of a genre like the mystery play, numerous scourging scenes memorialize dramatically the rule of the rod. The converse is equally plausible: if violent memory images of virtual performance could be translated into the speaking visions of the medieval and Renaissance stage, so too might violent theatrical imagery originating on the stage have gone on to inform the spectacle of pedagogy. Whether the arena was the classroom, the stage, or the stage of the world, *memoria* offered a deeply entrenched epistemology of violence with a performative potential in teaching that enhances our understanding of the medieval theater of cruelty.

In that sense, while Kubiak attributes to Bertolt Brecht the development of an equivalency between "seeing and the violence of language . . . in an almost seamless iconographic interplay of the visual with the enunciative" (*ST*, 64), antiquity and the Middle Ages had already identified the phenomenon in the *artes memorandi* that mediated between the visual and the enunciative and between image and delivered performance. Correspondingly, since memory is the canon that rehearses and enacts virtual violence, it nullifies some of the implicit distinctions posited by Deleuze and Guattari between a memory of words (*paroles*) and signs as opposed to a memory of things and effects (*Anti-Oedipus*, 144). Its routine violence extends beyond rhetoric, law, and theology to establish strong connections to medieval drama and pedagogy, where its tortures, catharses, and spectacular enactments were staged to the horror and glee of the public.

When it comes to the ubiquitous dramatic renditions of violence, it cannot be overemphasized that Murner's heavy-handed schoolmaster and his predecessors are part of a much larger conception of the pedagogical mnemonic as an edifying and enjoyable game—beatings included. As it happens, early dramatists repeatedly staged precisely those sorts of instructive "fun and games" in the Passion of Christ, the ordeals of saints, and even the farcical portrayals of university life. In all those genres, the performative potential of violent memory images of teaching made for good learning, good entertainment, and good drama. Especially in the theater, which retained its connections to torture and catharsis, the horrible dart games, dice, dances, and blind man's bluff display a whole array of the sights and sounds of the body in pain.

As we saw in Chapter 1, the French dramatic tradition is uncommonly rich in that respect, for the status of torture as memory game is consistently reinforced by the philological interplay between *batre* and *ebatre*. By far the greatest resonances with the master of grammar and his whips may be noticed when Christ's tormentors inflict His beating as a game. In the Sainte Geneviève *Passion*, the torturers associate *compter* (counting) with its homonym, *conter* (storytelling) as one chants, "Jhesu, tien ce cop a la chance! / Qui t'a feru? Car le me conpte!" (Jesus, try this blow on for size! Who hit you? Give me your account!) (1602–03). As if Murner's mnemonically inclined schoolmaster had been transformed into a metronome, audiences of several Passion plays witnessed another sort of rhythmic scourging of Christ, complete with the technical counting of beats on his body. The torturers who wish to be remembered count out the beats as if they were cuing a modern-day band: "Empreuf. / Et deux. / Et trois. / Et quatre. / et le cinquieme de surcois" (And one. And two. And three. And four. And the fifth for good measure) (Gréban, 22803–13).[179] Gréban's torturers alternate in a singsong fashion between chanting and scourging: "Ça, des verges! / Combien? / Deux paire; / les miennes ne vallent plus rien" (Hey, the whips! How many? Two pair; mine aren't worth anything anymore) (22769–76); and Pilate himself comes in with a refrain as he gives the order "Frappez fort, frappez, ribaudaille! / Homme ne se mecte en *oubly*! / Vous sembl'il donc que je luy faille? / Frappez fort, frappez, ribaudaille!" (Strike, strike, you scum! Let no one forget! You think I'm failing him [in this game]? Strike, strike, you scum!) (22755–762).[180] Malque of the Auvergne *Passion* is nothing if not explicit as he initiates the deadly count:

> Et ung et deux! Ton cas s'empire!
> Et trois et quatre! Est il mort?

[179] See also the Mons *Passion*, p. 330.

[180] See ibid., 292, where the torturers also invoke the mnemonic idea of the *coppie*; and the counting game for the robe in the Auvergne *Passion*, 2657–776.

Sirus
Nany; il faut fraper plus fort.
Cinq, six, vij, viij, ix, x, xj!

Malbec
Il est mort; de riens ne fait compte!
Toutesfoiz luy donrey je ung cop.
(Auvergne *Passion*, 3335–40)

And one and two! Your case is getting worse!
And three and four! is he dead yet?
Nay, nay: you've got to hit harder.
Five, six, seven, eight, nine, ten, eleven!
He's dead; he takes no heed of anything
But I'll give him another blow anyway.

While Rosemary Woolf has compared such scenes to the nursery-rhyme counting of "one, two, buckle my shoe" (255), it is imperative to recall here that one critical function of any nursery rhyme is pedagogical.[181] Its easy tempos, rhymes, rhythms, and refrains are designed to facilitate memorization of the most basic social lessons.

Such "lessons" were recognizable, moreover, in the realm of a farce like *Martin de Cambray* or the contemporaneous *Farce de Goguelu*. The entire plot of the latter play revolves around the reversal of victims and agents—another sine qua non of the ideology of torture.[182] On stage first is Goguelu's chambermaid-girlfriend, whose role is to open the action by being beaten by their blind master. On stage last is the blind master, whose role is to close the action when Goguelu and his gal pal avenge themselves by "playfully" punishing him with a beating of their own. Like the torturers in the Passion play, the pair enjoy the ludic process of correction and redress. "Esbatons-nous à quelque jeu" (381), she says as they lie in wait; and her paramour responds "A quel jeu sera / Que nous jourons encependant / Qu'i va par ce bois esbatant, / Dictes?" (Let's play a little game. And what game will it be that we'll play while he goes a-frolicking through the woods? Tell me, do) (386–89). When they wield their switches, the language that accompanies the farcical beating is virtually identical to that of the rhythmic scourgings of Christ—and then some: "Je commance encore à vous batre: / Enpreu, et deux, et trois, et quatre, / Et cinq, et six, et sept, et huyt. / A vous batre prendray deduit, / Neuf, dix, XI, XII., treze, / Estes-vous present à vostre aise?" (I'm going to start beating you again: And one, and two, and three, and four, and five, and six, and seven, and eight. I'm going to have a blast

---

[181] Woolf, *English Mystery Plays*, 254–55. See also Eric Havelock's treatment of musicality, rhythm, and nursery rhyme in *Greek Concept of Justice*, 25–27 and chap. 3.

[182] The *Farce de Goguelu* appears in Cohen, ed. *Receuil*, pp. 357–67, ll. 499–504. *Martin de Cambray* is the play in which the female sex partner is made of wax. See ibid., 415–17.

beating you. Nine, ten, eleven, twelve, thirteen. Comfy now?) (499–504). Their vengeance complete, both servants are pleased with the lesson they have imposed. So when they state, "Il a receu, / Ce croy, bonne discipline" (524–25), that phrase exploits the multiple connotations of the term *discipline*: the master has been disciplined, he has "learned his lesson," he has been taught well, he has gotten a good beating, and he has felt the good whip. In the end, the unnamed female character, initially the real victim of unjustified violence from her socioeconomic superior, becomes the complicitous agent in the beating of a blind man played for laughs. Pity and fear are subsumed by fun and games—in this case, on the backs of women and the infirm.

The rule of the rod is thus a great game which is executed by dramatists who oscillate relentlessly between violence and play and between physical and intellectual discipline. Likewise in the mystery play, Christ's torturers endeavor to "teach Him a lesson" on behalf of their hegemony as they themselves become the subject of the Christian dramatist's lesson. For example, Marquin and Haquin of the Sainte Geneviève *Passion* invite Christ to join in the fun by learning their game and by guessing the author of the blows He endures: "Nous te voulons *endoctriner*; / Mais il te convient deviner/ Qui t'a donné sy gros chopin" (We want to teach you; but you've gotta guess who has given you such a great big clobbering). "Bien ly plaist ce *jeu* a aprendre," they continue, "Fier fort! Il a la char trop tendre. / Qui t'a feru, roy? Car parole!" (Strike hard! He's just a tenderfoot. Who has struck you, king? Tell us, do!). And they offer this additional insight: "Il a esté a *bonne escole*! . . . / Il n'est pas hors de nos dengiers; / En nostre *jeu* moult se delite" (He's been well schooled [and] he's not out of danger from us yet; he's enjoying our little game a lot) (1605–18). Similarly, Jesus of the Amboise play speaks of his memory of a dismembering dice game played upon his body. It had been foretold by King David: "Or est du tout fait en verité / Que dist David en son dicté: / Que mes os *demembreroient* / Et ma robe *aux dez* joueroient" (They would dismember my bones and play a dice game for my robe) (Amboise *Passion*, 728–31) (emphases mine).

Occasionally the entire mnemonic scene is transposed into the register of the classroom, as when Gréban's torturer Broyefort inquires as to the proper weapon of chastisement to be wielded against Christ. Brayart responds that "Ce n'est point cy pour le pugnir: / verges ne sont que pour enfans. / A telz ribaulz gros et puissans / il faut bien restrainctes plus fortes" (This here isn't what you need to punish him! Whips are for kids. For big, strong jokers like this, you need much stronger restraints) (Gréban, 22787–90). In the Troyes *Passion*, Estonné mocks Christ's status as pedagogue: "Sus, troussez avant, *magister*! / Vous venrés sermonner ailleurs" (Go on, step right up, *magister*! You'll come preach elsewhere) (II, t. 2, 7233–34). A little later, the metaphor has a twist: "A peu se scet il remouvoir; / Est il en poinct pour sermonner? / Il ne se sçaroit demener, / tant est sarré pres du *pillier*" (He can barely move; is he in any state to preach? He can't even budge, he's bound so tightly to the pillar) (t. 2, 7752–55). Elsewhere, during the persecution of Saint Denis in the *Cycle des Premiers Martyrs*, Denis's beating is likened to that of a recalcitrant student who has outdone his professors. A stage direction calls for the bedeviled saint to be shown to his new "classroom," a prison cell (*En moustrant la chartre*). "Va rimachier en celle escole," cheer his enemies (Go do your doggerel in this here school) (*GSD*, 572) (emphases mine).

In the histories of both torture and pedagogy, investigation becomes punishment—just as it does for the thugs of religious drama. Not only do they alter the initial investigative mission of *la question* as the ostensible discovery of information into a quest for punishment, but their questioning-as-punishment is aesthetic, entertaining, and liberally interspersed with comic relief. A scornful Menjumatin proceeds in much the same way, adding excessive mockery to the violence of his lesson: "Vecy, veez dan chie-en-escole / Qui scet trop bien gens escorchier. / Je vueil son cul breneus torchier / (*En ferant*)" (Here you go, Mr. Shitter-in-school, who know so well how to gouge folks. I want to clean out his own turdy asshole [*striking*]) (*GSD*, 992–94). Even so, all their grim pedagogy presents a stark contrast to another moment in the life of Christ which is represented with comparable frequency in the mystery play.

The young Jesus appears as the model student during his debates with the doctors, praised in the *Mystère de la Résurrection* from Angers by Cleophas as follows: "Oncques si amoureux enffant, / Si doulx, si begnin ne si saige, / Ne de si gracïeulx langaige / Ne fut, car jusqu'a l'ame rendre / Tousjours povoit on bien aprendre / Par frequenter en ses escoles" (Never has there been such a loving child, so sweet, so kind, or so wise, or with such gracious language because, for all one's days, one could always learn well by frequenting his school) (Angers I, 11682–87). Christ's verbal victory against the Romans is an intellectual feat; and the physical indignities he will endure at their hands represent the dark underside of the same pedagogy. In the *Conversion Saint Pol*, a violent beating occurs after Roman torturers mock learned Christians for being poor students:

> Qui est ce fol qui la parole?
> Est ce ore histoire ou parabole,
> Dont il va ainssy sermonnant?
> Sachiez, c'est .i. cristicole,
> Qui a prins leçon a l'escole,
> Dont il va ainssy gergonnant.
> (*CPM*, 653–58)

Who is this nut who's speaking? Is it now some new story or parable that he's a-going sermonizing? Just know that's it's one of those Christers again who took lessons in school that he's running around telling in his jargon.

In all the examples above, mnemonic "facilitation" is violent and dramatic. Furthermore, such brutal instructional activities help the didactic dramatist to inscribe on the collective memory of his audiences a message of his own about Christian discipline.

Ultimately, the emphasis in many scourging scenes on invention, memory, and pedagogy incorporates within the Passion play all the anomalies of torture: in particular, its self-contradictory position in the rhetorical tradition as both factual and emotional, extrinsic and intrinsic, desired and despised. In their own way, the scourging scenes of early drama translate a memory of violence into a performance, which is then memorable enough to be reconsigned to the memory. But in the final analysis, if that is one of the principal anomalies of the countless didactic representations of the life of Christ, it is an anomaly shared by the violent mnemotechnics of medieval schoolmasters, who raised their rods in order to beat lessons *into* and *out of* a Christian public for its own good. Both spectacular modes of pedagogical violence betray the same self-contradictions inherent in the rhetoric that undergirds the theory of torture. Additionally, as the Christian dramatist harnesses those ignoble means to his noble ends, his answers to the following questions would have been known in advance. Why are Romans and Jews insidious when they raise their staffs against Christ, while the medieval French Bishop is virtuous when he is empowered to force men to accept Christ through flogging?[183] Why are the torturers of Christ poor teachers while the playwright who stages their sinister pedagogical practices is presumably a good teacher? And just what manner of message are they all beating *into* or *out of* their victims, their audiences, and even their twentieth-century readers and critics?

Late medieval religious writings sketch answers to those questions that are more complex than the critical commonplace of "violence was everywhere." They offer (or seem to offer) some happy endings about commemoration, civilization, and empathic audience response. Indeed, if they did not, a quintessential paradox of memory would remain unaltered, and that art could but continue to alternate between the desire to remember and the need to forget (or the need to remember and the desire to forget).

That paradox has proved particularly appealing of late in modern (if not postmodern) approaches to rhetoric and theater. For example, when placed under the critical scrutiny of Lynn Worsham, even Roland Barthes's thorough essay on "The Old Rhetoric: An *Aide-mémoire*" is transfigured into a more deeply felt critical wish to forget. For Worsham, Barthes's goal to expose rhetoric as "the desire for social control exercised through and imposed by language" is severely compromised by his choice to "[seal] Rhetoric's fate by placing it in the past as the dead art of an equally dead object, to be remembered only long enough to be forgotten. In this light, the title of his lecture notes—'The Old

---

[183] Goebel, *Felony and Misdemeanor*, 170–71.

Rhetoric: An *Aide-mémoire*'—is pure irony, and his memorandum . . . is also, and more important, an aid to forgetting." [184]

From a tongue-in-cheek perspective, Umberto Eco reports that, with some friends, he imagined a university in which the nonexistent discipline of an *ars oblivionalis* would be taught. Its function would be to "establish the principles of a technique and of a rhetorical art—and therefore principles of a process that was artificial and institutable at will—that would permit one to forget in a matter of seconds what one knew." As Eco looks back on his participation in this intellectual joke, however, his points are quite serious. He reasserts the problematic distinction between natural and artificial, accident and intention, desire and will, observing that "it is possible to forget accidentally, as a consequence of repression, drunkenness, drugs, cerebral lesions. But these are *natural* events, which do not concern us here" ("An *Ars Oblivionalis*?," 254). For Eco, the ways in which ancient memory treatises deploy the same "monstrous bleeding images" as aids to both remembrance and forgetting are doomed to fail: "When it is necessary to free a system of *loci* or memory to make room for other notions . . . one should imagine a man who removed images and tossed them out a window. But this technique allows one not to forget something but to remember that one wanted to forget it" (254). Elsewhere, DeLeuze and Guattari contend that when cultures "create a memory for man," they do so by suppressing and forgetting individual memories in favor of a more collective memory. As for Nietzsche, man is himself "constituted by means of an active faculty of forgetting [*oubli*]"; and for that reason, he must repress the biological memory in order to "create an *other* memory, one that is collective" (*Anti-Oedipus*, 144; emphasis theirs).

Here, the mortuary circulation of memory between life and death is replicated in the circulation of conservation and forgetting. Merleau Ponty made a similar point in his Monday Course when he taught that, as the body mediates between past and present, "the experience of a memory that is returning from oblivion stands at the center." Within that paradox, he concludes, lies a kind of answer which is pertinent to the ability of mnemotechnics to reanimate and create from death: "It appears that thanks to this conception we may be able to overcome the problematic alternative between a consciousness that conserves and a consciousness that constructs the past. For we bring both concepts into positive interrelation, and we say that through forgetting the past is present." [185] The memory of the medieval theater proved ideally suited to such an assignment. When the theater exploited mnemotechnics, it too engaged in conservation, construction, and reconstruction as its bodies mediated—as all memories did—among past, present, and future (*Confessions*, bk. 11, chap. 11).

[184] Worsham, "Eating History, Purging Memory, Killing Rhetoric," 152. Barthes also "forgot" the fifth rhetorical canon, delivery. See also Solterer, "Dismembering, Remembering, and the Châtelain de Couci;" and Carruthers on "eating the book," *BM*, 167.

[185] "Monday Course," cited in English in Krell, *Of Memory*, 101.

Somehow, audiences of all ages keep turning to theater to help them both to remember and to forget the violence of law and religion. "When the audience does gather in the accustomed spaces," muses Herbert Blau, "it seems more like a collective desire to forget or, with a lapse of memory about where we are in history, for the perpetuation of the most exhausted illusions" (*Blooded Thought*, xi). Jan Kott argues that playwright Tadeusz Kantor helps audiences to remember what they would like to forget: "Kantor, like very few artists in our time, succeeded in translating into theatrical signs a forgotten memory that is locked away in each and every one of us like a healed wound." [186] André de Lorde viewed madness as the only palliative to the memory of pain and pitied Edgar Allan Poe for its absence: "Less fortunate than Maupassant, he will not even know that forgetfulness of everything which is given by madness" (*TM*, 11). And, when the sixty-five-year run of the Parisian Theater of the Grand Guignol came to an end, John Callahan offered as an epitaph that it "entertained audiences through terror and laughter . . . [but] left the theatre world with many fond, if gruesome, memories" ("Ultimate," 174). In a medieval society in which the desire to forget pain was consistently thwarted by what Patrick Geary deems commemorative ways of "living with the dead," the paradoxes of an *ars memorandi* that staged the need to forget were especially poignant. That art circulated in a world in which the master trope of liturgical drama began with an empty tomb and in which Guibert of Nogent invoked a cruelty that helped him to forget the very violence that helped him to remember the love between master and disciple. The medieval theater of cruelty engaged masters and disciples of its own with its unforgettable memories of violence.

The Memory of Drama

Even today, the bloody images of the early theater attest to an epistemological process that is as painful to remember as it is difficult to forget. Tertullian noticed this as he memorialized for posterity the history of the very theater he deplored. "As for the Christian," he cautioned, "God forbid *he* should need further teaching to hate the spectacle. No one however can fully set out the whole story here, unless he be still a spectator. *I prefer to leave it incomplete than to remember*" (*De spectaculis*, 19; emphasis mine). In other words, one neither can nor should write the history of the theater, because one cannot remember what it is better to forget.

Yet one can only remember that it is better to forget the theater by remembering what there is to forget. One of the things audiences seem eternally to wish both to forget and to remember but can neither forget nor remember com-

---

[186] See Jan Kott's essay, "Kantor, Memory, Mémoire," in *Memory of the Body*, 55. See also David Marshall's superb chapter "Forgetting Theater" in *Surprising Effects of Sympathy* (hereafter *SES*).

pletely is the pleasure of pain. With its long-standing connections to birth, creation, creativity, law, and aesthetics, medieval drama demands that audiences remember pain even as the pleasures of its catharses urge forgetfulness of that
pain. At a minimum, if memory writes on bodies in the name of the law and does
them violence, such violence is accompanied by pleasure. Michel de Certeau
writes, for instance, that "the act of suffering oneself to be written by the group's
law is oddly accompanied by a pleasure, that of being recognized (but one does
not know by whom), of becoming an identifiable and legible word in a social
language" (*PEL*, 140). Oddly enough, however, it is in the remembering and the
forgetting of painful pleasure and pleasurable pain that one may discern a certain "happy ending" to the spectacular violence of mnemotechnics. The "final
act" of the memory play is to locate the violence of performance within dramatic and extra-dramatic models for empathy and civilization.

By way of conclusion, I turn to the ways in which theorists of literature, aesthetics, and moral philosophy transform violent mnemonic origins into the origins of civilized empathy. As the rhetorical arts of memory engendered rhetorical speech, dramatic action, and effective drama, all their violence and all their
theatricality had another important social purpose with which rhetoric was
charged. Notwithstanding a long history of what Jonas Barish termed the "antitheatrical prejudice," medieval rhetoricians and learned Christian dramatists
used theories of memory to equate acting good with good acting. As we have
seen, when the latter tapped the mnemonic lexicon, they too urged that theatrical imagery be translated into "real"—not "pretend"—behaviors. It thus
seems fitting to close this chapter by coming full circle to the mnemonic imagery of death and dismemberment with which it began and to the happy aesthetic finale which that imagery inspired. What memory teaches is that, for reasons that remain embedded in the language of rhetoric, violence, and aesthetics,
societies prefer to tell themselves stories of goodness, empathy, and civilization
rather than to unmask the ways in which those very stories promote the violence necessary to their own construction. That principle, foregrounded by
rhetoric and rehearsed in medieval drama, is also a principle that undergirds
much of what twentieth-century critics have come to understand about the
essence of acting.

In *An Actor Prepares*, a treatise that would inspire generations of "method
actors," Constantin Stanislavski traces the origin of his own vision of the "emotion memory" to a violent accident. When the actor Kostya learns from his director how to access the "memory of life" rather than the "theatrical archives"
of his mind, the young man's epiphany occurs when he recalls and relives the
experience of seeing the dismembered victim of an isolated streetcar accident:

On a boulevard we ran into a large crowd. I like street scenes, so I pushed into the
centre of it, and there my eyes fell on a horrible picture. At my feet lay an old man,
poorly dressed, his jaw crushed, both arms cut off. His face was ghastly; his old yel-

low teeth stuck out through his bloody moustache. A street car towered over its victim. . . . This picture made a deep impression on me. . . . In the night I awoke, and the visual memory was even more terrifying than the sight of the accident itself had been. Probably that was because at night everything seems more fearful. But I ascribed it to my emotion memory and its power to deepen impressions.[187]

For Kostya, the terror prompted by this violent accident engenders compelling, believable, persuasive acting. Emotion memory is important, his mentor explains, because "just as your visual memory can reconstruct an inner image of some forgotten thing, place or person, your emotion memory can bring back feelings you have already experienced" (*AP*, 168). Yet, long before Stanislavski codified such mnemonic principles of acting technique, classical and medieval theorists had accomplished much the same thing in their treatments of the imagery, the origins, the virtual performances, the justice, and above all, the violence of *memoria*.

When Kostya relives and remembers the terror prompted by the violent streetcar accident, the experience engenders not only good acting but "acting good" as it gives rise to the young actor's righteous indignation against the injustices of the world: the ultimate method acting. In the same way that the deadly incident experienced by Simonides sparked the genesis of a *techne*, Stanislavski's tale of arbitrary violence has a happy ending. A self-affirming, life-affirming, naturalizing dismemberment, it gives birth to empathy:

> I passed by the scene of the accident and involuntarily stopped to recall what had happened so recently. All traces were obliterated. . . . As I thought, my memory of the catastrophe seemed to become transformed. At first it had been raw and naturalistic, with all the ghastly physical details, the crushed jaw, the severed arms, the children playing with the stream of blood. Now I was shaken as much by my memory of it all, but in a different way. I was suddenly filled with indignation against human cruelty, injustice, and indifference. (*AP*, 171)

Here a method actor has learned to tap his emotion memory in order to develop acting techniques that are more natural and, by extension, more authentic, more persuasive, and more cathartic.

Historically, another important moment when such a happy cultural ending to violence is rationalized is the eighteenth century. In his *Theory of Moral Sentiments* (1759), for instance, philosopher Adam Smith even goes so far as to configure torture as the origin of empathy. In substituting empathy for cruelty, he evokes the incapacity of the senses to convey the suffering of "our brother upon the rack." Smith turns to the subject of torture for the purpose of demonstrating that empathic identification on the part of an observer/witness can only

---

[187] *An Actor Prepares* (hereafter *AP*), 165, 170–71. For an excellent discussion of this passage, see Cousin, "A Note on Mimesis," esp. 236. See also Diderot, "Paradoxe du comédien."

be achieved through the "imagination." Illustrated with such terms as "representations," "copies," and "impressions," his imagination is mnemonic:

> It is *by the imagination only* that we can form any conception of what are his sensations. Neither can that faculty help us to this any other way, than by *representing* to us what would be our own, if we were in his case. It is the *impressions* of our own senses only, not those of his, which our imaginations copy. By the imagination we place ourselves in his situation, we conceive ourselves enduring all the same torments, *we enter as it were into his body*, and become in some measure the same person with him, and thence form some idea of his sensations.[188]

Still, happy critical endings about communing bodies, faith, healing, and unity sometimes seem too pretty. Besides the question where empathy comes from, they raise the question as to why violent memory epistemology is necessary for the construction of empathy. They revive what Simonides revived: their need to kill something the better to make it live on. When it comes to the discipline of mnemotechnics (which had itself originated in the simultaneous deaths and rebirths, concealments and revelations of Simonides's crypt), empathy constitutes a kind of solution to the problem of violence. It surpasses even the rhetorical tendency described earlier to oppose the virtual violence of memory to the actual violence of performance. Since the virtual violence of memory can lead to the enactment of an unacceptable violence, which in turn leads to the performance of an acceptable empathy, then even the most violent performance is endowed with a positive valence. That strategy even gains currency in rhetoric's finale—which is delivery, the spectacular outcome of *inventio* and *memoria*.

If modern aesthetic theory has taken seriously the theatrical visions of empathy articulated by the likes of Stanislavski and Smith, then early mnemonic theory clearly needs to be taken just as seriously. It so happens that all the principles and paradoxes of empathic identification had already been systematized by theorists of rhetoric studying the role of the orator as *actor*.[189] For Cicero, the emotional and emotion-generating reenactments of *memoria* were to be achieved through empathic investment in the principals of a court case (*De oratore*, II, 189). The same held true for Quintilian, who directed that "the prime essential for stirring the emotions of others is . . . first to feel those emotions oneself" (*IO*, VI, 2.26). Since "emotions are not transferable at will, nor can we give the same forcible expression to another man's emotions that we should give to our own" (*IO*, IV, 1.47), the orator was to strive for a kind of "method acting" that exploited mental pictures as the precursors to the dramatic portrayal of emotion. Presaging the critical theories of a Diderot, an Artaud, or a

---

[188] Smith, *Theory of Moral Sentiments*, 2; emphasis mine; cited and discussed in Marshall, *SES*, 4–5. See also Pelias, "Empathy and the Ethics of Entitlement."

[189] Here I emphasize the full gamut of meaning of the term *actor* (rhetor, lawyer, prosecutor, histrionic speaker, etc.); see *ROMD*, 8.

Stanislavski, Quintilian advised that the orator assume the actual feelings of the personages in the case to be tried. With pain and theatricality dominating his analysis, he posits the following proposition: "Suppose we are impersonating [*agimus*] an orphan, a *shipwrecked* man, or one in grave peril. What profit is there in assuming such a rôle unless we also assume the emotions which it involves?" (*IO*, VI, 2.36; emphasis mine).[190] He likens that situation to that of actors who are still drowned in the tears of their role after the play is over, concluding that "we must identify ourselves with the persons of whom we complain . . . and must plead their case and for a brief space feel their suffering as though it were our own" (*IO*, VI, 2.34): "It is sometimes positively ridiculous to counterfeit [*ridicula fuerit imitatio*] grief, anger and indignation, if we content ourselves with accommodating our words and looks and make no attempt to adapt our own feelings to the emotions to be expressed" (*IO*, VI, 2.26).

Ridiculous or not, the counterfeit and the imitations that were rehearsed as tortured truths in *inventio* and pictorialized as violent imagery in *memoria* reached fruition in delivery. Whoever the recipient of violence or torture might have been, the mnemonic conception of brutality was considered rhetorically expedient only insofar as it endowed orators with the "power of vivid imagination, whereby things, words and actions are presented in the most realistic manner" (*IO*, VI, 2.30). In fact, orators had eternally exhibited their violent stories dramatically—first during the mnemonic and inventional process, and then, in their delivered performances. We "seem to ourselves not to be dreaming but acting (*facere*)," notes Quintilian (*IO*, VI, 2.30). But if an orator could turn mnemonic "hallucination to some profit" (VI, 2.30–31) by using "actions as well as words . . . to move the court to tears" (*IO*, VI, 1.30), it follows that his hallucinatory and violent mnemonic scene might readily be turned to profit in the stunning special effects and in the occasional real violence of the medieval and early Renaissance stage. There, it would help to spawn further performances of violence, the cathartic properties of which could then be exploited during *actio* only to spawn further inventions.

In the end, the ad hoc placement of torture in *inventio* and its post hoc representations in delivery were dependent upon the virtual performativity of *memoria*.[191] The place for imagining such violence, such theatricality, such catharsis was the inventional memory; but the place where it was acted out was delivery, the culmination of any rhetorical process. While empathy identifies rhetoric as a site for the fusion of good acting and acting good, however, it also poses the problem of audience reception to violence. It is one thing to visualize

---

[190] While Marshall seems unaware of the influence, the later reflections of Marivaux and Jean-Baptiste Du Bos owe much to Quintilian, as when spectators flock to see such direful spectacles as quadrilles, *shipwrecks*, and gladiatorial display because they "feel like theater" (*SES*, 24).

[191] Helpful contemporary perspectives on virtual performativity include Hernadi, *Cultural Transactions*, chap. 2; and Alter, *Sociosemiotic Theory*, 173.

a body in pain and to display an appreciation for what Eugene Vance terms "violence as semiosis" (*MS*, 54); but it is quite another to see what really happens when, as Kubiak writes, theater displays events " 'out there' in real bodies living and dying in real time" (*ST*, 11). And it is quite another thing when violence is enacted with the realism—and occasionally, the reality—for which medieval theater is notorious.

When it comes to the violence of the rhetorical scene, the idea that a memorable image might itself do violence and even torture is an old one. Lucian of Samosata, who had once elevated Mnemosyne to the premier skill of drama ("Saltatio," 36), conveys as much in his "Tyrannicide," where horrific imagery is employed to teach a tyrant a lesson. In a series of memorable, disfigured, and dramatic images of the law, Lucian narrates a punishment for tyranny that is all the more tyrannical in that it begins with the hypervisuality of torture. When the avenger/murderer tortures the tyrant with a series of real images of death which precede the latter's demise, all the participants are stained with blood: agent, victim, and the implied audience of this violent spectacle of retribution. Death and the imagery of death are protodramatic, dramatic, and, in this case, even pre-performative in their anticipation of a real death generated theatrically through violent visions:

> Even if you require bloodshed, that is not wanting either, and I am not unstained with blood; on the contrary, I have done a great and valiant deed in that I slew a young man in the fullness of his strength. . . . Look at the slain man himself! He was a tyrant's son, nay more, a harsher tyrant, an inexorable despot, a more cruel chastiser, a more violent oppressor. . . . I killed the tyrant by killing someone else. . . . First I *tortured* him with profound grief, *displayed full in his view* all that was dearest to him lying exposed in pitiable case, a son in his youth, wicked, to be sure, but in the fullness of his strength and the *image* of his sire, *befouled with blood and gore*. Those are the wounds of fathers. . . . To die forthwith, to know nothing, to see no such *spectacle* has in it nothing worthy of a tyrant's *punishment*.[192]

Of special interest here is the notion that the tyrant is not yet dead, but virtually dead and that the virtuality of his death resides in Lucian's memory. As his punishment, the tyrant must view the act of his son being murdered—a punishment that adds an actual dead body to the traditional forensic repertoire of "blood-stained swords, fragments of bone taken from the wound, and garments spotted with blood" (*IO*, VI, 1.30). Lucian's tyrant is punished with both a body and its imagery—and doubly so, for the body of his son is the image of himself. In a negative typology, evil son and evil father are sacrificed in an imaginary act of rebellion that punishes a despot with imagery.[193]

---

[192] Lucian, "Tyrannicide," 16–17; emphasis mine.

[193] Ironically, then, mnemotechnics might sometimes provide the means by which to restore a certain rhetorical agency to a disenfranchised or disempowered speaker/writer. But a learned author who had benefited from an education largely reserved for the elite was not necessarily disempow-

Ever since Plato identified the ideological force of memory when it is placed in the service of a hegemony, that *techne* has been implicated in the imposition of civilized rule—one of the primary concerns of rhetoric itself. Lawmakers were the rivals of poets because both were masters of illusion, a power that owed much to the exploitation of memory images. When Plato writes in the *Laws* that judicial and poetic communities correct the "foggy vision" of their charges by replacing one image of society with another, he implies that there was something coercive about the ways in which early cultures fused epistemology, invention, terror, and theatricality within the memory:

> Distance has the effect of befogging the vision of nearly everybody, and of children especially; but our lawgiver will reverse the appearance by removing the fog, and by one means or another—habituation, commendation, or argument—will *persuade people that their notions of justice and injustice are illusory pictures*, unjust objects appearing pleasant and just objects most unpleasant to him who is opposed to justice, through being viewed from his own unjust and evil standpoint, but when seen from the standpoint of justice, both of them appear in all ways entirely the opposite.[194]

The goal of Plato's lawmaker is to control and to correct the misguided mental pictures of a people by regulating their memory systems. Thus, before modern critics ever posed their questions about the memory of violence, ancient and medieval authors had already rehearsed the answers in a violent rhetorical scene that was didactic, disciplinary, corrective, coercive, and creative of new images of justice. Their insights considerably antedate Pierre Bourdieu's that, "if all societies . . . that seek to produce a new man through a process of 'deculturation' and 'reculturation' set such store on the seemingly most insignificant details of *dress*, *bearing*, physical and verbal *manners*, the reason is that, creating the body as a memory, they entrust to it in abbreviated and practical, i.e. mnemonic, form the fundamental principles of the arbitrary content of the culture." [195] Herewith, I conclude the rhetorical chronology of discursive events at the same place where rhetoric stops even as its cyclical life recommences: with delivered performance. As we shall see, a revitalized view of delivery suggests that the entire process of deculturation and reculturation is not arbitrary at all. Instead, it is intimately linked to a rhetorical performance that, by dint of its grounding in a mnemonic language of evolutions of culture, is designed to seem natural—even in its intermittent violence.

---

ered. Moreover, if an image can punish, it cannot kill—although I later examine incidents in which some medieval theatrical productions explore that very possibility.

[194] Plato, *Laws*, 663b–c. See also *Laws* 817b, cited earlier. While little is known about the availability of Plato's *Laws* to the Middle Ages, a text such as John of Salisbury's *Policraticus*, which staged the ruler's body in its own ways, was indeed known (see, e.g. 60–61).

[195] Bourdieu, "Structures and the Habitus," in *Outline of a Theory of Practice*, 94; also discussed by Paster in *Body Embarrassed*, 5.

The *ars memorandi* is concerned with orchestrating the desired social performances on the stage of the world by replacing one public picture with another, a vision consistent with the illusions of truth so violently prescribed during *inventio* and reimagined in *memoria*. The coercive ramifications of its modes of ideological substitution in various rhetorico-dramatic forms of indoctrination are the focus of the next chapter.

CHAPTER 3

The Performance of Violence

Nothing to be done: language is always a matter of force, to speak is to exercise a will for power; in the realm of speech there is no innocence, no safety.

—Roland Barthes, *Image / Music / Text*

As the legend goes, the art of rhetoric was born at the same moment as the political hegemony, its advent explained in terms of the need for a peacekeeping, mediatory discourse that simultaneously facilitated empowerment, domination, and discipline. Cicero believed, for example, that eloquence owed its genesis to the impossibility that a "mute and voiceless wisdom could have turned men suddenly from their habits and introduced them to different patterns of life." In the same way that Simonides's originary memory scene naturalized the unnatural, so too did a parallel scene of the first delivery. Accompanied by the first sacrifice, it designated the conceptual parameters of forensic rhetoric:

> How could it have been brought to pass that men should . . . become accustomed to obey others voluntarily . . . ? Certainly only a speech at the same time powerful and entrancing could have induced one who had great physical strength to submit to justice without violence, so that he suffered himself to be put on a par with those among whom he could excel, and abandoned voluntarily a most agreeable custom, especially since this custom had already acquired through lapse of time the force of a natural right.[1]

In the eighth century, the author/protagonist Alcuin agreed in his *Dialogue with Charlemagne* that civilization was founded when the first eloquent man discovered in rhetoric a linguistic means by which to subjugate the early inhabitants of the earth who were "made gentle and mild from being savage and brutal."[2]

---

[1] Cicero, *De inventione*, I, 1.3; see also his *De oratore*, I, 30–36.
[2] Alcuin, *Rhetoric of Alcuin and Charlemagne*, ll. 47–48.

It was rhetoric that turned them "against their previous habits, and [brought] them to the diverse pursuits of civilized life" (50–51). And, in a theological version of the legend, Eusebius observed in the *Ecclesiastical History* that, beginning with the Jews, "the minds of most of the heathen were softened by the lawgivers and philosophers who arose everywhere. Savage and unbridled brutality was changed to mildness, so that deep peace, friendship, and mutual intercourse obtained."[3] Ideologically consonant with rhetorical treatments of torture, delivery was associated with the intervention of the stronger upon the weaker and the empowered upon the disempowered. The first brutish inhabitants of the earth whom the first rhetor wished to educate and discipline were the first "willing" victims.

Implicit in all those narratives, however, is the identification of rhetoric in general and of its performance structures in particular with the imperialistic imposition of hegemonic, juridico-political, and theological constructs of civilization. In accordance with Cicero's dictum that orators are "the players that act real life" (*De oratore*, III, 214), the first rhetorician acted out the ideal of civilized life for the audience of his community.[4] With his first rhetorical performance, he changed, instituted, and regulated what Michel de Certeau terms the "practice of everyday life," Norbert Elias the "pacification of behaviour and the control of emotions," and, long before them, Eusebius the practice of religion.[5] Politics was more than the "management of language," as Jean-Pierre Vernant has written, by which "all questions of general concern that the sovereign had to settle . . . were now submitted to the art of oratory and had to be resolved at the conclusion of a debate. . . . There was thus a close connection, a reciprocal tie, between politics and *logos*."[6] It was the *dramatic* management of rhetoric and behavior.

In this chapter, I argue that, when it comes to enforcing the "voluntary submission" to the common good heralded by rhetoricians as the birth of civilization and to creating arguments that justify and perpetuate that submission, early theorists of rhetoric, dramatists, and practitioners of theater display the same behaviors of uncovering and repression evidenced in the previous chapters. They construct rhetoric as a nonviolent and spectacular way to mediate the violence that accounts for its own genesis. They then go on to denounce selected types of community violence that rhetoric's inherent violence is morally

[3] Eusebius, *EH*, I, 2.23.

[4] Juan Luis Vives also suggests that language and community originated simultaneously when speech bound the first inhabitants of the earth (*De tradendis*, 14). For the medieval notion of textual community, see, e.g., Stock, *Implications of Literacy*, and Ong, *RRT*, chap. 1. See also Knight, "Beyond Misrule."

[5] I refer here to de Certeau, *PEL*; and Elias, *Civilizing Process*. Elias is discussed by Chartier in "Social Figuration and Habitus," 74, and by Paster in *Body Embarrassed*, 16. See also in this connection Roland Barthes on law, speech, and delivery in *Image/Music/Text*, 192.

[6] Vernant, *Origins of Greek Thought*, 50. I return later to the concept of *logos* in the context of dramatic performativity.

obliged to extinguish. At the same time, theorists locate rhetorical violence within the drama of delivery—a drama that can be critiqued independently of memory or invention as a "mere" stylistic performance. By that time, once the violent theatricality of rhetoric has been masked by illusions of mediation and civilization, its systems of performance may more readily elicit pity, fear, and verisimilitude (the very activities rehearsed within a tortured inventional memory). So, a violent delivery ultimately ennobles the blood and gore that it exists to denounce. An innately violent and dramatic form of invention then perpetuates violence within the discipline of rhetoric, which presumably owed its origins to the need to mediate violence.

Seen from that perspective, the social situation of the first audience of rhetoric calls to mind René Girard's assertion that "social coexistence would be impossible if no surrogate victim existed, if violence persisted beyond a certain threshold and failed to be transmuted into culture."[7] Their story exemplifies Michel Foucault's insight that "humanity does not gradually progress from combat to combat until it arrives at universal reciprocity, where the rule of law finally replaces warfare; humanity installs each of its violences in a system of rules and thus proceeds from domination to domination."[8] It anticipates certain modern tenets of colonialist discourse, as when Carol Dougherty contends that "colonial tales that include murder displace the warlike violence of the colonial expedition itself and relocate it within the tale by virtue of a religious system which can address and expiate that violence."[9] It is compatible with other cultural institutions such as religion and politics, the former described by Jonathan Dollimore as having "historically served to legitimize systems of power and subjection";[10] and the latter by Vernant as having relied extensively upon the power of speech: "the system of the *polis* implied, first of all, the extraordinary preeminence of speech over all other instruments of power. Speech became the political tool par excellence, the key to all authority in the state, the means of commanding and dominating others" (*Origins*, 49). Whatever modern terminology one might choose to adopt, one crucial system of power and subjection that helped the legitimation of law, religion, and politics was rhetoric.

However "voluntary" the sacrifices of a given community, the performative status of a civilizing rhetoric often defies the concomitant theoretical articulation of that discipline as nonviolent and mediatory. Emerging from the apparent need to replace militaristic rule by force with democratic rule by participa-

---

[7] Girard, *VS*, 144.

[8] Foucault, *Language, Counter-Memory, Practice*, 51; see also William Ian Miller's discussion of this passage in *Humiliation*, 91.

[9] Dougherty, *Poetics of Colonization*, 41, in which she extrapolates from Vernant's notions of "The Pure and Impure." See also Fischer-Lichte, "Theatre and the Civilizing Process"; McConachie, "Using the Concept of Cultural Hegemony to Write Theatre History"; Mignolo, *Darker Side of the Renaissance*; and Roach, "Inscription of Morality as Style."

[10] Dollimore, *Radical Tragedy*, 14.

tion, rhetoric remains dependent nonetheless on the violence it claims to replace. In other words, the dominations, displacements, and legitimizations which have so captured the attention of modern theorists have long been associated with the originary moment of rhetoric, which signaled the birth of culture, consciousness, politics, language, and the law.

For that reason, I turn once again to the ideological contortions necessary to authorize subjection—in this case, to the theory and practice of performance in both rhetoric and drama. Contemporary resonances notwithstanding, what cultural and rhetorical historians alike have resisted exploring is the notion that the first rhetor's "surrogate victims" were also the first audience of *actio*: their status as victims was inextricably linked to their status as spectators.[11] Complicitous in the originary story of the first rhetorico-dramatic *actio* was the gaze of the audience—an audience that was called upon to judge but was simultaneously being judged. While Simon Goldhill has complained that "even recent attempts to reassert the priority of action over the word for Greek theatre have failed to reinscribe violence as a term of performance studies," *actio* specifically denotes performance and enables us to do just that.[12]

Similarly, Anthony Kubiak has framed the entire problem of legal origins in theatrical terms, proposing that "theatre is not merely a means by which social behavior is engineered, it is the *site* of violence, the locus of terror's emergence as myth, law, religion, economy, gender, class, or race, either *in* the theatre, or in culture *as* a theatricality that paradoxically precedes culture" (*ST*, 4–5; emphasis his). According to the originary narratives above, early theorists found specifically that it was the *theatricality* of rhetoric that preceded the codification of legal and social constructs of civilization. As such, rhetoric promises to illuminate the larger drama invoked by Victor Turner, who writes that

> what seems to happen is that when a major public dramatic process gets under way, people, whether consciously, preconsciously, or unconsciously, take on roles which they carry with them, if not precisely recorded scripts, deeply engraved tendencies to act and speak in suprapersonal or "representative" ways appropriate to the role taken, and to prepare the way for a certain climax that approximates to the nature of the climax given in a certain central myth of the death or victory of a hero or heroes in which they have been deeply indoctrinated or "socialized" or "enculturated."[13]

The reinforcement of social roles through enculturation, representation, engraving, scripting, and indoctrination was scripted and rehearsed within the

---

[11] A significant exception is Kubiak, who argues in *ST* that sociopolitical power is "impossible without some implied and already recognized structure of performance" (5).

[12] Goldhill, "Violence in Greek Tragedy," 15.

[13] *Dramas, Fields, and Metaphors*, 123. For a discussion of this view in classical theater, see Ober and Strauss, "Drama, Rhetoric, Discourse," 245.

epistemology of mnemotechnics; but delivery was its site of enactment. Indeed, Alcuin found that after the rhetorician had ordered (*dispositio*) and stylized (*elocutio*) materials discovered beforehand during *inventio*, "the last and highest [power is] to deliver what you have fixed in the memory" (Howell, *Dialogue*, 81–82). As the rhetorical canon devoted to the regulation of voice, mien, and gesture toward the production of meaning, *actio* incarnated a living script for the performance of law, civilization, and their social dramas.

Moreover, in the world of the medieval dramatist who was trained in rhetoric and for whom Christ's life was "one great drama," such unforgettably violent cultural events as the Simonides legend and the *quem quaeritis* trope took on special resonances as they fused the violence of representation with the representation of violence. If this returns us to Teresa de Lauretis's comment that "once a connection is assumed between violence and rhetoric, the two terms begin to slide, and, soon enough, the connection will appear to be reversible," it does so in the context of the quintessential representation of the liturgy.[14] In his oft-cited treatment of *De tragoediis* from the *Gemma animae* (c. 1100), for instance, which endures for many as the key to the "origins" of liturgical drama, Honorius Augustodunensis depicted the "representation" of the liturgy by a priest/*tragicus* who re-presents true events: "It is known that those who recited tragedies in the theaters represented [*repraesentabant*] to the people, by their gestures, the actions of conflicting forces. Even so, our tragedian [the celebrant] represents [*repraesentat*] to the Christian people in the theater of the church, by his gestures, the struggle of Christ, and impresses upon them the victory of his redemption."[15] The "social drama" of *actio* might thus have been reinforced by the social drama of the liturgy in ways that rendered a violent theatrical scene like the scourging of Christ all the more real and, at the same time, all the more dramatic.

After a brief résumé of some of the more powerful performance features of delivery, we shall see in this chapter that *actio* raises anew the questions of victimization, agency, law, aesthetics, and theatricality that have dominated this book. In yet another response to the tenacious question of how cultures attribute a positive valence to violence, rhetorical delivery functions by means of a counterintuitive yet no less effective combination of coercion, pain, and pleasure. As the Quintilianic *mentis index*, delivery "indexed" not only the rhetorician's performative power to civilize his audiences but his attendant anxieties about that process, during which violence commonly became an end in itself.[16] Perhaps that is why *actio* came to help theorists and practitioners of rhetoric to

[14] *Technologies of Gender*, 32; and Erich Auerbach's "great drama" of Christianity (*Mimesis*, 158).

[15] The passage is reproduced in many places, including Bevington, *Medieval Drama*, 9; Hardison, *CRCD*, 39–40; and Young, *Drama of the Medieval Church*, I, 83. In *ROMD*, I discuss another type of generic "shifting" between rhetoric and drama (50–54) which occurred centuries before Christianity.

[16] Quintilian, *IO*, XI, 3.62.

craft one of the greatest illusions of all: namely, that it is art or performance that aestheticizes violence when in reality violence has always and already been aestheticized in the *imitatio veritatis* of law and legal language (*IO*, V, 12.22).

In that sense, one of the most important cultural gestures of delivery is the reconfiguration of violence itself as impersonation, imitation, or representation. The fifth rhetorical canon cloaked the numerous paradoxes of violence by appearing to aestheticize the performances of law, politics, and religion. Consequently, it had the capacity to nurture the illusion that the coercive spectacle of violence was more part of aesthetics than it was of those same disciplines of law, politics, and religion. That phenomenon is apparent in several later rhetorical theories in which violent legal, political, and religious interventions are framed explicitly as civilized, cathartic, and poetic.

For example, in his Italian Renaissance treatise on the political foundations of civilized life, the philosopher Denores develops catharsis, invention, punishment, poetry, and the pleasures of pain into an aesthetic theory of politics. Poetry, he writes, is in some sense equal to moral and civil philosophy because "both attend with every care to the two most noble actions [the purgation of the passions, the inculcation of virtue]. It is superior insofar as the other proceeds by means of laws, penalties, and punishments, while this produces the same result with the greatest enjoyment and recreation of the spirit." [17] Denores underscores here the dramatic and potentially cathartic properties of violence within the law and its politics. In the statements above, poetry, law, and politics are compatible because they rely upon certain pleasures and pains, certain similitudes and verisimilitudes, certain inventions and reinventions of the law, including its own long-standing reliance on a tortured inventional system. After all, as Geoffrey of Vinsauf had maintained of his tortured psychodramatic struggle, that system was about giving birth to a legalistic rule of art in violence.[18] Medieval rhetoric also provided a site where theorists perceived a shift from the political theory of catharsis to the dramatic reception of torture. With its interplay of torture, invention, and drama, it promises to tell us as much about the political resonances of dramatic pleasure as it does about the problematic pleasures of torture in rhetoric, poetics, and the law—for makers and audiences alike.

To address those issues, I examine the long-standing rhetorical interplay among delivery, drama, politics, philosophy, law, aesthetics, and pain, which have always been portrayed as interdependent in the legend of rhetoric's origins. When their practitioners emphasized the mimesis of violence, they fostered the conception of violence as an object of desire and a thing of beauty. That is the subject of the first section, in which I problematize the fluid interrelations

---

[17] Denores, cited in Weinberg, *History of Literary Criticism in the Italian Renaissance* (hereafter *HLCIR*), I, 27. I thank Victoria Kahn for bringing this reference to my attention.
[18] Geoffrey of Vinsauf, *PN*, 1759–61.

between pleasure, pain, and dramatic catharsis as conceived and enacted in the scourging scenes of late medieval French Passion plays. If the first audience of the first rhetorical delivery constituted the first victims, it follows that, for the civilizing functions of rhetorical performance to work, theorists would have a vested interest in conditioning their target audiences (or attempting to condition them) to *enjoy* being civilized. The aesthetico-political register of forensic rhetoric provided an important means by which audiences could truly be persuaded that they derived pleasure from threatening discursive forms of real or staged hegemonies. As a powerful discourse steeped in the pleasures of pain, delivery was the crowning moment at which the tortured drama of invention and the memory of its pain came to life with the full force of their rhetorical probabilities and verisimilitudes.

Afterward, I show that that model was especially effective in foregrounding an important rhetorical theory of reception which configured the audiences of law, politics, and drama as witnesses to, participants in, and even victims of violence. The confusion among those roles was further cultivated by a rich repertoire of anecdotal evidence from the medieval stage. When medieval dramatic productions regaled spectators with an extensive repertoire of special effects that were designed to render pain and suffering as realistically as possible, they consistently pushed the limits of witnessing, impersonation, and violence. Much as forensic rhetors had done before them, they gave literal meaning to Quintilian's advice that the main thing future lawyers were to do was "exhibit an emotion that cannot be distinguished from the truth" (*IO*, XI, 3.62).

Finally, while theater historians have long puzzled over isolated tales of actual beatings, tortures, and even executions that were allegedly incorporated into the occasional medieval and early Renaissance play, such performances of violence hark back to the tortured aesthetics of invention and memory and may actually have threatened audiences. In light of the well-documented possibilities of real violence on stage along with the widespread staging of public chastisement as a form of spectacle, I argue for the viability of the Austinian concept of performativity as an approach to late medieval and early Renaissance drama.[19] A close reading of some of the imitated and actual tortures of representative scourging and crucifixion scenes suggests that, whether or not such testimony is credible, it prompts serious considerations about the presence of bona fide speech acts in the Austinian sense. It is no coincidence that Austin practically paraphrased the definition of delivery when he claimed of performativity that "there are a great many devices that can be used for making clear, even at the primitive level, what act it is we are performing when we say something—the tone of voice, cadence, gesture—and above all we can rely upon the nature of

---

[19] I return later to the notion of medieval performativity based on Austin's *HDTW*, *Philosophical Papers*, esp. chap. 10, "Performative Utterances"; and Baudrillard's "Simulacra and Simulations," in *Selected Writings* (hereafter *SW*). See also Derrida on the performative in the law in *Memoirs*, 24.

the circumstances, the context in which the utterance is issued" (*Philosophical Papers*, 244). Medieval dramatic imitations were so effective, so violent, and so dramatic that modern audiences find it difficult to make distinctions that rhetorical theory itself failed to make: between "real" and "realistic," true and verisimilar, imitation and enactment, drama and law. As it happens, nowhere is Bruce Wilshire's contention that theater is lifelike and life theater-like more compellingly elaborated than in the rhetorical foundations of a medieval theater of cruelty.

A rhetorical approach to performance ultimately suggests a slight modification of the views expressed by such theorists as Baudrillard and Kubiak to the effect that theater's special contribution to culture is the creation of a situation in which violence seems the most theatrical at the moment when it is the most real.[20] I assert instead that the hyperreality that characterizes so many early performances proves a particularly successful means by which to create the idea that the combination of pleasure and pain is aesthetic and desirable.

That analysis cannot proceed, however, without a preliminary overview of delivery. In antiquity and the Middle Ages, delivery was the site where the rhetorical materials conceptualized in invention and rehearsed in the memory were performed, says Aristotle, by means of the three basic skills of volume, harmony, and rhythm.[21] Those skills were refined by the Pseudo-Ciceronian author of the *Rhetorica ad Herennium* as voice, mien, and gesture, which merged with style, intonations, pauses, and proper breathing to produce meaning.[22] As the key to the performative register of rhetorical discourse, delivery encapsulated the interrelations among persuasion, mimetic impulse, and the power of the body itself to signify. *Actio* was dramatic "body language," a view exemplified by Cicero's assertion that "by action the body talks [*est enim actio quasi sermo corporis*], so it is all the more necessary to make it agree with the thought" (*De oratore*, III, 222).[23] Quintilian even went so far as to equate it with the corporeal movements of deaf-mutes and mimes: "signs take the place of language in the dumb, and the movements of the dance [*saltatio*] are frequently full of meaning, and appeal to the emotions without any aid from words" (*IO*, XI, 3.66).[24] The faculty that he called a *mentis index* was also a vocal and dramatic semiosis that enabled not only communication between speaker and audience but the crucial transfer of feelings: "the voice, which is

[20] See, e.g., Baudrillard, *SW*, 168; and Kubiak, *ST*, 160. See also Allen S. Weiss on Sadian torture and dissimulation in *Aesthetics of Excess*, chap. 4.

[21] Aristotle, *Rhetoric*, 1403b.

[22] [Cicero], *RAH*, I, 3; III, 22. On Roman vocal training, see Rousselle, "Parole et inspiration."

[23] For a helpful critical introduction to the *sermo corporis*, see Schmitt, *Raison des gestes*; and the essays in Bremmer and Roodenburg, *Cultural History of Gesture*.

[24] See also Lucian of Samosata, "Saltatio," 64–65; and Ruth Crosby, "Oral Delivery." Nor is it a coincidence that Denis Diderot wrote both a *Paradoxe du comédien* and a letter on the deaf and dumb.

the intermediary between ourselves and our hearers, will then produce precisely the same emotion in the judge that we have put into it. For it is the index of the mind, and is capable of expressing all its varieties of feeling" (*IO*, XI, 3.62).

So it was that, centuries before Judith Butler ever spoke of "corporeal style," classical and medieval rhetoricians had already systematized those terms in the "physical eloquence" or "styled action" of delivery (*IO*, XI, 3.1).[25] In the early world, its bodily performance style was directly connected to the kind of "styled misery" that Saint Augustine attributed to theatrical performance.[26] In the modern world, it is equally connected to the medieval "gestural semiosis" described by Peter Haidu as "inhabited by brutality and violence, even in the absence of infringement of the law."[27] Indeed, in spite of many rhetoricians' efforts to distinguish nobly violent conception from ignobly violent delivery, the paradoxes of enactment were too thorny to resolve.

Like invention and memory, delivery had a dark side. On the surface, it was about performance, mediation, community, communication, drama, imitation, and even music and impersonation.[28] It was impersonation or *hypokrisis*, a state embodied in Quintilian's unambiguous advice that the lawyer identify with his client by "draw[ing] a parallel from the stage" (VI, 1.26). Geoffrey of Vinsauf roused orators to assume the emotions of the characters they portrayed and to "arise a voice full of gall, a face enraged, and turbulent gestures" for "outer motion follows the inner, and the outer and inner man are equally moved. If you play this part [*quid recitator ages*], what shall you, the speaker, do? Imitate (*imitare*) genuine fury" (*PN*, 2049–53).[29] Likewise, delivery was music to the ears of Cicero, who advised that "the tones of the voice are keyed up like the strings of an instrument" which an orator might play (nam voces ut chordae sunt intentae quae ad quemque tactum respondeant) (*De oratore*, III, 216). For his part, Quintilian expanded that vision to a greater musico-philosophical harmony in which excellent deliveries might participate when he cautioned that the head "should derive appropriate motion from the subject of our pleading, maintaining harmony with the gesture and following the movement of the hands and side" (*IO*, XI, 3.69).

With such words, those writers helped to carve out a moral niche for delivery. Their goal was, in part, to anchor in questions of nobility, beauty, and character the precept that *hypokrisis* (denoting acting, feigning, or counterfeit) was

---

[25] In her discussion of "corporeal style," Butler remarks that the body is "a materiality that bears meaning" in a manner that is "fundamentally dramatic" ("Performative Acts," 272). See also Maud Gleason on delivery as "a language that anatomical males were taught to speak with their bodies" ("Semiotics of Gender," 402).

[26] Augustine, *Confessions*, bk. 3, chap. 2.

[27] Haidu, *SV*, 199.

[28] I reserve discussion of some of the coercive components of musical philosophy for a future study on the music of the medieval body in pain.

[29] For Quintilian and others, the key to capturing the essence of a character was to capture the emotions of that character (e.g., *IO*, VI, 2.34–35).

for orators while *hypocrisy* was for actors: "for a speech which is out of keeping with the man who delivers it is just as faulty as the speech which fails to suit the subject to which it should conform" (*IO*, III, 8.51). Later, that goal of moral harmony was to prove particularly attractive to such theorists as Tertullian, Cyprian, and Saint Basil as they pondered the morality of dramatic discourse. In his treatise on reading, for example, Saint Basil invokes a rich lexicon of aesthetic terms within a larger critique of the inconsistency between a public, theatrical self and a private, "real" one. He unites the venom of Tertullian with the famous dictum of *ut pictura poesis*, philosophizing that the virtuous man acting as himself is an accurate painter of himself:

> It seems to me that such harmony between profession and life is very much as if a painter had made a likeness of a man of quite wondrous beauty, and this same man should be such in reality as the painter had portrayed him on his panels. For brilliantly to praise virtue in public, and to make long speeches about it, but in private to rate pleasure before temperance, and self-interest before justice, resembles, as I would assert, those stage-folk who bring out plays and often appear as kings and potentates, although they are neither kings nor potentates, and perhaps not even free men at all.[30]

As we shall see, the desirable harmony among rhetoric, morality, and social praxis depended on the same kind of social regulation and control depicted by the originary tale of rhetoric. Delivery problematized for early cultures the interrelations among rhetoric, drama, and representation; but, insofar as its own originary moment concerned violence and mediation, delivery also proved exceptionally revealing about any discourse of power.

Above all, *actio* was power, a forceful network of social and dramatic performance practices to which Geoffrey of Vinsauf alludes in the *Poetria nova*: "force issues from the tongue, for death and life inhere in the hands of the tongue, as long as it enjoys the double guide of face and gesture" (*PN*, 2061–63). So great was its power that theorists of rhetoric consistently struggled (however unsuccessfully) to circumscribe its realm. Thomas Basin lobbied for the elimination of the entire oral component from the fourteenth-century French legal system so that the desirable yet fluid divisions between law, politics, and performance might be construed as discrete entities.[31] But even Aristotle had gathered that it was the special property of histrionic rhetorical performance to mutate into a defective drama precisely because of the imperfections of political life. Those who skillfully manipulated *hypokrisis*, he noticed, "nearly always carry off the

---

[30] *Saint Basil: The Letters*, 4, sec. 6. For recent phenomenological approaches to the spectacular creation and performance of personal identity, see Wilshire, *Role Playing and Identity* (hereafter *RPI*); and Walton, *Mimesis as Make-Believe*.

[31] I refer specifically to Basin, *Projet de réforme en matière de procédure* (1455), chap. 7, 51–54. The text appears in J. Quicherat's edition of *Histoire des règnes de Charles VII et de Louis XI*, vol. 4; and I discuss it in *ROMD*, 40–43.

prizes in dramatic contests, and as at the present day actors have greater influence on the stage than the poets, it is the same in political contests, owing to the corruptness of our forms of government" (*Rhetoric*, III, 1403b).[32] Quintilian too would blame histrionics for having forfeited the power rhetorical delivery must have possessed during the first subjections. When he called for control of a fashionable and "rather more violent [*agitatior*] form of delivery," he endeavored to distinguish serious pleading (*actio*) from mimicry (*imitatio*) and admonished his countrymen to control a discourse that was out of control when its very function was to control: It "requires to be kept under control. Otherwise, in our attempt to ape the elegances of the stage, we shall lose the authority which should characterise the man of dignity and virtue" (*IO*, XI, 3.184). The paradox was as follows: both rhetoric and theatricality were at their most powerful when violence overtook the probative value of argumentation during performance. Yet theorists denounced violence and theatricality for the very functions of displacement that actually served to empower their rhetorics.

When rhetorical theory grounds violence in dramatically induced cultural stereotypes of civilization and community, then even real violence seems like acting. Although such a combination undergirds the law, it is more easily perceptible as something that undergirds aesthetics. All those phenomena cause an inventional, imagined, rhetorical theater of cruelty to become an enacted medieval theater of cruelty that is grounded in an indispensable cultural impulse to denounce violence even as it relies on violence.

Pleasure, Pain, and the Spectacle of Scourging

At first glance, it is an exquisite image. The orator is a master musician, his body a lyre as Cicero describes him "playing" it by striking the chords of its harp: "The whole of a person's frame and every look on his face and utterance of his voice are like the strings of a harp [*ut nervi in fidibus*], and sound according as they are struck by each successive emotion. For the tones of the voice are keyed up like the strings of an instrument" (*De oratore*, II, 3.216).

Some six centuries later, Isidore of Seville spoke of a different kind of bodily harp in his discussion of torture. The victim of a particular sort of inventional "questioning" is brutalized by means of a stringed instrument known as the *fidiculae*: "Haec et *fidiculae*, quia his rei in *eculeo* torquentur, ut fides *inveniatur*" (And these things are called the strings or the reins, because, in order that the truth may be found, these kings are tormented on the rack).[33] Later, in the devotional context of his *Speculum caritatis*, Aelred of Rivaulx noted with alarm

---

[32] One need only pick up any contemporary American newspaper to find a plethora of references to the "theater" of politics or of justice—that is, when the word "circus" is not substituted for "theater." See, e.g., Longo, "Theater of the *Polis*."

[33] Isidore, *Etymologiarum*, I, bk. 5, 27.20–22; emphasis mine.

that the singing voice was often twisted, even "tortured" (*torquetur* et *retorquetur*) into unnatural histrionic acts and "the whole body is agitated by theatrical gestures, the lips are twisted [*torquentur*], the eyes roll, the shoulders are shrugged, and the fingers bent responsive to every note." [34] Once again, the shared vocabulary of torture (*torquere*) invention, and aesthetics raises several questions that provide the focus of this section: Who is playing whose body and to what end? How was the orator's body to deploy the codified *sermo corporis* of delivery in order to speak that which was born of pain? How was torture (as a violent search for a truth hidden in the body) to be translated into the pleasures—nefarious or otherwise—of music or drama? How could it happen that audiences could concentrate more on the beauty or melodiousness of scourgings than on their violence?

If Plato advised that "when men are investigating the subject of laws their investigation deals almost entirely with pleasures and pains" (*Laws*, 636d), medieval French dramatists took the representation of juridical culture to new heights (and depths). Within their Passion plays, they reconceived a rhetorical debate about the empathic memory of violence as one concerning the morality of its theatrical performance. Somehow, the rhetorician and the author of didactic drama needed to instill in audiences the conviction that the pain they witnessed or endured was pleasurable because it served a greater social good. To do so by configuring brutality as an origin of empathy—or, at the very least, as the pleasures of the appearance of empathy—was not enough. For early audiences to believe that, as Deleuze and Guattari put it, "even death, punishment, and torture are desired, and are instances of production," some kind of intervention was needed at the level of epistemology. [35]

While one of the clear functions of *inventio* and *memoria* was to transform violence and torture into aesthetic and enjoyable pictures and objects of desire, *actio* crowns the process with an enactment of the cathartic pleasures of pain. The inventional memory helped to normalize violence as a means of production; the deliveries that were cultivated by medieval scholasticism fostered spectacular literary narratives that stressed the desirability of that system of production. The ideological import of rhetoric thus lies somewhere between Gustave Cohen's complaint that audiences desire torture and Deleuze and Guattari's intuition that hegemonies intimidate various audiences into merely perceiving violence as desirable: "culture is not the movement of ideology: on the contrary, it forcibly injects production into desire, and conversely, it forcibly inserts desire into social production and reproduction" (*Anti-Oedipus*, 145). [36] Thanks to the violence, death, and dismemberment of its originary scenes, rhetoric then assists

---

[34] Robert Hayburn's translation of the Latin (*Corpus Christianorum, continuatio medievalis*, 1, 98, ll. 1233–42) appears in *Papal Legislation on Sacred Music*, 19. It has been brilliantly analyzed by Bruce Wood Holsinger in "Music, Body, and Desire," chap. 3.

[35] Deleuze and Guattari, *Anti-Oedipus*, 145.

[36] See, e.g., Cohen, *HMS*, 275–76.

in the engenderment of individual literary productions, aesthetic theories, and especially stage plays that emphasize the troubled connection between pain and desire. That emphasis occurs both in the concept of catharsis and in the interplay between *lier* (to tie up or bind) and *liesse* (joy); or between *batre* (to beat), *abbatre* (to slaughter), *rabatre* (to take down by force), and *esbatre* (to enjoy, to take pleasure in something or someone).

Focusing below on the scourging scenes of medieval religious drama, I suggest that such language complicates the pleasure and pain of performance as *memoria* did for epistemology. Dramatists reconfigure the spectacle of brutality as joyful, beautiful, civilizing, cathartic, curative, and even musical. Catharsis, as a rhetorical approach to the law, nurtures an association among torture, spectacle, and civilization (whether the latter was staged mentally during *inventio* and *memoria* or performed during the delivery of oratory or drama). Catharsis not only ties law to torture and invention: its violence foregrounds dramatic invention and performance. By extension, rhetoric is profoundly implicated in what René Girard calls the "banal role of violence in awakening desire" (*VS*, 144). But all its pains and pleasures hint that there was nothing at all banal about a violence that awakened a desire for drama. Dominant in a world in which so many real and fictional trials functioned as faits accomplis was what Bert States terms "the pleasure of the play."[37] Part and parcel of that pleasure were the long-standing associations among aesthetics, discipline, and the law. The medieval theater of cruelty reinvents those associations as it stages the useful pleasures of pain—or the painful pleasures of utility.

Nowhere is the phenomenon more striking, perhaps, than in the *Geu Saint Denis*, where *lier* and *liesse* alternate in a lyrical passage which invokes pain and joy, bondage and freedom. The Saint speaks immediately after a stage direction that he be bound (*Cy les ferrent*):

> Seigneurs, le corps povez *lier*
> Puis qu'a Dieu plaist, mez l'ame non.
> Les *liens* que nous soustenon
> Ou corps en *liee* pascïence
> Remetent l'estat d'innosence
> En l'ame et de mal la *deslient*
> Et a Dieu par amour la *lient*.
> Pour ce sommes joieus et *liez*
> Quant vous nous *liez* mains ou piez
> Car par vos durs *liens* de fer
> Dez fors et durs *liens* d'enfer
> Est nostre esperit *deslïe*.
> Par celuy qui pour nous *lié*
> Fut de durs *liens* a l'estache. (Emphasis mine)

[37] I refer to his book of the same title, *The Pleasure of the Play*; see esp. his Introduction and chaps. 1 and 12.

My Lords, you can bind my body, since it pleases God, but not my soul. The ligatures that we endure on our body in joyful patience put the soul in a state of innocence and unbind it from evil and attach it to God. For this, we are joyous and glad [bound] when you bind our hands and feet because, by your hard irons, our spirit is unbound from the strong and hard irons of hell by Him who was bound to the stake by hard irons.[38]

The saint asks his audiences to share the pain which he suffers with joy by experiencing their own joyful pains:

> Bonnes gens, *ne vous tristoiez,*
> *Se tourmenter vous me voiez,*
> Car par la *paine temporele*
> · Vient la *joye perpetuele.*
> Prenez bon cuer et hardiece;
> *Souffrez* tous maulz a grant *leece.*
> (*GSD*, 522–27; emphasis mine)

Good folk, don't be sad if you see me tormented because, through earthly pain comes eternal gladness. Take strength and courage in your hearts, and suffer all pains in great joy.

Naturally, medieval drama is by no means the sole cultural force to attribute a positive valence to violence; but its dramatizations of torture offer some illuminating rhetorical, pedagogical, and aesthetic strategies by which catharsis comes to be associated with rampant imagery of bodily mutilation. It provides a response to a question posed by Simon Richter. How, he asks, "can a representation be beautiful if pain is essential, but at the same time necessarily disfigures beauty and makes it different from itself?"[39] Early theorists had already explored that problem in such plays as the Amboise *Passion*, in which the joys of suffering are framed explicitly as catharsis. When one character bears witness to the murder of his family, his pain is transmuted into a pleasurable purgation "quant son pere et son enfant / Vit mourir a si grant tort. / Par son *plaisir* nous doint *effort / De purger nos vices et molestes /* Et que accepte noz requestes" (when he saw his father and his child die so wrongly. By his pleasure, may he [God] give us the strength to purge our vices and evils and that he accept our requests).[40] Here torture is so positive, so ennobling, so pleasurable that it produces not pain but the triumphant joy of sacrifice and, eventually, of the pleasures of witnessing such sacrifice on the medieval stage.

[38] *GSD*, 557–70; emphasis mine. I have reinterpreted some of Seubert's punctuation in favor of syntactic sense.

[39] Richter, *Laocoon's Body*, 48.

[40] Amboise *Passion*, 1–5; emphasis mine.

Nor is there any paucity of early English, German, Italian, or Spanish dramatic representations of torture. Countless plays stage beatings that imitate, reenact, and may even subvert the literal inscription of the law upon bodies. But the vicious *ébats* of the French Passion plays offer a particularly striking testimonial to the desire for and the desirability of violence. There, the depiction of torture as a violent *ludus* is consistently reinforced by the philological cohesion of bodily harm and pleasure. When the torturers of diverse Passion plays proudly announce their intent to concentrate on the fun and games of inflicting torture, they also articulate an important dramatic principle according to which pleasure is imbricated in the juridical representations of violence. That is to say that if the conjunction of violence, spectacle, and persuasion was the province of rhetoric, it was also the province of some medieval dramas to invent and reinvent the spectacular, persuasive powers of torture as a great dramatic game with all the ambiguous pleasures that derived from all the ambiguous pain.

As it happens, one feature that enhanced pain and pleasure was the musical playing of the body in pain. In numerous *mystères*, various representatives of the hegemony "play" the body of Christ or of other martyred characters by inflicting musical beatings as coercive "fun and games." The singsong refrains and relentless rhythmic beats that accompany a ludic *beating* are accentuated by a musical lexicon that aestheticizes violence in the ways implied by my opening reference to the *fidiculae*. For example, the torturers from the anonymous Troyes *Passion* invoke the concept of counterpoint: "Avant, villain, as tu ton conte? / Tu ne dis mot? Respons tu point? / Il chantera d'un contrepoint, / mais que soyons en jugement. / Vien ça, vien, hee, faulx garnement! / Est il vray ce qu'on a de toy / chanté aux princes de la loy?" (March, villain, have you had enough? Nothing to say? Got no answer? He'll soon be singing in counterpoint, but let us all agree. Come here, come on, you piece of fluff. Is it true what those princes of the law once sang/said about you?).[41] Beating the body is likened to playing a musical scale when "Rustique recorde sa gamme (*GSD*, 639); while, in the Auvergne *Passion*, the rounding up of martyrs inspires Maulbec to teaching his cronies the words of hunting songs. His offering imitates the sounds of wounded animals: "En voix casse / on leur dit: 'Bertrant, betoray!' / Lors la beste crye: 'Ay! Ay!' / quant l'a ung peu menassee" (in a hoarse voice, they said: 'Bertrant, betoray!' And the animal screams, 'Ay, ay,' when it's threatened a bit).[42] Shortly thereafter, Mallegueype strikes the cords of his instrument (*fugiendo ad cordas*) and sings a threatening tune: "Hay, hay, hay, hay, hay, hay, hay, hay! / Betoray, Girault, betoray! / Hay, hay, hay, hay, hay, hay, hay, hay! / Ou poueray yo fugir, meichante?" (nowhere to run, poor thing) (1396–99). Later still, Mal-

[41] Troyes *Passion*, II, bk. 3, 714. As Leo Treitler has shown in "Oral, Written, and Literate Process," medieval terminology did not distinguish between speech, singing, and chant.

[42] Auvergne *Passion*, 1356–59; also 1348–1406. On wild animals, see also Esther Cohen, *Crossroads of Justice*, chap. 7; Eusebius, *EH*, V, 1.38–42; and V. A. Kolve's comparison of Christ's torturers to animals in *PCC*, 190.

bec and Malegorge exercise their vocal chords as they beat Christ: "La, mon amy, la! / La, la la! / Veés cy tresbon commensement" (Now there's a good start) (2557–58). The torturer Sirus supplies song, dance, and percussion by beating out a rhythm (*Percutiat Sirus*) as his companion hammers nails into the body of Christ in tempo: "Malque, tourne de la le dos! / Tien la main et je frapparey. / Jhesus, tantost arés repos! / dormés vous et je chantarey" (Malque, turn his back over that way. Hold his hand down and I'll hit it. Jesus, soon you can relax. Fall asleep while I sing [you a lullaby]) (Auvergne *Passion*, 2593–96). And in the *Geu Saint Denis*, two torturers decapitate Saint Denis and hand him his head, which he picks up and carries off to the sound of music: "*Lors saint Denis prenge sa teste entre sez mains et lez anges le meinent un pou avant en chantant: 'Gloria tibi domine . . .' puis le metent souz .i. couverteur et s'en revoisent*" (Then Saint Denis is to take his head between his hands and the angels lead his way forward a little bit as they sing 'Gloria tibi domine' and then they place him under a blanket and return whence they came) (after v. 1041). The divine melody that survives and transcends all the pain is repeated in the final *Te Deum* (Chantez *Te Deum Laudamus*) (*CPM*, 2214).[43] It had been foretold in the Prologue, during which the narrator recounted to viewers that "Aprés fut mis hors des prisons; / Batus fut, la teste ot coupee! / Aussy eurent ses compaignons! . . . / En melodïeuses chançons / Ont les anges joye menee" (After that, he was taken out of prison, beaten, and beheaded! So too were his companions! And, with their melodious songs, the angels were joyful) (*CPM*, 123–28).

The veritable choreography of the buffetings of religious drama might just as well have had Thomas Murner's metronome beating the rhythm. With their mnemonic rhymes, rhythms, and melodies, the torturers of many *mystères* play out the dark side of *saltatio*. As they beat their tempos on Christ's body as "Empreuf. Et deux. Et trois. Et quatre. Et le cinquième de surcois" and chant their singsong counting refrains of "Ça, des verges! / Combien? / Deux paire; / les miennes ne vallent plus rien" (Gréban, 22769–76), they inflict their beatings quite literally as song and dance.[44] In the Mons *Passion*, Christ becomes a pathetic marionette for his tormentors, who taunt him crying: "Chà! maistre, chà! / sautés en place / Vecy dont vous serés vestu / Tendés les bras" (Go, master, go! jump in place! Here's how you'll be dressed, raise your arms!); and his companion Dentart joins in with "Ce pendant nous prenrons *esbat* / A luy crocqueter sus le teste / De roseaux" (While you're doing that, we'll amuse ourselves by boinking him on the head with reeds).[45] For the torturers of the Troyes *Passion*, the buffeting is a dance, its rhythm punctuated on Christ's body and echoed by the stage directions of the play: "Tien, va jouer! *Il frappe*. Tien, va dancer! *Il frappe*" (Hey, go play! *He strikes*. Hey, go dance! *He strikes*) (II, t. 2, 7842).

[43] Again, though edited separately, the *Geu Saint Denis* is part of the *CPM*.
[44] Sometimes Gréban's torturers even stage their choreography as a dumb show (after 22818).
[45] Mons *Passion*, 332–33; emphasis mine.

Elsewhere, in the Sainte Geneviève *Passion*, the Devil himself had called the tune: "Le dÿable sanz demourance / Leur fait faire *trop laide dance*. / Lez piez leur tient en contremont, / De dur aguillon lez semont" (Without hesitation, the Devil has them do a very ugly dance. He holds their feet up in the air and sprinkles them with hard needles).[46] In fact, it was all so much fun that Hapelopin of the *Geu Saint Denis* was afraid of being left out: "A quel pié, dea, va celle dance?" (Golly, how many beats [in what tempo] is this dance?) (1104–5; emphases mine).

Whether such moments are played for pity, for fear, or for laughs, they share an important feature that transcends their tonal differences. They stage the violent inscription of discipline on the body of an actor and on the minds of the audiences who flocked to the *mystères* to see the song and dance of their Savior being flogged time and time again. All concerned got a good strong dose of community-sanctioned performance as Christian dramatists helped to canonize the connections linking pain, pleasure, and play in a moral recontextualization of the old Aristotelian concept of catharsis.

For example, Bishop Annas of the Troyes *Passion* suggests that his guards curtail their boredom during the nightwatch over Christ by making a game of it: "afin qu'il ne vous ennuye, / esbattez vous a quelque jeu" (so that he doesn't bore you, take pleasure in some sort of game). The guards respond that, just as His trial has been predetermined, so too has their violent gaming. Rouillart answers that his only pleasure (*esbat*) will be in scourging (*battre*): "Nostre *esbat* est ja tout pourveu: / a riens ne nous voulons *esbattre*, / synon le bien torcher et *battre* / et nous en mocquer entre nous" (We've already provided for our diversion: we don't want to play at anything except punching and beating him soundly and poking fun at him among ourselves) (Troyes *Passion*, II, t. 2, 7772–77; emphasis mine).[47] In Gréban, one torturer reproaches his companion for cheating during their contest by getting in too many blows at once. "Griffon," he complains, "tu comptes sans *rabatre*: / pour ung coup tu en frappes trois. / Quand ce sont dix, fais une croix: / je ne le fais que pour *esbatre*. / Empreuf . . ." (Griffon, you're counting without starting over again; for each blow, you hit three. When you have ten, make a cross: I'm just doing it for the fun of it. And one . . .) (Gréban, 22807–11). Elsewhere, the Auvergne torturers exclaim of the prize for their own dice game, Christ's robe, "Jouons aux excés" (2689). And the torturers from the Angers *Résurrection* remember the beating as a "whodunit" in which the blindfolded Christ must guess the author of the blows he receives:

> Helas! Et quant il fut batu,
> Tant sur son chief que sur son col,

---

[46] Sainte Geneviève *Passion*, 883–86. These beatings also belong to the larger category of ritual drama that Richard Axton terms the "dancing game" (*European Drama*, chap. 3).

[47] Other references to *esbas* occur in II, bk. 2, 7742–45. See also Gréban, 19736–41; and the references to *rabatre* and *esbatre* in the Mons *Passion*, e.g., 323, 328, 366.

> Que on faisoit de luy *chapifol*
> En luy disant qu'il devinast
> Celluy qui plus fort le frapast,
> N'estoit ce pas chose *piteuse?*
> Las, si estoit! et angoisseuse![48]

Alas! And when he was beaten as much upon the head as upon the back and when they played *chapifol* on him, telling him to guess which one had hit him the hardest, was that not a piteous thing? Indeed it was, and anguishing! (Emphases mine)

Their game is nothing new to the torturers of the Sainte Geneviève *Passion*, who taunt Christ with "Qui t'a feru? Car le me devine! / Esgar com il besse l'eschine! / Le jeu, je croy, ly abelit" (Who struck you? Come on, can't you guess! Looky, looky how his back is slumping! Our game is pleasing him greatly) (1597–99). In the Mons *Passion*, that was part of the fun of it for Brayart and Griffon, the former stating that "nous le volons mener aux fleurs / Pour s'*esbatre* ung petit aux champs" (We want to take him out into the meadows to have a bit of fun in the fields) (323); and the latter, "A tel ju me voray-je *esbattre* / Et y frapper ale volée. *Ilz frappent tous*" (I'd like to play that game and strike a whole clutch of blows. *They all strike*) (328; emphases mine).

Another commonly exploited poetic pair is equally violent as *deduit* (delight) alternates with *deduire* (deducing logically). The Sainte Geneviève torturers delight in the dismembering of their victim: "En le detranchant se *deduirent*" (They amuse themselves by undoing and flogging him) (63). That is the beauty of the Mons play, as Clacquedent volunteered earlier when he derided his victim with "Fau(l)x prophe(t)te / Je prens à te ba(t)tre deduit" (False prophet, I take pleasure in beating you) (311). Of special interest in this respect are the dice games of the plays from Amboise and Mons, which further enrich the symbolism of violent, pedagogical play. While Jesus in the Amboise play recalls the pain of the dice games for his robe (Amboise *Passion*, 728–31), the torturers of the Mons play make the usual references to the pleasures of pain (*rabatre/esbatre*). Orillart even requests instruction in the rules of the game: "Il convient que Griffon *ensaigne* / Le sort et comment il se asorte" (Griffon should teach you the game and how it's played). His companion is only too happy to oblige with a perverse rendition of the judicial ordeal in which God or destiny (*le sort*) intervenes to select the victor: "Gettons troix dés et chil l'emporte / Qui le plus de poins gettera" (Let's throw three dice and the one who throws the most points is the winner) (375).[49] When Dentart asks who should begin, Griffon explains the significance of the three dice, casting God as the ultimate gamester in a pa-

---

[48] Angers *Résurrection*, I, Day 2, 11618–24. This play is interesting in that it stages pious reactions to the fun and games yet does not reenact the horrible games themselves.

[49] For more on the violent gaming of Christ's tormentors, see Woolf, *English Mystery Plays*, 254–55; Kolve's discussion of dice games and papse in *PCC*, 185–86; Davis, "Rites of Violence," 181.

rodic vision of the Holy Trinity: "Il n'en poeult chaloir, c'est tout ung. / Il y ara quelque adventure" (It doesn't make a difference, it's all one and the same. Something fun will happen here) (Mons *Passion*, 375; emphases mine).

In that way, the ignoble dice games of these *mystères* reverse the once-noble allegory of dicing, the troubled history of which had been expounded by Isidore of Seville in his own treatment of the "Figures of Dicing" (De Figuris Aleae). There, Isidore invokes the mnemonic and Christological terminology of past, present, and future in an allegorical interpretation of dice games played out on the vast stage of the history of humankind:

> Moreover, some dice-players deliberately play the game in an allegorical fashion [*per allegoriam*], as in Natural Philosophy, and make up explanations because of various resemblances between things [*rerum similitudine fingere*]. For they say that they use *three dice* because of the three divisions of time—*present, past, and future*—because they do not stay in place but always run away. And they even contend that the very rows on the board are marked off in six segments [*locis distinctas*] to match the ages of man, and in three rows to match the three divisions of time. (*Etymologiarum*, bk. 18, chap. 64)[50]

As Isidore has it, dice games were forbidden because "cheating and lying and even perjury are never absent from such gaming, culminating in the loss of both reputation and property. In consequence of such evils [*haec scelera*], dice-playing was finally prohibited by law" ("On the Prohibition of Dice Games," chap. 68). But the allegory of human life was forced to include the universal human traits of baseness, perjury, and evil—traits now attributed by the religious dramatist to the torturers of Christ. As they do their work and play their games, they pass easily into the realm of farce.

If the *deduit/deduire* pair calls up scholasticism, the *batre/esbatre* pair calls up the gallows humor of comedy as the torturers of Christ transform their nursery-rhyme beats and beatings into dancing games. Their farcical portrayal of extreme violence links the *mystère*'s farting, shitting, tortured bodies to such gleeful classical enumerations as that proposed in Aristophanes's *Frogs*. When the slave Xanthias changes roles with his master Dionysius, Xanthias urges that his "slave" be tortured: "Why anything! / The rack, the wheel, the whip. . . . Skin him alive. . . . Vinegar up his nose . . . bricks on his chest. . . . Or hang him by his thumbs."[51] A play like the *Geu Saint Denis* holds its own in this tradition when Denis's tormentors follow a stage direction to beat him with a stick (*en batant d'un baston*) and describe the saint as if he were a jumping bean:

---

[50] *Etymologiarum*, bk. 18, chap. 44, unpublished translation by Alexander P. MacGregor. Compare this passage to, e.g., Augustine's discussion of memory as uniting past, present, and future in the *Confessions*, bk. 11, chap. 11.

[51] For an insightful discussion of *Frogs*, 618–21, see duBois, *TT*, 29–31; and Peters, *Torture*, 15–16.

"Denis sy jeue a bonde cul / Pour ce vueil je qu'il ait du mien. / Tent t'escuele, cest os est tien. / *En ferant*/ Port'en la moitié a ta fame" (Denis, let's play leap-ass. That's why he's gotta get some of what I've got to give. Here, take your turn, this bone is for you [*striking*]. There you go, bring half back to your wife) (*GSD*, 635–38).[52] Such comic beatings also recall the ambiguous relationship of rhetoric itself to pain and its pleasures. Inventionally speaking, everything remains open to question in an oft-replayed scene like the scourging of Christ, in which the moral ambiguities of torture are compounded by the moral ambiguities of reception. If, as we have seen, the truth of torture was in the eye of the beholder, so too was its cruelty and its theater.

Scourgings like those from the *Geu Saint Denis* and the *Passions* from Angers and Auvergne show how readily farcical pleasure mutates into terror. Upon viewing the violent spectacle they themselves have enjoyed tendering, even the torturers of the *Geu Saint Denis* acknowledge the problems of reception. When the decapitated saint walks off with his own head to the songs of angels, they realize that, in trying to terrify Denis, it is they who have been terrified by him. "Il me fault ou fuir ou seoir," cries Masquebignet, "Car lez chans et lez braieries / Que j'ay environ ly oïes / *M'espoventens et desconfortent*" (I've either got to flee or stay, because the songs and bleatings around me terrify and grieve my hearing) (1063–66).[53] In the Angers *Résurrection*, the way in which Christ's inhuman tormentors (*gens inhumains*) poked and pulled and prodded him because "neither his feet nor his hands could stretch far enough to the holes that had been fashioned there" prompts Lucas to ask, "Was that not great cruelty?" (Quant il fust tout nu despoillié / Pour estre a la croix atachié / Et tiré par gens inhumains, / Pour ce que ses piéz ne ses mains / Pas assez loing ne s'estendoient / Aux pertuys qui fais y estoient, / Ne fut ce pas grant cruaulté?) (I, 11643–49). Before that explicit analogy of Christ's cross to the tortures of the rack, Cleophas had condemned the buffeting as an anguishing *chose piteuse* and a public mockery:

> Mais aussi fut ce grant *pitié*,
> Quant son visaige fut crachié
> Et son chief couronné d'espines
> Aussi persans qu'aguilles fines,
> Sa doulce face *buffectee*
> Et sa barbe a force tiree
> Et luy *moqué* publiquement
> (Angers *Résurrection*, I, Day 2, 11626–31)

[52] In my translations of these merry dances, I have tried to capture the spirit (colloquial, grotesque) at the occasional expense of a more literal interpretation.

[53] Drama shares with hagiography this technique according to which saintly torments are occasionally transferred from the body of the martyr to that of the tormentor, who experiences a different kind of "cure." See, e.g., "The Life of Agnes," in Brigitte Cazelles, trans., *Lady as Saint*, p. 98.

But it was also a great pity when they spat in his face and crowned his head with thorns as piercing as fine needles and buffeted his sweet face and viciously pulled his beard and mocked him in public.

Here the function of these sad and gruesome recollections of violent gaming is to evoke feelings of pity, pain, and pleasure in audiences who are simultaneously invited to resurrect that violent gaming from their own memories. Buffeting as buffoonery is farcical to the torturers and piteous to Cleophas (or to the right kind of spectator).

Similarly, in the Sainte Geneviève *Passion*, the Jews are typecast in the role of Isidore's immoral perjurers as they play their evil games: "Chiez Pilate fut ramenez; / La fut son corps moult malmenez. / Quant les Juïfz yllec le tindrent, / De *leurs mauvez geus* li aprindrent. / Tantost tout nu le despoullierent; / A une estache le lïerent" (He was taken to Pilate; and there his body was mistreated. When the Jews held him there, they gave him some lessons in their evil games. They quickly stripped him and tied him to a stake) (77–82). Whenever torture is enacted on the medieval and early Renaissance stage, it solicits horror, terror, fear, and trembling in some; pity, mercy, and empathy in others; and yucks and guffaws in those who, like the spectators at the Corpus Christi pageant in which Fergus is beaten, "used to produce more noise and laughter than devotion" (magis *risum* & clamorem causabat quam deuocionem).[54] In the Angers *Résurrection* the scourging is a *chose piteuse* (I, 11623); while in the Auvergne *Passion* it is pleasure for Christ's torturers and a *doleureux esbatement* (painful playing) for Maria, who is watching (2422). Christ's pain is pleasure for his tormentors, pain for the virtuous Christian (although, as in many hagiographic narratives, pain is sometimes a kind of reward for the victim and the good-hearted spectator), and, presumably, both painful pleasure and pleasurable pain for anyone who chose to attend a mystery play in early France.

In the context of medieval religious drama, however, it is difficult to fathom that the same dramatic genre could prompt sympathy for the pain of a martyr but no sympathy for the villains who eventually receive their just deserts. It is equally difficult to fathom how authors of such a genre could denounce in strangers, Jews, and women the same violent methods that they reenact in service to the pedagogical mission of Christian peace and harmony. Even when a religious drama contains explicit denunciations of ludic violence against Christ, that violence is staged nonetheless for the pleasure and edification of its audiences. The very sight or thought or memory of His horrific ordeal therefore arms the Christian dramatist (along with his audiences) with ludic materials apt

---

[54] This passage appears in the REED volumes on *York*, ed. Alexandra Johnston and Margaret Rogerson, I, 47–48 (Latin); and II, 732 (English). It was discussed by Ruth Evans in a conference paper titled "When a Body Meets a Body." Elsewhere, V. A. Kolve replaces the question of violence with that of dramatic characterization (e.g., *PCC*, 178–79).

to condemn the Jews (scourging, dancing, playing). At the same time, those methods are beyond reproach for his own purposes.

Characterized by the same *mise en abîme* as torture itself, ludic medieval scenes of punitive and interrogatory torture undermine the lessons of violence exhibited as pleasure and pain. Since its own truths are grounded in dramatic and affective interpretations, the *mystère* prompts an additional inquiry into the dark side of catharsis: specifically, the ways in which its ideology stages the pleasures of bodies in pain and enacts purgations within the context of anti-Semitism.

Historically speaking, the terminology of catharsis has been linked not only to torture, pleasure, politics, and hermeneutics but to medicine and pathology. Beyond Aristotelian catharsis and Platonic juridical pleasures and pains, numerous rhetorical, hagiographical, and dramatic representations of the law presented a vision of the body of the state in pain or sickness and in need of a cure. In fact, long before the theme of torment as cure informed Nazi ideology, it had been associated with the tortured bodies of early religion, rhetoric, and drama.[55] Eusebius recounts that, when one group of torturers decided to kill their victim, their efforts were thwarted as follows: "not only did nothing of this kind happen, but, beyond all human expectation, he raised himself up and his body was straightened in the subsequent tortures, and he regained his former appearance and the use of his limbs, so that through the grace of Christ *the second torturing became not torment but cure*" (*EH*, V, I.24; emphasis mine). The Renaissance philosopher Scipione Ammirato analogized the cultural function of political life to a grand medical purgation with poetic resonances: "the poet bears the same relationship to the physician as the legislator does to the surgeon" insofar as the "end of poetry is to induce virtue into the soul by driving vice out of it."[56] As late as 1857, Jacob Bernays formulated "an intriguing theory: the word 'catharsis' would be a medical metaphor, a purgation which denotes the pathological effect on the soul, analogous to the effect of medicine on the body" (*TO*, 28.) But, as the tortured bodies of Christian martyrs become the battlefield for a greater conflict between Christian and pagan forces and an incitation that viewers martyr themselves, the vision of torture as a social curative returns us to the politics of catharsis, to its relationship to the tortures of invention, and to its occasionally pathological relationship to the body.

---

[55] See, e.g., Eckstein's comment on the ways in which Nazi rhetoric "proposed killing as healing . . . a sick body plagued by the disease of Jewry," in *LFWP*, 80. See also Tatar, *Lustmord*, 55–56. Although the historical and literary realities of anti-Semitism constitute a topic far too vast to be treated adequately here, I refer the reader to Louise Fradenburg, "Criticism, Anti-Semitism, and the Prioress's Tale"; Nirenberg, *Communities of Violence*; Biddick, "Genders, Bodies, Borders"; and Hsia, *Myth of Ritual Murder*.

[56] Weinberg on *Il Dedalione overo del poeta dialogo* (1560) in *HLCIR*, I, 17. Compare this with, e.g., Plato's extensive comparisons of rhetoric and cosmetics, medicine and gymnastics, body and soul, illusion and reality, preventive and corrective in *Gorgias*, 464.

Philologically as well as historically, the emphasis within the rhetorical tra-dition on torture, catharsis, and politics supplies an epistemological model in which such violently curative visions could be conceived. Indeed, the spectacu-lar nature of rhetorical theory probably reinforced the doctrine that, when it came to serving the body of the state, some victims of violence were more de-serving than others. For many medieval dramatists, who had their own plea-surable ways of spreading the word that torment could constitute a type of medicine for the state, the Jews seemed particularly "deserving." Nor were they "deserving" in the benevolent way described by Alan of Lille in his thirteenth-century *Liber poenitentialis*. In a fascinating link between the signifying power of the body, the gestural body-language of delivery, and the healing of souls, he writes that "like the doctor, the healer of souls must in fact consider 'also the gestures of the body and the expression of the face, so as to understand the in-ner *disposition* via the external signs. . . . The face is, so to speak, the revealer of the soul.'"[57] This is a description about reading the signs of bodies in pain and finding and delivering materials discovered in bodily health and pathology.

On the French medieval stage, one example of anti-Semitism is the sinister conclusion of the *Mystère de Sainte Venice*. When the emperor Vaspasien is goaded by his son Titus into avenging himself on the Jews as a way of maintain-ing the health of the state, the play comes to a brutal close with an escalation of violence and the promise of future violence against them. Titus visualizes the cure of the state as the extermination of the Jews: "Pour tant, pere, il fault que mandez / Tous voz barons et commandez / Lever par toute vostre terre / Capi-taynes et gens de guerre / Pour *mettre a execution / Des Juifz toute la nation*" (And that's why, Father, you must send for all your barons and generals and raise troops throughout your land, captains and warriors to put to death the entire nation of the Jews).[58] Region then analogizes that brutality to kindness, implying that the tyrant's own healed body must commit to further brutally inflicted cures:

> Monstrez vous plain de *gentillesse!*
> *Abbattez* courroux et tristesse,
> Puis que vostre mezellerie
> Et griefve douleur a pris cesse
> Et est totallement *guerye*.
> Monstrez par tout vostre noblesse
> Et que tout le monde congnoisse
> De Dieu la puissance infinye.
> (855–62; emphases mine)

Show yourselves full of kindness. Extinguish anger and sadness because your tribu-lations and leprosy have come to an end and [are] totally cured. Show [it] by all your nobility, so that the whole world might know the infinite strength of God.

[57] Alan as cited in Pouchelle, *BSMA*, 147; emphasis mine.
[58] *Mystère de Sainte Venice*, 844–49; emphasis mine.

Torment is the cure offered by a pagan state, the means to purge its collective body, even as it becomes a part of a Christian cure that drives out pagan vices— whence another "happy ending."

The final words of the play uttered by Ferandon exhort his listeners to violence as a means of fostering health. Healthy bodies are to be maintained so that they may be known *en faictz et en dictz* that will admit them to paradise (874– 75): "Dieu ceste belle compaignye / Vueille garder totallement / De tout mal et encombrement! / Par le merite des bons sainctz / *Maintienne tousjours noz corps sains*" (May God wish to protect this noble assembly completely from all evil and obstacle! By the merit of the good saints, may he always keep our bodies healthy) (863–67; emphasis mine). In the homophony of *sain* (healthy) and *saint* (saint/saintly), a healthy individual body is a healthy, holy collective, body which is strengthened here by the purgative brutality it inflicts on selected victims.

In the final analysis, one of the premier features of such purgations is the implication that one can be guided toward distinguishing between deserving victims and worthy practitioners of violence. What was a Passion play if not a golden opportunity to purge audience emotion and give them pleasure by staging the unjust punishment of Christ and the presumably just punishment of the Jews for having punished him? Catharsis is associated here with a kind of pathology that is rehearsed within an equally pathological rhetoric. Yet the very introduction of metaphors of pathology into the rhetorical tradition proffers a strategy according to which audiences who experience the pleasure of pity and fear may be persuaded that violence and the threat of torture is not only fun to watch but good for them. In that sense, the greatest feat of the combined powers of memory and delivery may well be that they make it possible for rhetoric to persuade its various audiences that coercive messages are diverting. Sometimes, dramatic rhetoric may even convince audiences that they are being entertained when, often, they are being coerced. Threats and coercion may then appear to be so good for an audience that they could inspire future enthusiastic theatergoers and dramatists eager to continue to replicate the paradoxes of violence in new art forms.

Supporting that view is the fact that rhetorical theories of tortured catharsis shift to the audience's experience of painful emotions and to the moral considerations of the pleasure they experience (or were solicited to experience) while watching spectacles of justice and retribution. Especially when it came to a "real" event like Christ's Passion and some of its anti-Semitism, ambiguous theories of representation gave rise to a debate about the ambiguous reception of violence.

The question of audience has eternally posed rhetorical problems that are likewise problems of delivery, drama, and morality. If Cato's dictum was that an orator was "a good man skilled in speaking," then, presumably, an evil man could not be a good rhetorician (even though the Devil in the *Jeu d'Adam* is one of the most skillful orators to grace the medieval French stage). More important, the question whether audiences could distinguish good from evil obsessed the likes of Tertullian and Augustine, both of whom pondered the moral conundrum exemplified by the interplay among law, drama, and the spectacle of punishment. The former reserved special contempt for the amphitheater because of its indiscriminate solicitation of worthy pleasures in the innocent, unworthy pleasures in the guilty, and unworthy pleasures even in the innocent who would normally enjoy (as they ought) the virtuous spectacle of the law in action: " 'It is a good thing, when the guilty are punished.' Who will deny that, unless he is one of the guilty? And yet *the innocent cannot take pleasure in the punishment of another*, when it better befits the innocent to lament that a man like himself has become so guilty that a punishment so cruel must be awarded him." [59] Saint Augustine proved equally troubled by the topic as he agonized in his *Confessions* about the seductive power of stage plays to convert pain into pleasure: "What is the reason now that a spectator desires to be made sad when he beholds doleful and tragical passages, which himself could not endure to suffer? Yet for all that he desires to feel a kind of passionateness, yea, and his passion becomes his pleasure too [*et dolor ipse est voluptas eius*]. What is all this but a miserable madness [*insania*]?" (*Confessions*, bk. III, chap. 2).

As it happens, the violence of early drama and the amphitheater moved such eighteenth-century aesthetic theorists as Du Bos and Marivaux to take their concerns to the next logical stage. As David Marshall observes, they worried about the conjunction of cruelty and empathy within "the frame of theater [which] signals the pleasure of the audience in beholding of a spectacle of suffering, yet it does not signal the secret awareness that the spectacle is false. If the audience watches the spectacle at several removes, it is because of the self-interested sense of distance and safety that Lucretius describes, not because of the effects of mimesis" (*SES*, 25–26). André de Lorde later justified his excessively violent conception of a *théâtre de la peur* by arguing that terror brings audiences "a sort of consolation" (*TM*, 14).

For all his fears about "styled misery," even Augustine's complaint betrays a kind of optimism that feigned stage passions would elicit at least mercy or pity if not action. If there was no hope that good thoughts like mercy and pity could be translated into good works, then the divide between emotion and action would be unbridgeable. The problem, of course, was whether the pleasures of empathy were legitimate or merely self-congratulatory:

> Howsoever, when a man suffers aught in his own person, it uses to be *styled misery*: but when he hath a fellow feeling of another's, then 'tis mercy. But what compassion is to be shown at those feigned and scenical passions? For the *auditors here are not provoked to help the sufferer*, but invited only to be sorry for him: and they so much the more love the author of these fictions, by how much the more he can move pas-

---

[59] Tertullian, *De spectaculis*, 19; emphasis mine. See also Plass, *Game of Death in Ancient Rome*. It is worth emphasizing here that, since mine is a book about the rhetorical canons used by speakers, it is not about reception or reception theory.

sion in them. . . . Whereas no man is willing to be miserable, is he notwithstanding pleased to be merciful? (*Confessions*, bk. III, chap. 2; emphasis mine).

Augustine's madness and de Lorde's comforting terrors were regularly in evidence in the pleasures, pains, punishments, and purgations of the late medieval and early Renaissance stage. And whatever the valence attributed to audience affect, few things were more unpredictable than the responses of medieval spectators to dramatic scenes of torture. One could, however, predict their participation in pleasurable pity and pain—a response cultivated by forensic rhetoric itself.

From Aristotle to Lucian of Samosata to Marivaux to the current American reality-based crime shows, the pleasure of watching pain has endured and flourished. No matter what arguments are advanced about the just or unjust infliction of violence, drama scholars have tended to subscribe to such positions as Aristotle's that "accurate likenesses" of pain are enjoyable to see, Lucian's that the pantomime's pleasurable violence involved fewer risks than real violence, or Lucretius's that it was "sweet" to watch danger "while assured of one's own safety." [60] Be that as it may, in the Middle Ages, the ostensible safety of that distance was habitually compromised, as was its sweetness, while in the realm of rhetorical spectacle such safety was an illusion. In both theory and practice, the Aristotelian limits to "likeness" has known no bounds in classical, medieval, and even avant-garde drama.

The concluding sections of this chapter focus on specific medieval performances that capitalized on precisely that phenomenon of boundlessness. But the distinct juridical register of many such moments first prompts an analysis of one more feature of forensic rhetoric. Invariably caught up in the spectacular invention of pain, that genre also foregrounded audience response to violence in a whole series of discourses and practices associated with the pleasures of witnessing cruelty: pleasures for some, pain for others, problems for critics.

Witnesses at the Scene

Forensic rhetoric is, of course, not identical to dramatic rhetoric. The former ritually enacts a juridical proceeding with "real" results while the latter would presumably "just represent" them. But the similarities between certain legalistic and theatrical representations readily collapsed that distinction. Once the theatricality of medieval public ordeals is considered side by side with the "representations" of public ordeals in the theater, their interdependence is only too apparent. Both types of juridical spectacle exhort their audiences to experience

[60] Again, I refer to Aristotle, *Poetics*, 1448b; Lucian, "Saltatio," 71; and the Lucretian view as discussed in, e.g., Marshall, *SES*, 23.

the pleasures (voluntary or involuntary) of being witnesses to, participants in, and judges of acts of violence. I show in this section that, within a juridical context, the boundaries between fictional and nonfictional violence (if boundaries there were) were consistently blurred by the reliance of the legal process on spectacle and the reliance of dramatic spectacle on the legal process. That confusion was propagated in large part by a theatricalized forensic *actio*, which enacted the protodramatic powers of memory and directly invited its audiences to participate in rituals of retribution.[61]

Quintilian, for instance, was emphatic on the subject when he urged a costumed, gesticulating lawyer to assume the voice of a murdered victim and to display the instruments of his demise so that "our emotions will be no less actively stirred than if we were present at the actual occurrence" (*IO*, VI, 2.32): "We see blood-stained swords, fragments of bone taken from the wound, and garments spotted with blood, displayed by the accusers, wounds stripped of their dressings, and scourged bodies bared to view [*verberata corpora nudari*]. The impression produced by such exhibitions is generally enormous, since they seem to bring the *spectators face to face with the cruel facts* [in rem praesentem animos hominum ducentium]" (*IO*, VI, 1.30–31).

With such words, Quintilian affirmed the necessity of representing before witnesses crimes for which motives might have been "discovered" through torture: "a powerful effect may be created if to the actual facts of the case we add a plausible picture of what occurred, such as will make our audience feel as if they were actual eyewitnesses of the scene" (multum confert adiecta veris credibilis rerum *imago*, quae velut *in rem praesentem* perducere audientes videtur) (*IO*, IV, 2.123). He also praised Cicero for having brought "such a vivid image of the crime before their minds [repraesentavit imaginem sceleris], that Caesar seemed not to have been murdered, but *to be being murdered* before their very eyes" (*IO*, VI, 1.31; emphases mine). In other words, it was not enough to judge a murder: one had to experience its drama for oneself.

As medieval religious drama explores, explicates, litigates, and punishes injustices, it bears out Kubiak's insight, following Nietzsche and Foucault, that "the law has its *origin* in terror inscribed on the body, projecting the body and its pain as currency into an economy of punishment and correction whose primary pay-off is the pleasure of being witness, of *seeing* the violence" (*ST*, 40; emphasis his). Indeed, the pleasures of witnessing and participating in violence were routinely played out with all the power and all the theatricality with which delivery endowed them. That occurred not only in rhetorical orations but in many types of theoretical, meditational, and dramatic writings. For example, Longinus believed that the memory imagery that rehearsed delivery was most

---

[61] The notion of a cathartic drama of execution is consistent with Vico's "Tre spezie de giurisprudenze" (*Scienza nuova*, 588–89); see also Foucault on Vico, *DP*, 45. Again, my focus here is not anthropological but rhetorical, although it is clear that the two might fruitfully be considered together.

"Dyeing" for art

It's fairly easy to avoid swallowing poison. Yet imagine if poison was seeping out of the walls of your house! That's exactly what happened in the 19th century.

William Morris was an English artist and writer who designed colourful wallpapers. He didn't realize that some of the colours he used were made from toxic chemicals, including arsenic, lead, chromium and mercury.

A brightly coloured William Morris wallpaper design.

Deathly glow

In the early 20th century, people didn't know that **radioactive** chemicals were dangerous. The numbers on watch faces were often painted with glow-in-the-dark radium paint. Radium is radioactive. When the painters' teeth began falling out, they realized that radium is toxic.

radioactive   sending out powerful and dangerous rays

powerful when "you seem to see what you describe and bring it vividly before the eyes of your audience."[62] For Isidore of Seville, the genres of comedy, tragedy, and law each cast their audiences as witnesses to events that were tonally dissimilar but etymologically similar. Comic actors rendered private things public when they "represented by song and gesture the doings of men in private life" (comoedi sunt qui privatorum hominum acta dictis aut gestu cantabant).[63] Tragic poets performed in something like the juridical forum which Isidore invokes at the outset of Book 18 of the *Etymologiarum*. Their judges and juries are *spectators* of ancient crimes: "those who sang in mournful verses of the ancient deeds and crimes of wicked kings *while the people watched*" (qui antiqua gesta atque facinora sceleratorum regum luctuosa carmine spectante populo concinebant) (*Etymologiarum*, bk. 18, chap. 45). And, most pertinent here, much of medieval devotional literature emphasized the spectacular and commemorative aspect of the blood of Christ with what Thomas Bestul terms a heightened realism and "spectacularism." Contrary to some Western ideas about the private, interior scene of devotion, when twelfth-century treatises encouraged intense meditation on the Passion, they frequently recommended "that the meditator *place himself as though actually present at the events*, forming detailed pictures through the faculty of the imagination."[64] If "these developments belong to a form of devotion known as *imitatio Christi*," they also belong to rhetoric, to the inventional, mnemonic imagination, and to its enactment during delivery.

Learned medieval dramatists seem to have appreciated that principle enormously, as when the great medieval mystery plays recruited their own audiences as *témoins oculaires*. In the Prologue to the Third Day of his *Mystère de la Passion*, Arnoul Gréban's narrator announces that "La verrez inquisicions, / faulx temoingz, accusacions / et tous les tours qu'on puet querir / a faire ung innocent mourir" (There you will see inquisitions, false witnesses, accusations, and all the tricks that one can seek in order to make an innocent man die) (20076–79); and in the banns before the Chester Plays, there occurs a similar promise to reenact the pain and suffering of Christ: "You ffletchers, bowyers, Cowpers, stringers, and Iremongers, / see soberly ye make of Christes dolefull death, / his scourginge, his whippinge, his bloudeshett and passion / and all the paines he suffred till the last of his breath."[65] Elsewhere, in the realm of farce, the fifteenth-century *Farce nouvelle et fort joyeuse du pect* plays on the status of the human nose as the witness to a domestic spectacle in which a husband hauls his wife before a judge for farting in the foyer.[66] So, many sorts of spectacle stage eyewitness accounts to dramatize the legal or punitive investigations that are the plays' ob-

---

[62] Longinus, "On the Sublime," 15, 1–2.

[63] Isidore of Seville, *Etymologiarum*, bk. 18, chap. 46; trans. by Brehaut, *Encyclopedist*.

[64] Bestul, *Texts of the Passion*, 147; emphasis mine.

[65] *Chester Plays*, ed. Deimling, v. 138–41. See also Guilfoyle, "Staging of the First Murder in the Mystery Plays in England"; and Diehl, "Rhetoric of Witnessing," *Staging Reform*, chap. 7.

[66] I discuss this text in *ROMD*, 216–21, although again my focus is on religious dramas that set forth explicit didactic messages.

jects of inventional and creative investigations. Such instances hold out the possibility that the shifting boundaries between law and spectacle were especially well-suited to the violence of late medieval French drama.

Thanks to Michel Foucault's work in cultural studies, critics have widely accepted the theory that "from the point of view of the law that imposes it, *public torture and execution must be spectacular. . . .* The very excess of the violence employed is one of the elements of its glory: the fact that the guilty man should moan and cry out under the blows is not a shameful side-effect, it is the very ceremonial of justice being expressed in all its force" (*DP*, 34; emphasis mine). But while Foucault and his followers have directed the force of their attention to the early modern period, his theory is borne out by innumerable classical, medieval, and early Renaissance examples. For the evil pre-Christian emperor Gaius Caligula, the legal ceremonial of torture was a favorite form of drama. While the emperor was "lunching or revelling capital examinations by torture were often made in his presence, and a soldier who was an adept at decapitation cut off the heads of those who were brought from prison" (*LC*, I, "Caligula," chap. 32). In the Christian Middle Ages and Renaissance, that spectacle continued when one observer termed an execution in Brussels "la plus belle que l'on avait oncques vue" (the most beautiful ever seen). The citizens of Mons even purchased a criminal from a neighboring town so that he might be drawn and quartered before spectators—so compellingly that "le peuple fust plus joyeulx que si un nouveau corps sainct estoit ressuscité" (the people were more joyous than if a new holy body had been resurrected).[67] In 1534, Francis I demonstrated to the sounds of trumpet fanfare the spectacle of his power along with his power over punitive spectacle when he announced that "doresnavant brigans et meurtriers ne seroient plus penduz ne brulez, mais seroient brisez et auroient les membres cassez, puis seroient mis et liez sur roues, pour y achever leur vie tant qu'ilz y pourroient languir" (henceforth, brigands and murderers would no longer be hanged or burned but would be flogged and would have their limbs broken, then they would be taken and bound upon wheels, there to end their life for as long as they would be able to suffer there).[68]

Furthermore, among the more haunting features of the history of torture is the transmutation of the role of witness/spectator to that of participant/victim. That is, victims of torture are forced to view the staging of their own dismemberment. Elaine Scarry has analyzed the phenomenon in her work on the theatrical and cinematic lexicon of the Chilean "blue lit stage" (*BP*, 28), but the lexicon is as old as antiquity. Suetonius reports that Caligula was particularly fond of forcing the tortured to watch the spectacle of their own mutilation. He "seldom had anyone put to death except by numerous slight wounds, his constant order, which soon became well-known, being: 'Strike so that he may feel that he is dying'" (*LC*, I, "Caligula," chap. 30). During one of the many mar-

---

[67] Rey-Flaud refers to both of these incidents in *PDMA*, 152.

[68] *Journal d'un Bourgeois de Paris sous le règne de François I (1515–1530)*, ed. V. L. Bourilly, 376.

tyrdoms enumerated by Eusebius, a victim is converted synecdochally into one massive wound that is witnessing its wounding: "his body was a witness to his treatment; it was all one wound and bruise, wrenched and torn out of human shape" (*EH*, V, 1.22–23). In a much later episode analyzed by Michael Lieb, the order for punishment of Major General Thomas Harrison stresses the fact that the traitor must behold his mutilation: "you shall be hanged by the neck, and being alive shall be cut down, and your privy members to be cut off, your entrails to be taken out of your body, and, you living, the same to be burnt before your eyes, and your head to be cut off, your body to be divided into four quarters, and head and quarters to be disposed of at the pleasure of the king's majesty." [69]

When such moments of conscious spectacularity are connected to the pleasures of so-called civilized societies, one can reasonably assert that the connections among torture, executions, drama, law, and legal language would have been perceptible not only to readers of Isidore of Seville or Tertullian but to the numerous spectators of various public ordeals. By extension, medieval spectators familiar with the scourging scenes of religious drama would also have been aware of the problematic associations of torture and pleasure, law and drama, especially since those associations were sometimes deliberately enhanced. The citizens of Arles, for example, imported a professional executioner from Avignon to lend immediacy to the torture scenes of a Passion play they were staging.[70] Similarly, in a little-known study on Cornish drama, Anatole Le Braz went so far as to speculate that medieval theater audiences experienced the dramatic aesthetics of death metonymically through a kind of vicarious participation in the fashioning of implements of torture. Part of the delight of a crucifixion scene, he argued, was that an audience composed primarily of farmers, miners, and fishermen could identify with their fellow workers on stage. As some members of the audience did "in real life," the artisan characters fashioned whips, nails, and crosses.[71] Here, the hands of murderers, of actors playing murderers, and of craftsmen fabricating murder weapons combined to inflict violence much as Quintilian's dancing mnemonic visions were joined hand in hand (*IO*, XI, 2.20). The synecdochal imagery of the hands of memory thus comes alive during delivery and during rhetorically conceived dramas. Those hands are linked synecdochally to mnemotechnics, to the *communis sermo* of gestural delivery (*IO*, XI, 3.87), and to their languages of violence.[72]

---

[69] *Complete Collection of State Trials and Proceedings*, V, 1034. See Michael Lieb's discussion of this text in *MCV*, 76. Compare it with, e.g., the ordeal cited earlier from the *Vengeance de Nostre-Seigneur*.

[70] The Avignon incident is also discussed in Rey-Flaud, *PDMA*, 153.

[71] Le Braz, *Théâtre celtique*, 120. See also Eusebius on the hands of workers (*EH*, III, 20.2–3). Space constraints prevent an adequate treatment of the question of class, although it subtends this repertoire. See, e.g., the Pseudo-Cicero on the gestures of actors or day laborers (*RAH*, III, 26).

[72] Compare, e.g., Le Braz's theory to John of Garland's metonymic depiction of the sword as a "wound-making steel" in *Parisiana poetria*, II, 57–58.

As far as gesture is concerned, rhetorical treatises spotlight the role of the hands, which speak a universal language. Quintilian writes, for example, that "other portions of the body merely help the speaker, whereas the hands may almost be said to speak. . . . Though the peoples and nations of the earth speak a multitude of tongues, they share in common the universal language of the hands [*communis sermo*]" (*IO*, XI, 3.85–87). The hands that murdered victims before spectators, the hands that scourged Christ, the hands that Pilate washed, and the hands that re-created such violence on the medieval stage (in both real and realistic manners) spoke a language of bloodshed as they enacted the blooded thought of mnemotechnics. Indeed, forensic rhetoric cultivated the hyperreality and simulations that medieval religious drama would later put to such effective use.

Even as acts of violence blur the boundaries between drama and law, however, they complicate the nature of catharsis—not only on the stage but during the spectacle of public execution with which the stage alternates. During the scourging of Christ in a Passion play, audiences pleasurably purged their feelings about the unjust infliction of pain, while during spectacles of public execution, the pleasurable infliction of pain was ostensibly justified. Even so, if we accept the testimony of the *bourgeois de Paris*, at least one medieval audience was steadfastly determined to experience catharsis at a public execution—even when forced to invent their own pathos when the victim failed to provide it. When Pierre des Essarts offered little aesthetic assistance to observers as he was led giggling to the slaughter in 1413, the crowd managed nonetheless to see the drama they wanted to see, to generate their own pity and fear: "tous ceulx qui le veoient plouroient si piteusement que vous ne ouyssiez oncques parler de plus grans pleurs pour mort de homme, et lui tout seul rioit" (all those who saw him were weeping so piteously that you would never have heard tell of greater sobbing for the death of a man—all the while that he alone was laughing).[73] Their pity, their fear, and their empathy emerge from a self-generated drama in the face of a physical reality that offered something different.

Pierre Des Essarts's tale represents the antithesis of a number of contemporary assessments about the spectacularity of public executions. When the contrary fellow subverts his own role (or roles), he contradicts Karen Cunningham's remark that, at least by Marlowe's time, jurists, defendants, and even executioners were complicitous in "self-conscious accord with their roles in some cosmic morality play, a sort of 'Everyman Goes to the Gallows.'"[74] Des Essarts has clearly refused to play his part. But that does not matter to his audience, who also call into question Esther Cohen's later assertion about them. For Cohen, the

---

[73] *Journal d'un bourgeois de Paris 1405–1449*, ed. Tuety, 33; see also the accessible translation by Shirley, *Parisian Journal, 1405–1449*, 78. In his discussion of this particular incident, Rey-Flaud examines only the comportment of the criminal—not the audience's response to him (*PDMA*, 155).

[74] Cunningham, "Renaissance Execution," 212. See Marshall, *SES*, 23; and Gontier, *Cris de haine et rites d'unité*.

spectators of medieval executions resembled "any magician's audience" in that "they saw exactly what they were meant to see and only that: the majesty of the law in its full efficacy. What they recorded for us was not how the law worked, but how people saw it working" ("'To Die,'" 300). The fact that Des Essarts's audiences persisted in seeing the very drama he refused to provide makes one thing clear: even if Cohen is correct in insisting that medieval repentants knew their lines in advance ("'To Die,'" 289), they did not necessarily agree to recite them. Consequently, Des Essarts's conduct also undermines Foucault's appealing contention that the criminal on the scaffold attains moral dignity because spectators identify with him.[75] For all those watching the dramatic execution of Pierre Des Essarts, the identification is clearly false, invented, and, by extension, so too is their pity.

The execution of Pierre Des Essarts along with the other examples cited above present a conundrum which will inform the final pages of this book. When an audience participates so willingly in a *spectaculum crudelitatis* that it sees something that is not there, is it *acquiring* or *abandoning* agency?[76] Under such circumstances, does catharsis occur? And how is its status altered by real violence, represented violence, or misunderstandings about what an audience is really seeing? If catharsis occurs, who experiences it, and who is responsible for it? The individual audience member? The victim? The hegemony controlling the execution? The dramatist representing or reenacting executions on stage? How is it possible to delight in witnessing the law in action at the same time that that experience is purged? In light of those questions, even Karen Cunningham's illuminating exposures of the spectacle of torture fall short. In her work on Marlowe, Cunningham concludes that certain spectators of an execution might transform their pity into a subtle yet effective condemnation of torture: "if the doomed figures touch the hearts of others, if they establish themselves not as outcasts but as members of society, if they cause observers to identify with rather than against them, they imply alternative ways of viewing their deaths and destroy the sense of difference needed to justify their torture" ("Renaissance Execution," 211). As was the case in the ideology of torture, the truth of their perceptions—however empathic or correct—would be based on falsehood.

Additional questions remain, the most significant of which is surely this: Did theater borrow its violence from the widespread early tendencies to imbue public chastisements and capital proceedings with mimetic effect? Or did public executions borrow their mimetic tendencies from pre-existing theatrical models? Or are those the wrong questions? Kubiak has reframed them, preferring to speak of the "cross-penetration of theatrical structure and legal technique in the

---

[75] See *DP*, 9, 59–64. Barbara Eckstein refutes Foucault in her work on J. M. Coetzee: "no such dignity, identity, or equality is granted indigenous peoples as objects of torture" (*LFWP*, 71).

[76] Compare this with, e.g., the possibility (invoked in Chapter 2) of a memory of things that were never there. I borrow the term *spectaculum crudelitatis* from Isidore of Seville, *Etymologiarum*, bk. 18, chap. 59.

maintenance of limits on the acting body" (*ST*, 27). Nevertheless, it is true that the forensic rhetorical tradition provided an important catalyst for such cross-penetration as well as for the transgression of the limits it apparently pre-scribed. After all, rhetoric was the *techne* that had at its core a goal of *imitatio veritatis*. It placed spectators at the scene of torture so that they might respond cathartically to statements that were themselves based on catharsis and veri-similitude. But my subsequent analysis of the stage effects and textual language of impersonation shows that medieval drama nurtured those correspondences among the ambiguities of torture, the ambiguities of pleasure, the ambiguities of representation, and the ambiguities of reception.

Again, eighteenth-century aesthetic theorists pondered the problem when Jean-Baptiste Du Bos found that "the imitation always acts more feebly than the object imitated" and produces "phantômes de passions." For that reason, special efforts were regularly undertaken to endow the copy with emotional force: "It must excite a passion in our soul that resembles that which the imi-tated object might have excited. *The copy of the object must, so to speak, ex-cite in us a copy of the passion which the object would have excited."* [77] Ante-dating Du Bos's work by several centuries, the ordeals of Christ from medieval French Passion plays staged the scourging by reenacting dramatically an event which, for the Christian Middle Ages, was a copy of something "true." More-over, when producers, stage masters, and artisans deployed their technical vir-tuosity to render torture, beatings, murders, vivisections, dismemberments, ex-ecutions, and death as graphically as possible, they too rendered their audiences witnesses at the scene of that great crime.

The medieval theater of cruelty was a theater of rhetoric that proved eminently compatible with the rhetorical needs of the medieval stage. As we shall see, the *mystères* were staged with an impressive repertoire of special stage effects; and their torturers even scrutinized their own portrayals of violence within the framework of the plays. In that way, a highly juridical scene like the scourging of Christ actually came to cultivate the very confusion between realism and real-ity that forensic rhetoric had fostered in its contorted quest for truth. Occasion-ally, the confusion embedded in rhetorical and dramatic theory collided with the dramatic realism of staging, plunging headlong into the reality of violence.

Special Effects

Most scholars of the early theater are more than happy to share with their mortified colleagues the groan-provoking stories of what constituted entertain-ment in the fifteenth and sixteenth centuries. With an extensive repertoire of fake blood, soft clubs, dummies, dolls, and mannequins, medieval and early Renais-

---

[77] *RCPP*, I, 51, 26; emphasis mine; trans. Marshall, *SES*, 20.

sance stage masters and artisans took great pains to render violence, torture, and death as realistically as possible.[78] A veritable laundry list of special effects survives in a fascinating fourteenth-century manuscript in Old Provençal which details just how the Crucifixion would be staged with sponges drenched in red liquids, a metal cap, and a wig:

> Un bonet de fe[r]
> sul cap, e pueis
> des spongos sus
> aquel bonet de fe[r]
> totas plenas de
> vermelo ho de sanc
> e pueis metri-li la
> falsa paruqua
> susa la spongos.[79]

An iron cap, and then some sponges on that iron cap that are all full of vermilion or blood, and then placed atop those sponges will be a false wig.

Elsewhere, the actors in a 1547 performance of a Passion play at Valenciennes apparently followed a stage direction reading: "Item a l'occision des Innocents on voyait sortir le sang de leurs corps" (When the Innocents are killed, blood was seen issuing from their bodies).[80] And in his important essay " 'There Must Be Blood,' " John Gatton enumerates the representational practices of the *Mystère des actes des apôtres* (ascribed to the brothers Arnoul and Simon Gréban) as it was performed in Bourges in 1536. His summary of the plethora of props designed to lend realism to the multiple stonings, beatings, stabbings, and scourgings suggests that each graphic effect outdid the previous one. An array of fake rocks, cudgels, knives, daggers, and whips were "doctored with wet dye or paint" to give the appearance of inflicting grave bodily harm upon "realistic, life-size dummies called *faulx corps*, *charnières*, and *décollations*" (" 'There Must Be Blood,' " 86). In other words, when stage directions called for blood, blood was provided—and more.

Beyond Herodotus's dictum that the eyes were more "credible witnesses" than the ears, even the nose stands out as a witness during a medieval representation

[78] Petit de Julleville, *LM*, contains two helpful sections on "Acteurs et entrepreneurs des mystères" (I, chap. 10) and "La mise en scène et les spectateurs" (I, chap. 11). Other work on this rich topic includes Gatton, " 'There Must Be Blood' "; Meredith and Tailby, eds., *Staging of Religious Drama in Europe in the Later Middle Ages*, "Special Effects," 101–16; Tydeman, *TMA*, chap. 6, on "resources and effects"; Shergold, *History of the Spanish Stage*, esp. 54, 63–64; and William D. Young's dissertation, "Devices and *Feintes* of Medieval Religious Theatre in England and France."

[79] *Il quaderno di segreti d'un regista provenzale del Medioevo*, ed. Alessandro Vitale-Brovarone, v. 7–15, p. 34. I thank John Coldewey for bringing this text to my attention.

[80] The translation is from Gatton, " 'There Must Be Blood,' " 82. This Passion, which boasted a flame-breathing Lucifer, is also discussed in Petit de Julleville, *LM*, II, 155.

of the immolation of Saint Barnabas which stipulated "stuffing the required fake body 'full of bones and entrails,' as dictated by the property list: 'fauldra ung corps fainct plain d'os et de trippes.'"[81] Gatton surmises that "as the apparent internal organs of St. Barnabas spill onto the blaze, the stench of roasting flesh complement [sic] the sight of the body being consumed by the flames" ("'There Must Be Blood,'" 87). Otherwise, few special effects rivaled those deployed during a Pentecostal production of the *Mistere de la Sainte Hostie*.[82] According to Philippe de Vigneulles, who witnessed it in 1513 in Metz, one of its most impressive features was the liberal use of hidden devices that held an abundance of blood:

Alors par *ung secret*, qui estoit fait, sortit grand abondance de sang et sailloit en hault parmi ladite hostie, comme se ce fut ung enfant qui pissoit, et en fut le juif tout gaisté et dessaigné et faisoit moult bien son personnaige. Aprez non content de ce, il ruoit ladite hostie au feu et par ung engien, elle se levoit du feu et se ataichoit contre le *contre feu* de la cheminée et le traistre la perçoit derechef d'une daigue, et par ung aultre engien et secret, elle jectoit de rechief sang abondamment. Puis ce fait il la reprint et lataichoit avec deux cloz contre une estaiche et la vint fraipper d'un espieu et ladite hostie jectoit arrière sang abondamment et jusques tout emmey le parcque trinçoit [sic] le sang *et en fut le lieu tout ensanglanté*. Et alors comme enraigié print l'hostie et la ruoit en une chaudiere d'yaue boullant et elle se elevoit en l'air et montoit en une nueé et devint ung petit enfant en montant a mont et se faisoit tout ceci par engiens et secrets; et s'y fist encore ledit jour plusieurs choses que je laisse. (*LM*, II, 103–4; emphasis mine)[83]

Then, by means of a secret place which had been fashioned, there emerged a great abundance of blood and it shot upwards from the aforementioned host, as if it were a child pissing. And the Jew was all soiled and bloody and played his part very well. Afterward, not content with this, he shoved the aforementioned host into the fire and, by means of a mechanism, the host rose up out of the fire and affixed it-

---

[81] See Gatton, "'There Must Be Blood,'" 87; and, on Herodotus's dictum, transmitted via Lucian of Samosata, see, e.g., Nagler's translation in *Sourcebook*, 31. Such a moment is also consistent with a play such as the *Farce du pect*.

[82] By Petit de Julleville's account, the *Sainte Hostie* survives in several editions, which he lists along with a brief plot summary in *LM*, II, 574–76: two undated sixteenth-century Parisian editions in octavo and a reissue in Aix in 1817.

[83] Petit de Julleville's own citation (albeit with numerous orthographic variations) comes from Heinrich (Henri?) Michelant's edition of the *Gedenkbuch des Metzer Bürgers Philippe von Vigneulles*, 244–45. In my translation, I have assumed a small transcription error either by Petit de Julleville or by one of his sources: I read "le parcque trinçoit le sang" (in Michelant's version, "le paircque trinçoit le sancq" [244]) as "le parcquet rinçoit le sang." Since the verb *trincer* is not attested in any Old French dictionary I have consulted and since the closest thing would be "drinking" blood (by analogy to *trinquer* or to the German *trinken*), this possibility seems more logical. Finally, although a 1513 performance is, in the strictest sense, no longer "medieval," I submit that its subject matter is certainly more "medieval" in spirit than, e.g., such French Renaissance offerings as those of Garnier and Jodelle.

self to the fireguard of the hearth. And the traitor then pierced it a second time with a dagger and, by means of another hidden mechanism, again it spewed out an abundance of blood. After having done this, he took the Host again and attached it with two nails against a stake and went to strike it with a boar spear and, from behind, the aforementioned host abundantly spit out blood until the whole center stage glistened with blood and the whole place was full of blood. And then, like one enraged, he took the host and threw it into a cauldron of boiling water and it rose up into the air in a puff of smoke and became a little child as it rose to the top. And all this was accomplished by devices and hidden places; and there were other things that happened that day that I leave aside.

Such technical skills encourage one to assume that other references to blood-shed would also have attracted the attention of the props master. One thinks, for example, of phrases like those uttered by the torturers of the Mons *Passion*: "Regardés le sang rideler / Qui le musiel luy ensenglente. . . . / Je l'ay jà si fort apuignie / Que le char est venu apres / Et le cler sang" (Look at the blood running down that's bloodying his mug. I've pierced him so hard that the flesh came out after the bright blood) (336). The Prologue to the *Cycle des premiers martyrs* offers similar directives as to how Saint Denis should be roasted alive: "Fust desrompu et tourmenté, / En four chaut mis, sus greil *rostis*, / Aus bestes sauvages jeté, / Crucefié, en chartre mis" (He was broken and tormented and placed in a hot oven, roasted on a spit, thrown to wild animals, crucified, and then thrown into a cell) (*CPM*, 108–11).[84] And William Tydeman paused to ponder how early producers might have translated the horrors of hagiography onto the stage when a naked Saint Barbara was to "be shown bound to a stake, beaten, burnt, and deprived of her breasts, rolled in a nail-studded barrel, and dragged over a mountain by the hair before final execution" (*TMA*, 177).

There is every reason to suppose that performers in the *Consueta de Santa Agata* would have interpreted to the letter a stage direction instructing them to "simulate the cutting off of the saint's breasts, with, so the rubric says, 'the greatest possible cruelty'" (Shergold, *History of the Spanish Stage*, 64). The infamous Croxton *Play of the Sacrament* probably inspired similar effects. When its Jews try to disembody the symbol of Christ's embodiment, they subject the Host to a series of tortures with a boiling cauldron, a dagger, a pair of pincers, and other "tormentry":

> I shall with thes[e] pinsonys, withowt dowt,
> Shake this cake owt of this clothe,
> And to the ovyn I shall it rowte
> And stoppe him there, thow[gh] he be loth.
> The cake I have cawght here, in good sothe—

[84] Compare this citation with, e.g., Eusebius, *EH*, IV, 15.4.

> The hand is soden, the fleshe from the bonys—
> Now into the ovyn I will therewith. (701–7)[85]

Sometimes, however, such miraculous effects accidentally caused real pain, as in the "close call" that befell seigneur Nicolle de Neufchastel en Loraine in 1437 while he was playing Christ:

> Et portoit le personnaige de Dieu ung prestre appelé seigneur Nicolle de Neufchastel en Loraine lequel alors estoit curé de Saint-Victor de Mets. Et fut cestuit curé *en grant dangier de sa vie* et cuydoit mourir luy estant en l'arbre de la croix, car le cueur lui faillist, tellement qu'il fust esté mort, s'il ne fust esté secouru. Et convint que ung aultre prestre fut mis en son lieu pour parfaire le personnaige de Dieu, et estoit celluy prestre alors l'ung des bourreaulx et tyrans dudit jeu. Mais neantmoins on donnait son personnaige a ung aultre et parfist celluy du crucifiement pour ce jour. Et le lendemain, ledit curé de Sainct-Victor fut revenu a luy, et parfist la resurrection et fist très haultement son personnaige.[86]

> And the role of God was played by a priest called Nicolle de Neufchastel en Loraine who was the curé of Saint Victor of Metz at that time. And this parish priest's life was in grave danger and he thought he would die upon the wooden cross, for his heart failed him, so much so that he would have died if he had not been rescued. And it was agreed that another priest would be put in his place in order to complete [playing] the character of God; and he too was a priest, at that time playing one of the executioners and tyrants of the aforementioned play. But nevertheless, they gave his character to someone else and he completed the crucifixion on that day. And the next day, the aforementioned priest of Saint Victor returned to his senses, and managed to complete the resurrection scene, playing his role mightily well.

Assuming a role in mystery play was dangerous. Indeed, Miri Rubin has cautioned that, when peering through the "distorted lens" of ritual at certain Corpus Christi processions, one does well to recall that "rituals can go wrong; wrong, that is, for their planners. In fact, ritual, and especially processional ritual, possessed an inherent destabilising element."[87] Ritualistic instability was such that the same Petit de Julleville who criticized the Middle Ages for amplifying Christ's tortures to far beyond his original ordeal (*LM*, I, 375) acknowledges nonetheless that, for Nicolle de Neufchastel and his contemporaries, acting the scourging was physically demanding if not completely exhausting: "Even though the executioners only performed the appearance of the tortures that they inflicted on the divine character, this simulation of the passion [*ce simu-*

---

[85] I quote here from the accessible edition of the fifteenth-century Croxton *Play of the Sacrament*, which appears on pp. 754–88 of Bevington, ed., *Medieval Drama*, 701–7.

[86] The full report of this incident appears in Petit de Julleville, *LM*, II, 12–13 (also I, 375, with modernized syntax). It has been discussed in Tydeman, *TMA*, 176–77; and Cohen, *HMS*, 239. This performance was especially ill fated in that its Judas was also left hanging too long. Ruth Evans has explored the concept of "risk management" in early English drama in "When a Body Meets a Body," as will Sarah Beckwith in *Signifying God*.

[87] Rubin, *CC*, 265.

lacre de passion] must have been exhausting. . . . Other roles were no less wearisome or even dangerous because of the imprudence of the 'techies,' already very bold [in those days] but still very unskilled" (*LM*, I, 375).

Suspect, though, is Petit de Julleville's sense that this was "just an imitation," a conviction mirrored in Tydeman's paradoxical inference from his own consideration of the numerous stage directions calling for "beheadings, mutilations, burnings, drownings, and other bodily sufferings." "Human lives plainly could not be put at risk" (*TMA*, 177), he flatly determines. Plainly, they *could* be. Similarly, Bruce Wilshire asserts from a phenomenological perspective that for theater to exist, audiences must be able to distinguish between violent aesthetics and violent reality: "in the experience of violence in the world one realizes that his own and others' lives are in jeopardy. . . . While in the theatre, one is at least marginally aware, on the critical level of consciousness, that *the violence is not really happening*" (*RPI*, 250–51; emphasis mine). In the Middle Ages, on that critical level of consciousness, it is clear that, sometimes, the violence really *was* happening or, as we shall see in the next section, that it had, that it could, or that it would. Of course, not all medieval dramas contain scenes of violence. But in the numerous cases in which they do, there could be no such awareness of artistic limits if there were no limits. If anything, the language of many scourging scenes compounds the problem by raising the question whether the torturers are "really" beating Christ or "just pretending."

As if the potentially spurious nature of some eyewitness accounts were not enough, mystery plays sometimes blur the distinction between illusion and reality by their extensive metacommentary on the nature of representation. The torturers from the Sainte Geneviève *Passion* specify that the blows upon the body of Jesus must be genuine, not imitated, as they discuss the authenticity of the representation of the beatings the actors are in the midst of representing:

> Jhesu n'a pouoir de füir,
> Car il me semble que mort est.
> De vostre lance, qui forte est,
> Ou costé destre le poignez,
> Et gardez que ne vous *feignez*;
> Mais bien en parfont le plaiez.
> Nous voulons que vos essaiez
> S'il a en ly de vie point
> (Sainte Geneviève *Passion*, 3011–18).

Jesus has no power to escape, for it seems that he's dead. Stab him on the right side with your sharp lance, and take care not to fake it, but wound him very deeply. We want you to test whether or not there's still some life in him.

In the *Geu Saint Denis*, Fescennin assures his partners in crime (or is it justice?) that the price to pay for a fake beating will be a real death not for the intended victim but for *them*, his victimizers: "Je pry Mahon qu'il soit pendus / Qui de bien ferir se *faindra*" (I pray Mohammed that anyone who only pretends to be striking forcefully be hanged) (*GSD*, 629–30). The distinction between realism and reality preoccupies the true believers of the Amboise *Passion*, one of whom insists that "En toy je croy sans *faintise*" (I believe in you without pretense) (Amboise *Passion*, 639). The same distinction informs the entire prologue to the *Cycle des premiers martyrs* in which hagiographic drama (*les vies des sains et des saintes*) is conceived as a didactic genre which must engender real—not faked—good works:

> Pour les bonnes gens inciter
> A bonnes euvres non pas *faintes*,
> Et pour leurs cuers habiliter
> Envers Dieu par doulces complaintes,
> Afin qu'i les daigne habiter,
> Par quoy sauvez sont mains et maintes.
> (*CPM*, 37–42; emphases mine)

To incite good people to do good works that are not make-believe and to rehabilitate their hearts toward God by sweet lamentations so that He deigns to inhabit them, by which many men and women will be saved.

At the level of theory, the false imitations of torture and rhetoric can be saved only by the absolute truth of Christ's martyrdom—strictly true but strictly unprovable by anything but faith, despite the best efforts of scholasticism.

In the Mons *Passion*, the torturers imply that all the pleasure of watching imitated pain is nothing compared to that of watching real pain. As Roullart, Dentart, Gadifer, Griffon, Brayart, Orillart, Clacquedent, and Rabanus exchange the following words, each speaker's line except Gadifer's is accompanied by the stage direction *frappe* to punctuate the relationship between command and action. A wave of violence is visible even on the printed page:

> ROULLART *frap(p)e*
> Souffle!
>   DENTART *frappe*
>   Happe!
>   GADIFER
>   *Je te voy faindre*
> GRIFFON *frap(p)e*
> Torche!
>   BRAYART *frap(p)e*
>   Lorgne!
>   ORILLART *frap(p)e*
>   Or ampogne!
>   CLACQUEDENT *frap(p)e*
>   Abbat!
> RABANUS *frap(p)e*
> Rien! rien! tout cecy n'est qu'esbat
> Il en ara bien d'au[l]tre sorte.

Go for it! Seize him! I see you faking! Hurt him! Get him! Hit him! Knock him down! Come on, come on! you're just gaming! Soon he'll have the real thing.

(Mons *Passion*, 291–92)[88]

In addition to calling up the memory of the terrible gaming discussed in Chapter 2, such moments also connect the dramatic scourging to farce. For example, the violent domestic comedy known as the *Farce de Goguelu* proffers an analogous metacommentary on the "playing" of violence—in this case, for laughs. Goguelu's chambermaid paramour (herself the victim of violence) proves an excellent imitator of the shrieks that accompany a real beating. She can imagine it only too well from her own experience: "Puis sur le cul de ce villain / Frappés fort et estroitement, / Je crieray aussi haultement / Comme si sur moy tu frappois" (Then hit hard and directly on the ass of that creep. I'll scream just as loudly as I would if you were hitting *me*).[89] Equal virtuosity is displayed by the persecuted (and eventually prosecuted) wife of the *Farce des drois de la porte Bouldès*, who, when struck by her husband because she will not close the door, strikes back. To save her husband's reputation, she agrees to stage a little drama by pretending that it is *he* who is beating her by imitating a "most hideous scream" (ung cry treshideux).[90] She is quite gifted at her impersonation—maybe because her husband has really hit her just seconds before:

> Je vous entens bien: A la mort!
> Au meurdre! mon mary me tue,
> S'on ne m'aide, je suis perdue.
> Ha! le mauvais, ha! le truant!
> Me turas-tu, dy, chien puant!
> Helas! la teste il m'a assommée.
> (115–20)

I understand perfectly: Help! Murder! My husband is killing me! I'm lost if you don't help me! Ah, the fiend, ah! the criminal! Are you trying to kill me, you stinking dog? Alas! he has bashed my head in.

In the end, both the staging effects and the language of medieval dramatic violence so blurred the boundaries between representation and real life that one commentator avowed of a 1536 performance in Bourges of the *Mystère des actes des apôtres* that the performers were "hommes graves qui sçavaient si bien *feindre* par signes et gestes les personnages qu'ils representaient, que la plupart des assistants *jugeaient la chose estre vraie et non feinte*" (sage men, who knew

---

[88] In my translation, I play deliberately on the title of *Just Gaming*, by Jean François Lyotard and Jean-Loup Thebaud.

[89] The *Farce de Goguelu*, v. 360–63, appears in Cohen, ed., *Receuil de farces françaises*, pp. 357–67.

[90] The text of the *Farce des drois de la porte Bouldès*, v. 109, also appears in Cohen, *Receuil*, 159–64. I discuss it at greater length in *ROMD*, 210–16.

so well how to feign through signs and gestures the characters they were representing that most of the audience thought the whole thing was real and not feigned).[91] Not only is that description reminiscent of the definitions of drama offered by Aristotle, Isidore, and Honorius: it further implicates gesture—one of the principal components of delivery—into a larger generic shifting between rhetoric and drama. That is, just as rhetorical treatments of delivery equate eloquence with acting, extant didascalia and reports of actual performances equate acting with eloquence. The shifting or "slippage" is a two-way process that impelled rhetoricians to see that the visual semiosis of delivery caused eloquence to cross over into acting. Conversely, commentators on the theater found that performance caused dramatic acting to cross back over into "real life." If nothing could seem more "real" than the actor's ability to incarnate a role, nothing could be more dramatic than the orator's ability to invoke the actor's performance as he dealt in testimony, facts, and probabilities.

In his discussion of "Exécutions et tortures," Cohen reserves special revulsion for the prop masters, whom Aristotle had once excluded from his theory of tragedy, because they

> applied their ingenuity to reproducing horror with the greatest possible realism. At the moment of the execution, their habitual method is to replace the actor with his *feinte*, that is, with his fake image or by a simple dummy destined to represent him and upon whom the grimacing executioner, who is the damned soul of the mystery play, lets loose with all the cruelties these torturous ages could invent as they further upped the ante of the real torments which the martyrs had endured. One can readily imagine that these substitutions demanded great technical skill, so that the spectator might not be too *disillusioned*, the spectator in whom the exposure of fiction would have forestalled the desired emotional response. (*HMS*, 149; emphasis mine)

But what was the nature of the *disillusionment*? And what are the historical ramifications of a theater that provided the ultimate *dis*-illusionment through the patent introduction of reality? Sometimes even all the special effects and all the metacommentary were not enough.

In the aesthetics of violence (medieval or modern) it is important to distinguish between the following types of theatrical event: the realistic staging of faked pain created through special effects; the real but accidentally inflicted pain that resulted from "close calls" when staging proved "too realistic"; and the deliberate infliction of actual physical pain in the form of legally sanctioned physical punishments. It is one thing for actors in the Admont Passion play to follow a stage direction to bring "whips and rods dipped in red paint [so that when] they strike Christ's body it becomes bloody."[92] And it is quite another

---

[91] Jean Chaumeau's *Histoire du Berry* (1566), cited in Petit de Julleville, *LM*, II, 133. The translation is by John R. Elliot, Jr., who cites the text in "Medieval Acting," 241.

[92] The citation from the Admont play appears in Meredith and Tailby, eds., *Staging of Religious Drama*, 109.

thing when the Devil's derrière accidentally catches fire, as it did during the *Mystère de Saint Martin* in Seurre in 1496: "le feu se prist à son habit autour des fesses, tellement qu'il fut fort bruslé" (Fire broke out on his clothes near his buttocks, so that he was seriously burned).[93] It is one thing when, in Metz in 1437, the colleague of Nicolle de Neufchastel en Loraine—one Father Jehan de Missey—was left hanging too long while playing the role of Judas and almost died during his performance: "Mais pour ce qu'il pendist trop longuement, il fut pareillement transis et quasy mort, car le cueur lui faillist; par quoy il fut bien hastivement despendu et fut emporté en aulcun lieu prochain pour le frotter de vinaigre et aultre chose pour le reconforter." (But because he was hanging too long, he lost consciousness and was almost dead, because his heart failed. For that reason, he was taken down in great haste [unhanged] and taken to a nearby place so that he could be rubbed with vinegar and other things to ease his pain) (*LM*, II, 13). It is quite another thing again to substitute condemned criminals for actors so that the criminals could be burned alive on stage, as happened during a performance of the *Laureolus*.[94] If the avant-garde director Evreinov wrote that "the participant's blood must somehow come to circulate in what is represented on stage," medieval and Renaissance dramatists had already demonstrated that that principle could be taken literally.[95] Few things are more avant-garde and even postmodern than the medieval theater of cruelty.

In Philip Massinger's "The Roman Actor" (1626), one of the characters tells a remarkable tale about the ability of drama to do something that the law and its tortures cannot:

> I once obseru'd
> In a Tragedie of ours, in which a murther
> Was acted to the life, a guiltie hearer
> Forc'd by the terror of a wounded conscience,
> To make discouerie of that, which torture
> Could not wring from him.[96]

As well as his story about torture, drama, and truth, Massinger tells a story of boundaries erected and boundaries transgressed. Something about theater and its catharses so terrified a murderer in the audience that he was motivated to confess. Drama made the discovery that torture could not—perhaps because, drama lies so close to the violent, inventional construction of the appearance of truth.

Since the import of this book depends on the recovery of French legal culture, especially illuminating is the ultimate fusion of legal and dramatic performance:

---

[93] This text appears in Cohen, *HMS*, 240, and is mentioned by Rey-Flaud in *Cercle Magique*, 283.
[94] Baty and Chavance, *Vie de l'art théâtral*, 67.
[95] Helen Solterer quoted this passage in a lecture titled "A Sixth Sense."
[96] Massinger, "Roman Actor," Act 2, ll. 90–95.

specific moments when the theater itself becomes a site of the "real life" violence of public executions. In that respect, the European Middle Ages and Renaissance had an illustrious forebear in the emperor Augustus who, according to Suetonius, had readily demonstrated his power to transform the theater into a locus of spectacular punishment for any actor who displeased him. Wresting from his magistrates the "power allowed them by an ancient law of punishing actors anywhere and everywhere," Augustus restricted the punishment

> to the time of games and to the theatre. Nevertheless he exacted the severest discipline in the contests in the wrestling halls and the combats of the gladiators. In particular he was so strict in curbing the lawlessness of the actors, that when he learned that Sephanio, an actor of Roman plays, was waited on by a matron with hair cut short to look like a boy, he had him whipped with rods through the three theatres and then banished him. Hylas, a pantomimic actor, was publicly scourged in the atrium of his own house. (Suetonius, "Augustus," *LC*, chap. 45)

More is at stake here than the spectacularity of public executions. This is the interpolation of a real, dramatically inflicted, public punishment into a "properly" theatrical space. Augustus not only controls and censors public and private thespian performances: he creates them. And he does so by fusing law and punishment with theater. So too would medieval France.

John Gatton once came to the astonishing conclusion that the horrific scenes of medieval religious drama allowed simultaneously for both greater theatricality and greater authenticity ("'There Must Be Blood,'" 80). But even Gatton does not seem to be imagining what has emerged over the centuries as one of the most excruciating moments of any European drama. When there came to circulate a legend that, during one particular Renaissance performance of a medieval play, an actor actually killed another, it raised the haunting possibility that the realism of theater might culminate in the reality of death by drama.

Death by Drama

The tracks have long since gone cold but, however shadowy the source may be now, there exists a medieval tale of theatrical representation that seems almost impossible to believe. Did an on-stage execution really take place in 1549 in the city of Tournai? [97]

[97] This question sparked a lively e-mail debate in the PERFORM discussion group. It all began with a query from Jesse Hurlbut about the precise location of the source since Henri Rey-Flaud had failed to include it in his discussion of the Tournai incident (*PDMA*, 19). Hurlbut did much of the reconstructive footwork in a generous bibliographical contribution to PERFORM (3 February 1995) in which he determined that Rey-Flaud's unattributed source was Faber, *Histoire du théâtre en Belgique*, I, 14–15. In "Medieval Snuff Drama," I explore the complex genealogy of this incident in the context of the politics of medieval drama criticism, source studies, violence, pornography, and snuff films. Again, in using the term "medieval" to describe a Renaissance performance, I am emphasizing that the play itself is "medieval."

According to somewhat questionable evidence about the biblical drama of Judith and Holofernes performed in that city, the "actor" playing Judith actually beheaded a convicted murderer who had briefly assumed the "role" of Holofernes (the doomed Assyrian general in the story)—long enough to be killed during the "play" to thunderous applause.[98] In his early work on the history of French theater in Belgium, Frédéric Faber scrupulously reconstructs the festive circumstances of this incident associated with the royal entry of Philip II, a monarch who was to become all too well known for his cruelty.[99] Rich in details that betray the complete fusion of legal and theatrical performance, Faber's description is rather closer to what John M. Callahan terms in the context of the Grand Guignol the "ultimate in theatre violence." It is worth reproducing in its entirety:

> Jean de Bury and Jean de Crehan, duly in charge of decorating the streets, had imagined rendering in its purest form [*rendre au naturel*] the biblical exploit of Judith. Consequently, for filling the role of Holofernes, a criminal had been chosen who had been condemned to have his flesh torn with red hot pincers [*tenaillé*]. This poor fellow, guilty of several murders and ensconced in heresy, had preferred decapitation to the horrible torture to which he had been condemned, hoping, perhaps, that a young girl would have neither the force nor the courage to cut off his head. But the organizers, having had the same concern, had substituted for the real Judith a young man who had been condemned to banishment and to whom a pardon was promised if he played his role well. (Faber, *HTB*, 14)[100]

[98] In the book of Judith, the heroine saves her city from the Assyrian general Holofernes, whom she decapitates in his drunken sleep. As for the play itself, at least two short theatrical versions exist—one in the *Mistére du Viel Testament*, ed. James de Rothschild, V, 231–354, and more recently edited by Graham Runnalls as *Le Mystère de Judith et Holofernés*—and an as yet unpublished version discovered by Alan Knight in Wolfenbüttel. The 845-verse "Coment Judich tua Oloferne" appears in Codex Guelf. 9 Blankenburgensis, the same manuscript that contains the story of Tamar cited earlier.

[99] The term "French theater" for the medieval and Renaissance period designates the art form in what are now several countries, among them France and Belgium. Philip's visit was part of his crown-princely tour of the Netherlands, accounts of which may be found in Calvete de Estrella, *El felicissimo viaje*; and Alvarez, *Relacion del camino buen viage* (trans. M. T. Dovillée). Neither source makes any mention of the decapitation or of the play. Even so, Philip was surely reacting to *something* when, as Faber notes, he enacted legislation a scant three years later to ensure preapproval of any plays staged in the region (*HTB*, 15).

On the processional qualities of medieval drama, see Knight, *Aspects of Genre*, chap. 6; Kolve's well-known discussion of pageant wagons in *PCC*, chaps. 2 and 3; Rubin, *CC*, chap. 4, esp. 235–71; and Guenée and Lehoux, *Les Entrées royales françaises de 1328 à 1515*. Finally, this royal entry featured a fascinating early example of *Katzenmusik* (*HTB*, 4–5) of the sort made famous by Robert Darnton in *The Great Cat Massacre* (chap. 2; also 271 for his sources).

[100] See Callahan, "Ultimate in Theatre Violence." For ceremonial pardons and public contrition, see also Campbell, "Cathedral Chapter and Town Council"; and Esther Cohen, *Crossroads*, e.g., 189, 198–201. Within the scope of this book, I cannot adequately treat the historical complexities of the unknown heretic's unknown heresies except to acknowledge that they might have contributed to the "black legend" of Philip II. Of interest here is Maus, *Inwardness and Theater*, chap. 3; and Lebègue, *Tragédie religieuse*, 57.

Faber is concerned here with looking behind the masks of the biblical characters and with divining how the *metteurs en scène* might themselves have looked behind those masks—even before the spectacle began. Coerced into playing Holofernes, the convicted murderer and heretic is *un malheureux* and an object of theatrical pity in his own cathartic story.[101] As for Judith, "she" may not be strong enough to deliver the fatal blow described in the Apocrypha, so a different kind of inducement is provided for "him." A young male criminal convicted of an unknown crime is to receive a legal pardon if he comes across with acting so good that it is not "acting" at all.[102]

But acting what? The biblical tale in which Judith saves her city by killing her drunken enemy? A projection of that tale designed to communicate something to the imperialistic Philip? Or the crimes, punishments, and pardons of medieval criminals? Just which roles would be played? That of Holofernes or of the deserving criminal? That of Judith, of the penitent convict, or of the town's temporary executioner? The fantastic quality of the narrative culminates with Philip's arrival just as the axe is falling. Apparently, "Holofernes" was participating willingly enough in the spectacle of his own execution to *pretend* to be asleep, while the Judith character assumed his/her preassigned role of executioner. As real blood supposedly begins to flow, it prompts applause in some, indignation in others, and curiosity in the prince who remains implacable as the body of the Holofernes/convict goes through its last spasms:

> In fact, as Philip approached the theater where the mystery play was being represented, the so-called [*prétendue*] Judith unsheathed a well-sharpened scimitar and, seizing the hair of Holofernes who was *pretending to be asleep* [*qui feignait de dormir*], dealt him a single blow with so much skill and vigor that his head was separated from his body. At the [sight of] the streams of blood that spurted out from the neck of the victim, frenetic applause and cries of indignation rose up from amidst the spectators. Only the young prince remained impassive, observing the convulsions of the decapitated man with curiosity and saying to his noble entourage: *"bien frappé"* [nice blow/well struck]. The sang-froid of the prince in the face of this atrocity would serve to predict the cruelty of his reign. (Faber, *HTB* 14–15)

Apocryphal or not, the tale from Tournai testifies to the possibility of real juridical performativity on the medieval stage, to the presence of bona fide Austinian speech acts, and even *mala fide* threats against actors and audiences of

---

[101] For all we know, the Holofernes character/murderer/heretic may have been falsely accused; and the Judith character, whose crime is never specified, unjustly pardoned. See, e.g., Esther Cohen on the arbitrary medieval application of justice ("'To Die a Criminal,'" 285).

[102] This incident also raises questions about the history of women on the stage, although such matters lie beyond the scope of this book. See, e.g., Zeitlin, "Playing the Other"; Rackin, "Androgyny, Mimesis, and the Marriage of the Boy Heroine"; and Bibolet's introduction to his edition of the Troyes *Passion*. Otherwise, the possibility of a "true representation" returns us to the inventional *imitatio veritatis* and its own "fictional truths."

theater, who assume real risks. If true, Tournai provides proof of Kenneth Burke's suggestion that "the symbolic act of art overlaps upon the symbolic act in life" and of Kubiak's suggestion that "we forget that theatre is the primary condition of life, that life itself is 'always already' subsumed by the theatrical" (*ST*, 162).[103] If true, this moment would be part of the larger history of torture, which included the "castigation with rods, scourging, and blows with chains" enumerated in the Justinian *Digest*.[104] For if the Tournai criminal really died, he resembled all too closely the "actors" in Roman gladiatorial display who "affect dying even as death really occurs . . . [and] become actors who die for the pleasure of their spectators, and what seems worse, who must perform their own deaths with broad, theatrical strokes" (*SES*, 25). And he would render it possible to speak of real coercion, real performativity, real "speech acts" on the medieval stage. If there was at least the possibility that real death might occur on stage, then any line within a play calling for brutality, torture, punishment or death would not merely *describe* doing something. In the strict Austinian sense, it would actually *do* something: "the issuing of the utterance is the performing of an action—it is not normally thought of as just saying something" (*HDTW*, 6–7).

If false, Tournai testifies to the existence of a kind of medieval urban legend just as frightening and just as attention-getting as such contemporary American counterparts as the deep-fried rat at the fast-food restaurant, the alligator in the sewer, or the mouse in the Coke bottle.[105] As such, it would have functioned as a myth which, then and now, discloses more about spectators' fears about what *could* happen in the theater than about what actually *did* happen. As is the case in American urban legends, the proof of what has happened lies with an elusive source whose identity is impossible to nail down.[106] Tournai was and is an enormously appealing and scary story—even as it emerges as a privileged site for the construction of several conflicting cultural myths: that illegal or extra-legal violence is transgressive; that, in accordance with a hopeful

---

[103] Burke, *POLF*, 119. See also Rey-Flaud on the quotidial effacement of the distinctions between ritual and real life (*PDMA*, 75–79). Even Jules Michelet found that "real" or "complete" imitation (*l'imitation complète*) was the order of the day when it came to the "crazy representations" of medieval mysticism (*Histoire de France*, 330–31).

[104] The jurist Callistratus in the Justinian *Digest*, 48.19.7, as discussed by Peters in *Torture*, 35. If the Tournai death occurred, then its *unprofessional* executioner apparently followed through on the violence threatened by the executioner borrowed from Avignon.

[105] Indeed, perhaps the strongest indication that the tale from Tournai is false is the preposterous notion that a condemned man about to be beheaded would be kind enough to take the trouble to "play his part" so convincingly. On urban legends, see, e.g., Brunvand, *Vanishing Hitchhiker* (hereafter *VH*) and *Curses! Broiled Again*. I will return to the complexities of medieval urban legend in a future book.

[106] This is the "famous friend of friend," whose role is summarized by Brunvand in *VH*, xi. Since the authenticity of the source is a focus of my "Medieval Snuff Drama," suffice it to recall here that many of Faber's sources cannot be verified.

conservatism, criminals must deserve the punishments they receive; and that, for the medievalist, our period is better understood by its alterity than by some of its troubling similarities.

True or false, it is impossible to authenticate anything beyond the intuition that something happened in Tournai that was noteworthy enough, unique enough, or frightening enough to warrant its circulation as legend. And if Tournai can be proved to be neither true nor false, then that itself constitutes a kind of conclusion. It points those who study Tournai in the direction of Jean Baudrillard's work on "Simulacra and Simulations," according to which one might view the dramatic violence of Tournai as a kind of a watershed form of simulation. "*Feigning or dissimulating*," writes Baudrillard, "leaves the reality principle intact: the difference is always clear, it is only masked; whereas *simulation threatens* the difference between 'true' and 'false', between 'real' and 'imaginary*" (*SW*, 168; emphasis mine). He then explores how one might explain to the security guards in a department store that what they have witnessed is a simulated theft in which a playful "thief" has gone through all the real motions of stealing without intending to steal. Baudrillard determines that there is no "objective difference" between the two: "the same gestures and the same signs exist as for a real theft; in fact the signs incline neither to one side nor the other" (*SW*, 178). Nor do they incline one way or the other in Tournai. Its simulation has threatened so well that, in retrospect, there is no "objective difference" between the real execution, the dissimulated one, and the simulated one. Sometimes dramatic violence is an illusion, sometimes a reality, sometimes a simulation. Sometimes an actor acts deliberately, sometimes accidentally, and sometimes a non-actor is forced into an acting role.

By way of offering some closure to the mental structures of the medieval theater of cruelty, I take the Tournai incident as a point of departure for broader speculation about the phenomenology of theatrical violence, medieval and modern. The criteria of intentionality and choice are inescapable and raise a disturbing question: are feigning, doing, acting, witnessing, and threatening the stuff of dramatic speech or are they actual speech acts within drama? The late Paul Zumthor ascertained from his own reading of death on the medieval stage that it activated a "desymbolized one-way pseudo-communication" in which "the actor takes on the latent violence of the people for whom he dies." [107] Yet, if the Tournai incident is indeed an act of pseudocommunication, then one of its more falsified aspects is that the "actors" doing the communicating have not really chosen to communicate at all—even through the illusive communications of drama. For the criminal/executioner/Judith, a new chance at life is an offer he cannot refuse; for the beheaded criminal/Holofernes, there was per-

[107] Zumthor, "From Hi(story) to Poem," 238. See also Warning, "On the Alterity of Medieval Religious Drama," 282–85; and, for an earlier period, Coleman, "Fatal Charades." Moreover, as was the case for Pierre Des Essarts, it is likely that such instances of pseudocommunication would have been accompanied by instances of pseudoreception.

haps the long-shot hope of a narrow escape. At a minimum, the only real choice for the latter is *how* he will die and not *if* he will die—the very choice that many current opponents of the death penalty find even more barbaric than capital punishment itself (as when a convicted murderer in Delaware recently opted to be hanged). His story represents the real performance of a pseudocommunication based on a pseudochoice in what may well have been a pseudoevent. Since the Tournai criminal has *not* chosen freely to participate, he undermines a distinction proposed by Kubiak which is, at best, tenuous for the medievalist: "the *theatrical ordeal,* no matter how intense, *is undergone voluntarily,* while the very terror of torture rests in part on the victim's absolute lack of control" (*ST,* 158; emphasis mine). Just as the first rhetor had helped to impose civilization through performance, certain early dramatic performances exploited juridical culture in order to instill within varied audiences (peers, writers, populace) the reality of a crucial cultural illusion: that there was indeed such a thing as voluntary participation in civilized societies—or at least, in their dramas.

More significantly for the literary theorist, once the pseudochoice of the Tournai criminal leads to a real performance, the coerced performer becomes an object of aesthetic pleasure and a potential subject of theater history. Notwithstanding the later objections of such a critic as Amy Newman that "the aestheticist tendency to romanticize immediate experience translates easily into a trivialization or idealization of suffering," the pain of the Tournai criminal has already been aestheticized for us.[108] In fact, his pain is so aestheticized that it is unclear in retrospect whether it happened at all. And the credible lack of credibility remains unaltered—no matter how tempted one might be to follow Louise Fradenburg's advice that "if we deny to our interpretive work the use of concepts of ideology and fantasy we risk losing our ability to distinguish between competing representations of reality, and between the Real and our (mis)recognitions of it." [109]

In what follows, I argue that, whether or not the death at Tournai actually happened, the mere investigation of that question irrevocably compromises certain generic cornerstones of theater and its criticism that many scholars still hold dear: the illusion of theater's civility, the viability of catharsis, and the entire principle of moral or aesthetic distance which collapses under the weight of performativity.[110] In a world where legends about on-stage executions circulated, where public executions were orchestrated and attended as spectacles, and where the language of theater replicated the confusion between impersonation and reality, one troublesome conclusion would be that as a genre, early drama was tied to the larger history of torture, justice, punishment, and even the regu-

---

[108] Newman, "Aestheticism, Feminism, and the Dynamics of Reversal," 23.

[109] Fradenburg, "Criticism, Anti-Semitism, and the Prioress's Tale," 76.

[110] William B. Worthen, e.g., questions the civility of the stage in *Modern Drama,* 138–39; while Pywell and Graver question the principle of aesthetic distance in *SRT* and *Aesthetics of Disturbance,* respectively. See also Wilson, "Promissory Performances."

lation of public entertainments. The possibility of real violence in Tournai would then resonate with such events as the following: certain French medieval Bishops were empowered to force men to accept Christ through flogging—the same ecclesiastical dignitaries who might have been watching theatrical spectacles from on high.[111] Likewise, actors in the Angers *Résurrection* worried within their play that their words would trigger punishment outside the play:

> Je proteste publiquement
> Pour tous joueurs generaument
> De cest mistere, et pour chacun,
> Que ou cas qu'il seroit par aucun
> Contre la foy riens dit ou fait,
> Il soit reputé pour non fait.
> Car nous n'entendons dire ou faire
> Riens qui soit a la foy contraire,
> Ne qui la noble seigneurie
> De rien offende ou injurie,
> Nous soubmectans sans fiction
> A la bonne correction
> De la noble université
> D'Angiers, l'ancïenne cité.
> (Angers *Résurrection*, I, Day 1, 218–31)

I lodge a public protest on behalf of both the collectivity and the individual players in this mystery play that, in case anyone happens to say or do anything against the faith, that he is considered to have done nothing. For we intend neither to say nor to do anything contrary to the faith or which would offend or wound in any way our noble lords, submitting ourselves without pretense to the good discipline of our noble university of the old city of Angers.

Indeed, as Faber remarks of the Tournai incident, the king himself intervened in theatrical life to legislate the level of brutality to be enacted on the stage:

In any event, if such a barbaric act could have occurred in public and even before the person of the king, he did not always show himself to be quite so tolerant. In 1552, the town counselors received an order from the sovereign that, henceforth, they were not to permit any play without having had an official, or an ecclesiastical judge designated by the bishop first examine the composition of the repertoire of the actors seeking to obtain a license to play in the city. (*HTB*, 15)

[111] See Goebel, *Felony and Misdemeanor*, 170–71. Or consider the 1483 legislation in Troyes on guarding and closing the city gates during the *mystères de la Passion*; and the use of military personnel in Angers in 1486 to impose silence during dramatic performances "under threat of prison or other penalty" (in Petit de Julleville, *LM*, II, 44, 50). Such legislation sheds light on all those injunctions at the beginning of mystery plays that the audience "shut up" (e.g., Gréban, 4–5, 1721–24). Also touched by the history of these debates would be such events as the outlawing of the mystery plays in 1548. See also Holquist, "Corrupt Originals."

Faber also reproduces an account of the fiery tirade by the Bishop of Esne who, upon learning that actors had been granted permission to play "farces, comédies et tragedies," appeared before his local government in 1599. Like Christ in the Temple, he declared: "on ne debvoit avoir donné ladite grâce et licence sans luy en avoir parlé, disant avec grant collère, chaleur et béhement, par plusieurs fois, qu'il ne permectroit les dis jeux, ains que s'ilz jouoient il les tireroit jus du théâtre et renverseroit ledit théâtre, priant que Dieu lui en donna la forche" (*HTB*, 15) (indulgence and permission should never have been granted without speaking to him, saying with great anger, fire, and gall, on several occasions, that he would not permit the aforesaid plays and, moreover, that if the actors performed, he would pull them off the stage and would knock down the aforesaid theater, praying that God give him the strength to do so).

Just as the Mass was a real event, so too (for the more devoted spectators) was the mystery play a strictly true narrative chronicling the events of Christ's Passion. Spectators placed themselves on a Christian space–time continuum that was eternity, believed that they bore the mark of the sins of their forebears represented in the exemplary tales unfolding, and thought themselves to be subject to the earthly authority of contemporaneous enforcers of the law who might well have been observing the *mystère* and *them*. In other words, the watchers of the performance were themselves being watched—perhaps by a Bishop with a staff—as both the subjects and the objects of didactic pieces about leading a good Christian life. When we then recall that, within that ethos, medieval culture also included the spectacular juridical display of real punishment, it is all the more fitting to venture that the scourging scenes of Passion plays (along with Tournai and other episodes discussed below) would have tended to configure their audiences as both subjects and objects of coercion *within* and *without* the play.[112]

What really happened in Tournai? What really happened to Jehan de Missey, Nicolle de Neufchastel, or those players in Angers? Without oversimplifying the psychological complexities of the guilt, hopes, fears, and anxieties of the tellers of the tale from Tournai, one comes to perceive that modern commentators and commentaries have something in common with their medieval ancestors. If an urban legend "truly represents" real fears, then so too would a medieval allegation of real violence.[113] Consequently, it does not matter at some level who originated the legend of Tournai: a sixteenth-century commentator who thought the story of Judith saving her city from a tyrant would be a par-

[112] Here I follow Kenneth Burke on the *Eumenides* in *POLF*, 156. Faber also reproduces an edict indicting the "réthoriques, comédies et farces" performed in the Chambres de Rhétorique in Mons (*HTB*, 12). For the tight connection between rhetoric and theater in the Low Countries, see, e.g., Hummelen, "Boundaries of the Rhetoricians' Stage"; Cartwright, "Politics of Rhetoric"; Kramer, "*Rederijkers* on Stage"; and Waite, "Vernacular Drama and Early Urban Reformation."

[113] See Brunvand's discussion of the guilty pleasures of the largely white Anglo-American tellers of urban legends in *VH*, xi, and *Curses*, 37–39.

ticularly appropriate choice for a monarch encroaching on his territory; or a nineteenth-century critic who lost his manuscript source, but remembered something he had heard an archivist say. Regardless of whether the Tournai execution occurred, one still needs to come to terms with at least one speaker's belief that it *could have* happened.

Had real threats of real violence never been an issue, it seems unlikely that a frightened thirteenth-century audience would have run away from a violent *Ludus prophetarum* in Riga, fearful that the pugnacious characters in the play were about to attack *them*; or that Petit de Julleville would report that, in an early performance of the *Jeu d'Adam*, "the *demons*, that is to say, the individuals charged with representing that infernal role, ran amongst the rows of spectators several times, creating a levity mixed with fright." [114] Similarly, if audiences *did not* experience real fear for their lives at the theater, one wonders why Lucian of Samosata would have circulated the story of an actor playing Ajax gone mad. According to Lucian, the actor came down among the public and "seated himself among the senators, between two ex-consuls, *who were very much afraid that he would seize one of them and drub him*, taking him for a wether!" ("Saltatio," 83). It seems equally unlikely that Aeschylus could have introduced the chorus of the *Eumenides* into the orchestra in such a terrifying way that "children died and women suffered miscarriage." [115] In fact, André de Lorde was so struck by the *Eumenides* story that he cited as fact the "veritable panic" it activated—much as I too once cited Tournai as fact (*ROMD*, 103). De Lorde affirms that "women aborted spontaneously, children died, and several spectators went mad. The playwrights of the Grand-Guignol genres can thus claim an illustrious lineage" (*TM*, 13). Whether it be the tale from Tournai or the well-documented "close call" that befell Jehan de Missey, early commentators clearly believed that real violence could and did happen on the stage.

From the standpoint of urban legend (and indeed, from the materials discussed in the preceding section), one might be tempted to conclude that the Tournai execution *did not* occur. On one hand, medieval producers were eminently familiar with the use of dolls or mannequins devised for the purpose of representing dismemberment and death. Of special relevance here is a didascalic commentary from the Mons *Passion*, which calls for a doll to be sliced in half: "Lors elle prend le cariot et met l'enffant fuitif dedens" (Then she takes the cart and places the ersatz child inside). Upon completion, the torturer Achopart sounds almost like Philip at Tournai: "Le velà trenchié tout d'un cop / En deux pars: esse pas bien fait?" (There you go! In one blow, he's sliced in two: good job, huh?) (Mons *Passion*, pp. 103–4). [116] Even more germane to the Judith and Holofernes tale is the fact that one of the nine decapitations of the *Mystère des*

---

[114] The Riga incident of 1204 is discussed in Tydeman, *TMA*, 223–24; and the performance of the *Adam* by Petit de Julleville in *Théâtre en France*, 3.

[115] This incident of ca. 460 B.C. is reproduced in Nagler, *Source Book*, 5.

[116] See also Gatton's discussion of this moment in "'There Must Be Blood,'" 82.

actes des apôtres requires a false head from a real sheep: "une teste faincte pour une decollacion de Symon Magus, et fault que Daru descolle ung mouton au lieu de luy" (A false head is needed for the decapitation of Simon Magus [in the *Mystère des apôtres*], and Daru [the executioner] must cut off the head of a sheep in his place).[117] In addition, then, to sometimes questionable testimony about actual performance practice, the language of medieval dramatic texts themselves helps to create ambiguity.

It appears even more likely that the Tournai execution *did not* occur when we examine another incident related by Faber: the annual commemoration of the Crucifixion on Good Friday in Brussels. In a ceremony that has long perplexed theater historians, a condemned criminal was ritually pardoned in exchange for playing Jesus. As Faber summarizes (from another lost source), it all began with the placement of a large cross on a scaffold at the altar of the Eglise des Augustins. Three groups processed through the representative stations of the Cross (the *confrères de La Miséricorde*, prisoners with ball and chain, and clerics disguised as Jews). When the procession was over, the spectacle culminated in the chastisement of the pardoned criminal who was representing Christ. He was transformed by the event into another pitiable *malheureux* surrounded by the mob:

> They simulated [*simulaient*] the nailing to the cross. He was stripped of all his clothes, and he was stretched out on the implement of torture, upon which his hands and feet were nailed. The imitation even went so far as to simulate the blood that must have flown out [*On avait même poussé l'imitation jusqu'à simuler le sang qui aurait dû en couler*]. That effect was achieved by means of little bladders full of red liquid which were attached to his limbs and by which the condemned man was attached to the cross. (Faber, *HTB*, 4; emphasis mine)

Was the bloodshed real? Or have we entered the realm of simulation? Faber makes two such contradictory statements that it is difficult to tell the difference between *realism* (bladders filled with red liquid) and *reality* ("they nailed his hands and feet").

There lingers, moreover, another nagging possibility that complicates the apparent binary of real/realistic. What if, in Tournai or in Brussels, both versions— realism *and* reality—coexisted not only in different years but simultaneously during one and the same event? What if, in Brussels, the special effects of simulated blood were added to real blood for the purpose of enhancing something that was *already really happening*?[118] What if, in Tournai, the head of a sheep

---

[117] *Mystère des actes des apôtres*, p. 22; cited and translated in Gatton, "'There Must Be Blood,'" 87. It is not clear, however, whether the sheep is dead or alive. See also Hashim, "Notes toward a Reconstruction of the *Mystère des Actes des Apôtres* as Represented at Bourges, 1536." Additionally, Shergold records a beheading trick in the *Passió de Sant Jordi* (*History of the Spanish Stage*, 64); and Simon Magus appears in Jane Goodal, *Artaud and the Gnostic Drama*, 10.

[118] One is reminded of the *Dateline NBC* scandal in which incendiary devices were used to enhance the effects of real automotive explosions. Similar questions arise about that famous image of Saint Apollonia by Jean Fouquet, ca. 1420–1477/81 (see the frontispiece).

was really used but the executioner's hand slipped and "Holofernes" bled a little before escaping? At least one twentieth-century ritual suggests that these are viable theories: the Filipino Passion of Easter 1995 invoked at the outset of this book during which a group of believers allowed themselves to be nailed to crosses with thin, sterilized nails before a huge crowd.[119] In the end, uncertainty reigns no matter which version of the preceding stories we choose to believe. No matter how fortunate we are today to possess so much eyewitness testimony about deaths, *faintes*, and *secrets*, early productions still guard the secrets of their performances centuries later. Uncertainty also reigns as to how critics are to come to terms with all the uncertainty. The only thing that is crystal clear is that the moment of bloodshed is the high point of the spectacle. As Faber resolves of Brussels, "if one is to believe the manuscripts which report this event, the ceremony used to produce a tremendous effect upon the multitude" (*HTB, 4*). The effect remains tremendous for contemporary critics invested for various reasons in the violent tendencies of the medieval multitude.

At the most, exemplary of real dramatic practice and, at the least, indicative of the real fears associated with medieval and Renaissance drama, the Tournai incident has something to say about the role of theater in cultural questions of art, fear, intentionality, choice, and force. It invites us to reconsider Kubiak's theory that "the terror of theatre moves somewhere between the propositions of the axiom—what seems true is a lie—while deception itself seems to be the truth of what is seen" (*ST, 64*). But, insofar as that real fear may be based on false events, it also invites us to dismantle certain enduring critical illusions about the sociability of theater. If a criminal could truly be forced into an actor's role so that he might die on stage, if an audience could be forced, tricked, or seduced into the role of witness to his execution, or—in the worst-case scenario—if none of these things *ever* happened but some people believed that they did, they would, or they could . . . then, contrary to Augusto Boal's declaration in *Theater of the Oppressed*, the stage *does not* offer "harmless and pleasant discharge for the instincts that demand satisfaction and that can be tolerated much more easily in the fiction of the theater than in real life" (*TO, 29*). If anything, it seems that the medieval and Renaissance spectacles of pain might have dominated aesthetics not because the relevant instincts *could not* be tolerated in real life, but rather because they *could be*. They could be tolerated in both drama and real life not because "intolerable" instincts were acceptable in one venue and not the other, but because they were acceptable in both. Not only was the pleasure of pain acceptable: it was logical when present within an art form slippery enough to leave it unclear whether theater purged violent emotions by cultivating them or cultivated violent emotions by purging them. In either case, theater seems to have been capable of creating the violence it alternatively solicited and condemned.

[119] *12:00 News*, KCOY, Channel 12.

This is more than a medieval problem. For some years now Americans have debated whether television and the silver screen dissuade viewers *from* violence or impel them *toward* it. One thinks of the largely conservative desire to install V chips everywhere so that television violence can stop "inspiring" children to set their houses afire à la Beavis and Butthead. Earlier, in response to the 1976 exploitation film *Snuff*, the feminist attorney Brenda Feingen Fasteau cautioned that "we have to deal with the possibility that this film is going to create a demand for real snuff films and that real women are going to be murdered." [120] Similarly, Maria Tatar eloquently captures the essence of the debate in her work on sexual murder: "To what degree is the disfiguring violence presented in a sympathetic light, drawing attention to the perpetrator's entitlement to discharge his 'evil' urges and effacing the suffering of the victim? . . . Do the 'aesthetically pleasing' images of fictive victims contaminate our perception of the real-life victims, leading us to look at their corpses as works of art?" (*Lustmord*, 18).[121] No matter how nuanced the speaker's position, participants in these debates all allude to the possibility that the representational uncertainty of violence has the power to create a real audience demand for violent reality. "Did the violence happen or not?" and "If it did, how does it make us feel? What does it make us do?" are eternal questions to which medieval juridical and literary culture provides some spectacular answers. In so doing, it speaks to the pleasures of an unspeakable fear: that theater is somehow so dangerous that it leads to death.

To endeavor to address the questions of violence is to go straight to the heart of a problem involving urban legends, simulation, hyperreality, catharsis, performativity, community, and even madness. For Henri Rey-Flaud, for example, the Tournai incident bordered on madness (*PDMA*, 19); while Faber chose to contrast it ironically to the realism of the theater of his own 1870s. "If one subscribes to the teachings of a certain manuscript account," he writes, "the play of Judith and Holofernes was performed there with a realism which has not yet been attained in modern times when, nonetheless, people clamor to reach the pinnacle of that species" (*HTB*, 14). But, as I suggested in my Introduction, just as each generation singles out its theatrical violence as an aberration, each generation also seems to single out its theatrical madness. If Tournai exemplified madness, so too did the equally frightening, equally hyperreal, and equally apocryphal display of hyperreality related by Lucian of Samosata.

Situated somewhere between the illusions and realities experienced by a mad actor and the audience whom he confused, terrorized, or amused, Lucian's story serves as a kind of precursor to the various medieval legends about the threats posed by theater to the lives of individuals and institutions. Specifically, it con-

---

[120] Fasteau, cited by Johnson and Schaefer in "Soft Core/Hard Gore," 53. Of course, if it existed, the snuff film—as opposed to what I call "snuff drama"—would stage *il*legally inflicted pain.

[121] See also the earlier treatment by Marivaux, "Avis au lecteur," 3–9; cited and discussed in Marshall, *SES*, 15–27.

cerns the role of theater in the genesis of violence and madness. According to Lucian, a famous actor who was engaged in imitating the madness of Ajax actually went mad himself during his performance, running amok in the senatorial benches and frightening the audience, especially the riffraff:

> By some ill-luck, I know not what, he wrecked his *fortunes* upon an *ugly bit of acting through exaggerated mimicry*. In presenting Ajax going mad immediately after his defeat, he so overleaped himself that it might well have been thought that instead of feigning madness he was himself insane; for he tore the clothes of one of the men that beat time with the iron shoe, and snatching a flute from one of the accompanists, with a vigorous blow he cracked the crown of *Odysseus*, who was standing near and exulting in his victory; indeed, if his watch-cap had not offered resistance and borne the brunt of the blow, *poor Odysseus would have lost his life through falling in the way of a crazy dancer* ("Saltatio," 83; emphasis mine).

This is a story about an accidental death that almost occurs. It raises questions of sanity, natural intelligence, intentionality, reception, the social status of acting, and good vs. bad fortune. In fact, its own realities are so muddled that the life of the fictive Odysseus seems at risk rather than that of the endangered actor.

Comparably muddled are the responses of the audience. For those who are ignorant of "good taste," the otherwise pitiable madness of an individual provokes laughter; for those intelligent enough to know the difference, it prompts not a real reaction but a simulation of appreciation through insincere applause:

> The pit, however, *all went mad with Ajax*, leaping and shouting and flinging up their garments; for the riff-raff, the absolutely unenlightened, took no thought for propriety and could not perceive what was good or what was bad, but thought that sort of thing consummate mimicry of the ailment, while the politer sort understood, to be sure, and were *ashamed* of what was going on, but instead of censuring the thing by silence, they themselves *applauded to cover the absurdity of the dancing*, although they perceived clearly that what went on came from the madness of the actor, not that of Ajax. . . . The thing caused some to marvel, some to laugh, and some to suspect that perhaps in consequence of his overdone mimicry he had fallen into the real ailment ("Saltatio," 83).

As the tale spins further and further out of control, it is evocative of Artaud's proposal of "a theater in which violent physical images crush and hypnotize the sensibility of the spectator seized by the theater as by a whirlwind of higher forces" (*TD*, 82–83). The actor's unintentional imitation (which had occasioned some audience members' intentional imitations of heartfelt applause) comes to a climax. His real return from his temporary madness is itself only temporary. He is sane enough to feel so repentant about his temporary insanity that his real discomfort becomes an unintentional but permanent performance of madness: "Moreover, the man himself, they say, once he had returned to his sober senses, was *so sorry for what he done that he really became ill through distress and in all truth was given up for mad*" (84; emphasis mine).

Lucian also finds here an opportunity to discuss (however satirically) the question of good vs. bad taste, noting that, "as in literature, so too in dancing what is generally called 'bad taste' comes in when they [mimes] exceed the due limit of mimicry and put forth greater effort than they should" (82). Hence, the mad actor never danced Ajax again, even when supplicated, claiming that, "for an actor, it is enough to have gone mad once!" Indeed, one of his rivals went on to play Ajax's madness "so discreetly and sanely as to win praise, since he kept within the bounds of the dance and did not debauch the histrionic art" (84). More interestingly still, one glimpses a remarkable continuity in the question of taste from Seneca to Stanislavski. In the ever-variegated realities of audience response, theorists draw a kind of aesthetic line in the sand that ideally separates true from false, acting from reality, good from bad. Even for Stanislavski, knowledge of the precise location of that line becomes part of any actor's mastery of his craft: "Never lose yourself on the stage. Always act in your own person, as an artist. You can never get away from yourself. The moment you lose yourself on the stage marks the departure from truly living your part and the beginning of exaggerated false acting." [122]

The story of Ajax exemplifies the interest, the pleasure, and the crisis of simulation, each of which enjoyed a long and elaborate history in the Middle Ages and Renaissance. Nowhere is that history better illustrated than by yet another legend about the sad fate of the theater at Meaux. According to Petit de Julleville, one early historian attributed the short life span of that theater to the sad demise of some of its actors, whose deaths proffered ominous examples of life imitating art:

> After two years of performances, *says a historian of Meaux*, and in spite of their success, the theater was demolished and its land sold off. One does not see that stage plays in Meaux were taken up again for a long time. Perhaps the miserable end of several people who had taken part there was the cause of this: an end which, in the account of the chronicler, seems to impinge somewhat on the legendary. In fact, according to the account, those who had played the roles of devils died in great poverty. The man who had played the role of Satan, a certain Pascalus to whom the nickname "the Devil" had stuck, was hanged; and the man who had played Despair poisoned himself. [123]

While the commentator is apparently loath to "depoeticize" the legend, he does manage to venture a socioeconomic explanation for the death of the Devils and a political one for Pascalus. The poor working stiffs who had played the devils on stage could never have returned to their menial jobs after the thrill and

---

[122] Stanislavski, *AP*, 177.
[123] The full text appears in Petit de Julleville, *LM*, II, 143–44.

celebrity of acting. As for Pascalus, he ends his days "playing straight" a very serious role in the great political drama of the Reformation:

> Without wanting to depoeticize the legend too much, one might note that those who had played the demons were "poor devils" in whom the passion for play-acting had occasioned a distaste for the daily grind of their real jobs, as the author himself insinuates. As for Pascalus, we see him later during the [times of] religious and civil unrest. He is playing for keeps a more dangerous role that sometimes could (and, in this case actually did) lead him straight to the gallows, notwithstanding his diabolical antecedents. (*LM*, II, 144)

The solution proposed by at least one of the narrative voices of this text is to distinguish between the false drama of the stage and the far more dangerous but ostensibly much more verifiable drama of political life.[124] Still, since the evidence of Pascalus's crimes has also vanished, all that remains are eloquently expressed fears: fears about the genuine risks assumed by actors and audiences of the theater, and fears about theater's role in the purgation or perpetuation of those fears.

Along those lines, it behooves us to consider another intriguing aspect of Petit de Julleville's treatment of the Meaux legend: namely, what he chooses to omit without really omitting. Relegated to the final footnote of his two-page discussion is a companion legend which Petit de Julleville admits to finding "too legendary" for inclusion with the other legends:

> I would not dare to mention anywhere but in a footnote a legend that is well-known but vague and hardly authentic. A resident of Melun named "The Eel" [Languille] was playing the role of Saint Bartholomew in a mystery play. At the moment of the ordeal, he started screaming before the actor playing the executioner could even touch him. Whence the proverb: "He's like the Eel of Melun, 'frighted by false fire'" ["Il est comme Languille de Melun, qui crie avant qu'on l'écorche"]. (*LM*, II, 144n)[125]

No matter who it is who screams or jumps before being touched—The Eel, the audience, or the twentieth-century reader of what I have called elsewhere "snuff drama"—playing one's part on the medieval stage was dangerous.

---

[124] In light of such highly spectacular juridico-political "dramas" as Anita Hill vs. Clarence Thomas, Bill Clinton vs. Paula Jones, and Newt Gingrich vs. the Ethics Committee, it is unclear that the drama of political life is any more "verifiable" than these early deaths-by-drama.

[125] Here Petit de Julleville cites Leroux de Lincy, *Livre des proverbes*, 2d ed., II, 49. The cultural specificity of proverbial wisdom is, of course, notoriously difficult to translate. So, in favor of something like "shrieking before the skinning," "crying for nothing," "putting the cart before the horse," or "saying 'ouch' before the doctor gives you the shot," I have opted for these words spoken by Shakespeare's Hamlet to Claudius, who rises after seeing the deadly serious playacting of the murder of Gonzago, staged by Hamlet. I am indebted to Roze Hentschell for bringing this phrase to my attention.

Real or imagined, the tale from Tournai still stands out from all the apocrypha because it turns the absence of proof into a virtue.[126] Although the pardoned criminal/executioner/Judith character has supposedly been granted
some kind of amnesty for his earlier conviction to banishment, he has vanished
anyway and taken his story with him. Even as the executioner's disappearance
ensures the impossibility of confirmation or denial of the decapitation, the event
is justified, verified, and authorized by another legend related to the "black legend" of Philip. The pardoned criminal-turned-actor-turned-executioner is said
to have gone on to the role of a lifetime. He has become the special servant of
Philip, handling unnamed iniquitous deeds for a monarch whose reign would
be dominated by cruelty: "It was even said that he took into his personal service
the young man who had 'struck so well' and that he employed him in secret acts
of iniquity [il l'employa à des actes secrets d'iniquité]" (Faber, *HTB* 15).

The banished, vanished criminal's public performance of iniquity has become
a private but no less fearful performance of public fears about authoritarian-
ism, public and private. Nor does the ambiguous language of the passage make
entirely intelligible just what kind of private misdeeds are at stake here: awful,
secret iniquities against the public that fears the prince and his henchman; or
delightful secret iniquities *for* the prince to whose person "Judith" has been attached, perhaps in the privacy of Philip's bedroom. A Devil of Meaux goes to the
gallows, a Despair becomes suicidal, and Judith remains a woman for Philip.[127]

For Isidore of Seville, comic actors rendered publicly the acts that men
committed in private life (privatorum hominum acta) (*Etymologiarum*, bk. 18,
chap. 46). The tragedy of Tournai is to represent only the fear of the unrepre-
sentable private. And that fear bring us full circle to the question of whether the
Tournai execution happened as it returns to us other questions of torture, truth,
and verisimilitude. Critics are left with more questions than answers. What really happened in Tournai, Brussels, and Meaux? What really happened to Jean
de Missey, Nicolle de Neufchastel, Pascalus, and the despairing Despair? What
if the Eel of Melun was not wrong to cry out in pain before any pain was inflicted? To what elusive events are elusive witnesses pointing elusively? And
what are the consequences of their own belief (or lack of belief) in what they
saw or did not see? It may not be so easy to proffer hurried assent to William
Tydeman's claims that the celebrated image of the martyrdom of Saint Apollonia unquestionably depicts a play and that the tortured victim is "no doubt" a
feinte (*TMA*, 177). If nothing else, the numerous legends of death by drama
rule out use of the term "unquestionably." More to the point is Kubiak's argument that the relationship between seeing and the violence of language is "the

---

[126] I confess that my own discussion to some extent does the same: turns absence into a critical
virtue.

[127] See, e.g., Dollimore's discussion of transgressive sexualities in *Radical Tragedy*, xxxiii–xlv,
and chap. 15, on *The White Devil*. I am thankful to Joan Scott for exploring the gendered ramifications of this text with me.

most impossible of theatre's conundrums. For the violence that is speaking, multiplied by the 'ocular proof' that is theatre, is only 'positive' (in the Brechtian perspective) when the proof in the seeing is *true*" (*ST*, 64; emphasis his). Although Kubiak attributes the development of theory of "ocular proof" to Bertolt Brecht, its conundrum had long been rehearsed by forensic rhetoric and torture, both of which depended on the very type of verisimilitude hyperrealized in the events above. That conundrum was also investigated regularly by medieval drama.

At the most, the Tournai incident points to real dramatic practice and, at the least, to real fears (contemporaneous and contemporary) associated with the theater. It may point as well to something along the lines sketched by Peter Brook. All the while acknowledging that, in theater, "there is a deadly element everywhere," Brook concludes that "deceptively, the opposite seems also true, for within the Deadly Theatre there are often tantalizing, abortive, or even momentarily satisfying flickers of a real life." [128] Whatever we choose to believe about spectacular violence in the Middle Ages and the Renaissance, the reality of early dramatic realism is that it regularly staged its own capacity to blur any possible distinction between real and realistic. Accidental or deliberate, that blurring is clear and present in these legendary occurrences of death at the hands of drama. It is equally clear in the scourging scenes of early French religious drama which, now within the world of performativity, take on new meaning.

Violence and Performativity on the French Medieval Stage: A Retrospective

If Tournai's fusion of legal and dramatic spectacle sketches in broad strokes the hermeneutic difficulties of theater and violence, so too do the numerous beatings, tortures, and ordeals of medieval and Renaissance drama. Given the spectacular enactment of legal rhetoric and public castigation along with the anecdotal evidence that a theatrical performance could even lead to death, the menacing utterances of so many scourging scenes become performative in ways medievalists might never have suspected. While the term "performative" might initially seem a strange bedfellow of early dramatic "fiction," it is important to bear in mind that, to a medieval Christian spectator, the story dramatized by a mystery play was *not* fiction. Reminders of its truth were available everywhere: especially if that spectator were to glance up and see a priest, a bishop, a teacher with rod in hand, or if he were to recall their images. In a world where legends about Tournai, Meaux, and the Eel of Melun circulated, early theater audiences may well have believed that real speech acts could occur at any time during the plays they were watching. No matter how apocryphal the stories, if any given

[128] Brook, *Empty Space*, 17.

medieval spectator believed that when actors threatened violence, violence would be carried out literally and with real risks to actors and audience, then we may speak of performativity on the early stage.

In this section, I propose to reintegrate into the scourgings of medieval religious drama J. L. Austin's theory that the enunciation of specific words in highly ritualized settings constitutes "doing something." "The uttering of the words," he writes, "is, indeed, usually *a*, or even *the*, leading incident in the performance of the act (of betting or what not)" (*HTDT*, 8; emphasis his). For the sake of argument, one might imagine the following scenario. An act of violence is threatened within a medieval religious drama.[129] That act is then represented with all the graphic realism medieval and Renaissance dramaturgy had to offer. Occasionally, staging techniques result in real harm—accidentally to Jehan de Missey and deliberately (at least, so goes the legend) to the Tournai criminal. In those instances, which again occur under highly ritualized circumstances, one character's threats or promises to do violence to another become actual threats of real bodily harm to the real people playing the endangered and endangering roles. In addition, then, to the vivid reenactments advocated by forensic rhetorical theory, such acts become legitimate "warrants" in the Austinian sense which must be addressed as such. Those real threats can be assessed only in retrospect, however, because it is only in retrospect that it is possible (or impossible) to sort out what *really* happened or what producers and performers "intended" to happen.

Despite Eusebius's assertion that there was "nothing fearful where there is the love of the Father nor painful where there is the glory of Christ" (*EH*, V, 1.23), there was indeed something to fear on the medieval stage. And there was a reason why theatrical producers over the ages have found the semiotics of ecclesiastical space to be so conducive to scenes of violence. As John Callahan muses in regard to the heyday of the Grand Guignol, "in 1896 when Maurice Magnier converted the chapel into an intimate theatre, he retained the chapel *motif*. Thus some of the worst manglings, acid throwings and vile murders have been witnessed by carved cherubs and seven-foot angels, while the loges look vaguely like confessionals and the balcony seats like pews" ("Ultimate," 167). Following John Calvin's claim that "in order to hold Men's minds in greater subjection, clever men have devised many things in religion by which to inspire the common folk with reverence and strike them with terror," I conclude with the suggestion that one of those things was religious drama.[130]

From the Logos of Genesis to the Annunciation to the Tournai execution, there is no dearth of apparently performative utterances in the mystery play.

---

[129] Obviously, such a moment is equally plausible in farce. I submit, however, that real violence cannot function in the same way because the play would cease to be a farce.

[130] Calvin, *Institutes*, I, 3.2; cited and discussed in Dollimore, *Radical Tragedy*, 11.

"Faites tant que vous le trouvez; / Et sus ly si bien vous prouvez / *Que lez autres aient freeur,*" cries one of the torturers in the *Geu Saint Denis* (Do what you can to find him; and prove yourselves upon his body in order to raise terror in the hearts of the others) (361–63). "Punition de ce chrestïen, / Je vous *prometz,*" intones another character from the *Mystère de Saint Christofle,* "sanz faillir rien, / Que ce n'est qu'un droit enchanteur" (I promise to you unflinchingly the punishment of this Christian, because he's just a pure sorcerer).[131] In the *Martire Saint Estienne* from the *Cycle des premiers martyrs,* when the saint refuses to recant his views on the Creation during a punitive interrogation, an apoplectic Bishop Annas who is gnashing his teeth and pounding his ears ("en gregnant les dens et en estoupant sez oreilles") gives the order for torture: "Lïez, ferez, frapez dessus, / Froissiez la teste et la cervele, / Rompez les os et la bouele! / Hors de la ville a grosses pierres / Me lapidez ce sanglant lierres!" (Tie him up, shackle him, hit him, batter his head and his skull, break his bones and his spine. There are big rocks outside our city, so stone this bloody thief for me!) (*CPM,* 414–18). Estienne's beating begins directly after that performative utterance.

In the Sainte Geneviève *Passion,* the torturer Marquin warrants a similar fate: "Plus soef t'en yrons menant, / *Je te promet*; vecy la corde. / Haquin, garde qu'il ne me morde; / Tu me verras ja bien estraindre, / Et sy ne s'en osera plaindre" (Things are going to go much more nicely for you now, I promise you. Here's the rope. Haquin, you make sure he doesn't bite me. You'll see me shut him up good, so he won't dare to complain). His promise is followed immediately by a stage direction indicating that Jesus is to be bound (*Jésus est lié*) (1412–16). Elsewhere in the play, other scourging scenes depict threats of violence which occasion actual violence to victims as they exemplify the perceived power reversal on which torture depends. Herod threatens that "Tu as fain de te faire batre, / Se ne respons appertement" (you're asking for a beating if you don't answer clearly) (1890–91); and demands, "Respon, ou tu seras batu! / Tu ne m'as *pouoir d'eschaper.* / Comment te es tu lessé haper? / Se tu point de *pouoir* eüsses, / Pas lessé prendre ne te fusses!" (Answer, or you're going to be beaten! You've no power to escape me now. How'd you let yourself get caught this way anyhow? If you'd had any power at all, you could never have let yourself get taken like this!) (Sainte Geneviève *Passion,* 1940–44). Those threats prompt the issuance of another one: "nous te menon / La ou ton corps bien tourmentez / sera" (now we're going to lead you somewhere where your body's gonna be tortured good) (1994–96). Shortly thereafter, Caiaphas orders the beating of Christ:

> Marquin, gardez que bien te teignes!
> Celle robe du dos ly sache,
> Et puis tout droit a celle estache

---

[131] *Mystère de Saint Christofle,* 2107–9.

> *Le me va maintenant lïer,*
> *Car .i. pou le vueil chastïer.*
> Grans escourgees porterez,
> De quoy sez costez froterez;
> *Car je vueil qu'il soit bien batu.*
> (Sainte Geneviève *Passion*, 2304–11)

Marquin, take care to hold him well. Take off the robe from his back, and then, straight away, you'll tie him up for me now on that stake, because I want to punish him a little. You'll carry great switches with which you'll hit his sides. Above all, I want him beaten well.

Marquin obliges with the words "Roy, ton sermon est *abatu*" (My King, your word is law) (emphases mine).

Moreover, the close discursive connection between threat and action is often highlighted by stage directions which specify that beatings, tortures, or executions are to commence directly after a performative utterance. Malbec of the Auvergne *Passion* volunteers to hold Christ's feet while his partner strikes Him: "Or frape, car je tien les piés" (So hit him now while I'm holding his feet!). Malegorge responds: "Il fault qu'ilz soyent ensemble lié / Liget. / d'une *corde* pour le mieulx joindre. / *Pausa*" (They've got to be tied together [*They bind them*] with a cord the better to join them. [*They pause*]) (2613–15). Masquebignet and Hapelopin of the *Geu Saint Denis* practically whistle while they work at causing blood to flow: "*Lors lez batent en disant.* . . . Le sanc en sault de toutes pars; / Regardez s'ilz sont tains en rouge" (*Then they beat them while singing.* The blood is coming out all over the place; look at how they're all stained red with blood) (533–38).

Even more compelling is the medieval enactment of a practice discussed by Scarry in which the torturer displays his implements of mutilation as an enhancement of the promise of violence. When a torturer makes a verbal threat while raising a rod or pointing to an electrical switch, Scarry finds that "nowhere does language come so close to being the concrete agent of physical pain" (*BP*, 46). That very technique is illustrated by the torturers of the *Geu Saint Denis*: "Yllecques, enmy celle rue, / En ces tourmens lez estendez. (*En moustrant lez tourmens.*) / De pié en chief lez m'etendez / Comme en fait drap a la poulie" (And now in the middle of this street, stretch them out upon these implements of torture. *Showing the instruments.* Stretch them from head to toe like when you're making fabric with the pulley) (*GSD*, 601–14). In the *Martire Pere et Pol*, Agrippa feeds the same fears echoed by the Tournai incident when he swears by his own head that a decapitation will take place: "Par ma teste, ains qu'il soit souper / Sera fait, sire, cen [*sic*] que dites. / Avant prenez ces .ii. hermites; / Roulliez, ferez, frapez, lïez, / Ce bertondu crucifiez, / Et ad ce Pol coupez le col" (By my head, before it's suppertime, what you say will be done, sire. First take these two hermits. Beat them, shackle them, hit them, tie them up. Crucify this joker for me and cut off the head of that Paul). Masquebignet and Hapelopin oblige post haste *en ferant*; and their pal Menjumatin does one better, exhibiting the weapon with nefarious satirical resonances. Holding out the false lifeline to the "fisherman," he taunts "en ly monstrant *une corde: Delivre* toy; vecy ta ligne!" (showing him the cord, Go on, deliver yourself. Here's your lifeline!) (*CPM*, 1860–70; emphases mine).

When it comes to the interrelations among threats, language, and torture, however, the pièce de résistance may well be "Coment Judich tua Oloferne." Given what we now know about Tournai in 1549, the seemingly standard language of the dramatic prologue assumes strong connotations of performativity (or the promise thereof). According to the narrator of the play, during the particularly brutal siege of her city in which inhabitants are dying of thirst, Judith becomes a heroine for all time:

> Mais depuis Judich se venga,
> car de sa main le decola
> et aporta en Bethulie
> sa teste du corps departie,
> *conme vous verrez en presence,*
> s'il vous plaist a faire silence.

But then Judith avenged herself, for with her hand she beheaded him and brought to Bethulia his severed head, *as you will see shown before you* if you'll be kind enough to be quiet. (57–62; emphasis mine)

The city of Tournai was itself a contested site that changed hands from England to France to Spain. Hence Philip's victory visit to the city as an "exellent prince et redoubté" (a prince excellent and feared)—the very terms with which one of his knights addresses Holofernes (63). So, when Judith prays to God and explains her intentions, her words also constitute a statement to the intruding victor (of questionable sexuality). She will topple Holofernes while Tournai metacritically topples Philip: "Donne moy constance et coraige, / que sa vertu mette en servaige. / Lors sera de ton nom memoire / que en main de fenme soit victoire" (Give me the will and the courage to subjugate his strength. Then your name will live on in memory as the victory will lie in the hands of a woman) (365–68). At the moment of truth, Judith prays again, begging her God of Israel to comfort her and to see her plan through (670–78). Afterward, the stage directions read: "*Ce temps pendant Judich coppe la teste a Olofernés, puis dist:* and *Judich se part de l'ost et emporte la teste de Olofernés et vi[e]nt a la porte, puis dit:* Guettes! Guettes! Ouvrez la porte! / Bonne[s] nouvelles vous apporte" (Meanwhile, Judith cuts off Holofernes's head; Judith goes off, carrying the head of Holofernes and arrives at the gate of the city and says: "Look, look, I bring you glad tidings") (681–82). Holofernes, or a fantasized Philip, is dead.

Like the rhetorician who chose to avail himself of evidence extracted from torture, the medieval dramatist who invented and reinvented the tortures of Christ, saints, and Old Testament figures was translating physical pain into a performative construct—and with all the enormity that practice implied. In fact, the myriad dramatic representations of the tortures of Christ retrace the steps of the linguistic conversion that normally occurred during the *inventio* of torture. First, the speech of the tortured victim reverts to prelinguistic cries of pain; next those cries (and whatever confessions follow) are conceived by the dramatist as evidence; and finally, the dramatist retranslates those cries back into either a linguistic representation of torture or (most disturbing of all) into the performative reenactment of actual torture—which itself reverts back to the primordial utterances of a real pain now inflicted on the stage. The acknowledgement of the possibility of actual performativity in medieval religious drama thus calls into question such contemporary theories about the violence of language as those of Roland Barthes or Jacques Derrida. The former postulates, for example, that terrorist discourse can "simply be the wish to accomplish the lucid adequation of the enunciation with the true violence of language, the inherent violence which stems from the fact that no utterance is able directly to express the truth and has no other mode at its disposal than the force of the word." [132] Barthes hopefully deconstructs the phenomenon in which "an apparently terrorist discourse ceases to be so if, reading it, one follows the directions it itself provides" (208–9). But that intuition is itself deconstructed by the experiences of medieval spectators and spectatorship. Similarly, despite Derrida's remark that an originally violent discourse "can *only do itself violence*," [133] it is clear that some early audience members who had been exposed to legends about death by drama could counter that violence was not just about language.

The reintegration of Austinian performativity into medieval theater studies has at least three immediate critical consequences. First, as contemporary audiences are regularly treated to television shows on the order of *Rescue 911* and avant-garde productions such as those of the troupe that bills itself as the Real and True Theatre, the perennial debate about real violence as entertainment demonstrates a remarkable consistency over time. [134] Medieval dramatists were in the business of "credible threats," a concept that recently caught the attention of a group of social scientists. When they released the results of the National Television Violence Study in 1996, they identified the "credible threat" as one of three principal types of media violence: "Violence is defined as any overt depiction of the use of physical force—or the *credible threat* of such force—intended to physically harm an animate being or group of beings." [135] All the threats, all their credibility, all their promise of physical harm, all their danger-

---

[132] Barthes, *Image/Music/Text*, 208; see also Kubiak's discussion of this text in *ST*, 63.
[133] *WD*, 130; emphasis his.
[134] See, e.g., Pywell's discussion of the Real and True Theatre in *SRT*, 21.
[135] "Television Violence and Its Context," 3; emphasis mine.

ous consequences in the realm of entertainment were played out in classical, medieval, and early Renaissance literary theory and practice.

Second, the acknowledgment of medieval dramatic performativity might spur a renewed critique of metadramatic critique, as it were. Notwithstanding the current trend among scholars of the medieval, Renaissance, and early modern periods to view popular or civic festivities as sites of rebellion, it is not at all clear that ecclesiastical productions necessarily constitute displays of power while popular ones constitute displays of subversion.[136] Karen Cunningham contends that, when Christopher Marlowe "transfers violence from the executioner's to the theater's scaffold," he undermines the spectacular rhetoric of torture and "transform[s] a theater of pain into a drama of subversion" ("Renaissance Execution," 210). Today's nagging duplicity may well have eluded a medieval audience. If huge crowds flocked to festivities in which the possibility of real pain and suffering blurred the boundaries between drama and real life, it is also conceivable that they blurred the boundaries between so-called "popular" and "learned" forms. Consider the Brussels procession of chained Jews on Good Friday. From the standpoint of what went on inside and outside the Church, it is reasonable to submit that the exclusive association of violence with formal, learned, institutional structures of knowledge may be misleading when it comes to the endurance of violence in drama, law, and religion.

Although my contention throughout this book has been that violence is deeply embedded in the very language of classical and medieval rhetoric and its pedagogies, there is no reason to assume from the outset that coercion and terror are possible only under the hegemonic aegis of learned forms. Despite the critical politics in which oppressors are unilaterally condemned, one characteristic I hope to have shown is that the rhetoric of violence (which relentlessly alternates with the violence of rhetoric) transcends the sometimes all-too-facile categories of popular and learned. For the literary critic, a large part of the difficulty may derive from a presumably natural reluctance to participate in repressive structures. Amy Newman argues from that perspective that "when the distinction between art and life is dissolved, the oppressors, as much as the oppressed, become artists in their own right—and those with the upper hand in the game of dominance are, for the most part, profoundly uninterested in, and their victims unaffected by, the methodological cleverness of privileged, artistic intellectuals" ("Aestheticism, Feminism," 24). W. I. Miller even compares the complications of talking about violence to a great game: "violence may simply be what we accuse the Other of when we are contesting interests. It may be little more than a rhetorical play in the game of self-legitimation or the delegitimation of the Other" (*Humiliation*, 77). There was nothing simple and nothing

---

[136] For all their differences, one thinks of the common denominator of community formation in, e.g., Justice, *Writing and Rebellion*; Travis, "Social Body of the Dramatic Christ;" Beckwith, *CB*; Aers, *Community, Gender, and Individual Identity*; Farmer, *Communities of Saint Martin*; Rubin, *CC*.

quintessentially ludic about the violence and spectacle of rhetoric. As the tortures of its tradition have shown, its drama was deadly serious.

Third, the study of real violence permits a larger reintegration of performance as an interpretive category in medieval theater studies. If characters in a Passion play issue promises and threats that may or may not have tangible physical consequences, then certain thematic distinctions long held dear by theater historians begin to collapse. Rosemary Woolf's contrast of the "aristocratic villains . . . who assault Christ with words" with the "base figures, soldiers or Jews, who maltreat him" (238–39) become irrelevant—all the more so in that the tortured history of *la question* irremediably blurs distinctions between verbal interrogation and infliction of physical punishment.[137] The scourging scenes mean more in performance than even Kolve's emphasis on their role in characterization and plot. He notes, for example, of the Towneley scourging that "the dramatists were guided by another fact about the *tortores*, greater in importance, and richer in meaning: they had to develop characterization and dramatic action" (*PCC*, 179).[138] Tortured characterizations were characterizations in performance.

In that sense, performativity reproblematizes the aesthetics of violence at the levels of catharsis and reception. Since torture was an institution with a cultural force enhanced by its ability to threaten, perhaps drama more than any other medieval genre helps to create a situation in which a threat outside the play may function as a threat inside a play. Paradoxically, however, the presence of torture within medieval religious drama may also have served to camouflage the very fear on which torture relies. Since on-stage violence could be real, less real, "unreal," and even comical, the *mystère* was sometimes able to entertain its audiences by terrorizing them into believing that it was a form of entertainment.

In the epistemologically complex scourging scenes, the "doing" of violence regularly transcended the realm of discourse. Even if we assume briefly that the countless threats and promises of a genre like the *mystère* did *not* operate as performatives, frequent metacommentary about representation within drama would complicate that assessment. If the prospect of real violence, real death, real pain, and real dismemberment was possible or believable once, it was possible or believable again, endowing medieval drama with all the pity and terror that many spectators experience today at the circus (sometimes secretly hoping that the tightrope walker working without a net will fall). Given the medieval predilection for hyperreality, one thing seems evident (and this is true whether or not that hyperreality is intentional or accidental). To a medieval audience listening to the threats of torture against Christ or against other martyred characters, the terror was real.

While it is clear that, within the framework of medieval religious drama, threats of brutal chastisement would not always be carried out literally, it is

---

[137] Woolf, *English Mystery Plays*, 238–39.
[138] Richard Beacham comes to a similar conclusion in "Violence on the Street," 47, 53.

equally clear from the examples treated in this chapter that accidental violence was a definite possibility and that intentional, premeditated violence was a real fear. The terror, the pity, and the fear lie in the fact that the audience's anticipation is suspended until the very moment when they learn whether or not real violence will be inflicted (deliberately or accidentally) on a real body or merely staged with *faintes*. It is only at the moment when an individual dramaturgic choice has been prearranged by producers or improvised by the "torturer" that the audience knows for sure what is happening. And it is only when a violent event actually happens (or not) that they discover whether drama will imitate or enact performativity.[139] The problem is that we can never know with certainty who they really were and what they think they really saw. When dramatic scenes of torture and punishment collide with forensic witnessing, they betray an imminent danger, madness, and terror that one can only begin to imagine. And yet the violence is all too imaginable.

After all, in the contemporary American and English avant-garde theaters of pain, violence is no longer left exclusively to the imagination. By the time Geoff Pywell recounted his personal experience as a witness to the actual bloodshed and broken bones staged by the twentieth-century Real and True Theatre (RATT), the stakes were considerably greater than the dramatic imagination. Himself the victim of a senseless drunken driving accident, the late Pywell was a witness to theater's violent reality. As he recreates the trauma of RATT, he recalls that one of the actors

> strode to the nearest woman, grabbed her hair, and in a single, rapid motion brought her face down onto his raised knee. I could hear the sharp crack of a bone. Her nose opened up. He lifted her head, still held by the hair and showed us the blood covering her face as her knees went from under her so that she seemed to be swinging like a grotesquely abused doll from his grasp. He held her there for a few seconds and then let her drop unceremoniously to the floor. Without removing his eyes from us, he ground his heel into the face beneath him. She didn't move and I believe at that point she was unconscious. The other three women neither shifted nor flinched. (*SRT*, 21)

It is the degree of violence that motivates Pywell to reminisce that "the shock of realization was . . . mixed, adulterated, by its quite deliberate representative nature." He determines that the violence of RATT has decimated the handy categories of fiction and reality: "I couldn't divorce the knowledge of its real consequences, now inescapable perpetually, from its theatrical genesis so pointedly, even elegantly, signposted" (*SRT*, 21). In Meaux, in Brussels, in Tournai, in the

---

[139] See Alter on the "tension that always underlies all virtual performances, and threatens the stability of textual references" (*Sociosemiotic Theory*, 173). Part of the tension involved in performing the Tournai "heresy" betrays another great Reformation tension about the performativity of transsubstantiation.

scourging scenes of the *mystère*, medieval and Renaissance drama regularly sign-posted that genesis just as pointedly. Indeed, one of the special functions of the-atrical violence was to signpost barriers that did not, strictly speaking, exist be-tween thought and real life, morality and action, correct and incorrect, normal and transgressive. Perhaps that was and is the greatest threat of all.

Theater, ventures Kubiak, "has by and large resisted or covered over actual violence, simply because *real violence in performance*, as Girard shows us, is *not as efficient* as its mimetic representations: real violence in performance, then, is not transgressive, but merely inefficient" (*ST*, 160; emphasis mine). More re-cently, Joel Black has elaborated a theory of the "aesthetics of murder" (albeit in the eighteenth-century context of Edmund Burke). "The reason the audience abandons the theater for the execution," he surmises, "is because the latter is the more *theatrical* spectacle. It is not that art fails to match life, or that fiction can't compete with reality; in this particular instance [the execution of Lord Lo-vat], the public display of an actual killing simply has a greater aesthetic impact on its audience than the representation of violent death in a play." [140] Be that as it may, when an exasperated William Gruber endeavors to crucify Francis Barker for his "ungenerous moralizing" and "offensive piousness," Gruber's response resurrects a quarrel of the Ancients and the Moderns as he transforms a criti-cal question about violent, politicized aesthetics into a generational question: "so frequent nowadays is disparagement of writers on ethical grounds that one sometimes feels as if a generation of scholars is attempting—perhaps in des-peration—to convince themselves and their students that literature has a more than parenthetic relationship with real life." [141] Such a "desperate" effort to convince oneself of the physical and rhetorical powers of drama would scarcely have surprised anyone who had circulated the legends about the spontaneous abortions of the female spectators of the *Eumenides*, the mysterious deaths of the actors in Meaux, or the execution of a felon in Tournai. All such tales have long invited speculation about a relationship between theater and real life that has always been "more than parenthetic." Indeed, the fact that so many forms of violent entertainment play out on the barrier between real and unreal implies that, then and now, it is *the* relationship to investigate. Marvin Carlson cer-tainly believed that it was when he asserted that the link between theater and everyday life was almost totally neglected. [142]

In "The Avoidance of Love," Stanley Cavell launched one such investigation when he pondered the case of the local Southern yokel who rushes onstage to save Shakespeare's Desdemona from the evil black Othello. [143] Phenomenologi-cally speaking, that yokel might just as well have crashed into the frightened

---

[140] Black, *Aesthetics of Murder*, 4; emphasis his. See also Thomas de Quincey's celebrated mani-festo, *On Murder as One of the Beaux-Arts*.

[141] Gruber, review of Francis Barker's *Culture of Violence*, 532, 527.

[142] See Carlson, *Theatre Semiotics*, xiv–xvi.

[143] Cavell, *Must We Mean What We Say?* 326–37.

spectators from Riga as they were running away from scary soldiers. What it takes to "correct" both errors of ignorance is an explicit disavowal of the very "make believe" and "pretending" on which theater depends. After all, the medieval theater was well known for inviting its spectators within its bounds. It did so as early as the Fleury Playbook *Herod*, in which a didascalic commentary called upon the *populus circumstantem* to participate in the play: "Let them invite the people standing around to adore the child." [144] In all the stories analyzed above, the truth of violence (if truth there be) depends on the circumstances of the *circumstantes*.

And yet, when Cavell wraps up his meditation on the yokel, he makes a powerful assertion about the hyperreal theater which must give pause: "Neither credible nor incredible. that ought to mean that the concept of credibility is inappropriate altogether" (329). It seems that the only way to "correct" the yokel is to intervene at the epistemological level of virtual performance and at the precise moment when choices are made (to save or not to save, to correct or not to correct). Since the yokel is an otherwise ignoble racist who has nevertheless felt a noble impulse to save a woman's life, it becomes impossible for critics of his behavior to sustain three contradictory impulses. We cannot simultaneously instruct him that his noble instinct to save Desdemona is out of place at the same time that we correct his ignorance of theatrical conventions at the same time that we teach him about race relations. We cannot simultaneously exhort him to suspend both his belief and his disbelief. Even so, that is precisely what we must do if we wish to decide something about the medieval theater of cruelty.

The chronology is different, but the phenomenology is the same. It is neither "right" of Cavell's yokel to act nor right of Augustine's theatergoer to fail to act: "auditors here are not provoked to help the sufferer, but invited only to be sorry for him" (*Confessions*, bk. III, chap. 2). Along those lines, it is possible to endorse both Baudrillard's position that the theater occludes real violence and Kubiak's position that Baudrillard's comment is "obvious": theater "always seems to leave real violence behind because this is precisely theatre's function— to conceal violence even when (or especially when) it is seemingly exposing it in the violent spectacle" (*ST*, 160).

As I argued in the context of the philology of torture and drama, when the staging of torture in a mystery play is "realistic" rather than "real," it appears to incarnate a rhetorical strategy for proving truth that is more logical than the forensic strategies used to interpret the verisimilitude of confessions coerced through torture. In rhetoric, the truth of torture is illusory because it is validated with dramatic verisimilitude, while in the *mystère* a Christian truth seems to validate illusion with illusion and thus appears more "true" because it is more logically consistent in its analogies. The incidents discussed above destabilize any illusion of stability which might have been created by those ratiocinations.

[144] For this text, see Tydeman, *TMA*, 223.

When the question of performativity is raised by the medieval stage, it further jeopardizes the already fragile stability of intervention upon bodies as productive of truth. In Tournai and in Brussels, reenactments occur with such realism that they encroach on the real process of jurisprudence, which forensic rhetoric was designed to protect—but which forensic rhetoric also transgressed.

To put it another way, it is at the moment when theater is the least theatrical that it seems the most theatrical, its real violence masquerading as fiction. Theater seems to aestheticize violence because its own language has so much in common with the violence of rhetoric, and rhetoric seems to aestheticize violence because it has so much in common with theater. Whether or not the Tournai criminal was executed, whether or not Ajax went mad, whether or not the bedeviled actors died at Meaux, whether the image of the martyred Apollonia is a "photograph" of a real event, a dream, or a nightmare: those stories call into question the principle of reality. As for the special scenario of Tournai, it suggests that death is spectacular in the law and potentially legal in the theater. So even if Tournai is a fabrication, its spectacular representation of one outcome of the juridical process returns us to the invention of torture, truth, drama, and catharsis. As authenticity and reality evaporate in extensive medieval metacommentary about where theater ends and life begins (or where life ends and theater begins), the imposition of morality and justice seems the greatest illusion of all.

When a medieval play enacts performativity, when verisimilitude becomes reality, drama creates the same interpretative *mise en abîme* that characterizes the history of torture—especially in its exposures of the illusions and verisimilitudes of the law itself. Baudrillard's legalistic example of a simulated holdup is illuminating:

> A real hold up only upsets the order of things, the right of property, whereas a simulated hold up interferes with the very principle of reality. Transgression and violence are less serious, for they only contest the *distribution* of the real. Simulation is infinitely more dangerous since it always suggests, over and above its object, that *law and order themselves might really be nothing more than a simulation*. (SW, 177; emphasis his)

Here the insight that the law itself is the ultimate simulation sends the problem of performance back to its inventional place of origin as it sends the conclusion of this book back to its beginning. But one need not concur with Baudrillard's assessment that both reality and illusion are impossible. Nor need one wholly agree that "rediscovering an absolute level of the real" is as impossible as staging an illusion: "illusion is no longer possible, because the real is no longer possible" (SW, 177). Instead, one might endeavor to resolve the moral conundrum of rhetoric, law, and theater by sending rhetorical performance back to the memory of the theater.

Vicious Cycles

I am not one of those who believe that civilization has to change in order for the theater to change; but I do believe that the theater, utilized in the highest and most difficult sense possible, has the power to influence the aspect and formation of things.

—Antonin Artaud

There is now and there has always been something about violence.

That statement might have seemed relatively obvious from the outset of this book. But even today, as the boundaries of genre disappear in each new experimental theater production, even as illusion after illusion about the nobility and value of aesthetics is regularly called into question, a final observation is necessary.

The limits of genre are signposted daily by different types of artists inclined toward self-reflexivity. They enact their chosen modes of performance on the borderlines of theaters, courtrooms, books, the visual arts, and even in the U.S. Congress or on the computer screen. It all occurs without necessarily prompting the massive sociocultural malaise that appears eternally to accompany incidences and discussions of violence. To proffer a seemingly anodine example, when an actor eats an apple on stage in a scene that calls for an apple to be eaten, no critic to my knowledge has yet paused to contemplate what it means for the ontology of theater if the actor actually swallows a mouthful of apple, or what it means for thespian agency if he enjoys or loathes its taste, or what critical issues of reception are raised by the possibility of audience awareness of his preferences.[1] Nor has any spectator I have ever known reckoned that theater's illusions or suspensions of disbelief have been violated as a result of such a verifiable introduction of reality. The apple represents an acting problem; the

---

[1] I am inspired here by a remark made by one of the undergraduates in my medieval drama course, Samantha Flate.

Tournai execution or the black comedy of the scourging scenes, a moral one. While we may eat apples every day—indeed, some popular wisdom advises that we do just that—we do not every day witness or participate in violence on the streets (aestheticized or otherwise). At least, most of us do not. That latter statement would not hold true, of course, for the inhabitants of Bosnia, of some Latin American countries, of some American housing projects, or of some gang turfs in West Los Angeles.

Whence arise the complex problems of audiences, agents, actors, and writers; of the classes, races, and genders they represent in different locales and at different times; of their varied proximities to theater, its violence, and its degrees of violence; and of their relations in time and over time to behaviors that are flexibly deemed normative or transgressive.[2] Whatever the individual critical bent, many who scrutinize those problems of antiquity to the present day have found that the very ubiquity of violence almost renders it invisible. Richard Beacham observes of Plautus that the Roman dramatist's audience was "accustomed both to virtually continuous warfare, and from the mid-third century onwards, to the institutionalized violence of the gladiatorial displays. For such spectators, violence must have almost seemed commonplace, an element of everyday life."[3] Contemporary journalist Michael Silverblatt speculates of twentieth-century America that "audiences are inured to violence—when the violence is entertaining."[4] Elsewhere in the debate about violence, a successful television writer-director like Larry Gelbart mulls over the following question uneasily: "What is there in my imagination to rival the theatrics of reality?"[5] Anthony Kubiak traces theatrical violence all the way back to Euripides and finds that it "continues today in the incessant repetitions of violence in the video image—seems to describe an emptying out of violence, an attenuation that appears to make violence both absolutely ubiquitous and completely non-existent...." (*ST*, 160). And, with a different valence, William Gruber purports to share with Francis Barker an aversion to the huge death tolls detailed in the *Calendar of Assize Records*, but trots out the critical topos that, since violence was everywhere in the Middle Ages, it would have passed unnoticed: "it is likely, nevertheless, that in an environment where each year the plague, cholera, smallpox, syphilis, spotted fever, dysentery, rickets, and a host of other lethal but now *nearly forgotten* diseases took the lives of thousands of utter innocents, the executions annually of several hundred criminals would not have seemed as horrific to Shakespeare's imagination as they do to Barker's."[6] In spite of some of the similarities I have

---

[2] The medieval theater of cruelty is thus compatible with the critical frameworks so cogently elaborated in Haidu, *SV*; Stallybrass and White, *Politics and Poetics of Transgression*; and Kubiak, *ST*.

[3] Beacham, "Violence on the Street," 49.

[4] Silverblatt, "New Fiction of Transgression," 11. I thank Sharon Farmer for bringing this article to my attention.

[5] Gelbart, "Peering through the Tube Darkly . . . ," H, 33.

[6] Gruber, review of Francis Barker, *Culture of Violence*, 531–32; emphasis mine.

been investigating here between the respective pathologies of torture, rhetoric, and disease, there is no escaping the fact that death at the hands of disease is a radically different entity from death by drama or death at the hands of torturers who have specific motivations in selecting their victims. Gruber's implication is that, since the diseases mentioned are "nearly forgotten," then that fact would mitigate a certain medieval nonchalance toward violence as it mitigates modern nonchalance. Even if one were to believe that gruesome deaths by disease could be consigned to oblivion, that belief would surely disappear in the face of anyone's present-day assertion that, since we are so used to the reality of people dying of cancer, then something like the AIDS epidemic is easier to take. One cannot conveniently forget at the same time that one remembers.

While this book has focused on the medieval theater of cruelty, my principal contention has been that there is a more universal aesthetics of cruelty that rhetoric helps to identify because so much of cruelty is indigenous to rhetoric. The restoration of rhetoric to the study of the Middle Ages and its literatures thus sheds new light on the historical continuity of violence in aesthetic theory and practice. In other words, Gustave Cohen was right when he wrote that the savage genre of the mystery play grows out of "a universally cruel tendency."[7] He was right, albeit for the wrong reasons.

It really *is* a question of an ideological tendency that is "universally cruel," but the roots of that cruelty lie in the very language of some of the foundational narratives of Western civilization (or at least in the rhetorical expression of those foundations). From the migrating Lydians bringing torture and spectacle to the West, to the mutilated yet newly recreated cronies of Simonides, to the performative imposition of government by the first civilizing rhetorician, the rhetorical tradition has constituted a body of theory that intellectualizes a theory of violence by means of real violence (even if that real violence is only a legend). At the same time, it stimulates the practice of a real violence which has been nurtured by centuries of theory.

Moreover, if rhetoric's stories have prompted a natural attention here to the institutional structures and pedagogies of hegemonies, that is not the whole picture. Nowadays, as voices from all quarters are raised condemning violence of all sorts, other voices ensure anyone who will listen that violence "works" and is just what consumers demand. In his *Théâtre de la mort*, the ever-haunted André de Lorde tells the story of a young Soviet dramatist who was trying to please the European public of the Grand Guignol with the all the horrors of life in what was then the Soviet Union. De Lorde recalls that, "when the curtain went up, one could see the Red Guard torturing a miserable woman by grilling her feet in order to force her to reveal the hiding place of her valuables."[8] Appar-

---

[7] Cohen, *HMS*, 276.

[8] De Lorde, *TM*, 19. Compare this scene with, e.g., Augustine, *City of God*, bk. 1, chap. 10 (see p. 40 above).

ently, the tortures escalated so relentlessly that the Soviet missed the mark: "With all the necessary tact, he was given to understand that his play belonged more to the art of the butcher than, strictly speaking, to that of dramatist. He seemed surprised and declared ingenuously, 'and here I was scared that I hadn't made it horrible enough!'" (*TM*, 19). At least one artist trying to cater to popular taste feared that he would not include *enough* violence.

At stake here is the need to decipher far more than what it means when motorists slow down on the highway, transfixed by the sight of an accident, or when American television audiences gleefully follow murder trials on the Court Television Network in every grisly detail. At stake is the elucidation of arguments that are positively "medieval."

Or negatively medieval. When it came to clarifying the elusive reactions of medieval spectators to theatrical violence, Petit de Julleville had asked and answered certain tenacious questions many years ago. Pleasure is bipolar: "How could it happen that such a people—primitive but not ferocious—and who were profoundly religious—could have found such great pleasure in seeing displayed on the stage the interminable ordeal of the martyrs whom they venerated the most and of Christ himself whom they adored? This apparent contradiction has perhaps surprised literary critics to excess. In essence, the public of all ages remains the same." [9]

Nevertheless, when Richard Homan addresses the difficult topic of "Mixed Feelings about Violence in the Corpus Christi Plays," he judges, on one hand, that "violent activity on stage may inspire different emotions depending on its significance. In this regard, violent activities are no different from any other class of activities." [10] On the other hand, he concludes of the slapstick humor of the Croxton Crucifixion that "I doubt that the original audience laughed at the difficulties with which the soldiers do their work" (Homan, "Mixed Feelings," 94). Why wouldn't they have laughed, any more than many learned academic audiences alternatively laugh or groan when they first hear the story of the Tournai incident, or when they bristle at the suggestion that medieval audiences might have identified with wife beaters rather than with their victims? Notwithstanding Thomas Gould's assertion that Freud and Frazer were wrong "in supposing that 'we', whether in an audience or in our community, identify with the perpetrators rather than the victims of the 'sacrifice,'" [11] it is clear that some audiences do indeed identify with the perpetrators. It is also clear that, if the European Middle Ages is implicated in the linguistic and performative perpetuation of violence, so too is the contemporary West. By all accounts, it exists in a strange familial relationship to its medieval "parent," which is paradoxically viewed as the engendering child.

---

[9] Petit de Julleville, *LM*, I, 409.
[10] Homan, "Mixed Feelings," 93.
[11] Gould, "Uses of Violence in Drama," 11.

For example, when Petit de Julleville runs through the pleasures experienced by seventeenth- and eighteenth-century spectators as they watched Oedipus blind himself, he returns to the foundational principle of Aristotelian catharsis. That sweet sentiment purges and purifies emotions "by a sweet pity and by a terror of the imagination, which have nothing of the bitterness and violence of real terror and pity" (*LM*, I, 410). Petit de Julleville's solution to the historical problem of violence is a hopeful recourse to one of the great teleologies of literary criticism: medieval people were children while the critic and his peers are adults.[12] That topos enables him to preserve both "his God" and his relationship to his immature French ancestors from whom he distances himself:

> We may then believe that these were the complex and diverse sentiments that filled the souls of medieval spectators during the representation of the mystery plays. They laughed at the vulgar jokes of the executioners, beggars, and servants; they cried when they saw the Savior of mankind the butt of so many jokes, horrors, and such cruel tortures. They laughed and cried at the same time, alternatively and sometimes almost at the same time in the way that children do. (*LM*, I, 410)

Today, as critics enact the most radical revisions of early scholarship, their conclusions about violence have not always deviated much. So, in the current debate about violence on the medieval stage, one often sees that the invocation of concepts like "collective salvation," "affective piety," and "community-formation" replaces one vision of childlikeness with another.[13]

Closer to home is Stanley Cavell's allusion to another kind of child—a terrified child who is too young to understand the theatrical event to which he has been taken: "'They are only pretending' is something we typically say to children, in reassurance. . . . The point of saying it there is not to focus them on the play, but to help bring them out of it. It is not an instructive remark, but an emergency measure. If the child cannot be brought out of the play by working through the content of the play itself, he should not have been subjected to it in the first place."[14] Faced with the conceptual difficulties of late medieval religious plays that are staged on the tenuous borderlines between fiction, the "non-fiction" of Christ's Passion, and real life, we too are being "helped out" of the theater. But, as it happens, the very violence that "helps us out" may eventually help us back in.

In the year 1437, there was an accident in the city of Metz. Father Jehan de Missey was left hanging so long during his suicide scene that participants scampered to fetch smelling salts to revive him from his swoon. A little over a hun-

---

[12] See R. Howard Bloch on the critical perception that medieval people are children in "New Philology and Old French," 43–46. Martha Grace Duncan also explores the topos of the criminal as child in *Romantic Outlaws, Beloved Prisons*, 189.

[13] See, e.g., Rey-Flaud, *PDMA*, 153–54; or Victor Scherb, "Violence and Social Body," 69, 77.

[14] *Must We Mean What We Say?* 329.

dred years later, legends were circulating in Meaux to the effect that a Satan had been hanged and a Despair had poisoned himself. Shortly thereafter, there was supposedly a snuff murder in Tournai, carried out for a visiting prince to thunderous applause. And now, almost four and a half centuries later, America ponders whether or not the depiction of brutality within modes of entertainment causes the commission of brutal criminal acts in real life. One seems to have come back to the medieval future. Nor is that the only future at issue. Insofar as it is rhetoric that exposes both the theatricality of violence and the violence of theatricality, it is also rhetoric that may help to bring drama studies back to that future.

However different in tone, these tales have provoked an extensive meditation about the interplay among theatricality, pleasure, didacticism, morality, and real life. To return to one of the images with which I began, there was a reason why theatrical spectacles failed to pacify the blood lust of Caligula—as much as his father Tiberius held out the hope that "through these his savage nature might be softened." [15] The commingled histories of torture, theater, rhetoric, and aesthetics that I have endeavored to chronicle in this book suggest that the violent linguistic foundations of aesthetics offer no safe haven for spectators who seek release or sublimation in the arts. Seen from that perspective, theater would not purge our violent emotions at all, but rather funnel them right back into the violent ideological structures that presumably inspired such impossible purgations and catharses.

Even so, there endures a certain optimism about the cathartic process and the art forms which solicit it. Michael Silverblatt contributes a "handy guideline" for deciphering the complexities of violence in which the authorial imagination manages to emerge intact. "The false transgressor," he believes, "wants to give us an experience of virtual reality—but the author underlines the fantasy of the experience. The real transgressor will not feed our yearning for fantasy and distance.... The transgressive writer is more honest, knowing that all desire is unsafe, that all fantasy is trumped up style, that all transgression is a mixture of violations of style and personal risk" ("The New Fiction of Transgression," 11). The old casuistic argument of purity of intention has never been more in evidence. Yet, if violence is embedded in learned language, what else besides intention is left? That conundrum perplexes audiences today as do its companion questions. If violence was so enduringly ingrained in the very conceptualization of the rhetorical enterprise, then why was it necessary (then and now) to create a rhetorical counterdiscourse against violence? to create that counterdiscourse within the very discipline that so often depends on violence for its own genesis, as well as for its formative role in morality, law, religion, and aesthetics? If violence and drama have always been linked by the rhetorical tradition, and if

---

[15] Suetonius, "Gaius Caligula," in *LC*, chap. 11. Of course, whether Tiberius's hope was genuine remains open to question.

violence has been rehearsed and re-rehearsed in the inventional memories of rhetoric, pedagogy, drama, and aesthetics ever since their advent, then why is it so hard for postmedieval evaluators to acknowledge the connection? How can violence be simultaneously "natural" and "unnatural," beautiful and horrendous, commonplace and shocking?

Whatever optimistic response may be ventured to those questions, such a scholar as Kubiak comes to an archly pessimistic conclusion. Even when a revitalized focus on the intentionality of violence helps to identify the agents and perpetrators of pain, the pain never disappears. For Kubiak, even the self-inflicted violence of the avant-garde stage persists in compromising all safety because theater will always echo its originary violence: "Individual artists try to resist the violent commodification and objectification of the body in the 'real world' by resubjecting their own bodies to self-inflicted violence in the performative space. But. . . even this effort is doomed to failure in the representative tyranny of theatre" (*ST*, 161). Change in agency does not eliminate violence. One thing that might, however, is the dismantling of its epistemological foundations in rhetoric.

"No other art," writes Marvin Carlson, "seeks to absorb and *convert into interpretive structures* so much of the total human experience as the theatre does, its potential resources and meanings bounded only by the resources and meanings of humanity itself." [16] That statement is hard to dispute, but so are the equally boundless resources of inhumanity. William B. Worthen, for instance, likens Samuel Beckett's theater to "an instrument of torture on the protagonists" and determines that the playwright effects a "deconversion of an instrument of civility and sociality [theater] into a weapon" (*Modern Drama*, 138–39). Given the inherent violence of a spectacular rhetoric, there has been no deconversion because theater has always had the capacity to serve as a weapon that extracts, interprets, creates, enacts, and inflicts the discoveries of torture. Similarly, in Carlson's formulation, even the potential "conversion" of the social experience of coercion into drama is problematic. Once we infer from the interrelations among rhetoric, drama, and law that the coercive experience is itself conceived "theatrically," then the conversion of coercion is a tautology. Theater cannot convert itself into itself.

From the horrors of Aristotelian catharsis and inventional torture to the dismembered images of the memory of the body in pain to the pseudorepresentation of a real death in Tournai, the contortions of the rhetorical tradition suggest that empathy is as firmly entrenched in illusions of truth, creativity, and civilization as is the ideology torture. But that can never be all that there is to say. Even if violence so dominates the language of aesthetics that it can never be completely escaped and even if civilization is a myth, it is myth to which societies still cling. To understand contemporary mythologies, we may find it help-

---

[16] Carlson, *Theatre Semiotics*, xviii; emphasis mine.

ful to understand medieval ones. All the events discussed in the preceding pages have something to say about the spectacles of law, death, entertainment, and morality. They speak to us even now because, in theory and in practice, audiences somehow keep turning to theater for its presumed capacities to purge, to please, to frighten, to civilize, and to instill empathy as a response to the paradoxes of law, death, entertainment, and morality. The rhetoric of theater is crucial to the exploration of the ways in which the horrible generates the good and the good generates the horrible. And in the end, maybe that is what makes the rhetorical theater of cruelty good enough in and of itself. Or bad enough.

Works Cited

Primary Sources

Abelard, Peter. *Historia Calamitatum*. Ed. J. Monfrin. Paris: Vrin, 1967.

——. *The Story of Abelard's Adversities: A Translation with Notes of the* Historia Calamitatum. Trans. J. T. Muckle. Toronto: Pontifical Institute, 1964.

[Alan of Lille]. Alanus de Insulis. *The Art of Preaching*. Trans. Gillian R. Evans. Cistercian Studies 23. Kalamazoo: Cistercian Publications, 1981.

——. *Summa de arte praedicatoria*. In *Patrologia Latina*, ed. J. P. Migne, vol. 210, cols.
110–98. Paris: Vrin, 1855.

Albertus Magnus. "Commentary on Aristotle's De memoria et reminiscentia." *Opera
Omnia*. Ed. August Borgnet. Vol. IX. Paris: Ludovicum Vives, 1890.

Alcuin. *The Rhetoric of Alcuin and Charlemagne*. Ed. and trans. Wilbur Samuel Howell.
Princeton: Princeton University Press, 1941.

Alvarez, Vincente. *Relacion del camino buen viage que hizo el principe de Espana Don
Felipe*. Brussels, 1551.

Andreas Capellanus. *On Love*. Ed. and trans. P. G. Walsh. London: Duckworth, 1982.

Aristophanes. *Frogs*. Trans. R. H. Webb. In *Complete Plays of Aristophanes*, ed. Moses
Hadas, 367–415. New York: Bantam, 1962.

Aristotle. *The "Art" of Rhetoric*. Ed. and trans. John Henry Freese. Loeb Classical Library. 1926; Cambridge: Harvard University Press, 1975.

——. *De anima*. Ed. and trans. W. S. Hett. Loeb Classical Library, Cambridge: Harvard
University Press, 1935.

——. *De poetica liber Graece et Latine*. Ed. T. C. Harles. Leipzig: Siegfried Lebrecht
Crusius, 1780.

——. *Metaphysica Aristotelis: Translatio anonyma sive "media."* Ed. Gudrun Vuillemin-
Diem. Leiden: E. J. Brill, 1976.

——. *Poetics*. Ed. and trans. Stephen Halliwell. In Aristotle: *The Poetics*; Longinus: *On
the Sublime*; Demetrius: *On Style*. Loeb Classical Library. 1927; Cambridge: Harvard
University Press, 1946.

——. *The Poetics of Aristotle: Translated from Greek into English and from Arabic into
Latin*. Ed. and trans. D. S. Margouliouth. London: Hodder & Stoughton, 1911.

——. *Posterior Analytics and Topica*. Ed. and trans. Hugh Tredennick and E. S. Forster. 1960; Loeb Classical Library. Cambridge: Harvard University Press, 1966.

Augustine of Hippo. *The City of God against the Pagans*. Ed. and trans. George E. Mc-Cracken. 7 vols. Loeb Classical Library. Cambridge: Harvard University Press, 1957.

——. *Confessions*. Ed. and trans. William Watts. 2 vols. Loeb Classical Library. Cambridge: Harvard University Press, 1950.

——. *On Christian Doctrine*. Trans. D. W. Robertson, Jr. 1958. Indianapolis: Bobbs Merrill, 1980.

Avicenna Latinus, Liber de anima seu sextus de naturalium. Ed. Simone van Riet. 8 vols. Louvain: Peeters, 1972.

Saint Basil. *Saint Basil: The Letters*. 4 vols. Ed. and trans. R. Deferrari. Loeb Classical Library. Cambridge, Mass: Harvard University Press, 1961.

Baoin, Thomas. *Histoire des règnes de Charles VII et de Louis XI*. Ed. J. Quicherat. 4 vols. Paris: Renouard, 1859.

Beck, Jonathan. *Théâtre et propagande aux débuts de la Réforme: Six pièces polémiques du Receuil La Vallière*. Geneva: Slatkine, 1986.

Bernard of Clairvaux. *Opera*. Vol. IV, *Sermones*. Ed. J. LeClerq and H. Rochais. Rome: Editiones Cistercienses, 1966.

——. *Sermons on Conversion: On Conversion, A Sermon to Clerics, and Lenten Sermons on the Psalm "He who Dwells."* Trans. Marie-Bernard Saïd. Kalamazoo: Cistercian Publications, 1981.

Bevington, David, ed. *The Medieval Drama*. Boston: Houghton-Mifflin, 1975.

Bonaventure. *Bonaventura Opera omnia*. Quaracchi: Collegium S. Bonaventurae, 1882–1902.

——. *The Works of Bonaventure*. Vol. I, *Mystical Opuscula*. Trans. José de Vinck. Paterson, N.J.: St. Anthony Guild Press, 1960.

Bradwardine, Thomas. "De memoria artificiale adquirenda." Ed. Mary Carruthers. *Journal of Medieval Latin* 2 (1992): 25–43.

——. "De Memoria Artificiali," Fitzwilliam Museum, Cambridge, MS. McClean 169.

Brunetto Latini. *Li Livres dou Trésor*. Ed. Francis J. Carmody. Berkeley: University of California Press, 1948.

Calvete de Estrella, Juan Cristóbal. *El felícissimo viaje del muy poderoso príncipe Don Phelipe*. 2 vols. 1551; Madrid: Sociedad de bibliófilos españoles, 1930.

Cazelles, Brigitte, ed. *The Lady as Saint: A Collection of French Hagiographic Romances of the Thirteenth Century*. Philadelphia: University of Pennsylvania Press, 1991.

La Chanson de Roland: An Analytical Edition. Ed. Gerard J. Brault. 2 vols. University Park: Pennsylvania State University Press, 1978.

The Chester Mystery Cycle. Ed. R. M. Lumiansky and David Mills. 2 vols. Early English Text Society, S. S. 3. London: Oxford University Press, 1974.

The Chester Plays. Ed. Hermann Deimling. Early English Text Society. 2 vols. 1892, 1916; Oxford: Oxford University Press, 1968.

[Cicero]. *Ad C. Herennium*. Ed. and trans. Harry Caplan. Loeb Classical Library. 1954; Cambridge: Harvard University Press, 1977.

Cicero, Marcus Tullius. *De inventione, De optimo genere oratorum*, and *Topica*. Ed. and trans. H. M. Hubbell. Loeb Classical Library. 1949; Cambridge: Harvard University Press, 1968.

———. *De oratore* and *De partitione oratoria*. Ed. and trans. H. Rackham. 2 vols. Loeb Classical Library. 1942; Cambridge: Harvard University Press, 1976.

Cohen, Gustave, ed. *Le Livre de conduite du Régisseur et Le Compte des dépenses pour le "Mystère de la Passion" joué à Mons en 1501.* Paris: Champion, 1925.

———. *Receuil de farces françaises inédites du XVᵉ siècle.* Cambridge: Mediaeval Academy of America, 1949.

"Coment Judich tua Oloferne." Ed. in progress, Alan Knight. In Codex Guelf. 9 Blankenburgensis. Herzog August Bibliothek, Wolfenbüttel.

The Complete Works of the Pearl Poet. Trans. Casey Finch. Ed. Malcolm Andrew, Ronald Waldron, and Clifford Peterson. Berkeley: University of California Press, 1993.

"Conment Thamar fut violee par forche de Amon son Frere." Ed. in progress, Alan Knight. In Codex Guelf. 9 Blankenburgensis. Herzog August Bibliothek, Wolfenbüttel.

Coppée, Denis. *La sanglante et pitoyable tragédie de nostre Sauveur et Rédempteur Jesu-Christ.* 1624.

Le Cycle de mystères des premiers martyrs. Ed. Graham A. Runnalls. Geneva: Droz, 1976.

Cyprian, Bishop of Carthage. "To Donatus." In *Treatises*, trans. Roy J. Deferrari, 5–21. New York: Fathers of the Church, 1958.

Davidson, L. S., and J. O. Ward, eds. and trans. *The Sorcery Trial of Alice Kyteler: A Contemporary Account (1324).* Binghamton, N.Y.: Medieval and Renaissance Texts and Studies, 1993.

The Digest of Justinian. Ed. Theodor Mommsen and Paul Krueger, trans. Alan Watson. 4 vols. Philadelphia: University of Pennsylvania Press, 1985.

Drew, Katherine Fischer, trans. *The Lombard Laws.* Philadelphia: University of Pennsylvania Press, 1973.

Drouart la Vache. *Li Livres d'amours de Drouart la Vache.* Ed. Robert Bossuat. Paris: Champion, 1926.

Erasmus, Desiderius. *The Education of a Christian Prince.* Ed. L. K. Born. New York: Columbia University Press, 1936.

Eusebius. *The Ecclesiastical History.* Ed. and trans. Kirsopp Lake. 2 vols. Loeb Classical Library. 1926; Cambridge: Harvard University Press, 1959.

Fouquet, Jean. *Le Livre d'heures d'Etienne Chevalier.* Ed. Germain Bazin. Paris: Somogy, 1990.

Fournier, Edouard, ed. *Le Théatre français avant la Renaissance.* 1872; New York: Burt Franklin, 1965.

Geoffrey of Vinsauf. "The New Poetics (*Poetria nova*)." Trans. Jane Baltzell Kopp. In *Three Medieval Rhetorical Arts*, ed. James J. Murphy, 27–108. Berkeley: University of California Press, 1971.

———. *Poetria nova.* In *The "Poetria Nova" and Its Sources in Early Rhetorical Doctrine.* Trans. Ernest Gallo. The Hague: Mouton, 1971.

Le Geu Saint Denis du manuscrit 1131 de la Bibliothèque Sainte-Geneviève de Paris. Geneva: Droz, 1974.

Gréban, Arnoul. *Le Mystère de la Passion.* Ed. Omer Jodogne. Brussels: Académie Royale, 1965.

Guibert of Nogent. *Self and Society in Medieval France.* Trans. John F. Benton. Medieval Academy Reprints for Teaching 15. Toronto: University of Toronto Press, 1989.

Guillaume de Saint-Pathus, confesseur de la reine Marguerite. *Les Miracles de Saint Louis*. Ed. Percival B. Fay. Paris: Champion, 1931.

Howell, Thomas Bayley, ed. *A Complete Collection of State Trials and Proceedings for High Treason and Other Crimes and Misdemeanors from the Earliest Period to the Year 1783*. 21 vols. London: Longman, 1816–26.

Hugh of Saint Victor. *Didascalicon: De studio legendi: A Critical Text*. Ed. Charles Henry Buttimer. Washington, D.C.: Catholic University Press, 1939.

——. *The Didascalicon of Hugh of St. Victor*. Trans. Jerome Taylor. 1961; New York: Columbia University Press, 1991.

Isidore of Seville. *Etimologías*. Ed. José Oroz Reta and Manuel A. Marcos Casquero. 2 vols. Madrid: Biblioteca de Autores Cristianos, 1982.

——. *Isidori Hispalensis Episcopi Etymologiarum sive originum libri XX*. Ed. W. M. Lindsay. 2 vols. 1911. London: Oxford University Press, 1962.

James I. *The Political Works of James I, Reprinted from the Edition of 1616*. Ed. Charles Howard McIlwain. Harvard Political Classics 1. Cambridge: Harvard University Press, 1918.

Jean de Meun [and Guillaume de Lorris]. *Le Roman de la rose*. Ed. Daniel Poirion. Paris: Garnier-Flammarion, 1974.

——. *The Romance of the Rose*. By Guillaume de Lorris and Jean de Meun. Trans. W. Harry Robbins. New York: Dutton, 1962.

——. *The Romance of the Rose*. By Guillaume de Lorris and Jean de Meun. Trans. Charles Dahlberg. Princeton: Princeton University Press, 1974.

Jehan du Prier, dit le Prieur. *Le Mystère du Roy Advenir*. Ed. A. Meiller. Geneva: Droz, 1970.

John of Garland. *The "Parisiana Poetria" of John of Garland*. Ed. Traugott Lawler. Yale Studies in English 182. New Haven: Yale University Press, 1974.

John of Salisbury. *Metalogicon*. Ed. Clement C. J. Webb. Oxford: Clarendon, 1929.

——. *The* Metalogicon *of John of Salisbury: A Twelfth-Century Defense of the Verbal and Logical Arts of the Trivium*. Trans. Daniel D. McGarry. Berkeley: University of California Press, 1955.

——. *Policraticus: The Statesman's Book*. Ed. Murray E. Markland. New York: Frederick Ungar, 1979.

Johnston, Alexandra, and Margaret Rogerson, eds. *York*. 2 vols. Records of Early English Drama 2. Toronto: University of Toronto Press, 1979.

Journal d'un bourgeois de Paris, 1405–1449. Ed. A. Tuety. Paris, 1881. Published in English as *A Parisian Journal, 1405–1449*. Trans. Janet Shirley. Oxford: Clarendon, 1960.

Le Journal d'un bourgeois de Paris sous le règne de François I (1515–1530). Ed. V. L. Bourilly. Paris: Picard, 1910.

Kilwardby, Robert. *On Time and Imagination. De Tempore. De Spiritu Fantastico*. Ed. P. Osmund Lewry. Auctores Britannici Medii Aevi 9. Oxford: Oxford University Press, 1987.

Kors, Alan C., and Edward Peters, eds. *Witchcraft in Europe, 1100–1700: A Documentary History*. 1972; Philadelphia: University of Pennsylvania Press, 1986.

Kramer, Heinrich (Institoris). *Malleus Maleficarum*. Trans. Montague Summers. 1928; London: Pushkin, 1951.

——. *Malleus Maleficarum 1487*. Ed. Günter Jerouschek. Hildesheim: G. Olms Verlag, 1992.

Libanius. *Selected Works*. Ed. and trans. A. F. Norman. Loeb Classical Library. Cambridge, Mass: Harvard University Press, 1977.

Longinus. "On the Sublime." Ed. and trans. W. Hamilton Fyfe. In *Aristotle: The Poetics*; *Longinus: On the Sublime*; *Demetrius: On Style*. Loeb Classical Library. 1927; Cambridge: Harvard University Press, 1946.

Lucian of Samosata. "A Professor of Public Speaking." Ed. and trans. A. M. Harmon. In *Works*, vol. IV. Loeb Classical Library. 1925; Cambridge: Harvard University Press, 1969.

——. "Saltatio." In *Works*, vol. V. 1936; Cambridge: Harvard University Press, 1972.

——. "The Tyrannicide." In *Works*, vol. V. 1936; Cambridge: Harvard University Press, 1972.

Ludus Coventriae or the Plaie called Corpus Christi. Ed. K. S. Block. Early English Text Society. London: Oxford University Press, 1922.

Lydgate, John. *The Minor Poems of John Lydgate*. Vol. I. Ed. H. N. MacCracken. Early English Text Society, E. S. 107. London, 1909.

Marivaux, Pierre Carlet de Chamblain de. *Oeuvres de jeunesse*. Ed. Claude Rigault. Pléiade. Paris: Gallimard, 1972.

Martianus Capella. *De Nuptiis Philologiae et Mercurii*. Ed. Adolfus Dick. 1925; Stuttgart: Teubner, 1969.

Massinger, Philip. "The Roman Actor." In *The Plays and Poems of Philip Massinger*, vol. III. Ed. Philip Edwards and Colin Gibson. Oxford: Clarendon, 1976.

Meredith, Peter, and John E. Tailby, eds. *The Staging of Religious Drama in Europe in the Later Middle Ages: Texts and Documents in English Translation*. Early Drama, Art, and Music 4. Kalamazoo: Medieval Institute Publications, 1983.

Minnis, A. J., and A. B. Scott with David Wallace. *Medieval Literary Theory and Criticism, c. 1100–1375*. Rev. ed. Oxford: Clarendon, 1991.

Mirk, John. *Mirk's Festial: A Collection of Homilies by Johannes Mirkus*. Ed. T. Erbe. Early English Text Society, E. S. 96 (1905).

Le Mistére du Viel Testament. Ed. James de Rothschild. 6 vols. 1878. New York: Johnson Reprint Corp., 1966.

[Molinet, Jean?]. *Le Mystère de Judith et Holofernés: Une édition critique de l'une des parties du "Mistere du Viel Testament."* Ed. Graham A. Runnalls. Geneva: Droz, 1995.

Murner, Thomas. *Logica memorativa*. Nieuwkoop: Miland, 1967.

——. *Logica memorativa, Chartiludium logice, sive Totius dialectice memoria; et Nonus* [i.e. *novus*] *Petri Hispani textus emendatus, cum iucundopictasmatis exercitio. . . .* Strasbourg, 1509.

Murphy, James J., ed. *Three Medieval Rhetorical Arts*. 1971; Berkeley: University of California Press, 1985.

Le Mystère d'Adam (Ordo Representationis Ade). Ed. Paul Aebischer. Geneva: Droz, 1964.

Le Mystère de la Passion: Texte du Manuscrit 697 de la Bibliothèque d'Arras. Ed. Jules-Marie Richard. 1891; Geneva: Slatkine, 1976.

Le Mystère de la Passion à Amboise au moyen âge: représentations théâtrales et texte. Ed. Graham A. Runnalls. Montreal: CERES, 1990.

Le Mystère de la Passion de Troyes. Ed. Jean-Claude Bibolet. 2 vols. Geneva: Droz, 1987.

Le Mystère de la Passion Nostre Seigneur du manuscrit 1131 de la Bibliothèque Sainte-Geneviève. Ed. Graham A. Runnalls. Geneva: Droz, 1974.

Le Mystère de la Résurrection Angers: (1456). Ed. Pierre Servet. 2 vols. Geneva: Droz, 1993.

Le Mystère des actes des apôtres représenté à Bourges en avril 1536. Ed. Auguste-Theodore de Girardot. Paris: Librairie Archéologique Victor Didron, 1854.

Le Mystère de S. Bernard de Menthon. Ed. A. Lecoy de la Marche. 1886; New York: Johnson Reprint Corp., 1968.

Le Mystère de Saint Christofle. Ed. Graham A. Runnalls. Exeter: University of Exeter, 1973.

Le Mystère de Sainte Venice. Ed. Graham A. Runnalls. Exeter: University of Exeter, 1980.

La Passion d'Auvergne. Ed. Graham A. Runnalls. Geneva: Droz, 1982.

La Passion de Palatinus: Mystère du XIVᵉ siècle. Ed. Grace Frank. Paris: Champion, 1922.

——. In *Jeux et sapience du Moyen-Age*, ed. Albert Pauphilet, 211–78. Paris: Pléaide, 1951.

Plato. *Cratylus*. In *The Dialogues of Plato*, trans. Benjamin Jowett, vol. I, 173–229. 1892; New York: Random House, 1937.

——. *Gorgias*. Trans. B. Jowett. In *The Dialogues of Plato*, vol. I. 8th ed. New York: Random House, 1937.

——. *Laws*. 2 vols. Loeb Classical Library. 1926; Cambridge: Harvard University Press, 1942.

——. *Phaedrus*. Trans. R. Hackforth. 1952; Cambridge: Cambridge University Press, 1972.

——. *Theaetetus*. Trans. Francis MacDonald Cornford. 1957; Indianapolis: Bobbs-Merrill, 1977.

Plotinus. *Enneads*. Trans. S. Mackenna. London: Medici Society, 1969.

La Poissance damours dello Pseudo-Richard de Fournival. Ed. Gian Battista Speroni. Pubblicazioni dell Facoltà di Lettere e Filosofia dell'Università di Pavia 21. Florence: La Nuova Italia, 1975.

[Quintilian]. *Declamationes XIX Maiores. Quintiliano Falso Ascriptae*. Ed. Lennart Hakanson. Stuttgart: Teubner, 1982.

Quintilian. *Institutio oratoria*. Ed. and trans. H. E. Butler. 4 vols. Loeb Classical Library. 1920; Cambridge: Harvard University Press, 1980.

Rabelais, François. *Oeuvres complètes*. Ed. Guy Demerson. Paris: Seuil, 1973.

Suetonius. *The Lives of the Caesars*. 2 vols. In *Works*, ed. and trans. J. C. Rolfe. Loeb Classical Library. 1913; Cambridge: Harvard University Press, 1951.

Tacitus. *Dialogus de oratoribus*. Ed. and trans. Sir W. Peterson. Rev. M. Winterbottom. Loeb Classical Library. Cambridge: Harvard University Press, 1980.

Tertullian. *De spectaculis*. Ed. and trans. T. R. Glover. Loeb Classical Library. 1931; Cambridge: Harvard University Press, 1977.

Tissier, André, ed. *Recueil de farces (1450–1550)*. 8 vols. Geneva: Droz, 1986–94.

The Towneley Plays. Ed. George England and Alfred W. Pollard. Early English Text Society, E.S. 71. Oxford: Oxford University Press, 1897.

La Vengeance de Nostre-Seigneur. The Old and Middle French Prose Versions. Ed. Alvin E. Ford. Toronto: Pontifical Institute, 1993.

Vico, Giambattista. *La Scienza nuova*. 2d ed. Torino: Unione Tipografico-Editrice Torniese, 1968.

Vigneulles, Philippe de. *Gedenkbuch des Metzer Bürgers Philippe von Vigneulles aus den Jahren 1471–1522*. Ed. Heinrich Michelant. 1852; Amsterdam: Rodopi, 1968.

Villon, François. *Oeuvres*. Ed. André Mary. Paris: Garnier-Flammarion, 1965.

Viollet-le-Duc, M., ed. *Ancien Théâtre français*. 3 vols. 1854; Nendeln, Liechtenstein: Kraus, 1972.

Vitale-Brovarone, Alessandro, ed. *Il quaderno di segreti d'un regista provenzale del Medioevo: Note per la messa in scena d'una Passione*. Allessandria: Orso, 1984.

Vitruvius. *Ten Books of Architecture*. Trans. M. H. Morgan: Cambridge: Harvard University Press, 1914.

Vives, Juan Luis. *Vives on Education: A Translation of the "De tradendis disciplinis" of Juan Luis Vives*. Trans. Foster Watson. 1913; Totowa, N.J.: Rowman & Littlefield, 1971.

——. *Vives on the Renascence Education of Women*. Trans. F. Watson. New York: Edward Arnold, 1912.

The Wakefield Pageants in the Towneley Cycle. Ed. A. C. Cawley. Manchester: Manchester University Press, 1958.

Secondary Sources

Aers, David. *Community, Gender, and Individual Identity: English Writing, 1360–1430*. New York: Routledge, 1988.

Alter, Jean. *A Sociosemiotic Theory of Theatre*. Philadelphia: University of Pennsylvania Press, 1990.

Andrews, William. *Old-Time Punishments*. London: Simpkin, Marshall, Hamilton, Dent, 1890.

Arendt, Hannah. *Between Past and Future: Eight Exercises in Political Thought*. New York: Viking, 1968.

Artaud, Antonin. *Le Théâtre et son double*. Vol. IV of *Oeuvres complètes*. 2d ed. Paris: Gallimard, 1978. Published in English as *The Theater and Its Double*, trans. Mary Caroline Richards. New York: Grove Weidenfeld, 1958.

Asad, Talal. *Genealogies of Religion: Discipline and Reasons of Power in Christianity and Islam*. Baltimore: Johns Hopkins University Press, 1993.

——. "Notes on Body, Pain and Truth in Medieval Christian Ritual." *Economy and Society* 12 (1985): 287–327.

Ashley, Kathleen M., ed. *Victor Turner and the Construction of Cultural Criticism: Between Literature and Anthropology*. Bloomington: Indiana University Press, 1990.

Auerbach, Erich. *Mimesis: The Representation of Reality in Western Literature*. Trans. Willard R. Trask. 1953; Princeton: Princeton University Press, 1974.

Austin, J. L. *How to Do Things with Words*. Ed. J. O. Urmson and Marina Sbisà. 2d ed. Cambridge: Harvard University Press, 1978.

——. *Philosophical Papers*. Ed. J. O. Urmson and G. J. Warnock. 2d ed. Oxford: Clarendon, 1970.

Axton, Richard. *European Drama of the Early Middle Ages*. London: Hutchinson, 1974.

Bachelard, Gaston. *The Poetics of Space*. Trans. M. Jolas. Boston, 1969.

Barish, Jonas. *The Anti-Theatrical Prejudice*. Berkeley: University of California Press, 1981.

——. "Shakespearean Violence: A Preliminary Survey." In *Violence in Drama*, ed. James Redmond, 101–22.

Barker, Francis. *The Culture of Violence: Essays on Tragedy and History*. Chicago: University of Chicago Press, 1993.

Barthes, Roland. "L'Ancienne Rhétorique." *Communications* 16 (1970): 172–229.

——. *Image/Music/Text*. Trans. Stephen Heath. 1977; New York: Farrar, Straus & Giroux, 1992.

Bartlett, Robert. *Trial by Fire and Water: The Medieval Judicial Ordeal*. Oxford: Clarendon, 1986.

Baty, Gaston, and René Chavance. *Vie de l'art théâtral des origines à nos jours*. Paris: Plon, 1932.

Baudrillard, Jean. *Selected Writings*. Ed. and trans. Mark Poster. Stanford: Stanford University Press, 1988.

Beacham, Richard C. "Violence on the Street: Playing Rough in Plautus." In *Violence in Drama*, ed. James Redmond, 47–68.

Beckwith, Sarah. *Christ's Body*. London and New York: Routledge, 1994.

——. *Signifying God: Social Relations and Symbolic Action in York's Play of Corpus Christi*. University of California Press, forthcoming.

Benjamin, Walter. *Denkbilder*. Frankfurt am Main: Suhrkamp, 1974.

Bennett, Benjamin. "Performance and the Exposure of Hermeneutics." *Theatre Journal* 44 (1992): 431–47.

Berlin, James A. "Revisionary Histories of Rhetoric: Politics, Power, and Plurality." In *Writing Histories of Rhetoric*, ed. Victor Vitanza, 112–27.

Bestul, Thomas H. *Texts of the Passion: Latin Devotional Texts and Medieval Society*. Philadelphia: University of Pennsylvania Press, 1996.

Biddick, Kathleen. "Genders, Bodies, Borders: Technologies of the Visible." *Speculum* 68 (1993): 389–418.

Black, Joel. *The Aesthetics of Murder: A Study in Romantic Literature and Contemporary Culture*. Baltimore: Johns Hopkins University Press, 1991.

Blau, Herbert. *The Audience*. Baltimore: Johns Hopkins University Press, 1990.

——. *Blooded Thought: Occasions of Theater*. New York: Performing Arts Journal, 1982.

Bloch, Marc. *Feudal Society*. 2 vols. Trans. L. A. Manyon. 1961; Chicago: University of Chicago Press, 1974.

Bloch, R. Howard. *Etymologies and Genealogies: A Literary Anthropology of the French Middle Ages*. 1983; Chicago: University of Chicago Press, 1986.

——. *Medieval French Literature and Law*. Berkeley: University of California Press, 1977.

——. "New Philology and Old French." *Speculum* 65 (1990): 38–58.

Blumenfeld-Kosinski, Renate. *Not of Woman Born: Representations of Caesarean Birth in Medieval and Renaissance Culture*. Ithaca: Cornell University Press, 1990.

Boal, Augusto. *Theater of the Oppressed*. Trans. Charles A. and Maria-Odilia Leal McBride. New York: Urizen, 1979.

Bourdieu, Pierre. *Outline of a Theory of Practice*. Trans. Richard Nice. Cambridge: Cambridge University Press, 1977.

Braccesi, Lorenzo. *Poesia e memoria: nuove proiezioni dell'antico*. Roma: L'Erma di Bretschneider, 1995.

Brehaut, Ernest. *An Encyclopedist of the Dark Ages: Isidore of Seville*. Studies in History, Economics, and Public Law 48. New York: Columbia University Press, 1912.

Bremmer, Jan, and Herman Roodenburg, eds. *A Cultural History of Gesture: From Antiquity to the Present Day*. Cambridge: Polity, 1991.

Briscoe, Marianne G., and John C. Coldewey, eds. *Contexts for Early English Drama*. Bloomington: Indiana University Press, 1989.

Bronfen, Elisabeth. *Over Her Dead Body: Death, Femininity and the Aesthetic*. New York: Routledge, 1992.

Brook, Peter. *The Empty Space*. New York: Atheneum, 1969.

Brown, Frederick. *Theater and Revolution: The Culture of the French Stage*. New York: Viking, 1980.

Brown, Peter. *The Body and Society*. Princeton: Princeton University Press, 1988.

———. *Power and Persuasion in Late Antiquity: Towards a Christian Empire*. Madison: University of Wisconsin Press, 1992.

Brunvand, Jan Harold. *Curses! Broiled Again: The Hottest Urban Legends Going*. New York: Norton, 1989.

———. *The Vanishing Hitchhiker: American Urban Legends and Their Meanings*. New York: Norton, 1981.

Burke, Kenneth. *Attitudes toward History*. 3d ed. Berkeley: University of California Press, 1984.

———. *The Philosophy of Literary Form: Studies in Symbolic Action*. 3d ed. 1941; Berkeley: University of California Press, 1973.

Burns, E. Jane. *Bodytalk: When Women Speak in Old French Literature*. Philadelphia: University of Pennsylvania Press, 1993.

Butler, Judith. "Performative Acts and Gender Constitution: An Essay in Phenomenology and Feminist Theory." In *Performing Feminisms*, ed. Sue-Ellen Case, 270–82.

Bynum, Caroline Walker. *Fragmentation and Redemption: Essays on Gender and the Human Body in Medieval Religion*. New York: Zone Books, 1991.

———. *Jesus as Mother: Studies in the Spirituality of the High Middle Ages*. Berkeley: University of California Press, 1982.

Callahan, John M. "The Ultimate in Theatre Violence." In *Violence in Drama*, ed. James Redmond, 165–76.

Campbell, Thomas P. "Cathedral Chapter and Town Council: Ceremony and Drama in Medieval Rouen." *Comparative Drama* 27 (1993): 100–113.

Caplan, Harry C. "Memoria: Treasure-House of Eloquence." In *Of Eloquence: Studies in Ancient and Medieval Rhetoric*, 196–246. Ithaca: Cornell University Press, 1970.

Carlson, Marvin. *Theatre Semiotics: Signs of Life*. Bloomington: Indiana University Press, 1990.

Carruthers, Mary. *The Book of Memory*. Cambridge: Cambridge University Press, 1990.

Cartwright, John. "The Politics of Rhetoric: The 1561 Antwerp 'Landjuweel.'" *Comparative Drama* 27 (1993): 54–63.

Case, Sue-Ellen, ed. *Performing Feminisms: Feminist Critical Theory and Theatre*. Baltimore: Johns Hopkins University Press, 1990.

Cavell, Stanley. *Must We Mean What We Say?: A Book of Essays*. New York: Scribner's, 1969.

Céline, Louis-Ferdinand. *North.* Trans. Ralph Manheim. New York: Delacorte, 1972.

Certeau, Michel de. *The Practice of Everyday Life.* Trans. Steven Rendall. Berkeley: University of California Press, 1988.

Chambers, E. K. *The Mediaeval Stage.* 2 vols. Oxford: Oxford University Press, 1903.

Chartier, Roger. "Social Figuration and Habitus: Reading Elias." In *Cultural History: Between Practices and Representations.* Trans. Lydia G. Cochrane. Ithaca: Cornell University Press, 1988.

Clanchy, M. T. *From Memory to Written Record: England, 1066–1307.* Cambridge: Harvard University Press, 1979.

Clark, Robert L. A. "Courtly versus Bourgeois Dramaturgy: The *Mystère du roy Advenir* and the *Miracle de Barlaam et Josaphat.*" Paper presented at the International Congress on Medieval Studies, Kalamazoo, 13 May 1990.

Clerval, Jules Alexandre. *Les Ecoles de Chartres au moyen-âge du Ve au XVIe siècle.* Chartres: Selleret, 1895.

Clover, Carol J. *Men, Women, and Chain Saws: Gender in the Modern Horror Film.* Princeton: Princeton University Press, 1993.

Cohen, Esther. *The Crossroads of Justice.* Leiden: Brill, 1993.

———. " 'To Die a Criminal for the Public Good': The Execution Ritual in Late Medieval Paris." In *Law, Custom, and the Social Fabric in Medieval Europe: Essays in Honor of Bryce Lyon,* ed. Bernard S. Bachrach and David Nicholas, 285–304. Studies in Medieval Culture 28. Kalamazoo: Medieval Institute Publications, 1990.

Cohen, Gustave. *Histoire de la mise en scène dans le théâtre religieux français du Moyen-Age.* 2d ed. Paris: Champion, 1951.

Coleman, Janet. *Ancient and Medieval Memories.* Cambridge: Cambridge University Press, 1992.

Coleman, Kathleen. "Fatal Charades: Roman Executions Staged as Mythological Enactments." *Journal of Roman Studies* 80 (1990): 44–73.

Copeland, Rita. "The Pardoner's Body and the Disciplining of Rhetoric." In *Framing Medieval Bodies,* ed. Miri Rubin and Sarah Kay, 138–59. Manchester: Manchester University Press, 1994.

———. *Rhetoric, Hermeneutics, and Translation in the Middle Ages: Academic Traditions and Vernacular Texts.* Cambridge: Cambridge University Press, 1991.

———, ed. *Criticism and Dissent* in the *Middle Ages.* Cambridge: Cambridge University Press, 1996.

Corbett, Edward P. J. *Classical Rhetoric for the Modern Student.* New York: Oxford University Press, 1990.

Cousin, Geraldine. "A Note on Mimesis: Stanislavski's and Brecht's Street Scenes." In *Drama, Dance and Music,* ed. James Redmond, 235–47.

Covino, William. "Alchemizing the History of Rhetoric: Introductions, Incantations, and Spells." In *Writing Histories of Rhetoric,* ed. Victor Vitanza, 49–58.

Crosby, Ruth. "Oral Delivery in the Middle Ages." *Speculum* 11 (1936): 88–110.

Cunningham, Karen. "Renaissance Execution and Marlovian Elocution: The Drama of Death." *PMLA* 105 (1990): 209–22.

Curtius, Ernst Robert. *European Literature and the Latin Middle Ages.* Trans. Willard R. Trask. Bollingen 36. 1953; Princeton: Princeton University Press, 1973.

Darnton, Robert. *The Great Cat Massacre and Other Episodes in French Cultural History.* New York: Vintage, 1984.

Davis, Natalie Zemon. *Society and Culture in Early Modern France*. 1965; Stanford: Stanford University Press, 1975.

Davis, Tracy C. "Questions for a Feminist Methodology in Theatre History." In *Interpreting the Theatrical Past*, ed. Postlewait and McConachie, 59–81.

Deleuze, Gilles, and Félix Guattari. *Anti-Oedipus: Capitalism and Schizophrenia*. Minneapolis: University of Minnesota Press, 1983.

De Quincey, Thomas. *On Murder as One of the Beaux-Arts*. In *Collected Writings*, vol. XIII. Ed. David Masson. Edinburgh: A. and C. Black, 1889–90.

Derrida, Jacques. *Memoirs for Paul de Man*. Trans. Cecile Lindsay, Jonathan Culler, Eduardo Cadava. New York: Columbia University Press, 1986.

——. *Of Grammatology*. Trans. Gayatri Chakravorty Spivak. Baltimore: Johns Hopkins University Press, 1976.

——. *Writing and Difference*. Trans. Alan Bass. Chicago: University of Chicago Press, 1978.

Diderot, Denis. *Paradoxe sur le Comédien*. In *Oeuvres esthétiques*, ed. Paul Vernière, 299–381. Paris: Garnier, 1968.

Diehl, Huston. *Staging Reform, Reforming the Stage: Protestantism and Popular Theater in Early Modern England*. Ithaca: Cornell University Press, 1997.

Dionisotti, A. C. "From Ausonius' Schooldays? A Schoolbook and Its Relative." *Journal of Roman Studies* 72 (1982): 83–125.

Dollimore, Jonathan. *Radical Tragedy: Religion, Ideology, and Power in the Drama of Shakespeare and His Contemporaries*. Brighton: Harvester, 1984.

Dorey, T. A. "Honesty in Roman Politics." In *Cicero*, ed. T. A. Dorey, 27–45. London: Routledge & Kegan Paul, 1964.

Dougherty, Carol. *The Poetics of Colonization: From City to Text in Archaic Greece*. Oxford: Oxford University Press, 1993.

duBois, Page. *Sowing the Body: Psychoanalysis and Ancient Representations of Women*. Chicago: University of Chicago Press, 1988.

——. *Torture and Truth*. New York: Routledge, 1991.

Du Bos, Jean-Baptiste. *Réflexions critiques sur la poésie et sur la peinture*. 1770; Geneva: Slatkine, 1967.

Duncan, Martha Grace. *Romantic Outlaws, Beloved Prisons: The Unconscious Meanings of Crime and Punishment*. New York: New York University Press, 1996.

Durkheim, Emile. *L'Evolution pédagogique en France: Des origines à la Renaissance*. Paris: Félix Alcan, 1938. Published in English as *The Evolution of Educational Thought*, trans. Peter Collins. London: Routledge & Kegan Paul, 1977.

Eckstein, Barbara J. *The Language of Fiction in a World of Pain: Reading Politics as Paradox*. Philadelphia: University of Pennsylvania Press, 1990.

Eco, Umberto. "An *Ars Oblivionalis*? Forget It!" *PMLA* 103 (1988): 254–61.

Ede, Lisa, Cheryl Glenn, and Andrea Lunsford. "Border Crossings: Intersections of Rhetoric and Feminism." *Rhetorica* 13 (1995): 401–41.

Eden, Kathy. *Poetic and Legal Fiction in the Aristotelian Tradition*. Princeton: Princeton University Press, 1986.

Elias, Norbert. *The Civilizing Process*. Vol. I of *The History of Manners*. New York: Urizen, 1978.

Elliot, John R., Jr. "Medieval Acting." In *Contexts for Early English Drama*, ed. Marianne G. Briscoe and John C. Coldewey, 243–44.

Emeljanow, Victor. "Grand Guignol and the Orchestration of Violence." In *Violence in Drama*, ed. James Redmond, 151–63.

Enders, Jody. "Delivering Delivery: Theatricality and the Emasculation of Eloquence." *Rhetorica* 15 (1997): 253–78.

———. "The Feminist Mnemonics of Christine de Pizan." *Modern Language Quarterly* 55 (1994): 231–49.

———. "Medieval Snuff Drama." *Exemplaria* 10 (1998): 171–206.

———. "Music, Delivery, and the Rhetoric of Memory in Guillaume de Machaut's *Remède de Fortune*." *PMLA* 107 (1992): 450–64.

———. *Rhetoric and the Origins of Medieval Drama*. Rhetoric and Society 1. Ithaca: Cornell University Press, 1992.

———. "The Theatre of Scholastic Erudition." *Comparative Drama* 27 (1993): 341–63.

———. "Violence, Silence, and the Memory of Witches." In *Violence Against Women in Medieval Texts*, ed. Anna Walecka Roberts, 210–32. Gainesville: University of Florida Press, 1998.

Erdman, Edward. "Imitation Pedagogy and Ethical Indoctrination." *Rhetoric Society Quarterly* 23 (1993): 1–11.

Evans, Ruth. "When a Body Meets a Body: Fergus and Mary in the York Cycle." Paper presented at the Modern Language Association Convention, Chicago, 30 December 1995.

Faber, Frédéric. *Histoire du théâtre en Belgique depuis son origine jusqu'à nos jours: D'après les documents inédits reposant aux Archives Générales du Royaume*. Vol. I. Brussels: Olivier; Paris: Tresse, 1878.

Fantham, Elaine. "The Concept of Nature and Human Nature in Quintilian's Psychology and Theory of Instruction." *Rhetorica* 13 (1995): 125–36.

Farmer, Sharon. *Communities of Saint Martin: Legend and Ritual in Medieval Tours*. Ithaca: Cornell University Press, 1991.

Fiorelli, Piero. *La tortura giudiziaria nel diritto commune*. 2 vols. Milan, 1953–54.

Fischer-Lichte, Erika. "Theatre and the Civilizing Process: An Approach to the History of Acting." In *Interpreting the Theatrical Past*, ed. Thomas Postlewait and Bruce A. McConachie, 19–36.

Foucault, Michel. *Discipline and Punish: The Birth of the Prison*. Trans. Alan Sheridan. New York: Pantheon, 1977.

———. *Language, Counter-Memory, Practice*. Trans. Donald F. Bouchard and Sherry Simon. Ithaca: Cornell University Press, 1977.

Fradenburg, Louise O. "Criticism, Anti-Semitism, and the Prioress's Tale." *Exemplaria* 1 (1989): 69–115.

Fradenburg, Louise O., with Carla Freccero. "The Pleasures of History." Introduction to special issue of *Gay and Lesbian Quarterly* 1 (1995): 371–84.

Frazer, Sir James George. *The Scapegoat*. Vol. VI of *The Golden Bough*. 3d ed. 1913; London: Macmillan, 1920.

Fredell, Joel. "The Three Clerks and St. Nicholas in Medieval England." *Studies in Philology* 92 (1995): 181–292.

Frye, Northrop. *Anatomy of Criticism*. 1957; Princeton: Princeton University Press, 1973.

Fumagalli, Vito. *Landscapes of Fear: Perceptions of Nature and the City in the Middle Ages*. Cambridge: Polity, 1994.

Fumaroli, Marc. *L'Age de l'éloquence: Rhétorique et "res literaria."* Hautes études médiévales et modernes 43. Geneva: Droz, 1980.

Garner, Stanton B., Jr. *Bodied Spaces: Phenomenology and Performance in Contemporary Drama.* Ithaca: Cornell University Press, 1994.

Garnsey, Peter. *Social Status and Legal Privilege in the Roman Empire.* Oxford: Clarendon, 1970.

Gatton, John Spalding. " 'There Must Be Blood': Mutilation and Martyrdom on the Medieval Stage." In *Violence in Drama*, ed. James Redmond, 79–92.

Geary, Patrick J. *Living with the Dead in the Middle Ages.* Ithaca: Cornell University Press, 1995.

Gehl, Paul F. *A Moral Art: Grammar, Society, and Culture in Trecento Florence.* Ithaca: Cornell University Press, 1993.

Gelbart, Larry. "Peering through the Tube Darkly . . . " *New York Times*, 16 April 1995.

Gellrich, Jesse M. *The Idea of the Book in the Middle Ages: Language Theory, Mythology and Fiction.* Ithaca: Cornell University Press, 1988.

Gibson, Gail McMurray. "Writing Before the Eye: The N-Town *Woman Taken in Adultery* and the Medieval Ministry Play." *Comparative Drama* 27 (1994): 399–407.

Gibson, Joan. "Educating for Silence. Renaissance Women and the Language Arts." *Hypatia* 4 (1989): 9–27.

Girard, René. *Violence and the Sacred.* Trans. Patrick Gregory. Baltimore: Johns Hopkins University Press, 1977.

Gleason, Maud W. "The Semiotics of Gender: Physiognomy and Self-Fashioning in the Second Century C.E." In *Before Sexuality*, ed. David M. Halperin, John J. Winkler, and Froma Zeitlin, 389–415.

Glorieux, Palémon. *La littérature quodlibétique de 1260–1320.* 2 vols. Bibliothèque Thomiste, 5 and 21. Vol. I: Le Saulchoir, Kain, Belgium, 1925; vol. II: Paris: Vrin, 1935.

Goebel, Julius, Jr. *Felony and Misdemeanor: A Study in the History of Criminal Law.* Philadelphia: University of Pennsylvania Press, 1976.

Goffman, Erving. *Frame Analysis: An Essay on the Organization of Experience.* Cambridge: Harvard University Press, 1974.

Goldhill, Simon. "Violence in Greek Tragedy." In *Violence in Drama*, ed. James Redmond, 15–34.

Goldmann, Lucien. *Pour une sociologie du roman.* Paris: Gallimard, 1964.

Gontier, Nicole. *Cris de haine et rites d'unité: La Violence dans les villes, XIII–XVIᵉ siècles.* Turnhout: Brepols, 1992.

Goodal, Jane. *Artaud and the Gnostic Drama.* Oxford: Clarendon, 1994.

Gould, Thomas. "The Uses of Violence in Drama." In *Violence in Drama*, ed. James Redmond, 1–14.

Graver, David. *The Aesthetics of Disturbance: Anti-Art in Avant-Garde Drama.* Ann Arbor: University of Michigan Press, 1995.

Gruber, William. Review of Francis Barker, *The Culture of Violence. Comparative Drama* 28 (1994–95): 527–33.

Guenée, Bernard, and Françoise Lehoux. *Les Entrées royales françaises de 1328 à 1515.* Paris: Centre National de la Recherche Scientifique, 1968.

Guilfoyle, Cherell. "The Staging of the First Murder in the Mystery Plays in England." *Comparative Drama* 25 (1991): 42–51.

Haidu, Peter. *The Subject of Violence: "The Song of Roland" and the Birth of the State.* Bloomington: Indiana University Press, 1993.

Hajnal, Istvan. *L'enseignment de l'écriture aux universités médiévales.* Budapest: Academia Scientarum Hungarica Budapestini, 1954.

Halperin, David M. "Why Is Diotima A Woman? Platonic *Eros* and the Figuration of Gender." In *Before Sexuality,* ed. Halperin, John J. Winkler, and Froma Zeitlin, 257–308.

Halperin, David M., John J. Winkler, and Froma Zeitlin, eds. *Before Sexuality: The Construction of Erotic Experience in the Ancient Greek World.* Princeton: Princeton University Press, 1990.

Hanson, Elizabeth. "Torture and Truth in Renaissance England." *Representations* 34 (1991): 53–84.

Hardison, O. B., Jr. *Christian Rite and Christian Drama in the Middle Ages: Essays in the Origin and Early History of Modern Drama.* Baltimore: Johns Hopkins University Press, 1965.

Hashim, James. "Notes toward a Reconstruction of the *Mystère des Actes des Apôtres* as Represented at Bourges, 1536." *Theatre Research* 12 (1972): 29–73.

Havelock, Eric A. *The Greek Concept of Justice: From Its Shadow in Homer to Its Substance in Plato.* Cambridge: Harvard University Press, 1979.

Hayburn, Robert. *Papal Legislation on Sacred Music 95 A.D. to 1977 A.D.* Collegeville, Minn.: Liturgical Press, 1979.

Hernadi, Paul. *Cultural Transactions: Nature, Self, Society.* Ithaca: Cornell University Press, 1995.

Holquist, Michael. "Corrupt Originals: The Paradox of Censorship." *PMLA* 109 (1994): 14–25.

Holsinger, Bruce Wood. "Music, Body, and Desire in Medieval Literature and Culture, 1150–1400." Ph.D. dissertation, Columbia University, 1996.

Homan, Richard L. "Mixed Feelings about Violence in the Corpus Christi Plays." In *Violence in Drama,* ed. James Redmond, 93–100.

Homans, George Caspar. *English Villagers of the Thirteenth Century.* 1941; New York: Norton, 1975.

Hsia, R. Po-chia. *The Myth of Ritual Murder: Jews and Magic in Reformation Germany.* New Haven: Yale University Press, 1988.

Huizinga, Johan. *Homo Ludens: A Study of the Play Element in Culture.* 1950; Boston: Beacon, 1972.

Hummelen, W. M. H. "The Boundaries of the Rhetoricians' Stage." *Comparative Drama* 28 (1994): 235–51.

Huot, Sylvia. *From Song to Book: The Poetics of Writing in Old French Lyric and Lyrical Narrative Poetry.* Ithaca: Cornell University Press, 1987.

Illich, Ivan. *In the Vineyard of the Text: A Commentary to Hugh's "Didascalicon."* Chicago: University of Chicago Press, 1993.

Irvine, Martin. "Literate Subjectivity and Conflicting Gender Positions in the Writing of Abelard and Heloise." In *Criticism and Dissent,* ed. Rita Copeland, 87–114.

——. *The Making of Textual Culture: 'Grammatica' and Literary Theory, 350–1100.* Cambridge: Cambridge University Press, 1994.

Jauss, Hans-Robert. "Adam intérrogateur (pour une histoire des fonctions du modèle question/réponse)." *Texte* 3 (1984): 159–78.

———. "The Alterity and Modernity of Medieval Literature." *NLH* 10 (1979): 181–227.

Jed, Stephanie. *Chaste Thinking: The Rape of Lucretia and the Birth of Humanism.* Bloomington: Indiana University Press, 1989.

Johnson, Eithne, and Eric Schaefer. "Soft Core/Hard Gore: *Snuff* as a Crisis in Meaning." *Journal of Film and Video* 45 (1993): 40–59.

Justice, Steven. *Writing and Rebellion: England in 1381.* Berkeley: University of California Press, 1994.

Kamuf, Peggy. *Fictions of Feminine Desire: Disclosures of Heloise.* Lincoln: University of Nebraska Press, 1982.

Kastely, James L. "Violence and Rhetoric in Euripides's *Hecuba.*" *PMLA* 108 (1993): 1036–50.

Kaster, R. A. *Guardians of Language: The Grammarian and Society in Late Antiquity.* Berkeley: University of California Press, 1988.

Kelly, Douglas. *The Arts of Poetry and Prose.* Typologie des sources du moyen âge occidental 59. Turnhout, Belgium: Brepols, 1991.

———. *Medieval Imagination: Rhetoric and the Poetry of Courtly Love.* Madison: University of Wisconsin Press, 1978.

———. "The Scope of the Treatment of Composition in the Twelfth- and Thirteenth-Century Arts of Poetry." *Speculum* 41 (1966): 261–78.

Kelly, Henry Ansgar. *Ideas and Forms of Tragedy From Aristotle to the Middle Ages.* Cambridge: Cambridge University Press, 1993.

Kennedy, George A. *Classical Rhetoric and Its Christian and Secular Tradition from Ancient to Modern Times.* Chapel Hill: University of North Carolina Press, 1980.

Kennell, Nigel M. *The Gymnasium of Virtue: Education and Culture in Ancient Sparta.* Chapel Hill: University of North Carolina Press, 1995.

Kinneavy, James L. *Greek Rhetorical Origins of Christian Faith: An Inquiry.* New York: Oxford University Press, 1987.

Kline, Daniel T. "Structure, Characterization, and the New Community in Four Plays of Jesus and the Doctors." *Comparative Drama* 26 (1992–93): 344–57.

Knight, Alan E. *Aspects of Genre in Late Medieval French Drama.* Manchester: Manchester University Press, 1983.

———. "Beyond Misrule: Theater and the Socialization of Youth in Lille." *Research Opportunities in Renaissance Drama* 35 (1996): 73–84.

Knott, John R. *Discourses of Martyrdom in English Literature, 1563–1694.* Cambridge: Cambridge University Press, 1993.

Kolve, V. A. *The Play Called Corpus Christi.* Stanford: Stanford University Press, 1966.

Koopmans, Jelle. *Le Théâtre des exclus au Moyen Age: hérétiques, sorcières et marginaux.* Paris: Imago, 1997.

Kors, Alan C., and Edward Peters. *Witchcraft in Europe 1100–1700: A Documentary History.* Philadelphia: University of Pennsylvania Press, 1972.

Kott, Jan. *The Memory of the Body: Essays on Theater and Death.* Evanston: Northwestern University Press, 1992.

Kramer, Femke. "*Rederijkers* on Stage: A Closer Look at 'Meta-theatrical' Sources." *Research Opportunities in Renaissance Drama* 35 (1996): 97–109.

Krell, David Farrell. *Of Memory, Reminiscence, and Writing: On the Verge.* Bloomington: Indiana University Press, 1990.

Kristeva, Julia. *Powers of Horror: An Essay on Abjection.* Trans. Leon S. Roudiez. New York: Columbia University Press, 1982.

Kubiak, Anthony. *Stages of Terror: Terrorism, Ideology, and Coercion as Theatre History.* Bloomington: Indiana University Press, 1991.

Langbein, John H. *Torture and the Law of Proof: Europe and England in the Ancien Régime.* Chicago: University of Chicago Press, 1977.

Lauretis, Teresa de. *Technologies of Gender: Essays on Theory, Film, and Fiction.* Bloomington: Indiana University Press, 1987.

Lea, Henry Charles. *The Inquisition of the Middle Ages: Its Organization and Operation.* 1887; London: Eyre & Spottiswoode, 1963.

Leach, A. F. *The Schools of Medieval England.* 1915; New York: Benjamin Blom, 1968.

Lebègue, Raymond. *La Tragédie religieuse en France; Les Débuts (1511–1573).* Paris: Champion, 1929.

Le Braz, Anatole. *Le Théâtre celtique.* Paris: Calmann-Lévy, n.d.

Le Goff, Jacques. *La Civilisation de l'Occident médiéval.* Paris: Arthaud, 1967. Published in English as *Medieval Civilization, 400–1500,* trans. Julia Barrow. New York: B. Blackwell, 1988.

Lentricchia, Frank. *Criticism and Social Change.* Chicago: University of Chicago Press, 1983.

Lesser, Wendy. *Pictures at an Execution: An Inquiry into the Subject of Murder.* Cambridge: Harvard University Press, 1993.

Lieb, Michael. *Milton and the Culture of Violence.* Ithaca: Cornell University Press, 1994.

Longo, Oddone. "The Theater of the *Polis.*" In *Nothing to Do with Dionysos,* ed. John J. Winkler and Froma I. Zeitlin, 12–19.

Lorde, André de. *Théâtre de la mort: "Les Charcuteurs," "Le Vaisseau de la mort," "L'Homme mystérieux."* Paris: Eugène Figuière, 1928.

Lucas, Robert H. "Medieval French Translations of the Latin Classics to 1500." *Speculum* 45 (1970): 225–53.

Lyotard, Jean François, and Jean-Loup Thebaud. *Just Gaming.* Trans. Wlad Godzich. Minneapolis: University of Minnesota Press, 1985.

Marin, Louis. *Utopics: Spatial Play.* Trans. Robert A. Vollrath. Atlantic Highlands, N.J.: Macmillan, 1984.

Marshall, David. *The Surprising Effects of Sympathy: Marivaux, Diderot, Rousseau, and Mary Shelley.* Chicago: University of Chicago Press, 1988.

Maus, Katharine Eisaman. *Inwardness and Theater in the English Renaissance.* Chicago: University of Chicago Press, 1995.

Mazzaro, Jerome. "*Mnema* and Forgetting in Euripides' *The Bacchae.*" *Comparative Drama* 27 (1993): 286–305.

McConachie, Bruce A. "Using the Concept of Cultural Hegemony to Write Theatre History." In *Interpreting the Theatrical Past,* ed. Thomas Postlewait and McConachie, 37–58.

McLuhan, Marshall, and Quentin Fiore. *The Medium Is the Message.* New York: Random House, 1967.

La Médecine au Moyen Age. Ed. Marie José Imbart-Huart et al. Paris: Editions de la Porte Verte, 1985.

Mellor, Alec. *La Torture.* Paris, 1949.

Michelet, Jules. *Histoire de France*. Vol. II. Paris: A. Lacroix, 1876.

———. *La Sorcière*. Ed. Lucien Refort. 2 vols. Paris: Marcel Didier, 1952.

Mignolo, Walter D. *The Darker Side of the Renaissance: Literacy, Territoriality, and Colonization*. Ann Arbor: University of Michigan Press, 1994.

Miller, William Ian. *Humiliation: And Other Essays on Honor, Social Discomfort, and Violence*. Ithaca: Cornell University Press, 1993.

Miner, John N. *The Grammar Schools of Medieval England: A. F. Leach in Historiographical Perspective*. Montreal: McGill-Queen's University Press, 1990.

Minnis, A. J. *Medieval Theory of Authorship: Scholastic Literary Attitudes in the Later Middle Ages*. London: Scholar, 1984.

Mullini, Roberta. *La Scena della Memoria: Intertestualità nel teatro Tudor*. Bologna: Cooperative Libraria Universitaria Editrice Bologna, 1988.

Murphy, James J. "Aristotle's *Rhetoric* in the Middle Ages." *QJS* 52 (1966): 109–15.

———. "The Influence of Quintilian in the Middle Ages and Renaissance." Seventh Conference of the International Society for the History of Rhetoric, Göttingen, 27 July 1989.

———. *Rhetoric in the Middle Ages: A History of Rhetorical Theory from Saint Augustine to the Renaissance*. 1974; Berkeley: University of California Press, 1981.

Murray, Alexander. *Reason and Society in the Middle Ages*. Oxford: Clarendon, 1978.

Nagler, A. M. *A Source Book in Theatrical History*. 1952; New York: Dover, 1959.

National Television Violence Study, 1994–95: Executive Summary. University of California, Santa Barbara; University of North Carolina, Chapel Hill; University of Texas, Austin; and University of Wisconsin, Madison. Studio City, Calif.: Mediascope, 1996.

Newman, Amy. "Aestheticism, Feminism, and the Dynamics of Reversal." *Hypatia* 5 (1990): 20–32.

Nichols, Stephen G. *Romanesque Signs: Early Medieval Narrative and Iconography*. New Haven: Yale University Press, 1983.

Nietzsche, Friedrich. *The Birth of Tragedy and the Genealogy of Morals*. Trans. Francis Golffing. Garden City, N.Y.: Doubleday, 1956.

———. *The Will to Power*. Ed. Walter Kaufmann. Trans. Kaufmann and R. J. Hollingdale. New York: Random House, 1967.

Nirenberg, David. *Communities of Violence: Persecution of Minorities in the Middle Ages*. Princeton: Princeton University Press, 1996.

Ober, Josiah, and Barry Strauss. "Drama, Political Rhetoric, and the Discourse of Athenian Democracy." In *Nothing to Do with Dionysos*, ed. John J. Winkler and Froma I. Zeitlin, 237–70.

Ong, Walter J. *Interfaces of the Word: Studies in the Evolution of Consciousness and Culture*. Ithaca: Cornell University Press, 1977.

———. *Orality and Literacy*. New York: Methuen, 1982.

———. *Ramus, Method, and the Decay of Dialogue*. 1958; Cambridge: Harvard University Press, 1983.

———. *Rhetoric, Romance, and Technology: Studies in the Interaction of Expression and Culture*. Ithaca: Cornell University Press, 1971.

Otter, Monika. *Inventiones: Fiction and Referentiality in Twelfth-Century English Historical Writing*. Chapel Hill: University of North Carolina Press, 1996.

Padel, Ruth. "Making Space Speak." In *Nothing to Do with Dionysos*, ed. John J. Winkler and Froma I. Zeitlin, 336–65.

Paetow, Louis John. *The Arts Course at Medieval Universities, with Special Reference to Grammar and Rhetoric.* Champaign: University of Illinois Press, 1910.

Paster, Gail Kern. *The Body Embarrassed: Drama and the Disciplines of Shame in Early Modern England.* Ithaca: Cornell University Press, 1993.

Paxson, James J. *The Poetics of Personification.* Cambridge: Cambridge University Press, 1994.

Pelias, Ronald J. "Empathy and the Ethics of Entitlement." *Theatre Research International* 16 (1991): 142–52.

Peters, Edward. *Inquisition.* Berkeley: University of California Press, 1989.

———. *The Magician, the Witch, and the Law.* Philadelphia: University of Pennsylvania Press, 1978.

———. *Torture.* New York: Basil Blackwell, 1986.

Petit de Julleville, L. *Les Mystères.* Vols. I and II of *Histoire du théâtre en France.* 1880; Geneva: Slatkine, 1968.

———. *Le Théâtre en France: Histoire de la littérature dramatique.* Paris: Armand Colin, 1923.

Plass, Paul. *The Game of Death in Ancient Rome: Arena Spirit and Political Suicide.* Madison: University of Wisconsin Press, 1995.

Postlewait, Thomas, and Bruce A. McConachie, eds. *Interpreting the Theatrical Past: Essays in the Historiography of Performance.* Iowa City: University of Iowa Press, 1989.

Pouchelle, Marie-Christine. *Corps et Chirurgie à l'apogée du Moyen-Age.* Paris: Flammarion, 1983. Published in English as *The Body and Surgery in the Middle Ages,* trans. Rosemary Morris. New Brunswick: Rutgers University Press, 1990.

Poulakos, Takis. "Human Agency in the History of Rhetoric: Gorgias's *Encomium of Helen.*" In *Writing Histories of Rhetoric,* ed. Victor Vitanza, 59–80.

Pywell, Geoff. *Staging Real Things: The Performance of Ordinary Events.* Lewisburg, Pa.: Bucknell University Press, 1994.

Rackin, Phyllis. "Androgyny, Mimesis, and the Marriage of the Boy Heroine on the English Renaissance Stage." *PMLA* 102 (1987): 29–41.

Redmond, James, ed. *Violence in Drama.* Themes in Drama 13. Cambridge: Cambridge University Press, 1991.

Rey-Flaud, Henri. *Le Cercle magique: Essai sur le théâtre en rond à la fin du Moyen-Age.* Paris: Gallimard, 1973.

———. *Pour une dramaturgie du Moyen-Age.* Paris: Presses Universitaires de France, 1980.

Reynolds, L. D., ed. *Texts and Transmissions: A Survey of the Latin Classics.* Oxford: Clarendon, 1983.

Riché, Pierre. "Le Rôle de la mémoire dans l'enseignement médiéval." In *Jeux de mémoire,* ed. Paul Zumthor and Bruno Roy, 133–48. Paris: Vrin, 1985.

Richter, Simon. *Laocoon's Body and the Aesthetics of Pain: Winckelmann, Lessing, Herder, Moritz, Goethe.* Detroit: Wayne State University Press, 1992.

Riffaterre, Michael. *Fictional Truth.* Baltimore: Johns Hopkins University Press, 1990.

———. "The Mind's Eye: Memory and Textuality." In *The New Medievalism,* ed. Marina S. Brownlee, Kevin Brownlee, and Stephen G. Nichols, 29–45. Baltimore: Johns Hopkins University Press, 1991.

Roach, Joseph R. "Power's Body: The Inscription of Morality as Style." In *Interpreting the Theatrical Past,* ed. John J. Postlewait and Bruce A. McConachie, 99–118.

Roberts, Michael. *Poetry and the Cult of the Martyrs: The "Liber Peristephanon" of Pru-dentius*. Recentiores: Later Latin Texts and Contexts. Ann Arbor: University of Michigan Press, 1993.

Rousselle, Aline. "Parole et inspiration: Le travail de la voix dans le monde romain." *History and Philosophy of the Life Sciences* 5 (1983): 129–57.

Rousset, Jean. *La littérature de l'âge baroque en France: Circé et le paon*. Paris: Corti, 1953.

Rowland, Beryl. "The Art of Memory and the Bestiary." In *Beasts and Birds in the Middle Ages*, ed. Willene B. Clark and Meradith T. McMunn, 12–25. Philadelphia: University of Pennsylvania Press, 1989.

——. "Bishop Bradwardine, the Artificial Memory, and the *House of Fame*." In *Chaucer at Albany*, ed. Russell Hope Robbins. New York: Burt Franklin, 1975.

Rubin, Miri. *Corpus Christi: The Eucharist in Late Medieval Culture*. Cambridge: Cambridge University Press, 1991.

Saenger, Paul. "Silent Reading: Its Impact on Late Medieval Script and Society." *Viator* 13 (1982): 367–414.

Scarry, Elaine. *The Body in Pain: The Making and Unmaking of the World*. New York: Oxford University Press, 1985.

Schechner, Richard. *Between Theater and Anthropology*. Philadelphia: University of Pennsylvania Press, 1985.

——. *Performance Theory*. 2d ed. New York: Routledge, 1988.

Scherb, Victor I. "Violence and the Social Body in the Croxton *Play of the Sacrament*." In *Violence in Drama*, ed. James Redmond, 69–78.

Schmitt, Jean-Claude. *La Raison des gestes*. Paris: NRF, 1990.

Schneider, Press. E. "Fading Horrors of the Grand Guignol." *New York Times Magazine*, 17 March 1957.

Shergold, N. D. *A History of the Spanish Stage from Medieval Times until the End of the Seventeenth Century*. Oxford: Clarendon, 1967.

Silverblatt, Michael. "The New Fiction of Transgression." *Los Angeles Times Book Review*, 1 August 1993.

Slater, William J. "The Theatricality of Justice." *Classical Bulletin* 71 (1995): 143–57.

Smith, Adam. *The Theory of Moral Sentiments*. 11th ed. London, 1812.

Smith, D. Vance. "In Place of Memory: Remembering Practices after 1348 and 1983." Paper presented at the International Congress of Medieval Studies, Kalamazoo, 5 May 1994.

——. "Irregular Histories: Forgetting Ourselves." *NLH* 28 (1997): 161–84.

Snyder, Jon R. *Writing the Scene of Speaking: Theories of Dialogue in the Late Italian Renaissance*. Stanford: Stanford University Press, 1989.

Solterer, Helen. "Dismembering, Remembering, and the Châtelain de Couci." *Romance Philology* 46 (1992): 103–24.

——. *The Master and Minerva: Disputing Women in Old French Literature*. Berkeley: University of California Press, 1995.

——. "Revivals: Paris 1935." *Alphabet City* (1995): 74–80.

——. "A Sixth Sense: Evreinov, Artaud, and Medieval Theatricality." Paper presented at the Third Colloquium on Medieval Theatricality, Bad Homburg, Germany, 28 March 1994.

———. "The Waking of Medieval Theatricality: Paris, 1995." *NLH* 27 (1996): 357–90.

Spierenburg, Pieter. *The Spectacle of Suffering.* Cambridge: Cambridge University Press, 1984.

Stallybrass, Peter, and Allon White. *The Politics and Poetics of Transgression.* Ithaca: Cornell University Press, 1986.

Stanislavski, Constantin. *An Actor Prepares.* Trans. E. R. Hapgood. New York: Routledge, 1936.

States, Bert O. *Great Reckonings in Little Rooms: On the Phenomenology of Theatre.* Berkeley: University of California Press, 1985.

———. *The Pleasure of the Play.* Ithaca: Cornell University Press, 1994.

Steiner, Wendy. *The Scandal of Pleasure: Art in an Age of Fundamentalism.* Chicago: University of Chicago Press, 1995.

Stock, Brian. *Implications of Literacy: Written Language and Models of Interpretation in the Eleventh and Twelfth Centuries.* Princeton: Princeton University Press, 1983.

Svenbro, Jesper. "The 'Interior' Voice: On the Invention of Silent Reading." In *Nothing to Do with Dionysos,* ed. John J. Winkler and Froma I. Zeitlin, 366–84.

Swearingen, C. Jan. "Plato's Feminine: Appropriation, Impersonation, and Metaphorical Polemic." *Rhetoric Society Quarterly* 22 (1992): 109–23.

———. "Plato's Women: Alternative Embodiments of Rhetoric." Paper presented at the International Society for the History of Rhetoric Conference, Saskatoon, 22 July 1997.

Tatar, Maria. *Lustmord: Sexual Murder in Weimar Germany.* Princeton: Princeton University Press, 1995.

Teskey, Gordon. "Irony, Allegory, and Metaphysical Decay." *PMLA* 109 (1994): 397–408.

Travis, Peter. "The Social Body of the Dramatic Christ in Medieval England." *Acta* 13 (1985).

Treitler, Leo. "Oral, Written, and Literate Process in the Transmission of Medieval Music." *Speculum* 56 (1981): 471–91.

Trible, Phyllis. *Texts of Terror: Literary-Feminist Readings of Biblical Narratives.* Philadelphia: Fortress, 1984.

Trimpi, Wesley. "The Quality of Fiction: The Rhetorical Transmission of Literary Theory." *Traditio* 30 (1974): 1–118.

Turner, Victor. *Dramas, Fields, and Metaphors: Symbolic Action in Human Society.* Ithaca: Cornell University Press, 1974.

———. *From Ritual to Theatre: The Human Seriousness of Play.* 1982; New York: PAJ, 1992.

Tydeman, William. *The Theatre in the Middle Ages: Western European Stage Conditions, c. 800–1576.* Cambridge: Cambridge University Press, 1978.

Ullman, Walter. "Reflections on Medieval Torture." *Juridical Review* 56 (1944): 123–37.

Valesio, Paolo. *Novantiqua.* Bloomington: Indiana University Press, 1980.

Vance, Eugene. *Mervelous Signals: Poetics and Sign Theory in the Middle Ages.* Lincoln: University of Nebraska Press, 1986.

———. "Roland, Charlemagne, and the Poetics of Memory." In *Textual Strategies,* ed. Josué Harrari, 374–403. Ithaca: Cornell University Press, 1978.

Vernant, Jean-Pierre. *The Origins of Greek Thought.* Ithaca: Cornell University Press, 1982.

Vernant, Jean-Pierre, and Pierre Vidal-Naquet. *Tragedy and Myth in Ancient Greece.* Trans. Janet Lloyd. Atlantic Highlands, N.J.: Humanities Press, 1981.

Vickers, Brian. *In Defense of Rhetoric.* Oxford: Clarendon, 1990.

Vitanza, Victor, ed. *Writing Histories of Rhetoric.* Carbondale: Southern Illinois University Press, 1994.

Waite, Gary K. "Vernacular Drama and Early Urban Reformation: The Chambers of Rhetoric in Amsterdam, 1520–1550. *Journal of Medieval and Renaissance Studies* 21 (1991): 187–206.

Walton, Kendall L. *Mimesis as Make-Believe.* Cambridge: Harvard University Press, 1990.

Ward, John O. "Quintilian and the Rhetorical Revolution of the Middle Ages." *Rhetorica* 13 (1995): 231–84.

Warning, Rainer. "On the Alterity of Medieval Religious Drama." *NLH* 10 (1979): 265–92.

Weber, Joseph G. "The Poetics of Memory." *Symposium* 33 (1979): 293–98.

Weinberg, Bernard. *A History of Literary Criticism in the Italian Renaissance.* 2 vols. Chicago: University of Chicago Press, 1961.

Weiss, Allen S. *The Aesthetics of Excess.* Albany: State University of New York Press, 1989.

Wilshire, Bruce. *Role Playing and Identity: The Limits of Theatre as Metaphor.* 1982; Bloomington: Indiana University Press, 1991.

Wilson, Luke. "Promissory Performances." *Renaissance Drama* 25 (1996): 59–87.

——. "William Harvey's *Prelectiones*: The Performance of the Body in the Renaissance Theater of Anatomy." *Representations* 17 (1987): 62–95.

Winkler, John J., and Froma I. Zeitlin, eds. *Nothing to Do with Dionysos? Athenian Drama in Its Social Context.* Princeton: Princeton University Press, 1990.

Winterbottom, Michael. "Schoolroom and Courtroom." In *Rhetoric Revalued: Papers from the International Society for the History of Rhetoric*, ed. Brian Vickers, 59–70. Binghamton, N.Y.: Medieval and Renaissance Texts and Studies, 1982.

Woods, Marjorie Curry. "Among Men—Not Boys: Histories of Rhetoric and the Exclusion of Pedagogy." *Rhetoric Society Quarterly* 22 (1989): 18–26.

——. "In a Nutshell: *Verba* and *Sententia* and Matter and Form in Medieval Composition Theory." In *The Uses of Manuscripts in Literary Studies: Essays in Memory of Judson Boyce Allen*, ed. Charlotte Morse, Penelope Doob, and Marjorie Woods, 19–39. Studies in Medieval Culture 31. Kalamazoo: Medieval Institute Publications, 1992.

——. "Rape and the Pedagogical Rhetoric of Sexual Violence." In *Criticism and Dissent*, ed. Rita Copeland, 56–86.

Woolf, Rosemary. *The English Mystery Plays.* 1972; Berkeley: University of California Press, 1980.

Worsham, Lynn. "Eating History, Purging Memory, Killing Rhetoric." In *Writing Histories of Rhetoric*, ed. Victor Vitanza, 139–55.

Worthen, W. B. *Modern Drama and the Rhetoric of Theater.* Berkeley: University of California Press, 1992.

Wright, Stephen K. *The Vengeance of Our Lord: Medieval Dramatizations of the Destruction of Jerusalem.* Toronto: Pontifical Institute of Medieval Studies, 1989.

Yates, Frances. *The Art of Memory*. Chicago: University of Chicago Press, 1966.

Young, Karl. *The Drama of the Medieval Church*. 2 vols. Oxford: Clarendon, 1933.

Young, William D. "Devices and *Feintes* of Medieval Religious Theatre in England and France." Ph.D. dissertation, Stanford University, 1959.

Zeitlin, Froma I. "Playing the Other: Theater, Theatricality, and the Feminine in Greek Drama." In *Nothing to Do with Dionysos*, ed. John J. Winkler and Zeitlin, 63–96.

Zumthor, Paul. *Essai de poétique médiévale*. Paris: Seuil, 1972.

——. "From Hi(story) to Poem, or the Paths of Pun: The Grands Rhétoriqueurs of Fifteenth-Century France." *NLH* 10 (1979): 231–63.

Zumthor, Paul, and Bruno Roy, eds. *Jeux de mémoire: Aspects de la mnémotechnie médiévale*. Paris: Vrin, 1985.

Index